Linking Home and School

LINKING HOME AND SCHOOL

A New Review

3rd Edition

Edited by

Professor Maurice Craft
University of Nottingham

Dr John Raynor
The Open University

Professor Louis Cohen
Loughborough University of Technology

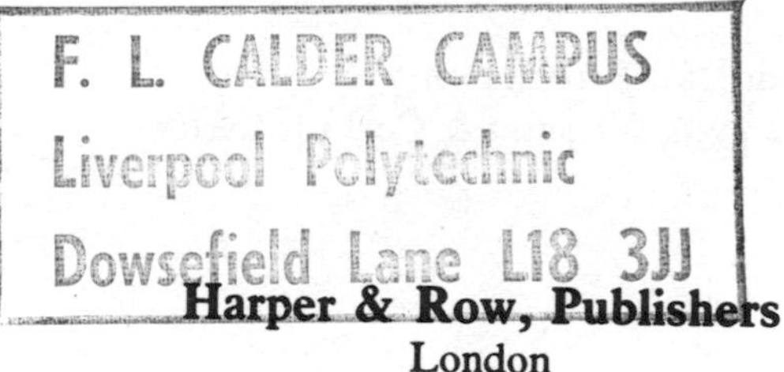

Harper & Row, Publishers
London

Cambridge
Hagerstown
Philadelphia
New York

San Francisco
Mexico City
Sao Paulo
Sydney

First published 1967 (Longman)
Eighth impression 1971
Second edition 1972
Third impression 1975
Third edition 1980 (Harper & Row Ltd, 28 Tavistock Street, London WC2E 7PN)

British Library Cataloguing in Publication Data

Linking home and school – 3rd ed. –
(The Harper education series).
1. Home and school
I. Craft, Maurice II. Raynor, John
III. Cohen, Louis
371.1'03 LC225

ISBN 0-06-318136-3
ISBN 0-06-318149-5 Pbk

Typeset by Inforum Ltd, Portsmouth
Printed and bound by A Wheaton & Co Ltd, Exeter

CONTENTS

EDITORS' PREFACE

Linking Home and School, first published at the time of the Plowden Report in 1967, has been completely revised for this third edition. Of the twenty-five chapters it now includes, two have been reprinted from the second edition, eighteen have been specially written for this revision, and all the remainder have been brought up to date. As before, each of the contributors is a specialist, and most have published authoritatively in their respective fields.

The book has been extended and restructured to take account of new developments in both theory and practice. A central assumption of both the previous editions, for example, was that many children, and particularly those from working-class homes and those in inner-urban areas, are 'deprived' materially or culturally, and that schools must compensate for these deficiencies through the development of closer home-school links. In recent years, this view has been heavily criticized from a variety of points of view. Some have argued that the relatively modest short-term benefits of compensatory programmes suggest that we need to look to the *home* rather than to the school, if we are to make any real headway in overcoming educational disadvantage. This is a broadside, for it implies that the focus should be on employment, housing, and the whole spectrum of existing social priorities, and that tinkering is futile. A less extreme view has proposed that the regional allocation of educational resources is where our scale of priorities and the distribution of power really counts, and that intervention should be made at this point. Others have argued a less 'macro' and more 'micro' view. It is the *school*, they suggest, which is the crucial agency, both in the way it defines what is acceptable language, behaviour, and knowledge, and in the way it groups children or uses other more subtle means of engendering differential responses; for all such strategies lead to the designation of many working-class (or ethnic minority) children as educationally inept. To use compensatory devices such as PTAs, home visiting, or counselling is to blame the victim, it is claimed. Ken Roberts (Chapter 3) and Jack Demaine (Chapter 7) each offer echoes of a number of these recent debates on educability.

On the other hand, the more pragmatic view of hard-pressed teachers, and especially those in urban secondary schools, might be that, regardless of broader questions of social and political ideology, many children lack the competencies they will need in the marketplace, and many parents lack the information and skills with which to support them. John Mays' analysis (Chapter 4) is unfortunately probably as relevant today as it was in the 1960s. In these circumstances, it seems irresponsible not to develop compensatory devices which might be of help. As a number of theorists have suggested, underprivileged children may speak, think, and behave in ways that are 'different' rather than 'deficient'; but either way they are at a *disadvantage* in the real world which confronts them. It may well be necessary to review our teaching strategies so as to avoid the erosion of self-esteem and the loss of talent which has been claimed by critics to be widely the case; perhaps we should be more willing to take a 'bicultural' or 'bidialectal' view in schools. But this third edition of *Linking Home and School* has sought to explore a number of perspectives on bridging the gap which can exist between teachers and parents, on the assumption that there often *is* a gap, and many of the contributors in Parts Two and Three take up this theme.

Another important development in recent years has been the expansion – and the refinement – of school welfare provision. This is now a significant aspect of home-school relations, and one which encompasses children from all social backgrounds, and we are fortunate in being able to include accounts by many of the leading contemporary exponents, in Part Four. But here, too, the compensatory assumptions do not pass without comment, and they are considered, for example, by Daphne Johnson and Elizabeth Ransom in Chapter 11, and by Tony Marshall in Chapter 19. There are also important functional issues: whether the emphasis should be on cure or prevention; the gap between bureaucratic intent and realization; the shared skills and objectives of teaching and social work, and discussion of such questions appears in Parts Five and Six.

Finally, this third edition of *Linking Home and School* has tried to take account of some of the salient pressures of the contemporary social context which have immediate relevance for parent-teacher relations: falling school rolls, the changing needs of a multicultural society, and the developing ethic of participation and of accountability. These find expression in the chapters by Gerald Fowler (Chapter 2), Sally Tomlinson (Chapter 12), Eric Midwinter (Chapter 13), and William Taylor (Chapter 1).

We hope this will prove a useful symposium, and we are greatly indebted to our contributors, to Alma Z. Craft for many comments and suggestions, and to Sue Hellier for expert secretarial help. But, as always, the responsibility for the final shape of the work must fall to us.

December 1979

MAURICE CRAFT
JOHN RAYNOR
LOUIS COHEN

CONTRIBUTORS

ROBERT BAILEY is a Senior Lecturer in the Department of Educational Development at the Oxford Polytechnic. He is past Chairman of the National Home-School Liaison Association.

DEREK BIRLEY is Rector of Ulster Polytechnic, and was formerly Deputy Director of Education in Liverpool. His publications include *An Equal Chance* (with Anne Dufton) (Routledge & Kegan Paul 1971), and *Planning & Education* (Routledge & Kegan Paul 1972).

PHIL CLIFT is Lecturer in Curriculum Studies at The Open University, and was formerly a Principal Research Officer at the NFER. His publications include *Parental Involvement in Primary Schools* (joint author) (NFER 1980).

MAURICE CRAFT is Professor of Education at Nottingham University. His publications include *School Welfare Provision in Australia* (Aust. Govt. Pub. Service 1977), and *Guidance & Counselling in British Schools* (co-editor, with Prof. Hugh Lytton) (Arnold 1974).

RICHARD CYSTER is an Assistant Research Officer at the National Foundation for Educational Research, and is joint author of *Parental Involvement in Primary Schools* (NFER 1980).

PETER DAWS, Professor and Head of the School of Applied Social Studies at Ulster Polytechnic, was formerly Director of counselling courses at Keele University. His publications include *A Good Start in Life* (CRAC 1968).

JACK DEMAINE is a Lecturer in Education in the Department of Education at Loughborough University of Technology. His publications include *Contemporary Theories in the Sociology of Education* (Macmillan 1980).

KATRIN FITZHERBERT is SSRC Research Fellow at West London Institute of Higher Education, and was formerly a Child Care Officer. Her publications include *Child Care Services & the Teacher* (Temple Smith 1977).

GERRY FOWLER is Deputy Director, Preston Polytechnic. He was formerly Professor of Education at The Open Univeristy, and a DES Minister of State. His publications include *British Political Parties & Education* (ed.) (Falmer 1980).

ROGER HARRIS is Head Teacher at the Fulfen Middle School, Staffordshire, and was formerly Deputy Head of a large middle school in an educational priority area in Bradford.

DAPHNE JOHNSON is Senior Research Fellow in the Educational Research Unit at Brunel University, and is joint author (with Ransom et al.) of *Secondary Schools & the Welfare Network* (Allen & Unwin 1980).

JAMES LYNCH, Head of the School of Education, Newcastle College of Advanced Education, Australia, was formerly Head of the School of Education, Bradford College. His publications include *Parents and Teachers* (Macmillan 1976).

KAREN LYONS is Senior Lecturer in Social Work at the North East London Polytechnic, and was formerly an educational social worker. Her publications include *Social Work & the School* (HMSO 1973).

KEITH MACMILLAN is Director of Studies (Masters Programme) at the Administrative Staff College, and was formerly a teacher and college of education lecturer. His publications include *Education Welfare: Strategy & Structure* (Longman 1977).

PATRICK McGEENEY is a Lecturer in Education in the Manchester University School of Education. His publications include *Parents Are Welcome* (Longman 1969), and (with Michael Young) *Learning Begins at Home* (Routledge & Kegan Paul 1968).

TONY MARSHALL, Principal Research Officer, Home Office Research Unit, was previously Senior Research Officer on the Central Lancs. Family & Community Project. Co-author (with Prof. Gordon Rose) of *Counselling & School Social Work* (Wiley 1975).

JOHN BARRON MAYS is Professor of Sociology at the University of Liverpool, and was formerly Warden at the University Settlement. His many publications include *Education and the Urban Child* (Liverpool University Press 1962).

ERIC MIDWINTER is Head of the Public Affairs Unit, National Consumer Council, and was formerly Director of the Liverpool E.P.A. Project. His many publications include *Education & the Community* (Allen & Unwin 1975).

JOHN PIMLOTT is Lecturer in Industrial Relations in the University of Southampton Department of Extra-Mural Studies. His publications include *Parents & Teachers* (Macmillan 1976), which he co-authored with James Lynch.

GEOFF POULTON is Lecturer in Applied Social Studies at the University of Southampton. His publications include *Pre-School Learning in the Community* (Routledge & Kegan Paul 1975), and *Learning Networks in Adult Education* (Routledge & Kegan Paul 1979).

ELIZABETH RANSOM, now at the SSRC, was formerly with the Educational Research Unit at Brunel University, and is joint author of *Secondary Schools & the Welfare Network* (Allen & Unwin 1980).

KEN ROBERTS is a Senior Lecturer in the Department of Sociology at the University of Liverpool. His publications include *The Working Class* (Longman 1978) and *The Fragmentary Class Structure* (Heinemann 1977).

MARGARET ROBINSON is Director of the Social Work Studies Course at Chelsea College, University of London, and was formerly a psychiatric social worker. Her publications include *Schools & Social Work* (Routledge & Kegan Paul 1978).

ANNE SHARROCK, a social worker and later a teacher, subsequently became a Research Officer at the National Foundation for Educational Research. Her publications include *Home-School Relations* (Macmillan 1970).

WILLIAM TAYLOR is Director, London University Institute of Education, and was formerly Professor and Director of the Bristol Institute of Education. His many publications include *Research & Reform in Teacher Education* (NFER 1978).

The late J.W. TIBBLE was Professor of Education at the University of

Leicester, and Chairman of the National Interprofessional Working Party. His many publications included *The Future of Teacher Education* (Routledge & Kegan Paul 1971).

SALLY TOMLINSON, a Lecturer in the Lancaster University Department of Educational Research, was formerly Senior Research Fellow at Warwick University. Co-author (with Prof. John Rex) of *Colonial Immigrants in a British City* (Routledge & Kegan Paul 1979).

PART ONE

Context

CHAPTER 1

FAMILY, SCHOOL AND SOCIETY

William Taylor

*This opening chapter places the discussion of home-school relations, and of the means by which closer cooperation and more efficient liaison may be achieved, in the context of broader social and political issues and assumptions.**

If one thing is clear from the variety of contributions by teachers, social workers, administrators, trainers, and researchers that follow (and from the fact that this is a third and much revised edition of a book first published nearly fifteen years ago), it is that very general acceptance exists of the desirability of forging links between home and school, of clearing away barriers to communication and sources of misunderstanding between teachers and parents about the education of their children.

At the practical level, such acceptance seems unproblematic. The child held back in his school work by inadequate care at home, or by bad housing, needs help. Some combination of educational and social guidance and practical assistance is needed to overcome the handicaps to educability to which he is exposed. The value of attaching teacher/social workers to schools where they are required and where resources permit, of trying to secure the cooperation of apathetic and uninterested parents in helping children to take advantage of the schooling they are offered, seems too obvious to require justification. Discussions among educationalists as to the merits or otherwise of so-called 'deficit theories', arguments about cultural hegemony or the definition of deprivation provoke irritation and even contempt on the part of the harrassed teacher and the overworked social

* This is a revised version of a paper originally published in *Linking Home and School* (Longman, 1972).

worker. The need for improved provision is so obvious, the supply of suitably trained people so inadequate, that time devoted to what many see as the academic smallprint is time wasted.

Yet understandable as this impatience may be, the fact remains that the way in which even the most practical person defines and perceives 'needs' and seeks to provide for them is powerfully influenced by the concepts and ideas that he or she has about the problems confronted. The ways in which these problems are identified, the strategies felt appropriate to their solution, the terms in which success or failure are evaluated are coloured by experience itself acquired in relation to particular expectations, assumptions, and beliefs. Bad theory may misdirect and distort perceptions and actions. But without theory of some kind, no understanding is possible.

I want in this introductory chapter to suggest that our efforts to build better links between home and school will be more useful and more successful if we try to define more clearly what we mean by educational opportunity before we try to furnish more of it; to recognize that the social discontinuities between the roles of families and schools, parents and teachers are important; to relate the home-school link to wider aspects of the social structure; and to take into account the historical background of the relationship between the parent and the teacher in our society.

Educational opportunity

The whole business of home-school relationships cannot be discussed realistically if our context is merely that of providing more educational opportunity for the individual child, of satisfying certain needs which the individual child is believed to possess, or removing handicaps to his or her educability. We are concerned here with a fundamental social relationship between the primary socializing role of the family and the inducting function of the school. It is this relationship that determines the ground on which many of the battles between private and public interest are fought out, and which provides the context within which occupational roles are assumed and social character built up. The questions that need most often to be asked about home-school relationships are not sociological, nor psychological, nor biological. They are political and moral. They are concerned with the legitimacy and justification of the means by which the individual is inducted into the wider society, the extent to which the family is entitled to sequester certain social advantages that are not universally available (either because they are scarce resources or because they are not recognized as advantages at all), with the respective rights and obligations of the individual and the family on the one side, and the school and the society on the other.

It is obvious that in many respects the goals and objectives of individual and family, teacher, school, and State coincide. It is equally obvious that there are many ways in which conflict may occur between what each assumes to be action best likely to maximize interests. These conflicts have to be resolved by the judgements of judges and juries, administrators and teachers, social workers and educational welfare officers. All must possess certain criteria by means of which decisions are evaluated, principles upheld, and particular problems and difficulties resolved.

Many considerations of home-school relationships give too little attention to this aspect of the matter, being based on a facile assumption that the interests of parent and teacher in the development of the child are the same – or can be made to be so through efficient liaison and communication – and all that stands in the way of complete cooperation in a common endeavour is the existence of certain misunderstandings of purpose and mutual lack of information.

But we must be very cautious in assuming that freeing the channels of communication will make it easier for parents and teachers to work together, especially if by more intimate contact the discrepancies in the value orientations and aspirations of the two roles are more clearly exposed. It is possible, of course, that what we are after is not just better communication and understanding, but some degree of redefinition of the rights and duties of the parties concerned. This brings us back to the problem of discovering criteria by means of which these rights and duties can be defined and made operational.

Nowhere is this problem of criteria greater than with respect to the provision of educational opportunities. 'Equality of opportunity in education' has been a dominant policy consideration for the past thirty years. It has been exposed to systematic examination and criticism by sociologists and philosophers. The impact of policies designed to improve educational access has been carefully evaluated by economists, psychologists, and other social scientists.

The effect of all this work has been to show that we can no longer espouse equality of opportunity as a simple unproblematic good to be secured by, for example, making secondary education universal and free and providing grants or loans to enable needy students to attend university or college.

Many recent discussions of the issue have been influenced by the work of the social philosopher John Rawls (1967 and 1972), whose 'two principles of justice' are formulated as follows:

> . . . first, each person . . . has an equal right to the most extensive liberty compatible with a like liberty for all; and second, inequalities as defined by the Institutional structure or fostered by it are arbitrary unless it is reasonable to expect that they will work out to everyone's advantage and provided that the positions and offices to which they attach or from which they may be gained are open to all. (Rawls 1967, p.61)

It will be noted that this does not require that everyone receive equal amounts of education, or master equal volumes of content or acquire similar credentials. It *does* demand that such inequalities of treatment as *do* exist be justified. So the aim is not to remove inequality, but to substitute, according to accepted democratic principles, distinctions and differences that are reasonable for those which are not.

Thus, we are obliged to identify the criteria relevant to determining who shall receive what kind of education. At the risk of following one quotation by another, let me suggest that the nature of this problem was clearly and unambiguously stated by Benn and Peters (1958) more than twenty years ago:

> The man who presses for 'equality of opportunity' is urging that certain factors, like wealth, which have hitherto determined the extent of an individual's opportunities, should be neutralised. But he may very well be urging at the same time discrimination according to other criteria. Because in the mouth of the egalitarian 'equality' is a term of approval, he is bound to distinguish between differences in treatment that are reasonable, and therefore compatible with equality and those that are not, and are thus 'inequalities'. His procedure is to criticise established criteria, and to elaborate new and more reasonable ones; and there is nothing wrong with it. But the statement of his objects in terms of 'equality', when his aim is to substitute reasonable for objectional distinctions, is frequently misleading, not least to himself. His position is not greatly clarified by saying that he seeks not 'equality of treatment' but 'equality of opportunity'; neither phrase means very much unless we know the nature of the criteria under attack.

The criteria we employ to discuss opportunity have altered a great deal over the years, and in ways that in certain respects do little to aid the clarification of our ideas and practices. Tawney and the Trades Union Congress knew what it was that they wanted when they urged the claims of 'secondary education for all' during the first two decades of this century. The extent to which children who could have benefited from continued education were being denied this was plain enough to see.

During the 1930s, Lindsay, Gray and Moshinsky, and others supported criticism of this state of affairs with statistics showing that large numbers of children of good ability were not catered for by existing provision. Setting out to examine the problem of 'how far the education ladder is effective; whether in fact it is, as it has been described, a greasy pole; and what are the main difficulties that beset the path of the child, parent, and teacher and the local education authority', Lindsay (1926, p.7) found that 'proved ability to the extent of at least 40 per cent of the nation's children is at present being denied expression'.

The 1930s hardly provided the sort of political and economic background for reforms designed to improve this situation. The problem was one of finding enough jobs for the educated, and the spectre of the political dangers of an underemployed intelligentsia was frequently invoked. But the war again highlighted the wastage of talent that, despite the existence of the special place and scholarship system, had characterized educational provision during the first four decades of the century. The 1943 White Paper and the 1944 Education Act attempted to remedy this wastage by providing a wider range of opportunities in secondary and higher education, and in removing some of the financial handicaps to a longer period of education for those from homes of humble means.

The criteria employed to discriminate amongst those who could benefit from such extended education and those who could not were based largely on the work that psychologists had done during the interwar period on the classification and measurement of abilities. It was reflected in the recommendations of consultative committees regarding the wider use of objective and standardized tests as a means of reducing the effect of such educationally 'irrelevant' factors as home background, wealth, and the occupational level of parents.

Such criteria were in their essence simple: age, ability, and aptitude. These provided the basis from which the earlier criteria of inherited social advantage could be attacked. They had the great advantage of being regarded by many as largely hereditary themselves. But from the economic and strategic point of view it was irrelevant whether intelligence and attainment owed most to heredity or to environment. What mattered was to identify early those with superior capacities, to give them an appropriate education, and to make them available to do the work of a technologically advancing society.

From the standpoint of the egalitarian, the assumptions regarding the hereditary basis of ability remained important, particularly since it appeared that the distribution of such ability was not the same as the distribution of existing social advantage. For the teacher, the I.Q. had the great merit of being readily measurable, apparently independent of the quality of teaching provided, and supportive of forms of school organization that reflected the existing provision of school buildings and divisions within the teaching profession itself. We have still to estimate the effects of a generation of teaching a particular type of differential psychology in training colleges on teachers' attitudes to children's abilities, and of the influence of statements implying that the educator must accept the constancy of the I.Q. and the fact that he was powerless to alter it.

There were, of course, plenty of cases where I.Q. and performance were discrepant, and where children performed a good deal better or worse than their measured score indicated. To deal with these, a complex vocabulary of terms such as 'late developers', 'premature burn-outs', and, at a lower level, 'smart Alecs', was developed in lecture theatre and staff room; and it was recognized – just as Lindsay had recognized in 1926 – that the home background of the pupil could affect the extent to which he might attain or fall below his scholastic and intellectual potential. But such cases were still discussed in the context of a set of assumptions about ability that regarded it as something qualitatively distinct from, if perhaps quantitatively affected by, differences in home background and cultural level. There still existed a more or less clear-cut criterion in terms of which the existence of opportunities could be measured, deficiencies exposed, barriers to educability recognized and removed. While this criterion remained legitimate, it helped to mediate the relationship between school and home, providing an external standard to which teachers could refer, a standard of judgement that was, albeit grudgingly, accepted by many parents as 'fair', even when it worked against their own first preferences. Whereas wealth and social advantage were unreasonable bases for discrimination in educational provision, ability, so defined, was not – as long as it could be assumed to have a substantial hereditary component and was susceptible to accurate prognostic measurement.

Within the last few years we have seen the crumbling of many of the assumptions that provided the rationale for the educational arrangements of the early postwar decades. The criteria of what constitute reasonable against unreasonable distinctions have changed. We have learned to speak, as did

Lord Boyle in his celebrated foreword to the Newsom Report, of the need to provide all children with the opportunity to acquire intelligence, not simply to manifest it. We have become much more aware of the role of the social determinants of educability, of the relationship of early socialization, language development and school performance, of how achievement motivation is fostered in the child, and the effect of all these and many other factors on aptitude and response to scholastic and academic work. We have lost a great deal of our faith in the prognostic value of objective tests, interviews, and other selective devices. Sometimes, indeed, we have gone too far in repudiating what are still valuable diagnostic and assessment techniques.

The effect of this has been to leave us without any generally agreed set of criteria in terms of which the provision of educational opportunity may be discussed. Whilst recognizing that children still differ in their performances and response to schooling, and that the advantages of a cultivated background and parental 'support' (itself a rather ambiguous term), will count for a great deal, we are unsure as to the way in which home, school, peer group, and hereditary endowment interact to produce performances of different kinds and at different levels. A growing awareness in both the United States and in this country that the variegated patterns of home influence on attainment are mirrored by those of the school has spawned a great deal of research on educational outcomes, the results of which are by no means statistically clear cut, but which have been heavily and in some cases illegitimately drawn upon to sustain particular ideologies and policies. It has been against this background that more recent work showing substantial and significant interschool differences has been welcomed by those who believe, contrary to interpretations of earlier evidence, that the impact on educational opportunity of what goes on in classroom and school is of major importance. These new findings, however, have not escaped criticism (Goldstein 1979). The relative influence on life-chances of home and school still remains an open question.

Arguments about the organization of secondary schools are a long standing feature of educational debate in this country. During the 1960s it seemed that, although we might still be a good way from implementing a fully comprehensive and unselective system, the debate about the principles on which such a system would be based was over. The general election of 1979 showed that this was by no means the case. Perhaps this is inevitable, given the saliency of the moral and political considerations involved in the organization of secondary schooling. But although the movement towards a fully comprehensive, nonselective system of secondary schooling may have been slowed, it has not been halted.

The discrediting of the I.Q. means that we no longer possess a criterion that will legitimize early selection, allocation, and the subsequent differentiation that follow them. Thus it becomes morally imperative to shift the basis of the allocation procedures from performance in intelligence and attainment tests and response to primary schooling, towards a more flexible procedure operating *within* secondary and postsecondary education, where the range of choices available is such as to make it easier for child, parent, and teacher to match interests, attainments, and a suitable type of course.

Lacking legitimate criteria of need or desert by means of which we may justify differences in the provision of opportunities, some have found themselves pushed in the direction of policies and principles that stress equality of outcome. Not everyone is willing or able to go as far as this. For many, the selective process is seen as continuing during the process of secondary education in a comprehensive school; but in a way that is less personally traumatic and socially divisive than selection at 11+ and segregation in a separate and poorly esteemed type of school. The evidence accumulates gradually, and what Burton Clark (1961) calls in another context 'the cooling out' process can be brought into play.

> . . . whereby systematic discrepancy between aspiration and avenue is covered over and stress for the individual and the system is minimised. The provision of readily available alternative achievements in itself is an important device for alleviating the stress consequent on failure and so preventing anomic and deviant behaviour. The general result of cooling-out processes is that society can continue to encourage maximum effort without major disturbance from unfulfilled promises and expectations.

During the thirty-five years since the 1944 Education Act – an Act which will still, in the 1980s, provide the legislative framework for much of our educational provision – certain things have become clear. First, despite the emotional attachment the parties of the left have to the idea of equality, it generates more than one educational policy. Equality is much more complex than it seems. Furthermore, social and political reforms designed to achieve greater equality may not be best served by kinds of educational provision that are fully 'democratized' in the sense of being open-access and nonselective.

Second, the democratization of access to education involves more than conferring *rights*, more than providing *opportunities*, more even than furnishing the institutional and financial *means*. If the members of hitherto underprivileged and under-represented groups are to benefit fully from improved access, and obtain the credentials that will enable them to secure positions of responsibility, power, and influence, then attention has to be paid to the *motivational* structure of such groups.

Third, neither in their 'weak' (in the sense of open access) or their 'strong' (in tending towards equal outcomes) senses, do extensions of educational opportunity in themselves do much beyond a certain point to alter chances of citizens and the power structures of society. For radicals, the so-called 'long march through the institutions' is a very time-consuming route indeed.

Fourth, despite the fact that they provide for only five or six percent of the overall school population, independent fee-paying schools outside the state system have maintained a hold on prestigious postsecondary opportunities, and their former students record a high rate of success in examinations for entry to senior branches of the public service and in achieving highly rewarded positions in industry and commerce. Twenty percent of sixth-formers are in independent schools. A somewhat higher proportion of university undergraduates are recruited from such schools. Many independent schools undoubtedly provide an education of very high quality. Classes are smaller, teaching is often better, there are few distracting social problems, students are highly motivated to succeed, and parents are supportive. The existence of such schools undoubtedly contributes to the maintenance of an educational and social élite. There are many, especially on the left, who would like to see their abolition. But it is increasingly recognized that the choice is not between a society with élites and one without; but between those kinds of élites that best foster open, democratic, flexible, and non-bureaucratic structures and those that do not. The simple abolition of the independent sector is impracticable, unless accompanied by legislation that would compel parents to have their children educated in a school provided by the State. It seems unlikely that voucher schemes, of the kind that have been tried in the United States and with which at least one large local education authority in England has dallied, would be a feasible means of so enhancing parental choice as to avoid the political and social disadvantages of compulsory state education for all.

Unless some major and unforeseen upset in the social and political structure takes place, change in educational provision over the next decade is likely to be evolutionary rather than revolutionary. It follows that efforts to reduce educational inequalities, to enhance opportunity and secure greater equality of outcome are likely to be piecemeal and ameliorative rather than thorough-going and radical. It is in this respect that the work of the professional groups and liaison personnel discussed elsewhere in this volume takes on significance. Teachers, social workers, and community agencies that bridge the gap between school and home contribute to the processes of educational guidance that reconcile the social claims of the family, the particular dispositions of the individual child, and the requirements of society and the occupational milieu.

The roles of parent and teacher

The need for careful analysis of the home-school relationship does not end with a definition of what we mean by educational opportunity. There are other and perhaps more fundamental issues. Historically, the school has often served to separate the child from the home, sometimes with the partial cooperation or at least the acquiescence of parents, sometimes without. During the nineteenth century, the public schools were able to increase in number and prestige largely because of the demands of the new middle class for a type of education that would provide the attributes of cultivation that first generation members of this class did not possess. These were boarding schools, reflecting the Victorian conviction that the family did not constitute the best environment for the growing child. Within the publicly provided system of education, state and church schools served to civilize a brutalized proletariat. In country areas schools were among the instruments of rural depopulation, giving pupils the literacy and the wider perspectives that would enable them to leave the kinship group and seek their futures elsewhere. More recently, the school has become a factor in social mobility, and if it has given parents new opportunities to feel satisfaction and fulfilment in the success of their young, it has also served to separate the child from the family and to offer the possibility of failure and social disesteem.

Psychologically, as well as socially and historically, the school has tended to divide children and parents. The primary school class emancipates the child from the basic emotional ties with his own family, encourages the internalization of social values and norms other than those current in the family home, and begins the process of selection and allocation relative to the adult role-system that will be continued and given great emphasis in later stages of schooling.

Given these tasks, the orientation of teachers must necessarily be different from that of parents. The latter are concerned with the whole child in a way that is different from the teacher's concern, not simply because the parent has two or three children to deal with while the teacher has thirty, but because there are certain differences in role-disposition built into the parental and teaching functions. The parental role emphasizes acceptance of the child, warts and all, irrespective of standards of performance or of levels of attainment. The provision of short-term incentives such as the eleven-plus bicycle, and the willingness of some parents to accept the teacher's evaluation of their child and to make it their own, may distort but do not fundamentally change the essentially ascriptive, subjective basis of the parent-child relationship.

For the teacher the situation is different. However much her training may have emphasized the need to give individual attention to the whole child, and however much she may be disposed to follow this prescription, her role imposes upon her a more objective, achievement-oriented approach, where performance will be evaluated and the claims of the family and the child adjudicated in accordance with criteria such as those referred to earlier in this chapter.

Once again, the question of criteria is crucial. It may be illustrated by reference to what might happen if a fire were to break out in the classroom whilst the teacher was talking with the parent of one of the children in the room. If there was time to save only one child, the parent would have no difficulty in deciding who should be saved – her own. But if the decision was the teacher's, presumably there would not be a single survivor. In this situation, the teacher has no *relevant* criteria by which to select one child rather than another. At one level, the family and the school, the latter representative of community values, committed to the principles of social justice, the former properly and selfishly concerned with the welfare of its own members, stand in clear opposition to one another. Better communication between parent and teacher, more liaison roles, and an attempt to remove grosser handicaps to educability will not eliminate this opposition, which is a basic characteristic of a society in which occupational access is formally open, kinship relationships beyond the nuclear family are attenuated, but the family is still regarded as the basic unit of association, with full rights over the socialization and training of its children.

The Taylor Report, with its recommendations concerning a broader basis of community and parental representation on school governing bodies, reflects a more general move towards openness and participation. There is no doubt that the problems of governing institutions and systems are more difficult when conducted in an atmosphere of critical questioning; but it could be argued that the erosion of trust in professional judgements, the desire to be kept in the picture – whether as rate-payer, patient in hospital ward, or in relation to the educational progress of one's young – is a coming to fruition of the critical process that has been encouraged and fostered by longer and deeper schooling.

The requirement in the Conservative Government 1979 Education Bill that parents be provided with more information about schools, and that opportunities for parental and community participation in their government be improved, reflects the growing importance that has been attached to those notions during the past ten years. Participation is likely to be a continuing theme of political discussion in the next decade. There are continuing fears about the bureaucratization and ungovernability of the modern State, and of many of its institutions. People as diverse as Heads of State, leaders of student movements, grass-root populists, syndicalists, and Marxists join forces in believing that people can and should take a more significant part in the making of decisions that affect their lives. The motives of such groups are, of course, very mixed. For some, greater participation will reduce disaffection with capitalism or social democracy. For others, such participation will diminish alienation, help to equalize power in society, and furnish a new basis for social and industrial relationships. For others still, it will hasten the coming of the revolution.

The demand for participation serves many diverse and sometimes conflicting ends. It is difficult to categorize along simple party lines the positions that people take up on the issue of participation in educational government. The demand that parents and representatives of the community play a greater part in decision-making in schools has both radical and conservative origins and motives. For some, 'parent power' is a right-wing slogan. Which parents are the ones likely to get the power? None but the articulate, the concerned, the middle-class mothers and fathers who already dominate the work of parent-teacher associations; who are first in the queue for interviews with the children's teacher on open days; and who contribute generously to the swimming pool appeal or sponsored walk.

Participation is not a one-dimensional concept. Some usages of this rather slippery term imply a normative ranking between elective autocracy on the one hand, where the citizen exercises his vote once every five years and keeps quiet in between, and a fully 'participant democracy' at the other, where all the significant decisions are taken by the factory council or the school general assembly. But the sense of felt participation in the operation of a general assembly may be no greater than in the processes of elective autocracy, while opportunities for power to fall into the hands of a few individuals are certainly no less. There may be degrees of participation, but they are not along a single scale. Participation means many things to many people. A single rhetoric can legitimize very different kinds of institutional arrangement, some of which have heavy costs attached.

Those concerned about the dangers of espousing 'participation' as an unequivocal good have pointed to the dangers of giving power to the mob, of creating false expectations, of encouraging minorities and the members of different interest groups in the view that all their demands are capable of being met simultaneously, that with a sufficiently radical restructuring of society the need for sacrifice can be avoided. Such critics have suggested that some contemporary models of participative government ignore the darker side of human nature. The self-seeking, irrational, wilful, and suggestible nature of man is all too readily enlisted in the service of attractive and plausible ideas. It is argued that to institutionalize more participative modes of institutional government would affect everybody, including those who are perfectly happy to leave the task to, and trust the judgement of, professionals. Even those with no desire to participate might be obliged to do so in order to balance the work of activists and the committed. Many teachers, many parents, many citizens want to get on with their work, not be constantly called upon to take part in what they may regard as time-wasting and ineffectual committee discussion.

Even when formal provision for greater participation is made, this does not always satisfy those whose interests it is designed to serve. Pupils, students, parents, citizens are sensitive to the smell of paternally imposed ritualistic participation, whether in the form of the works council agenda that never includes important items, the rigged meeting of the parent-teacher association, the 'consultative committee' that limits itself to trivia, or the school council that is persuaded to concentrate on coach trips rather than curriculum. For many, such window dressing is more offensive than the autocracy or oligarchy that it purports to replace.

None of this is to argue against greater participation by parents and citizens in the work of education, to deny the importance of ensuring good relations between teachers and parents, home and school. It *is* to suggest that relationships reflecting genuine participation and power-sharing need, if they are usefully to serve educational goals, to be reflected in carefully thought-out institutional structures, procedures, conventions, and understandings. Good intentions and goodwill concerning home-school relations are indispensable to the creation of such forms and procedures. They are no substitute for them. Given its deep roots in the theory of democracy, in contemporary humanism, and in the evolving character of our political institutions, the press to participate is not one of the fads or cults which, if ignored or gently patronized, will quietly go away. There is little sign of loss of momentum in the movement which towards the end of the 1960s introduced the notion of participation as something to which legislator and administrator might attend. This being so, it is important that we identify the levels and modes of participatory activity relevant to the achievement of greater satisfaction by teachers, parents, and students, and to the improvement of educational outcomes.

It is useful in this connection to analyse participation in educational decision-making in relation to the *groups* that might be involved in different *tasks* and at particular *levels*, as illustrated in the following diagram (Figure 1.1).

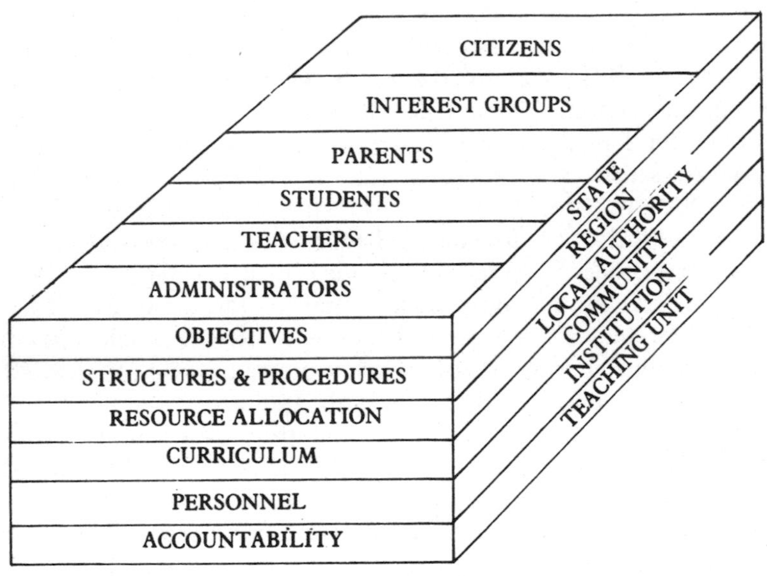

Figure 1.1

In these terms, whilst it might be perfectly proper for parents to play a part in the determination of curricula at the level of the community, the local authority, the region, or the State, it could be inappropriate for them to be directly involved in deciding what goes on in particular classrooms or schools. Teachers need to be free to carry on their work on a day-to-day basis without outside interference. The purpose of this kind of analysis is to disaggregate the notion of participation, to stress the significance of embodying it in well-understood procedures and appropriate modes of participatory activity – which can include attending, writing, speaking, manipulating symbols and physical action – in respect of the activity of particular *groups* concerning relevant *tasks* at appropriate *levels*.

In subsequent chapters, details are given of research that is exposing the continuing inadequacies of an educational system formally dedicated to the fullest possible provision of educational opportunity, and of efforts being made to secure greater understanding between teachers, pupils, and parents, between home and school. There is much more that could be done. The admirable work of teachers, social workers, educational welfare officers, and all those other individuals and agencies which seek to break down barriers between home and school needs all the support it can get. What I have tried to do in this chapter is not to belittle the importance of such efforts, but simply to point out the need for us to keep very clearly before us the fact that work of this kind can only be performed within the context of a complex set of traditions, value assumptions, and attitudes regarding the roles and relationships of family and society, individual and State.

A proper recognition of the difficulty and intractability of the tasks of reconciling differences in the structured role-performances of individuals and groups, in ameliorating the negative aspects of institutional forms and procedures that have taken many generations to develop (and which for all their faults, may still offer greater benefit and present less threat than some more radical and largely untried structures) need not and should not prevent us from pressing ahead with action designed to secure educational improvement. But such recognition may be helpful in tolerating the failure that will inevitably attend some of our efforts, and remind us that procedures and techniques without roots in an adequate theory are, in the long run, unlikely to be helpful or enduring.

References

Benn, S. and Peters, R.S. (1959), *Social Principles and the Democratic State*, London, Allen & Unwin.

Clark, B.R. (1961), 'The "cooling-out" function in higher education', in Floud, J.E., Anderson, C.A., and Halsey, A.H., *Education Economy and Society*, New York, FKE ?ress.

Goldstein, H. (1979), ' "Fifteen thousand hours": A review of its statistical procedures', in *Journal of Child Psychology and Psychiatry*.

Lindsay, A.D. (1926), *Social Progress and Educational Waste*, London, Routledge & Kegan Paul.

Rawls, J. (1967), 'Distributive justice', in Laslett, P. and Runciman, W.G., *Philosophy, Politics and Society*, Oxford, Basil Blackwell.

Rawls, J. (1972), *A Theory of Justice*, Oxford, Clarendon Press.

CHAPTER 2

FALLING SCHOOL ROLLS AND HOME-SCHOOL LINKS

Gerry Fowler

This chapter presents a detailed analysis of what may prove the most significant contextual influence upon educational provision in the 1980s and beyond – falling school rolls – and examines its likely impact upon home-school relationships.

The demographic context

The total school population will fall until the end of the 1980s. In 1979 it was a little under 9 million; it will be about 8 million in 1983, and there will be further decline thereafter to between 6½ and 7½ million by the end of that decade. The figures up to 1983 are certain, within very narrow parameters, since the children who will then be in the schools are already born. Only marginal factors, such as changes in the rate of infantile mortality, the rate of emigration, or the proportion of children of school age receiving private education, can affect them. From 1984 onwards, the number of children in primary schools can only be estimated subject to progressively wider margins of error; the same applies to the secondary sector from 1990 onwards. Changes in staying-on rates beyond sixteen, or in the proportion of rising-fives admitted to the schools, are likely to have only a marginal effect upon the size of the total school population, in default of a substantial and unlikely alteration of the law.[1]

The number of live births in 1978 was higher than in 1977, and the increase has continued in 1979. This is the first reversal of a continuous decline from the peak of 1964, but is not yet of great significance. It was always probable that the number of births would rise, since it is the product of the fertility rate – the number of children borne by each woman in the population – and the number of women of child-bearing age. The number of births increased sharply in the few years immediately following the Second World War, then declined until 1956, when an increase began which continued in each year up to 1964. We are now therefore in a period when the number of women of child-bearing age is high, and will continue to be high for several years. Therefore, if the fertility rate does not recover much from its historically very low point of 1.7 in 1977, the number of live births is likely to be some 120,000 per annum higher early in the 1990s than it was in that year. It could of course be very much higher; for the population merely to replace itself, which would require a fertility rate of 2.1, the number of births would by then have to be some 240,000 higher than the 1977 figure. Thereafter it may well again fall, as the number of women of child-bearing age declines; but by then the school population will again be rising. Both the number of births and the total school population manifest a 'wave-effect', with peaks and troughs, the peak in school population coming several years after that in births, with maximum numbers in secondary schools following seven years after those in primary schools have reached their zenith.

In the 1950s and 1960s we became accustomed to a constant if not steady rise in the school population. Even the lower number of births in the early 1950s was higher than the prewar and wartime figures, and it resulted in no more than a hiccough in the growth of the school population in the early 1960s, the consequences of which were in any event masked by the extension of the teacher's certificate course from two years' to three years' duration. The primary school population did not peak until 1973. A sharp fall in secondary numbers begins only in 1980. It is therefore only in recent years that educational planners have devoted attention to what for all of them now in service is a new problem, how to cope with falling school rolls. In one respect, i.e., the reduction of teacher-training places necessary if we were not to have a gross oversupply of teachers by comparison with any likely or practicable demand for their services by LEAs, serious planning began too late. One reason for this was that the decline in the number of births briefly levelled off in the early 1970s, so that it was reasonable to fear that precipitate cutbacks in teacher education could lead to renewed teacher shortage. In fact, the fall in the number of births then resumed at a much steeper rate. When the Ossa of cuts in the planned increase of local authority expenditure was piled in the mid-1970s upon the Pelion of teacher overproduction, there were inevitably loud protests about unemployment among teachers.[2]

Yet planning for a decline in the school population from a peak of nearly 9 million to a nadir of perhaps 6½ million is exceedingly difficult. The fall is not even throughout the country. Because of population shift (movement from the inner cities to suburban estates, New or Extended Towns; regional displacement of population in consequence of changing employment patterns; rural depopulation; and the continuing spread of a static population thanks to declining household size), it is necessary to continue building new schools while closing others. Thus, even when the number of births in the catchment areas of schools is known to the LEA with precision, it does not follow that it can calculate with equal precision primary intakes four years hence, nor that, knowing admissions to primary schools, it knows equally admissions to the secondary schools which they feed six years thereafter.[3]

Costs, staffing, and the quality of education

Theoretically, if we took the proportional decline in the school population in isolation, and matched it to the numbers employed in the education service and to expenditure on it, startling savings would be possible. The teaching force might be reduced by more than 100,000. We might make do with some 6,500 fewer schools than in the peak years (1973 for primary, 1980 for secondary, and 1977 overall). There might be a reduction of some 170,000 in the nonteaching staffing of schools (caretakers, cleaners, administrators, technicians), and of some 80,000 in cooks and supervisors employed in the school meals service. Some £130 million per annum, at constant prices, might have been saved on the cost of school meals by 1988-1989, even if the system operating before the Education (No.2) Bill 1979 had continued.[4] Savings of some £1600 million per annum could be achieved, again at constant prices, in the recurrent expenditure on schools in the ten-year period following 1978.[5]

Even were such savings practicable, it would be undesirable that we should seek to realize them. The benefits stemming from falling rolls – more space in crowded schools, and in overcrowded urban playgrounds, the possibility of smaller teaching groups, the extension of in-service education and training for teachers, or the admission of a higher proportion of 'rising-fives' to the schools – would all be lost. Further, it would perhaps be impossible even to maintain the quality of education, since such savings would entail that schools should always be closed at the earliest moment that it became possible to redistribute their pupils among other schools, whatever disruption that caused to their studies. Such a programme would require the denial of any element of parental choice of school or of curriculum; LEAs could look only to maximum efficiency in the deployment of resources rather than to the effectiveness of the education they provided; and home-school links would often be an inevitable casualty.

But it is impossible in any event to realize such savings. Some reasons for this are obvious. Natural wastage among teachers is capricious in its incidence, varying from year to year and between LEAs and schools. A programme of school closures designed to maximize savings would inevitably entail teacher redundancies on a substantial scale, more particularly since wastage rates declined in the mid-1970s, perhaps initially because of the Houghton increase in teachers' pay and subsequently because of higher levels of general unemployment, reducing opportunities for more congenial employment elsewhere.[6] Redeployment of the remaining teaching force so as to achieve a perfect match between demand and supply within a travel-to-work area will usually be impossible. Even if it were possible, it would have two undesirable consequences. It would increase the number of teachers who lived so far from the school in which they taught that they could not easily forge links, out of school hours, with the community which it serves. Secondly, the more successful is redeployment, the fewer are the opportunities for new entrants to the profession. The number of newly qualified teachers will fall from the September 1980 level of 20,000, but it is undesirable that their rising quality (measured in terms of academic achievement) should be matched by a decline in their employment prospects, especially in areas of proper educational concern, such as the teaching of mathematics, the physical sciences, craft, design and technology, and modern languages. If this were to happen, teacher education institutions would find it increasingly difficult to recruit students of the right calibre, and the schools themselves would suffer both from promotion blocks and from an ossification of both the content and the method of teaching.

Voluntary redundancy is most readily achieved when it takes the form of early retirement, and even then it has a cost attached to it, since pension is paid at an earlier date and after receipt of lower total contributions. Savings are thus reduced. But in any event, only 10% of primary teachers and 8% of secondary teachers were in 1977 aged 55 or over; 60% of schoolteachers were under 40. Compulsory redundancy will always be resisted by the teacher unions, sometimes with the threat or the reality of disruption of the education service,[7] and it must be bought.

Nor is it possible to reduce the teaching force each year commensurately with the decline in pupil numbers. Let us take a simple example. Imagine that a town has four comprehensive secondary schools, none of which is in 1979-1980 overcrowded, having to use temporary accommodation, but all of which are 'full', in the sense that no or almost no additional pupils could be admitted without bringing such accommodation into use. Further imagine that the total number of pupils will decline by one-quarter by 1984-1985. The LEA can decide to keep all four schools open until that year, when one will close and all of its pupils be transferred to the other three.[8] More sensibly, it can decide that in 1980 or 1981 it will seek to amalgamate two of the schools under a single head and a single governing body, progressively to integrate their work and to concentrate it upon one site, with the closure (and preferably the sale) of existing buildings as this becomes practicable. Notional catchment areas for the town's schools, taken into account in meeting or refusing parental choice of school, would be redrawn each year.[9] Again, it can decide that after (say) 1981 there will be no further intake to one of the four schools; this is easy, since clearly the fall in the numbers affects the younger age-groups first, but it leaves a 'rump' school, finally consisting of a fifth- or a sixth-form only – and still occupying the premises which once accommodated the whole secondary age-range.[10] Alternatively, if all the schools were for ages eleven-eighteen and there was some surplus daytime capacity at the local FE college, it may decide to reconstitute that as a tertiary college in 1982 or 1983, lop off the sixth-forms from all its four schools, and close one of them, although that will still leave it with excess capacity in the long term. Or it may prefer the early closure of one school and the temporary use of demountable classrooms at the other three – a proposal which is certain to maximize parental opposition throughout the town.

This imaginary situation is schematic and oversimplified, and the list of possibilities is not exhaustive; but it will be apparent that none of them would permit the achievement of reductions in the teaching force commensurate with the fall in pupil numbers throughout the period (let alone a commensurate reduction in nonteaching costs). If a reasonably broad curriculum is to be offered to all pupils in all schools up to the point when one school can be closed, then each option necessitates an 'improvement' in the pupil:teacher ratio (from the financial point of view, a 'worsening') in the intervening period. It was for this reason that even the new Conservative Government of Mrs. Thatcher, dedicated to achieving the maximum possible savings in public spending, announced in 1979 expenditure plans which assumed a reduction between 1978-1979 and 1980-1981 of the teaching force in maintained primary and secondary schools of 3.7%, although the pupil population of these schools would over the same two years fall by 4.7%.[11] It is doubtful if this reduction can itself be achieved without some narrowing of curricular options.[12] Even if it were, the savings on teacher salaries would not be exactly proportionate to the reduction in their numbers. This is not simply because the average age of the profession is likely to be marginally higher in 1980-1981. It is also because the Burnham system of fixing the salaries which teachers can be paid is based upon the numbers (and ages) of children in each school. The more there are, the more the head can be paid, and the higher the number of promoted posts for assistant teachers. But if numbers in the school subsequently fall, there is salary protection (as well as what amounts to permanent tenure in default of negotiated redundancy). It follows that at least the same proportion (or a somewhat higher proportion) of those in promoted posts as of those in nonpromoted posts would have to leave the educational system if savings commensurate with the reduction in overall numbers were to be made. But, by definition, these are exactly the teachers who have been judged (by their heads or governors or LEA) to be the 'better' or 'more responsible' teachers.

There are other difficulties in the way of the redeployment of the teaching force. Some 20% of teachers in the maintained sector work in voluntary schools. They are appointed by the governors of the school, not the LEA, who usually would not accept a teacher without the desired denominational allegiance. The teachers themselves may be unwilling to accept employment in a school which does not have the same religious affiliation. For all teachers, we lack an agreed definition of working hours or days beyond the hours of opening and the terms of schools, which makes it possible to argue that an improvement in pupil:teacher ratios is not just desirable but necessary if out-of-school-hours activities (including contact with parents) are to be maintained, despite falling rolls. (To ask how much teacher time must be devoted to such activities in a school of a given size is, in the absence of any such agreed definition, logically the same as asking the length of a piece of string.) Finally, the teacher unions, both nationally and locally, will naturally see falling rolls as an opportunity for a further improvement in pupil:teacher ratios (especially in educational priority areas, such as those inner-city areas where pupil numbers are declining most rapidly), and for an increase in in-service education and for work with industry.[13] These problems are perhaps not insuperable. But the management of contraction will be doubly difficult if it is accompanied by a grumbling guerrilla war between teachers and their employing LEAs. More seriously still, a depressed teaching profession, suffering from job insecurity and poor promotion prospects, as well as some collective hardening of the arteries, will provide a poorer education to their children than many parents hope and expect.

This is the gravest problem attached to falling school rolls. If, as Professor Rutter's research suggests, some 50% of the differences between the educational performance of schools can be attributed to 'in-school' factors,[14] then clearly the morale of teachers, their dedication to their jobs, and their relationships with parents, the community of which they are part, and its elected representatives, must affect materially the value which the nation receives for the money it invests in the educational system. It follows that, if an attempt is made to maximize the savings which falling rolls theoretically make possible, the quality of education is certain to suffer.

School closures and contractions

Teachers' salaries accounted in 1976-1977 for nearly three-fifths of the total cost of primary and secondary education in England and Wales. About 15% went on school meals, milk, transport, and support for individual pupils. The remaining 25.5% was accounted for by the nonteaching costs of schools, and of total expenditure under this head some two-thirds was expenditure upon the upkeep of premises, including the salaries of nonteaching staff concerned with premises.[15] Significant reductions in this area of expenditure can only be achieved by the closure of schools, since the cost of heating, lighting, cleaning, and repair does not vary much even if the number of pupils declines sharply. The cost of loan charges on capital borrowed in order to build a school does not vary at all. (Indeed, for this last reason, it is only the sale of premises or their transfer to another local authority account which can maximize savings to the education budget.) A a *proportion* of local authority spending on schools, nonteaching costs must rise as rolls fall, unless either the teaching force remains implausibly large or school closures keep pace precisely with the decline in the number of children in the education system.

There is historic evidence for the proposition advanced in the last paragraph. Between 1966-1967 and 1976-1977 there was a rise in the unit nonteaching costs of primary schools, in real terms, of 40%, whereas the corresponding figure for the secondary sector was only 15%. There can be little doubt that part of the explanation of this difference is that numbers in primary education peaked in 1973, and were in steep decline for the rest of the period. This view is confirmed by the behaviour of the secondary figures, which show the peak of their increase in 1972-1973, followed by a fall the following year, when the school-leaving age was raised and the population of the secondary sector increased. A fall in the number of pupils throughout the system is likely to lead to an increase in unit nonteaching costs, as well as unit teaching costs.

School closures are notoriously difficult to achieve. One chief education officer has written: 'You should not believe what employers say about schools. You should listen to parents – or better still – try to close their school! You will then obtain an indication of the esteem in which the school is held.'[16] The scale of the problem is easy to demonstrate. In 1978, some 100 schools were closed in England and Wales. In each of the following five years, the rate of closure would need to be five or six times that figure, with the same average size of school closed, in order to maximize savings from falling rolls arising from the disposal of premises. (Precision is here impossible, since the number of closures necessary must depend in part upon births which have not yet happened, since they will help determine LEA views of the viability in the long term of primary schools in particular.) The last Government proposed that an orderly run-down of the school system should be achieved by fixing planned admission limits for all schools.[17] This would have had the effect of setting an upper limit to the capacity of any school, so that popular schools did not exacerbate the difficulties of less popular by 'robbing' them of the number of pupils necessary to maintain curricular choice and to contain unit costs. When it was necessary to close a school, it would thus be possible to plan and to discuss the closure some years in advance. The new Conservative administration proposes a radically different approach, designed both to make it easier for LEAs to close schools quickly (in theory at least), and simultaneously to increase parental choice between schools.

Section 13 of the 1944 Education Act required that each closure proposal should be published by the LEA, and must receive the approval of the Secretary of State after the elapse of a statutory period for objection. School amalgamations always entail closure proposals: one school is to expand, while another closes. Objection may be raised by ten local government electors; it is of interest in the context of local representative democracy (as opposed to a 'second circuit' of community democracy) that the law prescribes 'electors' rather than 'parents'.[18] The Education (No.2) Bill, 1979, introduced into Parliament in the autumn of that year, embodied an attempt to streamline this procedure by providing that proposals would require the approval of the Secretary of State only if he gave notice to that effect to the LEA. Similarly, the LEA itself is to consider objections by electors, unless the Secretary of State, to whom they must be transmitted, decides that he wishes to do so. It is doubtful if this change will of itself significantly ease the difficulties attached to school closures, which stem primarily from the strength of local, and above all, parental support for 'their' schools. Local councillors who wish to secure re-election will often align themselves with those they represent rather than with their party colleagues on closure proposals, and minority party groups will often oppose them in order to win electoral favour. In many local education authorities, party control changes every few years, and the new majority is not committed to proposals espoused by the old. The new law may therefore even lead in some cases to an extended period of local consultation and altercation, and even to changes of heart, simply because 'the buck stops' with the LEA.

The Government proposed that where an LEA wished to cease to maintain a voluntary school, which would normally mean its closure, then the scheme would still require the approval of the Secretary of State. Parents frequently have even stronger emotional ties with a voluntary school than is normally the case with county schools, especially if they are devout adherents of the denomination which runs it. Opposition to closure has a ready-made core in the voluntary body or its nominees on the governors. Further, in a period of contraction, LEAs might be suspected, even where the suspicion was unjustified, of preferring to close voluntary schools rather than their 'own' county schools. The Secretary of State, removed from such local pressures, must therefore continue to act as the final arbitrator between the parties. But we may note that this makes it impossible for even a determined LEA to plan for contraction several years ahead, since it is not fully master in its own house and cannot predict the verdict of the Secretary of State.[19]

Similar procedures to those described in the last two paragraphs are to operate where an LEA or the governors of a voluntary school propose that the numbers admitted to it in any year shall be four-fifths or less of the 'standard number', which is defined as (in most cases) the admissions in

September 1979.[20] There is a difficulty here, as we shall see, since it is often likely to be parents who unconsciously determine that the number of admissions shall fall below this level. The scheme is however clearly intended to prevent LEAs from running down schools to the point where the curriculum is inevitably narrowed, while the nonteaching costs remain broadly the same, without at least consciously thinking through the consequences of this decision. Since the Secretary of State can, in the case of a county school, and must, in the case of a voluntary school, take the final decision, he can in effect force the closure of a school where admissions are running down below the 'standard number', if he deems that necessary in order to achieve the best deployment of resources. It is still up to the LEA to cope with the consequences of such a decision, such as teacher redundancy. Where the previous Government proposed to allow LEAs to set an upper limit to admissions, so as to plan the contraction of its school system as a whole, the successor administration believes that the Secretary of State should have *de facto* power, through the setting of a lower limit for admissions, to control to some degree the mode and pace of contraction. Further, he shall have the right to deny parental choice of school where parents opt for an 'unpopular' school, a right which is denied to the LEA itself. Put another way, if an LEA wishes to convert a five-form entry school, where each admission class was 30 in 1979, to a four-four entry school with the same size admission classes, the Secretary of State can prevent it doing so; but if it wishes to expand total entry to 170 instead of 150, with each admission class having 34 pupils, he cannot intervene. Clearly, resource management here takes precedence over the maintenance of LEA freedom, the provision of effective education, or the maximization of parental choice.

Parental choice and involvement

Elsewhere in the same Bill, the Government sought to extend parental choice. They proposed that LEAs must make arrangements for parents to express a preference for a particular school and that they and governors of voluntary schools must comply with it, except where to do so would (a) prejudice the provision of efficient education or the efficient use of resources, (b) would be incompatible with admission arrangements agreed between the governors of an aided or special agreement school and the LEA, or (c) would be incompatible with admission arrangements based upon selection by reference to ability or aptitude. Each LEA must establish an appeals committee to adjudicate in cases where the first preference of parents is denied and they appeal against the decision, and it must consist of persons other than those who made the original decision. Finally, parents are to be helped to express a preference by the publication each year of a wide range of information about each school, its mode of operation, and its 'successes' or 'failures'.[21]

It is this system which led the Chief Education Officer of Coventry to suggest that the new Government had replaced the planned admission limits of its predecessor with parents' admission limits. For it is the sum total of individual parental preferences which in urban areas at least (rural areas will be considered presently) will be the principal determinant, perhaps over several years, of which schools shall remain open and which close. The Government has thus opted for constraining elected local democracy by the creation of a 'second circuit' of popular or parental democracy; on school policy parents have in effect two votes, one cast in the ballot box when they elect their councillors who will form the LEA, and a second when they express a preference as to the school which their own children shall attend.[22] It is however still a majority system of voting, since, as we have seen, the wishes of a minority who opt for a school less popular with most of their fellows may be overridden, and the school closed. Again, the freedom and ability of LEAs to plan ahead for the contraction of a school system is constrained, although the very vagueness of the phrases 'the provision of efficient education' and 'the efficient use of resources' gives it, or its appeals committee, some hope of preventing parental choice becoming a strait-jacket on school policy-making. This is not to criticize the new scheme; it is however to state a necessary consequence of it. It is ironic that it is exactly at the moment when LEAs face the most difficult problems of contraction that they should find these problems have been artificially increased by the extension of parental choice.

It would be comforting to believe that parents will always pick 'good' schools for their own children. It seems certain that few will consciously choose schools which seem to be 'bad' when judged by the simplest criteria – poor examination results, poor sporting results, few successful out-of-school-hours' activities, and indiscipline among pupils. We have, however, to remember that such evidence may reveal as much about the composition of the catchment area of the school hitherto as about the quality of teaching within it, and that some such evidence is susceptible of more than one interpretation: a high number of canings may be a mark of unruliness or a sign of an excessively disciplinarian headteacher, and a high number of subject passes in external examinations show either that the school is academically successful or that it is too examination-oriented.[23] Free parental choice is likely to favour conformism among schools, helping to preserve those which seem to score highest on the simple interpretation of what may be complex data. In so far as the apparent difficulties of a school stem from external factors, its closure will of course simply move the problem elsewhere. More seriously, the encouragement of conservatism in school education by this means will reinforce the effect of having a teaching force which is static (relative to that of the past thirty years) and plagued by job insecurity.

Parents are also to enjoy another right, never before conferred on them by law, although conceded by some LEAs – that of electing a governor or governors to the school which their child attends. County, voluntary, controlled, and special schools should, it was proposed, have at least two parent governors, and voluntary-aided or special-agreement schools at least one. They would be elected by secret ballot of the parents of present registered pupils at the school.[24] (Every school would also have at least one, or if it had more than 300 pupils, two teacher governors.)[25] Nevertheless, not only would an LEA be required to appoint governors itself, but it would have the right to appoint as many governors as it wished, whether from the categories specified in the Bill or outside them.[26] That is to say, any LEA could if it wished continue to control through its own members or nominees the governing body of any school, effectively restricting or nullifying parent (and teacher) power. Such a system is markedly different from the 'balance of interests' approach recommended by the Taylor Report, which would have left LEA direct appointees in a minority on governing bodies, and different too from the scheme of defined proportional composition advanced by the Callaghan Labour Government.[27] Further, no attempt was made, contrary to the recommendations of Taylor, to specify the minimum powers (over the curriculum, for example) which governing bodies should enjoy.[28]

Two features of this system are worthy of note. First, the election of one or two parent governors, and of teacher governors, to a body which is dominated by LEA appointees is an extension of the cooptative or 'some representation for interest groups' principle which has operated in the composition of LEA education committees since the 1944 Act, and does not signal the arrival of 'second circuit' or participatory democracy in the government of schools.[29] The power of the LEA is in essence undiminished, since it cannot only control the decisions of governing bodies through its own appointees, but it can so restrict their powers that they are little more than talking shops in any event. Second, the election of parent governors by the secret ballot of all parents is itself borrowed from the practices of 'first circuit' representative democracy. Thus, the oft-quoted words of Burke (albeit delivered in a very different electoral context) apply to such representatives as much as they apply to any Member of Parliament or local councillor: 'Your representative owes you, not his industry only, but his judgement; and he betrays, instead of serving you, if he sacrifices it to your opinion.'[30] Put another way, a parent governor is a representative of parents, but is not delegated by them; a parent representative is not a representative parent, were such a creature imaginable. The election of parent governors therefore rests on a quite different principle from the extension of parental choice of school; in the one case we see the embodiment of the representation principle of modern western democracy, and in the other an example of popular, or participatory, or 'Athenian' democracy, in which all parents collectively determine by the 'vote' they cast on an issue (not in an election), namely the choice of school for their children, which schools shall survive and which be closed.

For these reasons, it is my view that the elections of parent governors must usually prove little more than a cosmetic exercise, not serving effectively to provide a link between the school and the families which it serves. If a parent has a specific problem with regard to the education his child is receiving, or a view about the organization or conduct of the school which he wishes to express, it is not clear what gain there would be to him or her in approaching a parent governor rather than his county/metropolitan district councillor (also likely to be a governor), the head teacher, or any other governor of the school. The choice of 'representatives' available to him is extended, but otherwise there is no change. By contrast, he exercises real and direct power when he expresses a preference for the school his child shall attend.

Rural schooling

In sparsely populated rural areas the effect of wider parental choice, of the election of teacher governors, and of falling school rolls is likely to be somewhat different from that in the towns. Even at primary level, let alone secondary, there is likely to be for most parents no effective choice of school, since most parents will wish their young children to attend the nearest available school. The inevitable closure of many small village schools as rolls fall may mean that the nearest school is in any event several miles away from the home. Furthermore, not all small rural communities will be able to secure the election of a parent representative to the governing body of the primary school which serves them, and few to that of the secondary school. Since the village remains to most people in such areas the community with which they identify most readily – not the nearest town, or the district, or the county – links between home and school, or between community and school, are likely often to be even weaker in the future than in the past.

At secondary level, falling rolls will mean that the average distance travelled to school must increase, as some schools are closed. But here the opportunities for school closure are much more restricted than they are in the towns, simply because it is unreasonable to expect pupils to travel more than (say) ten or twelve miles to school. Sometimes the problem will be exacerbated by rural depopulation (for example, in mid-Wales), meaning that the rate of decline in the school population will be faster than in many other areas. There may be no alternative but to maintain what are by national standards small and overstaffed schools, if pupils are to have a reasonable range of curricular choice. The practicable savings from falling school rolls will be proportionately less than in urban areas, free parental choice of school will be nugatory in its impact, and most communities must find themselves unrepresented on the governors of the secondary school which serves them.

The difficulty of improving liaison between home and school will in rural areas be exacerbated by the Government's intention to make substantial savings in public expenditure on school transport and meals.[31] LEAs are to be empowered to charge what they will for the provision of transport to and from school, except in respect of children from families in receipt of supplementary benefit or family income supplement. This must increase local opposition to the closure of either primary or secondary schools in areas where parents are to be charged significant sums (sometimes more than £1 a week per child) for the privilege of losing 'their' school and having their children transported to the nearest school which remains open. Further, some of these same parents will find that the child who previously came home for lunch will now have to take school meals (if he does not take sandwiches to school), and pay an economic price for them. Whatever the merits and demerits of seeking to charge more economic rates for these public services, and whatever the true cost computation (lunches at home do not have a nil cost), the new system must often create acrimony. Smouldering resentment at an increased burden on family finances, perhaps following upon an emotional campaign to retain a local school, can only impair relationships between home and school.

Falling school rolls allied to sharply increased school meal charges must have one other simple and direct effect on community-school links. As pupil numbers decline, fewer school meals will be eaten, whatever the charge for them. Similarly, the higher the price, the fewer the families who will think, rightly or wrongly, that they can afford school meals for their children. These two factors together will result in a steep fall in the number of women employed as part-time school meals assistants and supervisors. The number of posts lost cannot be quantified, since it will depend upon the varying policies of LEAs, here enjoying a new freedom, towards the school meals service. The effect upon family incomes does not here concern us. But such part-time employees, drawn from the local community, have provided one effective link between it and the school which serves it. Some of them have been the mothers of present, past, or future pupils of the school in which they have worked; they have come to know teachers informally, as fellow workers in a school which is as much 'theirs' as the teachers' or the pupils'. This useful link between school, home, and community will not be broken, but it will become more tenuous.

The education of sixteen- to nineteen-year-olds

There is no proposal for any change in the law governing that part of the educational service where the problems caused by falling rolls may ultimately prove most acute, namely the education of sixteen- to nineteen-year-olds. Yet here LEAs themselves, if a reasonable number of subject options is to be maintained, may be forced to amalgamate in one way or another the sixth-forms of otherwise separate schools, or the work with sixteen- to nineteen-year-olds of both schools and FE colleges. Sometimes sixth-form colleges may be established in the premises of an otherwise redundant secondary school, while remaining schools cater for the secondary age-groups of compulsory school age only. Sometimes one school for eleven- to eighteen-year-olds will provide sixth-form facilities for other schools catering only for eleven- to sixteen-year-olds, although this system has the disadvantage that the school with the sixth-form is likely to be perceived by parents and perhaps by some teachers as the *de facto* grammar school. Schools may share sixth-form facilities, including specialist teachers. There may be more tertiary colleges, uniting school sixth-forms and FE colleges, and operating under FE regulations.

In this welter of possibilities, two propositions alone seem probable. Firstly, the school regulations seem likely to be amended to permit the part-time attendance of pupils, who may also be enrolled at an FE college (or another school in addition to their 'home' school), if the widest possible range of subjects is to be taught at the lowest possible cost. This implies that some pupils/students will no longer identify with a single institution. Secondly, more young people than in the past are likely to have an additional institutional break in education at the age of sixteen, which will mean for them and for their parents (where they maintain a concern in their children's educational progress) the necessity to establish relationships with a new head teacher or principal and with new teachers and lecturers, in a new physical setting.

The problem of achieving the most effective use of the resources devoted to the education of sixteen- to nineteen-year olds is exacerbated by the existence of quite separate salary scales for schoolteachers and for FE lecturers. Sharing of staff is thus made more difficult. There may therefore be attempts on the part of employers (LEAs and indirectly the DES) to make the School and FE Burnham salary scales compatible, if not the same – attempts which the sectional interests represented by the teacher unions must resist. In FE, the principal union has long accepted prescription of the number of contact hours expected of each grade of teaching staff, while, as we have seen, there is no agreement on standard working hours within the school system. Improvement of pupil:teacher ratios in the schools has meant fewer contact hours for staff, as well as reduced teaching-group sizes, which has arguably made possible better preparation of lessons, increased education and training of teachers, and greater contact with parents and the community. The analogy of FE suggests that the teacher unions, which have in the past resisted the introduction of standard contact hours, might be willing to discuss it if they were generous (i.e. low), and were allied to a defined right to secondment for in-service training.[32] But any attempt to assimilate School and FE Burnham arrangements is a potential source not only of discontent in the profession but also of disruption in the schools and colleges, which can serve only to sour relationships between parents and teachers. Parental sympathy for teachers is unlikely, if only because the issue, unlike straightforward salary disputes, is to the layman so obscure.[33]

Again the root cause lies in the declining school population.

Accountability

Falling school rolls, legislative change, and restraints on public expenditure in combination must produce sharp changes in the relationship of parents, teachers, LEAs, and the DES. In the past, teachers have been responsible directly to their own head teacher, and through him to the governors and the LEA; indirectly they could be said to be responsible to parents and the electorate. In future, teacher representatives will serve upon governing bodies; in alliance with other groups they may even be able to defeat their own head teacher. But there will also be parent representatives on the governing body, sometimes presenting a collective parental view, where one exists, and thus acting as a constraint on the freedom of both head and assistant teachers. Parents collectively will exercise a massive influence on the shape of the school system through the preferences they express for the schools which their children should attend. Yet, whatever their views, closure decisions, as rolls fall, will in the end be taken by the LEA, and sometimes the Secretary of State. He will in some circumstances – for example, when a school's intake is about to fall to below four-fifths of its 'standard number' – be able in effect to force closure. He and the Government collectively will be able through financial controls to enforce upon LEAs a policy of contracting the school system as rapidly as possible, with a consequential denial of parental choice and of teacher autonomy.[34]

If we ask who is accountable to whom in such a system, there can be no clear answer. The old rule that ministers, Parliament, and LEAs alike are ultimately accountable to the electorate still stands. But they will equally be accountable to a section of the electorate, parents, in an unpredictable fashion, which will vary from area to area. The old principle that teachers are professionals accountable primarily to their consciences and their peers is to be reinforced. Yet at the same time they are to be made directly accountable to the representatives of parents and indirectly accountable to the totality of parents in the area of their school. The LEA will be accountable to parents, as they seek unconsciously to predetermine its decisions by choice of school, to teachers as they resist redundancy, and to the Secretary of State who may fine them for overspending and force closures upon them. They are the piggy-in-the-middle.

This chapter is not an exercise in crystal-ball gazing. But it seems likely that the diffusion of accountability and responsibility will lead to greater tension in the administration of the school system. As the school population falls, some schools must be closed against the wishes of parents and teachers alike, and others closed because of the indirectly expressed wishes of parents, with attendant teacher opposition. As many are likely to be dissatisfied with the decisions of the LEA as are satisfied, and it may resent the decisions imposed on it by the Secretary of State. In theory, falling school rolls should create an opportunity to extend and improve relationships between home, school, and the administrators of education. In practice, because the fall has come at a time of acute economic difficulty and of the testing of new political doctrines, the 1980s will more probably witness less collaboration and greater hostility between the many 'partners' in the government of education in Britain than in any period since the 1944 Education Act.

References

1. Vid. DES *Reports on Education*, No.85 'The Future School Population', June 1976; No.92 'School Population in the 1980s', June 1978; and No.96 'Trends in School Population', November 1979.
2. Hencke, D. (1978), *Colleges in Crisis*, Harmondsworth, Penguin Books; Fowler, G.T. in Bernbaum G.(ed.) (1979), *Schooling in Decline*, London and Basingstoke, The Macmillan Press, pp.62-63.
3. The problems of forward planning are analysed in Briault, E., 'The Management and Financing of a Contracting Educational System', and Fowler, G.T., 'Falling Rolls: Policy Options and their Resource Implications', both in *Educational Analysis* Vol.1, No.2 (1980).
4. Clause 22 of that Bill was intended to remove from LEAs the duty of providing school meals to those who wanted them, except where a pupil's parents were in receipt of supplementary benefit or family income supplement.
5. The figures given here are somewhat lower than those of Aitken, R., address to CIPFA Conference, London, November 1979 (typescript only). But he assumed a decline in the school population to no more than 6 million, which now seems unlikely.
6. *Report of the Committee of Inquiry into the Pay of Non-University Teachers* (1974) (The Houghton Report), Cmnd.5848, London, HMSO.
7. Thus, in autumn, 1979, the Avon LEA, which had declared that 400 teachers must be made redundant and had in consequence been threatened with industrial action by the teacher unions, found that after all only 4 redundancies were necessary.
8. Briault (*op.cit.*) rightly points out that this alternative 'has disadvantages which increase with each successive year'.
9. Although Clause 6 of the Education (No.2) Bill 1979 imposed upon LEAs the duty of complying with parental choice of school, it also offered them escape-routes, one of which was that choice could be denied when conceding it would

be incompatible with the 'efficient use of resources'. Thus, where a school is clearly oversubscribed, an LEA will have to establish criteria by which some pupils may be accepted and others rejected, and one of these is likely to be place of residence.

10. Briault calls this 'the ultimate nonsense', and says that 'the prospect of a so-called school consisting only of fifth-formers hardly bears thinking about'. Yet it was not unknown in schemes of comprehensive reorganization for a selective school to be run down in this way (e.g., Wellington Grammar School, Salop, 1974-1978).
11. *The Government's Expenditure Plans 1980-81* (November 1979), Cmnd.7746, London, HMSO, para.31; and address by the Minister of State at DES, Baroness Young, to CIPFA Conference, London, 5 November 1979 (typescript only).
12. It would be easier if in-service education of teachers were reduced, but the Government (Cmnd.7746 para.31, *ibid*) denied that this was its intention. An alternative might be an increase in contact ratios – the amount of teaching done by individual teachers.
13. Successive Governments have pointed to the failure of schools to encourage in their pupils positive attitudes to work in manufacturing industry and to the lack of understanding of it among teachers: e.g., speech of the Prime Minister, James Callaghan, at Ruskin College, Oxford, 18 October 1976, reported in *Times Educational Supplement*, no.3203, 22 October 1976, pp.1-3, and 72. Yet in 1979 the Government announced the withdrawal of 75% grant to LEAs in support of the secondment of teachers for in-service training.
14. Rutter, M., Maughan, B., Mortimore, P., Ouston, J., with Smith, A. (1979), *Fifteen Thousand Hours*, London, Open Books.
15. cf. *Statistical Bulletin* 1/79 (1979), London, DES; *Statistics of Education 1976*, Vol.5., 'Finance and Awards' (1978), London, HMSO; and Fowler, G.T., *op.cit.*
16. Aitken, R., *op.cit.*
17. Education Bill 1978, Clause 6.
18. Education Act 1944, s.13; for a discussion of the 'second circuit' of democracy, see Kogan, M., 'Educational planning perspectives: some definitions appropriate to the participative elements of educational government', in OECD (1974), *Participatory Planning in Education*, Paris, OECD.
19. Education (No.2) Bill 1979, Clauses 12 and 13.
20. Education (No.2) Bill 1979, Clause 15.
21. Education (No.2) Bill 1979, Clauses 6-8.
22. See n.18 above.
23. cf. *Aspects of Secondary Education in England, A Survey by HM Inspectors of Schools* (1979), London, HMSO, cap.10, pp.241-250, esp. p. 249: 'The exclusive pursuit of examination success does not necessarily promote work of quality. Nor can the quality of work in schools be assessed solely by examination results.'
24. Education (No.2) Bill 1979, Clauses 1 and 2, esp. c.2 subsections (4) and (5).
25. *Ibid.*, subsection (6).

26. *Ibid.*, subsections (2) and (8).
27. *A New Partnership for Our Schools* ('The Taylor Report') (1977), London, HMSO, cap.4; *The Composition of School Governing Bodies* (1978), White Paper, Cmnd. 7430, London, HMSO; and Education Bill 1978, Clause 2.
28. 'The Taylor Report', n.27 above, paras. 3.11-3.18, and caps.6 and 7.
29. Education Act 1944, First Schedule, Part II (5 and 6), and n.18 above.
30. Speech to the Electors of Bristol 1774, in Hill, B.W. (ed.) (1975) *Edmund Burke on Government, Politics and Society*, Glasgow, Fontana, pp.156-158.
31. *The Government's Expenditure Plans, 1980-81 (op.cit)*, para.32; and Education (No.2) Bill 1979, Clauses 22-25.
32. In 1979 there were signs that the teacher unions might be willing to discuss such a system; but the prospects for any increase in in-service education looked bleak (n.13 above).
33. An analogy may be found in disputes involving refusal by teachers to supervise school meals; cf. Coates R.D. (1972), *Teachers' Unions and Interest Group Politics*, London, CUP, pp.67-70.
34. The Local Government, Planning and Land Bill 1979, Clauses 48 to 50, would give the Secretary of State power to reduce the grant paid by central Government (Rate Support Grant), were a local authority to overspend by reference to a standard level of expenditure for authorities of the same type.

PART TWO

Theoretical Perspectives

CHAPTER 3

SCHOOLS, PARENTS AND SOCIAL CLASS

Ken Roberts

The study of social class differences in attitudes and behaviour has traditionally been a focal point in the discussion of variations in educability. In this chapter, Ken Roberts seeks to review recent changes in perspective.

Working-class attitudes as an educational problem

Numerous texts draw attention to the advantages of being born middle class: having articulate and confident parents who recognize the relevance of education for life-chances, who formulate high aspirations and encourage their children towards them, and who are prepared to present themselves at school not only on official open days but also at their own initiative to smooth their children's progress. Middle-class parents do not treat success as a prize reserved for the intellectually brilliant but act on the assumption that it lies within the grasp of any industrious child of their own. In the days of the 11-plus, Jackson and Marsden noted how middle-class parents who feared their children might fail to obtain grammar school places would visit the primary schools to discuss the problem and arrange special coaching when desirable.[1] Sometimes, as a last resort, they bore the costs of private education; the sacrifices were considered worthwhile. Some writers claim that schools in middle-class areas are normally 'community schools' whether so planned and officially designated or not: parents and teachers work in tandem, value education and demand success, push the pupils in a common direction, and reinforce each other's influence.[2]

In stark contrast, working-class parents have been characterized as uninterested, even discouraging. Researchers have drawn attention to their modest aspirations, how they accept signs of failure passively as evidence that a child lacks the required ability, and voice reservations about interfering in the school's business. In schools with predominantly working-class intakes, when not overwhelmed and resigned to a custodial role amidst a hostile culture,[3] it is commonplace for teachers to acknowledge a need to work continuously at home-school relations if they are to have any hope of engaging parental support. Parental attitudes have been identified as a persistent source of working-class underachievement that, some argue, teachers stand powerless to overcome.

The leading programme of British research in terms of drawing public and government attention to social class differences in parents' attitudes has unquestionably been that conducted on behalf of the Central Advisory Committee for Education, and incorporated in its report, *Children and their Primary Schools*, (the 'Plowden Report').[4] This research involved over 3000 children from a national sample of 173 schools, and stressed the importance of home as opposed to school factors such as class size in explaining variations in attainment. Furthermore, as regards the home, the research emphasized the role of attitudes, the interest and encouragement parents offered, as opposed to material conditions. In the Plowden enquiries, working-class parents were less likely than their middle-class counterparts to have visited the schools to discuss their children's performances, and a follow-up study four years later found all the expected relationships between the children's home backgrounds and their educational progress.[5]

No sociologist has ever pretended that the class structure is really as simple as juxtaposing the middle and working classes, the white-collar and manual strata, might appear to imply. Some overlapping of income and occupational prestige, income inequalities, status differences, and variations in life-style within each class have always been acknowledged. Nevertheless, sociologists have argued, the working-class/middle-class dichotomy remains useful in drawing attention to a genuine cleavage where class cultures diverge.

Postulating a qualitative break between working- and middle-class attitudes towards education harmonizes with other class phenomena.[6] Manual work, in general, is less prestigious and is otherwise ill-rewarded compared with white-collar employment. Manual families receive less of the resources that others enjoy. But the manual strata are not merely 'scaled-down' models of more privileged groups. They interpret and react to their positions in the social structure in distinctly 'proletarian' ways, exemplified above all by feeling that they belong to a working class. They see the main division in society as separating their own from more privileged classes, as their political sympathies demonstrate. Manual voters often explain their support for Labour in terms of it being a 'working-class party'.

No one pretends that this middle-class/working-class cleavage is crystal clear. Some manual workers do not exhibit proletarian attitudes, whilst some white-collar employees identify with the working class. Nonetheless, incorporating the working- and middle-class concepts into sociological analysis draws attention to a genuine schism, and educational sociology's conventional wisdom has maintained that attitudes towards schooling separate as part of the same cleavage that divides the population according to its types of work, subjective class identities, and party political loyalties.

As already indicated, the working class has never been portrayed as a homogeneous body. Numerous writers have distinguished the 'respectable' from the 'rough'.[7] But both have been seen as unmistakably working class if only by virtue of an awareness of their separation from 'them'. The demise of traditional communities, rehousing, greater economic security, and rising standards of living have inspired discussion about the appearance of a privatized, home-centred working class. Some researchers claim that these 'new' working-class families are 'status dissenting' rather than resigned, and that they resemble the middle classes in adopting purposive approaches to child-rearing, in their hopes that their children will remain at school beyond the statutory leaving-age, and in their willingness to cooperate with teachers.[8] In comparison with white-collar samples, however, even these 'new' working-class parents have been judged more willing to lower their sights and withdraw encouragement at the first setback, such as no more than modest progress during a child's initial terms in secondary school.[9]

The above contrasts between middle- and working-class attitudes towards education have been restated sufficiently to attain the status of taken-for-granted knowledge in education's everyday folklore. Beginning teachers 'know' from their training that schools in working-class areas will be 'difficult', and that working-class pupils will arrive 'disadvantaged'. As we shall see, the caricatures contain grains of truth, but the aim of the following analysis is to show that in a number of important ways the stereotypes are misleading. They underestimate working-class parents' ambitions to see their children succeed, present too harmonious a picture of middle-class home-school relations, ignore the difficulties that teachers often face when dealing with middle-class parents, and underplay the anxieties these parents feel for their children's progress.

Social class values and images of society

There is no dispute that parental attitudes are related to social class. What needs to be questioned, however, is whether our understanding of the known variations in parents' attitudes is really helped by emphasizing the middle-class/working-class dichotomy. It cannot be denied that these terms tap a juncture in the social hierarchy where class cultures separate and harbour politically opposed values. But do these same class cultures foster qualitatively distinct attitudes towards education?

A number of writers have alleged a basic lack of symmetry between, on the one hand, working-class values and images of society, and on the other, the middle-class values enshrined in education. According to this school of thought, the middle classes acknowledge the virtue of individual enterprise, and recognize and seek to exploit opportunities for personal advancement not only in education, but in employment as well. In contrast, it is claimed, the working class adheres to a collectivist outlook with individuals seeking to improve their circumstances only as members of the groups to which they already belong. They join trade unions to defend and enhance mutual interests, and cast their votes for a Labour Party committed to collectivist economic and welfare policies.

Elizabeth Bott's research has become a classic support for this theory that the middle and working classes subscribe to different mobility ideologies, although her fieldwork covered only 20 London families.[10] Bott juxtaposed the 'prestige imagery' of the middle classes in which the social hierarchy is regarded as a series of emulative layers inviting the individual to climb, against the 'power model', dichotomous, 'us-them' imagery of the working class which allows fatalistic acquiescence or a search for collective betterment but militates against any desire to join the 'other side'. Lockwood[11] makes a similar contrast, though again on the basis of little systematically assembled evidence, arguing that a disinclination to seek personal mobility is a feature of all working-class images of society. Michael Lane also attributes different models of the world, with contrasting implications for their evaluations of education opportunity, to the working and middle classes.[12] He suggests that as a result of their different income careers, manual and nonmanual families develop radically opposed views on the possibility and desirability of personal social ascent. White-collar careers, he argues, tend to be secure and progressive, and encourage broader views of society incorporating these features. Blue-collar careers, in contrast, are uncertain and fluctuating, resulting in perceptions of society as an unstable and unpredictable place where investing effort in education in the hope of reaping long-term rewards appears scarcely rational.

Once an antithesis between working-class images of society and individual ambition is accepted, the implications for education become readily apparent; working-class parents' disinterest and apathy cease to appear remarkable. Teachers begin to understand why posts in working-class schools involve an uphill struggle. Working-class children come to be labelled as 'socially handicapped' and 'culturally deprived', as requiring compensatory programmes to make good their deficiencies. The Plowden Committee developed this reasoning in its proposals for positive discrimination in favour of designated educational priority areas to which additional resources would be channelled, and for the appointment of school-based social workers and greater parent-teacher contact to replace culture conflict with the supportive home-school relations that occur normally in middle-class districts.

The failure of compensatory programmes

In an action research project conducted whilst the Plowden Committee was in existence and based on one London junior school, Young and McGeeney pioneered methods of improving home-school relations in a working-class locality.[13] The 'action' in the project included open days with exhibitions of work, talks between parents and head, class teachers, and the librarian, meetings at which teaching methods were discussed, and home visits by some teachers. During the lifetime of the project the average I.Q. scores of the pupils improved, but as is always a problem with single case studies, whether this was entirely due to the project's action could not be conclusively proved.

The major steps towards operationalizing the Plowden philosophy occurred in a subsequent, government-sponsored action research programme based on five designated educational priority areas. The eventual report[14] describes initiatives in preschool and primary education which included applying the community school concept in working-class districts. The aim in community education is to break down the cultural walls between a school and its locality. This can mean encouraging pupils to study their local environments, displaying children's work in local shops and pubs, inviting parents to school coffee mornings, and producing school magazines. The intention, in the first instance, is to make education *relevant* to children and their parents. This is seen as worthwhile in itself given the probability that most children from working-class districts will remain in such areas, in which case it is desirable to help them understand their milieux. Simultaneously, however, the intention is to trigger a chain reaction. It is hoped that relevant curricula and closer home-school relations will result in parental attitudes pulling alongside rather than against the schools, thereby boosting levels of attainment.

Treating parents' attitudes towards education as rooted in broader social class images of society not only offers a plausible account of the attitudes themselves, but can also explain the distinctly modest achievements of the very remedies that this theory has inspired. Whilst exponents of the view that the values nurtured in working-class homes and neighbourhoods inhibit the development of children's potential have often been enthusiastic supporters of compensatory programmes, even apologists have been able to claim only promising results. Sceptics prefer to say that the recorded improvements in children's performances have been no more than marginal. There are a number of obstacles. To begin with, it can be difficult to deliver positive discrimination on target, for the intended beneficiaries are not tidily concentrated in a limited number of districts.[15] Apart from this, however, if the bulk of the social class variance in children's performances is better explained by home rather than school factors, this suggests that changes in the latter will make little difference. Parental attitudes are unlikely to be quickly changed, particularly if rooted in broader value orientations and images of society. Although attitudes rather than material circumstances might have the most powerful direct effects on children's progress at school, the attitudes themselves are likely to be rooted in material conditions. Evidence from America suggests that, in so far as it can be successful, changing parents' attitudes is an expensive business. A sustained improvement can require intensive casework over a period of years at a cost well beyond the scale of positive discrimination envisaged in the Plowden Report.[16]

Although their project is reported enthusiastically, Young and McGeeney's research illustrates how difficult it can be to involve working-class parents in their children's schooling.[17] Seventy-five percent of the parents attended individually arranged talks with the class teachers, but only 40 percent of the children had a parent who visited an exhibition of work and public talks by the head and librarian, whilst only 15 percent attended a discussion on teaching methods. A survey of parents found that most were satisfied with the school and their children's attainments, though the school had been selected for the research project because of its pupils' low achievements. The parents' main complaints concerned lax discipline and too much play. Expectations were modest and easily satisfied. Parental attitudes can smother researchers' in addition to teachers' efforts.

In fairness to the parents it must also be said that, despite an enthusiastic head, Young and McGeeney encountered some comparable difficulties in persuading the teachers of a problem whose solution required their active collaboration. It is a misconception to regard the teaching force as composed of would-be missionaries awaiting a lead to stimulate parental interest and raise levels of working-class attainment. Young and McGeeney found that many teachers resented open days and special meetings encroaching on their own time, and only three could be persuaded to visit pupils' homes.

Starting from different rungs

Is it time to lay the argument to rest, to abandon hopes of interesting the working class, and to accept that class cultural differences must leave an inevitable impact in education? The conventional account of class differences presented above invites such a conclusion, but there is an alternative explanation now on offer as to why parental attitudes should be related to social class. Rather than composed of discrete segments, this alternative explanation conceptualizes the class structure as a continuous ladder, and spells out the implications of starting out in life from different rungs. Similar 'success values' are attributed to all strata; then it is argued that, in contrast to those situated towards the summit, from a position nearer the base an equivalent desire for success will result in lower absolute levels of aspiration and less interest in climbing to the very top. In relative terms, to rise from unskilled to skilled manual status or from the latter to a routine white-collar job can represent as great an achievement as for the son of a bank clerk to become a doctor.

In the United States, a number of investigators[18] have examined levels of student aspiration and shown that, *relative to their respective starting points*, working-class ambitions are actually higher than middle-class aspirations. It is also the case that when students are questioned about their fantasy hopes for the future the gap between middle- and working-class aspirations closes substantially.[19] Caro and Philblad[20] have shown that lower-class students' relatively modest ambitions result more from their perceptions of the difficulties that would be involved in rising to higher levels than from any working-class evaluations of job opportunities according to different criteria than those employed among the middle classes.

Manual workers in Britain who identify with the working class are just as likely as middle-class adults to seek upward mobility for their children. Furthermore, they are equally aware of the role education plays as a channel for ascent.[21] Working-class parents are just as likely as the middle classes to see education as a means of 'getting on' and value it for this reason. The point is that achievements that arouse pride in manual households, such as obtaining an apprenticeship following CSEs or O-levels, would be regarded as failure in many middle-class families.

In Britain there is plenty of evidence showing that, irrespective of parental and pupil values, individuals from working-class backgrounds face exceptional obstacles en route for success. Few working-class children have parents and relatives capable of offering the advice and information that middle-class homes can furnish on how to manipulate the educational system. Parents who do not understand new school subjects, who are unaware as to whether higher education will eventually pay off in job opportunities, and who, in the absence of any experience of student grants, worry over whether they will be able to afford to send a child to university, are obviously ill-placed to supply the support that could help their children survive to the final stages of the educational competition. The personal educational experience of most present-day working-class adults was a story of failure. Given such histories, is it any surprise that they hesitate before 'interfering' and anticipate being summoned by teachers only in the event of 'trouble'? We do not need to postulate any antipathy towards the principle of getting on to explain either working-class parents' apparent uninterest in education when set against middle-class levels of involvement or their readiness to subdue fantasy hopes. The known facts can be explained simply in terms of the implications that follow starting from a working-class position.

The working and middle classes do subscribe to contrasting images of society, but their cognitive worlds are not totally divorced. Elements of a common culture pervade all classes,[22] and the analysis now being presented insists that attitudes towards education and social mobility are rooted in common values rather than the configurations that divide the two sides of industry and underwrite class-based politics. The issues at stake here are of more than academic interest, for once common success values are attributed to all classes it becomes less plausible to blame working-class parents for their children's failure, and to identify working-class culture as an impediment that schools are powerless to overcome.

Education as the problem

Have we grown too accustomed to asking why working-class children fail? An alternative is to ask why teachers fail with working-class children. Are there grounds for treating education rather than the working-class child's presenting culture as the source of the latter's difficulties? At the end of the 1960s a 'new sociology of education' appeared with an alternative paradigm which insists on *making* rather than simply *taking* and attempting to answer the educational system's questions.[23] In education, working-class children are considered a problem. They are often difficult to control, let alone teach. Conventional educational sociology took this problem and endeavoured to solve it. Investigators sought to discover exactly which factors in the working-class child's make-up or background militate against success, and in this research education itself along with its definitions of success was simply taken as given. The new sociology of education has insisted on questioning what was formerly unquestionable. Why are certain types of knowledge and performance regarded as educationally legitimate? Asking these questions has cast working-class underachievement in a new light. Could it be that education systematically favours children from middle-class homes? Having discovered the 'culturally deprived' child in the 1960s, a great deal of subsequent sociological effort has been devoted to discrediting the concept. There is now a literature applauding the strengths of the inner-city child, including his ability to 'get by' and cooperate with peers.[24] The creators of the new sociology of education have argued that working-class culture is not incompatible with educability, and that labels such as 'disadvantaged' and 'deprived' can only be applied by imposing the values of a dominant class.

As members of the middle class themselves, maybe we must expect teachers to feel most at ease with middle-class children and their parents. Teachers have never been more than marginal members of the middle class, and their occupation has always contained a greater proportion of upwardly mobile recruits than traditional professions, but there is evidence that this very marginality has operated as an added incentive for teachers to set themselves apart from the working-class communities in which many have always taught.[25] In the early days of state education, teachers of working-class children were selected and trained specifically to ensure that they would uphold middle-class values.[26] Recent research among urban teachers has revealed a minority who deliberately and with political conviction adopt a fraternal stance towards working-class pupils and parents. The majority, however, remain firmly on the middle-class side, no longer mainly in response to overt controls, but under the less visible constraints of examination syllabuses and traditional notions of what constitutes 'good teaching'.[27]

Education is a fertile ground for self-fulfilling prophecies. In a widely reported enquiry, Rosenthal and Jacobson[28] have demonstrated how children whose teachers are led to expect intellectual gains do improve their test scores even when pupils are allocated to their classes at random. Children tend to perform according to what is expected of them, and there is evidence that self-fulfilling prophecies operate to the net disadvantage of working-class children. Murphy[29] argues that teachers are rarely insensitive to their pupils' social origins and, furthermore, that within their classrooms teachers become sufficiently familiar with their pupils to distinguish ability from acceptable behaviour, making it unlikely that working-class children will be type-cast as possessing limited potential merely because they are noisier, dirtier, or otherwise less well-behaved than their middle-class peers. In addition, Murphy argues, teachers' assessments of children are made tentatively, always subject to modification, thereby muting the operation of self-fulfilling prophecies. But the evidence from other studies suggests otherwise. Teachers do rate working-class children as less promising than their middle-class counterparts[30] even when their I.Q. scores are identical.[31] A working-class background is considered a handicap and teachers align their expectations accordingly. It is almost certainly the case that sociology will have unintentionally aggravated the working-class child's handicaps by sensitizing teachers to the relationship between social origins and educational failure.[32]

Rather than tinkering with the children's presenting culture, maybe we need to devote more effort to making teachers and curricula more responsive to working-class interests. The majority of working-class parents have positive attitudes towards education. If teachers find these attitudes an obstacle rather than a base from which to build, these are grounds for inviting teachers to re-examine *their* ideas about what constitutes concern, interest, ambition, and encouragement.

Middle-class anxieties

Our conventional stereotypes can easily create the impression that working-class pupils encounter school as a totally alien culture within which they never settle, whilst middle-class children glide smoothly up the educational escalator under the benevolent and harmonious gaze of teachers and parents. Nothing could be further from the truth. Working-class pupils do not find schooling particularly stressful.

Witkin's research amongst over 3000 secondary school fourth-formers found no consistent relationship between positive evaluations of lessons and social class.[33] The main social class difference that Witkin discovered was that middle-class pupils possessed the more firmly developed superordinate aspirations, meaning that they judged their schooling in terms of their own longer-term objectives such as university entry. These aspirations made middle-class pupils the more capable of recognizing and exploiting educational opportunities, but also the more critical of individual teachers' performances.

Middle-class parents often criticize their children's schools for identical reasons. They set high goals for their children, measure the schools' efforts accordingly, and are not prepared to leave their children's futures in the hands of experts in the classrooms. Many middle-class parents not only enjoy higher occupational status but are better educated than their children's teachers, and are uninhibited when voicing their concern and opinions.[34] 'Pushing parents' who harass teachers in classrooms and staff rooms, insist that their children receive favourable attention, and complain to the head when these demands are not met are familiar figures in schools in up-market areas.

Teachers in middle-class schools do not enjoy a quite life, and middle-class parents' anxieties are not ill-founded. Their children run a genuine risk of demotion. Education is regularly discussed in terms of facilitating upward mobility. We more rarely note that it can also be a route down the social scale. When commentators draw attention to how children fail, this invariably prefaces a call to unlock the doorways to success. Although researchers have diligently enquired why more working-class children do not climb higher up the educational and social ladders, it has been rare for investigators to consciously explore why schools fail to downgrade more middle-class children. Of course, upward mobility is the more palatable subject. It sustains a better image for education to treat it as an avenue to success rather than a slide to failure. Campaigning for the schools to fail more middle-class children would hardly make a popular election platform. Nevertheless, there can be no ignoring the fact that upward and downward mobility are complementary processes. Changes in the shape of the occupational structure such as the relative expansion of white-collar employment, and also an influx of immigrants, can make it possible for upward mobility amongst the native population to exceed downward movements; but pulling more working-class recruits into higher strata than structural and demographic trends require must mean pushing more middle-class children down.

This is a prospect that few middle-class parents relish. Downward mobility is sought by virtually no one. Despite complaints about the 'rat race', surveys of parents' aspirations find negligible proportions naming educational and occupational levels beneath their own.[35] There has been some debate as to whether social mobility *per se* leads to interpersonal and social maladjustment. There is evidence that upward mobility can be anticipated and institutionalized to minimize potential strains.[36] With downward mobility, however, the evidence points unequivocally to a relationship with mental illness,[37] and several enquiries have found 'skidders' refusing to acknowledge their descent and retaining attitudes characteristic of their origins.[38] For their part, parents with privileges to conserve will do everything possible to ensure their children do not slip, and these parents' worries have a solid foundation. From a position near the top of the class structure, the dangers of demotion are inevitably more threatening than when viewed from other levels. Despite persistent inequalities of opportunity, children born to privilege are anything but secure. In a social hierarchy containing many more positions around the base and centre than the top, the chances of any individual becoming mobile into the élite must be slender, whilst individuals starting their lives at the summit can nevertheless stand a good chance of descent. The implications of starting from different rungs illuminate the fears of the privileged as well as the attitudes of underdogs.

If it was only a matter of persuading people to vote for the principle, equality of opportunity would have arrived long ago. In absolute terms, working-class educational standards have risen over recent generations. The longer-term life-chances of working-class pupils have not improved commensurately because levels of attainment among the middle classes have also risen, keeping them as far ahead as ever. Raising general educational standards stimulates middle-class parents to set their aspirations and encourage their children to still higher levels. Could this be prevented? We can be sure that measures to restrict middle-class educational opportunities and increase the rate of downward mobility would encounter opposition, and sociologists of education have no ground for righteousness. Generations of sociology students have attended seminars and searched their minds and souls for ways of improving working-class children's life-chances. Few have contested the principle of equal opportunity. But in the final analysis it is deeds rather than words that weight the prospects of children born into different classes, and these same generations of sociologists have mostly become middle-class parents and done all the things that middle-class parents normally do to enhance their own children's prospects.

Conclusions

The impediments identified in the above passages offer an alternative to blaming working-class parents in particular or working-class culture in general for the continuing relationship between children's social origins and their success at school. It would be agreeable to conclude with a straightforward formula that could be painlessly applied to equalize opportunity, but all that can be offered is a clearer view of the obstacles.

Some writers insist that, whilst we inhabit a class society, it is inevitable that educational opportunities will be correspondingly stratified; and that the only effective remedies will involve narrowing class inequalities themselves, thereby drawing the rungs from which children commence closer together, minimizing the social distance between teachers and their working-class pupils, and making descent less traumatic for the middle classes.[39] This conclusion is realistic, but it is also politically expedient. Its phrasing continues to mask the class interests that inequalities of opportunity serve.

Working-class parents' attitudes are a base on which the schools *could* build. This would require appropriately trained and motivated teachers, plus measures to prevent middle-class parents cornering the opportunities necessary to retain their children's advantages. Whether or not we implement these requirements is a political choice. Crudely stated, middle-class interests rather than working-class culture are responsible for the persistence of inequalities in educational opportunity.

References

1. B. Jackson and D. Marsden (1962), *Education and the Working Class*, Routledge & Kegan Paul, London.
2. E. Midwinter (1972), *Priority Education*, Penguin, Harmondsworth.
3. See J. B. Mays (1962), *Education and the Urban Child*, Liverpool University Press.
4. Central Advisory Council for Education (1967), *Children and their Primary Schools*, HMSO, London.
5. J. M. Bynner (1972), *Parents' Attitudes to Education*, HMSO, London.

6. For further evidence and argument see K. Roberts (1978), *The Working Class*, Longman, London.
7. See J. Klein (1965), *Samples from English Cultures*, Routledge & Kegan Paul, London.
8. D. M. Toomey (1969), 'Home-centred working class parents' attitudes towards their sons' education and careers', *Sociology*, 3, pp.299-320.
9. J. H. Goldthorpe et al., (1969), *The Affluent Worker in the Class Structure*, Cambridge University Press, London.
10. E. Bott (1957), *Family and Social Network*, Tavistock, London.
11. D. Lockwood (1966), 'Sources of variation in working class images of society', *Sociological Review*, 14, pp.249-267.
12. M. Lane (1972), 'Explaining educational choice', *Sociology*, 6, pp.255-266.
13. M. Young and P. McGeeney (1968), *Learning Begins at Home*, Routledge & Kegan Paul, London.
14. A. H. Halsey (1972), *Educational Priority*, HMSO, London.
15. See H. Acland (1971), 'What is a bad school?' *New Society*, 9 September. 'Does parent involvement matter?' *New Society*, 16 September.
16. *Ibid.*
17. M. Young and P. McGeeney, *op.cit.*
18. L. T. Empey (1956), 'Social class and occupational aspiration', *American Sociological Review*, 21, pp.703-709; R. H. Turner (1964), *The Social Context of Ambition*, Chandler, San Francisco.
19. See Wan Sang Han (1969), 'Two conflicting themes: common values versus class differential values', *American Sociological Review*, 34.
20. F. G. Caro and C.T. Philblad (1964), 'Aspirations and expectations', *Sociology and Social Research*, 49, pp.465-474.
21. For a review of the evidence see K. Roberts et al., (1977), *The Fragmentary Class Structure*, Heinemann, London.
22. D. Lawton (1975), *Class, Culture and Curriculum*, Routledge & Kegan Paul, London.
23. See M. F. D. Young, ed., (1971), *Knowledge and Control*, Collier-Macmillan, London.
24. L. Eisenberg, 'Strengths of the inner-city child', in J. Raynor and J. Harden, eds., (1975), *Cities, Communities and the Young*, Routledge & Kegan Paul, London.
25. H. Himmelweit (1955), 'Socio-economic background and personality', *International Social Science Bulletin*.
26. G. Grace (1978), *Teachers, Ideology and Control*, Routledge & Kegan Paul, London.
27. *Ibid.*
28. R. Rosenthal and L. Jacobson (1966), 'Teacher expectancies: determinants of pupils' I.Q. test gains', *Psychological Reports*, 19, p.115.
29. J. Murphy, (1974), 'Teacher expectations and working class under-achievement', *British Journal of Sociology*, 25, p.326.
30. N. Keddie, 'Classroom knowledge', in M. F. D. Young, ed., *op cit*; R. Nash, (1973), *Classrooms Observed*, Routledge & Kegan Paul, London.

31. J. C. Barker-Lunn (1970), *Streaming in the Primary School*, NFER, Slough.
32. N. Keddie, ed. (1977), *Tinker, Tailor . . . the Myth of Cultural Deprivation*, Penguin, Harmondsworth.
33. R. W. Witkin (1971), 'Social class influences on the amount and type of positive evaluation of school lessons', *Sociology*, 5, p.169.
34. See G. Baron and A. Tropp, 'Teachers in England and America', in A. H. Halsey et al., eds. (1961), *Education, Economy and Society*, Free Press, New York.
35. K. Roberts, et al., *op cit*.
36. R. H. Turner, *op cit*.
37. R. J. Turner and M. O. Wagenfeld, (1967), 'Occupational mobility and schizophrenia', *American Sociological Review*, 32, pp.104-113.
38. H. L. Wilenski and H. Edwards, (1959), 'The skidder', *American Sociological Review*, 24, pp.215-231; K. Roberts, et al., *op cit*.
39. R. Boudon (1973), *Education, Opportunity and Social Inequality*, Wiley, New York.

CHAPTER 4

THE IMPACT OF NEIGHBOURHOOD VALUES

John Barron Mays

*Professor Mays' classic study takes up a number of the issues raised in the previous chapter, and is included as representing a continuing theme in the interrelationship of home and school in inner-urban areas.**

Most of the empirical material to be presented in this chapter was collected some years ago in relation to the work of a set of schools in one of the older and least favoured parts of residential Liverpool called Crown Street.[1] Since the data were collected and the original report written and published, there certainly have been changes in the survey area, although personal observation does not suggest that these changes have yet been substantial enough to modify to any considerable extent the generalizations which were made on the basis of the original enquiry. Figures regarding admissions to selective schools are no longer available or relevant since the city's educational service has mainly been reorganized on a comprehensive basis, and now almost all maintained schools are neighbourhood-based. But the pattern of disadvantage that I commented on then is still in being in many other ways; although several of the schools I studied have since been closed and a large new comprehensive opened to cater for a shrinking child population, the grosser manifestations of physical inequality are still observable in the locality. Housing is still often unsatisfactory; damage and vandalism are clearly visible; and there is still a lack of community facilities for leisure activities and recreation such as well-equipped youth clubs or a swimming pool.

*This is a revised version of a paper originally published in *Linking Home and School* (Longman, 1972).

The central theme of this chapter is the relationship between the norms upheld by the local residents and the institutionalized values of formal education; the differential attitudes of teachers and educational administrators, on the one hand, and many of the pupils and parents, on the other; and, above all, the ways in which these various social and normative standards interact and modify each other to produce the typical ethos of the downtown school in the underprivileged neighbourhood. As an educational sociologist, I am interested in how purely social influences outside the school condition what goes on in the classroom, and more especially, why in some localities the apparent influence of formal education is so slight in comparison with other and better-off districts. A number of general assumptions underlie my discussion and had better be exposed at the start. These assumptions are by no means novel and, to varying degrees, have been demonstrated in the writing of many educational researchers. The basic position is that children's behaviour (including their response to the experience of schooling) is substantially conditioned by influences emanating from the home, the school, and the peer-group in the immediate locality. Different writers have emphasized these influences to varying extents, and the American literature at least seems to suggest that the family and the peer-group are usually predominant.

Hollingshead (1949) in *Elmtown's Youth*[2] discovered a functional relationship between the class position of the adolescents' families and their social behaviour, and, in particular, how they fared at school. He also found that behaviour and behaviour traits tended to develop along lines approved by their clique mates who were themselves invariably members of the same social class and status group. James Coleman (1961)[3] in his study of American high school teenagers decided that they were strongly oriented to one another, although not entirely so. American adolescents, for Coleman, comprise a society, or rather a series of societies within a society, with the focus upon inward-looking teenager interests rather than upon the responsibilities and goals approved by the wider community. J.W.B. Douglas (1964)[4] in Britain has shown that very interested parents can, by their help and support, enable children to overcome the disadvantage of a lower ability level than is normally consonant with grammar school admission. One would imagine that sustained family care could also assist children to overcome the contrary pull of the local peer-group. It is when the peer-group works against the school and where the family itself fails to supply the necessary support that the work of the schools and the teachers becomes most extraordinarily difficult.

It will be apparent that in a situation in which influences deriving from three separate and powerful institutional sources are operating there will be a possibility of a series of conflicts of values arising, and that such a conflict will be a continuous process, seldom if ever finally resolved so that one dominant force prevails. The values of the school may conflict with those of the home, and those of the peer-group with both. The norms of the latter may on the other hand conflict with the school's but be harmonious with those of the home in many important regards. The situation is complex and many-faceted; so far, to the best of my knowledge, no writer has gone very far in analysing and describing *all* the possible permutations. A thorough institutional analysis of the school as a school and in relation to family life and parental attitudes, and in relation to the norms of the peer-group and the local youth culture, still remains to be effected.

Clearly the way different people perceive their roles is of crucial significance to any understanding of what is really involved in the educational process. People, moreover, have complex roles to play. There is, for example, both a personal and a formal or institutional aspect of the professional role. A teacher perceives himself as a teacher in an educational system; he also must regard himself as a particular teacher in relation to a specific group of pupils and their families in a particular milieu. Thus, one often hears the lament go up from many a harassed teacher to the effect that he is permitted to do everything in the school except teach.

The teacher, then, has a generalized and a specific aspect to his role. He has an idea of what being a teacher in general involves and also, possibly in some ways conflicting with this conception, there is his own assessment of his job in face of a particular group of individual pupils and families, not in the abstract but in the here and now, in relation to whom he must make decisions and exert influence. Parents, too, have complicated ideas of what their duties are, and of how they ought to behave. They may have a general impression of what the school and the local education authority expect of them. They may also have a fairly clear idea of what the neighbours think, or of what grandma did, or again, if they are members of a worshipping community, of what the priest enjoins upon them. Possibilities of confusion, of misunderstanding, of underlapping and overlapping, of conflict and disagreement arise from every side. And doubt and anxiety and uncertainty are often the result for all the parties involved in the bringing up and training of the young.

My own research has been confined to working-class areas and to the children of manual workers. These children, it has been shown in many researches, do less well in the academic sense than the offspring of professional and middle-class parents in general. So gross are the differences of performance that the idea that some kind of basic psychological inferiority is the cause of this must be ruled out. I found in Liverpool, for example, that the children of the inner-city wards in what we called the Crown Street district obtained a ridiculously small proportion of selective secondary school places in comparison with pupils at schools in good suburban areas, the range between inner and outer areas being in the region of 8 to 63 percent for the relevant age group. Dr. Crawford's[5] careful psychological study of a small sample of the children of all districts of the city showed that pupils in the Crown Street district were, as far as basic endowment goes, only fractionally inferior to children in better-class areas who gained much higher marks in the now obsolete General Entrance Examination, which allocated children to either secondary modern or grammar school places. The only possible explanation for such a disparity of achievement must lie in the social environment itself, in the quality of schooling being offered, in the nature of family life, and in the social influences emanating from other children in the neighbourhood. Further substantial support for such a contention comes from Dr. Douglas's work, already mentioned, on over five thousand children born in March 1946 in England, Wales, and Scotland, whom he and his collaborators have followed systematically from their birth into adolescence. He has shown that children from manual worker backgrounds seem to be most prone to environmental differences in the junior school between the ages of eight and eleven, and that those with parents who take a considerable interest in their school work improve their test performance, whilst those lacking such parental support tend to fall away. Hence a child's capacity to prosper academically depends to a considerable extent on the amount of parental support he receives and the quality of home he is lucky or unlucky enough to inherit. (The academic record of his school is also a strong determinant, but will not be pursued here.)

Furthermore, Elizabeth Fraser's (1959)[6] important study of schoolchildren in Aberdeen highlighted the fact that home environment is rather more closely connected with progress at school even than I.Q. She suggested that the factors in the home environment which are most influential in this respect are only partly economic, but that they are also partly emotional and partly motivational.

We therefore arrive at a general presumption, based on a growing crowd of informed witnesses, that type of home and type of neighbourhood are two of the most powerful, if indeed not the two most powerful, conditioning forces, which determine to a large measure a child's school performance and further the general quality of his life and attitudes. The question now before us, then, is how do these two forces interact? How far do school and home work together, to what extent do they pull in the opposite directions, and how do the values of the neighbourhood operate on both fundamental institutions?

There is a fair amount of evidence to show that many residents in traditional working-class neighbourhoods seriously undervalue education. A.B. Wilson (1959)[7] showed this very clearly in his study of high school boys in America. He found that educational achievement was comparatively devalued in working-class neighbourhoods, to such an extent, in fact, that even the products of middle-class families in the same area felt the draught of this influence. A process of what might be called pessimistic anticipatory socialization seemed to occur. What influences will predominate in any one case seems to depend to some extent upon whether the working-class pupils have middle-class peers to emulate or not. Where working-class peers' values are more conspicuous in a neighbourhood they tend to draw the others down with them. There is thus in any socially mixed area a potentiality for cultural conflict where the children attend common schools. Where they do not attend the same schools, it seems fair to assume, the influence of the home and the parents should be sufficient to counteract the adverse attractions of the peer-group and the local neighbourhood, providing, of course, as has so often been stressed, they are giving adequate support and encouragement in academic matters.

Evidence available in this country substantiates the view that education is often undervalued, and there is no doubt that a great many teachers working in schools in the poorer districts would take it as a self-evident fact. In my own limited enquiries in Liverpool I found that few parents seemed to make any positive demands on the schools and that, for the most part, they seemed to leave educational decisions to the teachers and to accept their advice more or less unquestioningly. It was, in a way, a compliment to the teaching profession, which indicated the high social status they enjoyed in the area. But such an attitude is very different from that which characterizes the higher-class neighbourhoods, where teachers find themselves under constant and often embarrassing parental pressure to concentrate on pupils' academic performance. As D.F. Swift (1964)[8] has shown, it is the socially aspirant middle-class and lower middle-class parents whose own careers have been unsatisfactory and whose personal ambitions have been frustrated who make such a fuss about schooling, and who overactively co-operate with the more limited aims of schools, in the way, that is to say, of passing examinations rather than in terms of widening children's cultural interests.

As far as the schools in the Crown Street district went, there was little to suggest that either teachers or parents pressurized children to become academic high-achievers, or even, at a more humble level, to do well at the then existing General Entrance Examination and obtain a place at either a technical or a grammar school. There were a few cases which teachers could cite in which parents had actively worked against the wishes of the school and refused to allow their children to sit the eleven-plus, or, when their children had obtained a grammar school place, had refused to let them take it up. Michael Carter (1962) hinted at the same kind of anti-educational attitude on the part of some families in his Sheffield study where parents expressed 'doubts about the worth of examinations . . . and dark pictures were drawn of the amount of studying that would be necessary'.[9] The general attitude of the teachers may be summed up by saying that if a child had obvious ability and came from a supporting home background he should be encouraged to do well academically; otherwise no special influence should be exerted one way or the other. Practices varied from school to school, but in the main seemed to reflect the social aspirations of the locality. In some schools all children were given a limited amount of experience in intelligence tests, but others would not go this far. A little over half the junior departments in my survey area gave prospective candidates some practice in answering intelligence tests, but in none did this involve anything remotely resembling cramming. Furthermore, some schools set homework for those taking the eleven-plus, but others refrained. A few schools organized special learning groups and gave some coaching. Homework, even in schools where it was set and marked, was usually confined to children about to sit the examination. Of all Crown Street children who were doing some homework at the time of the survey (1957), some 60 percent were doing it at the request of their parents, which indicates a fair degree of family interest. One cannot help wondering whether the schools themselves might not have done more at a somewhat earlier stage to encourage this interest, and to what extent the reluctance to set work was related to the dislike of the extra marking and correcting entailed.

Head teachers' views on the desirability of homework throughout the junior school, as opposed to homework specially set for those about to take the examination, were conflicting. The majority were against it, and only two of the ten questioned were in favour. Thus, it can be seen that the emphasis upon academic performance and measured attainment varied to a considerable extent with head teachers' interpretation of their duties. One head stressed the need to care for the backward pupils – a most laudable attitude surely, provided it does not in turn imply that the more able and advanceable children are allowed to drift. In some schools and departments there were teachers keen to encourage a high academic standard and eager to assist the more gifted pupils to get on via the examination system. I met at least one very keen man who was chafing at the lack of impetus in the schools he was serving, and who felt very keenly that not all was being done that could be done to promote the future prospects of the children. It is perhaps not very surprising that, very soon after, he left the district to work in a new school with better equipment and a higher level of endeavour.

It is clear that inequality and differential treatment exist on every hand, and especially in the downtown schools in poorer-class neighbourhoods. The degree of interest on the part of the parent is one side to this differential process; the other side of the coin is the extent of the teachers' and particularly of the head teachers' zeal and enthusiasm to do more than an average routine job.[10]

Parental apathy was frequently commented on by teachers when questioned about their work in downtown schools and the many problems associated with their work. Many of the teachers criticized parents and considered them to be seriously failing in their duties. There is little doubt, also, that an overcensorious attitude on the part of teachers, where it exists, must make relations between school and home more difficult than they might otherwise be.

But some of the criticisms of teachers could be substantiated, and they reveal emphatically the divergence between what we may term the standards of the wider community and those of the local subculture. They show also that to some extent the work of the schools must be thought of as being in opposition to the surrounding subculture. It is a nice question to determine how far some of the teachers accept this as a challenge to promote social change, or how far they merely accept the adverse influences as excuses for their own dislike of becoming too involved? How many accept that the notion of their standing *in loco parentis* commits them to something much more thorough-going than a disciplinary function and the right to administer punishment? How many are willing to reach out imaginatively and creatively into the lives of the local families, as the settlement movement, for example, attempted to do for nearly a century, and strive to raise the prevailing standards of family care so that their pupils may have a better chance to polish and exploit their talents in their own and in the country's interests?

Evidence against parents rests on the failure of many of them to cooperate actively. Even when it is objectively clear that they ought to come to the school, many stay away for one reason or another. All the Crown Street schools invited parents to attend when the school nurses or doctors were examining their children, but the response varied. In one all-age school it was stated that all the juniors were accompanied by a parent or relative when being medically examined, but few of the seniors received similar support. In another senior department no more than 15 percent of the parents were said to attend these sessions. The general impression of the area as a whole can best be summed up by saying that only a minority ever attended; for the most part the parents left it to the school to do their share of the job without overt support. This is a serious indictment, but one which is not necessarily confined to the parents who failed to respond. One would like to know to what extent the schools impressed on the parents the fact that not only was it their duty to attend such interviews but that they would be warmly welcomed when they came. What steps were taken to overcome parental diffidence or to arrange mutually convenient times for the inspection? How far is the medical review laid on in a routine way without any special build-up and publicity? It is dangerously easy to use a phrase such as 'parental apathy' and leave it at that.

Visits were made by officials of the Youth Employment Service to interview school-leavers during their last year. The purpose of this service is much more than job placement and aims at vocational guidance. Vocational guidance involves a tripartite collaboration between school, home, and youth employment officers, and this in turn should mean that all three are enabled to meet to discuss the future careers of leavers in the light of the pupils' abilities, temperaments, and aptitudes, and also in relation to the local labour market. Procedures to effect this varied between the various schools I surveyed. In a few schools the parents were invited to attend meetings with the vocational guiders, but it is undeniable that full collaboration was not possible in a majority of cases, nor was it even attempted. For schools to invite parents to attend meetings especially concerned with their own children's welfare and future and to find them not interested enough to come must be a most depressing experience. By the same token, for parents not to be asked to come to such meetings is to suggest that they are not regarded as partners in shaping the destinies of their own offspring. It is idle to claim that parents are not interested in what the schools are attempting to do if the latter are not themselves doing everything in their power to foster a responsible and collaborative relationship. The relationship must be structured so that all concerned at least have the opportunity to be present and to make their contribution. Anything less may be regarded as a failure on the part of those responsible to meet the minimum needs and rights of the pupils.

Parents will lean on the schools if the teachers encourage leaning. If, in important areas of pupils' lives they fail to elicit parental support and don't even try to get it, then they have less excuse for lamenting that 'the parents leave it all to us around here'. Hard-pressed parents, not unnaturally, seize on whatever voluntary or statutory help is available to them, and no doubt, being weak and human, they tend to leave as much as they can to those who have the skill and training to perform such services. If a child has an accident in school it is assumed that it is the teacher's job to go with him to the outpatient clinic. Cases were reported in Crown Street of pupils receiving injuries during the lunch hour and being sent back to the school by their mothers to obtain first aid whilst they themselves went off to their own work or went out shopping.

From what I have just been saying, it will be clear that there was disagreement and misunderstanding about the function of the school and the role of its staff in relation to the immediate environment. I have no doubt in my own mind that the role of the teacher in socially deteriorated districts must incorporate aspects of the role of the welfare officer, and that academic achievement will itself improve only when teacher and parent work in close harmony with each other towards the attainment of commonly understood and agreed objectives. Teachers need to spend time out of the classroom getting to know parents. Parents need to be brought more and more into the schools so as to realize that they are vitally connected with the whole educational process and not mere touchline figures. Concomitant with such attitudinal and organizational changes, and indeed an inseparable part of the development of the teacher's function and role, is the pressing urgency for an expansion of extracurricular activities and organizations. Most of our Crown Street schools undertook such out-of-school activities involving a sacrifice of time and energy on the part of members of the staff. Boys were much better catered for in this way than girls, men presumably having fewer additional responsibilities than women in out-of-school hours. Extracurricular events ranged from the organization of holiday camps to participation in civic music festivals. They included the ever popular football and swimming for boys, and, much more rarely, tennis and netball for girls.

The most important additional activity from the viewpoint of linking school and home is the organization of 'at home' days, special displays in the schools, and parent-teacher associations. In spite of the firm support for the latter expressed by representatives of the local education authority, Crown Street schools, at the time of the enquiry, with one notable exception, were either against the idea or claimed to have tried them and abandoned them as failures. Most of the reasons given for the fact that the schools were not running PTAs seemed to be merely excuses and rationalizations of prejudice. Whilst there was unanimous agreement amongst teachers on the need for more support from the home and many complaints about the adverse nature of the environment, only four out of ten heads, when asked the question 'Do you feel the need for a closer link and more cooperation with the parents of your pupils?' said 'Yes'. The prevailing attitude towards PTAs seemed to be extremely confused and illogical. One head said that he wanted to form one, but simply could not rely on obtaining the necessary backing from his colleagues. It is true, moreover, that, even if the majority of the staff should want an association, it could be forbidden by fiat from the head, and that would be an end to the matter.

So far I have said very little about family life or about the contents of the subculture as it affects the work of the schools in areas such as Crown Street. A great deal has been written about this, but if I may summarize a whole series of data, I think it is still true to say that the inhabitants of these older slum areas have comparatively narrow horizons and humble aspirations. The local and the concrete loom large in their eyes: they are fixated on the home and the neighbourhood. The family is still a fairly tightly-knit group of immediate relatives surrounded by an outer fringe of friends and neighbours who seldom cross each other's thresholds. Neighbours tend to borrow from one another. Standoffishness is acutely disliked, and life is social in the narrow sense that people seem to dislike doing things on their own or being conspicuously individualistic in their behaviour. 'They go through life with their arms linked, holding one another up,' commented one head teacher somewhat tartly. But, at the same time, the security and solidarity afforded by the group cannot so lightly be dismissed. Young people are especially gregarious and are invariably seen in small groups and clusters about the streets of the city. At an early age they are apprenticed to the neighbourhood peer-group, and they come to dislike being cut off from their associates to such an extent that they have little desire to do well in examinations if it means that they are then likely to be translated into another social setting and obliged to mix with unfamiliar faces. In terms of middle-class norms, the early years tend to lack consistent discipline and active training. Routines are neglected and a happy-go-lucky, sometimes a spendthrift, atmosphere prevails. Male and female roles still tend to be sharply segregated on outmoded Victorian lines. Housework and child care are mainly female spheres of interest; the man's duty is to bring home the money, deal out exemplary justice in the last resort, and, in his off-duty hours, enjoy himself relaxing at the local or watching football in the company of similarly placed males. Girls are expected to help at home and assist in looking after the infants. Boys are, by contrast, like their dads, much more fancy-free. Family life tends to be segmented, even the meals are seldom shared, and there is no tradition for group discussion or long-term planning. This does not mean that there is any lack of emotional warmth or of personal regard. It does mean, however, that since most of these families are comparatively large, children are left very much to their own resources, bringing one another up, and so become extremely vulnerable to influences emanating from the surrounding milieu. Mothers are especially overburdened, and, where the husbands are away from home for long periods or have abandoned the family, they find the load too much to bear. Small wonder, then, that they turn eagerly towards the school and the social services to get what help they can!

In general, then, we may say that the pattern of life in deteriorated inner-city localities is in many ways the antithesis of the more carefully organized middle-class suburban existence and, in so far as this is true, is simply not geared to secondary education as it has developed in this country during the past fifty or so years. Admittedly, I am painting the extreme in such a picture. There is a proportion of ambitious small families in such areas who are keen to rise socially, and who see education as a way to achieve their ambitions and a higher social status. But such households are the ones which are most willing to move away into the newer neighbourhoods, for the very reason, as they say, that in suburban localities their children will be healthier and get a better education.

What we are seeing is, I believe, no less than an elaborate exercise in social segregation, unwittingly promoted by rehousing and redevelopment policies, in which the aspirant families are given a degree of opportunity to get on and get out, whilst the residual group of less ambitious, possibly of less able and more inert families, remain behind to perpetuate a tradition of underprivilege and inferiority which will, unless I am very much mistaken, prove most difficult and stubborn to eradicate. We are living, in the central-city neighbourhoods, in the long twilight of the Two Nations; the divided groups are no longer the rich and the poor of former times, but the culturally deprived and intellectually divided of today and tomorrow. The final impression is somewhat depressing. Inferior physical provision, plus ineffective home background, plus schools with poor academic traditions, plus peer-group indifference or even hostility, add up to a total of disadvantage which is a formidable challenge to any kind of social engineering, as the comparatively ineffectual efforts to provide some kind of compensatory education have unfortunately shown.[11] Small wonder that the teacher at times feels helpless and inclined to give up the fight.

The problems that confront teachers in these downtown schools are multiple and complex in their mode of presentation and deeply grounded in the psycho-social matrix. They are not in fact purely educational problems. They certainly are not the kind of problems that many of them have been trained to cope with in their professional careers. As we have already said, faced with a seemingly impermeable barrier of public indifference and private apathy, some teachers cut their losses and get away by seeking transfers to schools in neighbourhoods where at least they will feel that the parents understand what they are trying to do and the authorities are supporting them. Give a school or a locality a bad name and it will increasingly be seen to live up to its reputation.

How can we hope to break into so vicious a circle? Are there any general administrative actions which might usefully be taken to improve the situation? Are any changes in the traditional conception of the teacher's role worth making?

Evidence accruing, for example, from Dr. Douglas's research, from Professor Fraser's, and from the investigations in Manchester and Salford described by the late Professor Wiseman,[12] seems to indicate that, in spite of adversities and manifold disadvantages, neither parents nor teachers are completely helpless in the face of neighbourhood norms unpropitious to educational objectives. The task resolves itself into ways of making school more intelligible to pupils and more attractive to parents. We have got to try to diminish, in the atmosphere of formal education, what Frank Riessman (1962) called 'the hidden dissuaders'.[13] They are potential in every school, and they are to be found much more extensively than we like to admit. A child's years at school have got to be made more and more a meaningful experience for him. The policy of drift which characterizes our general attitude to education has got to be halted and something more positive substituted.

The recently published research findings of Michael Rutter (1979)[14] and his colleagues permit me to end this chapter on a cautiously optimistic note. We have had two extremely influential and widely studied government-sponsored reports on the nation's primary and secondary schools: namely, the Newsom and Plowden Committee Reports. These highlighted many aspects of the general problem and in many ways bracketted the central target for us. But in the event surprisingly little positive work or practical results followed on their publication. The Educational Priority Area programme was something of an exception, but in the end it was allowed to peter out in a variety of minor activities and occasionally gimmicky ideas.

But *Fifteen Thousand Hours*, which abundantly confirms most commonsense views long held by practising teachers, perhaps points a possible way of improvement ahead and for once without the expenditure of large sums of public money. The findings of Rutter's team underline the vital importance of the right kind of schooling being available to disadvantaged children and the key role that teachers play in influencing children's academic work and also in modifying their general behaviour.

It is beginning to look as if schools during the past few years have tended to concentrate on the wrong objectives. Much more attention should perhaps have been given to imparting knowledge, ensuring sound learning and similar traditional pedagogical tasts, not excluding reasonable and firm discipline. Certainly the evidence produced by Rutter and his colleagues indicates that when teachers make a determined and concentrated effort to produce a sound working relationship with their pupils and to organize to that end, encouraging friendliness and cooperation as necessary elements in the process, children seem not only to produce better scholastic results but delinquency outside the school is also considerably reduced.

There are then grounds for limited optimism even for schools in the older and most disadvantaged inner-urban localities.

References

1. J.B. Mays (1968), *Education and the Urban Child*, Liverpool University Press, 3rd impression.
2. A.B. Hollingshead (1949), *Elmtown's Youth*, John Wiley, New York.
3. James S. Coleman (1961), *The Adolescent Society*, The Free Press, Glencoe.
4. J.W.B. Douglas (1964), *The Home and the School*, MacGibbon & Kee.
5. See *Education and the Urban Child*, op cit., pp.133-150.
6. E. Fraser (1959), *Home Environment and the School*, University of London Press.
7. A.B. Wilson (1959), 'Residential Segregation of Social Classes and Aspiration of High School Boys', *American Sociological Review*, Vol. 24.
8. D.F. Swift (1964), 'Who Passes the 11-Plus?', *New Society*, 5 March.
9. M.P. Carter (1962), *Home, School and Work*, Pergamon, p. 86.
10. R. Herriott and N.H. St.John's book *Social Class and the Urban School*, Wiley, 1966 showed that the influence and skill of head teachers were significantly important in determining the results of schooling in city neighbourhoods.
11. See A.H. Halsey, *Educational Priority*, HMSO, 5 vols. 1972-75.
12. S. Wiseman (1964), *Education and Environment*, Manchester University Press.
13. Frank Riessman (1962), *The Culturally Deprived Child*, Harper & Row, New York.
14. M. Rutter, B. Maughan, P. Mortimore and J. Ouston (1979), *Fifteen Thousand Hours*, Open Books, London.

CHAPTER 5

PARENTS AND TEACHERS: AN ACTION-RESEARCH PROJECT

James Lynch & John Pimlott

This chapter presents an account of a significant recent project, in which parents and teachers were involved in a systematic attempt to raise the level of awareness of the opportunities offered by closer home-school links.

Background

The project described in this chapter drew on the Plowden Report on primary education for its conception and sustenance. That report recognized that a broader social strategy was necessary if relationships between schools and their pupils' parents were to be improved and necessary professional networks extended.

The action research carried out in Southampton between 1972 and 1974 was aimed at assessing and improving community commitment to and involvement in education, by seeking to deliberately foster closer links between parents and teachers and by encouraging parental interest and involvement in the aims, objectives, and methods of their children's school. It was particularly aimed at seeking to detect existing levels and modes of interaction of parents and teachers and the satisfaction of both parties with these. The team sought to design and develop strategies that would enable schools, through improvements in home-school cooperation and coordination, to answer better the educational and *social* needs of children. It was thus concerned with an area of work which, at least since the publication of the Plowden Report, had attracted increasing attention, but little concrete activity. In this sense, the research described here followed closely the findings of Plowden and was complementary to the subsequent EPA research programme. The objective was to probe further a highly political and controversial area, one where head teachers, schools, parents' associations, and the teaching profession held strong and in some cases intransigent views.

If the research had to take account of the work outlined above and of the local and national political context, it equally had to come to terms with the developing research literature in the field of home-school relations. There was, for example, a mass of evidence highlighting the link between the child's home and his performance at school. Government reports from *Early Leaving* (1954) onwards had gradually and systematically exposed the substantial correlation between social class and academic ability and achievement, and more recent work had sought to account for this by reference to cultural standards and opportunities, levels of parental aspiration and the language style of the home, as well as the background of parents. The conclusion reached by the Plowden Report had been that the influence of background factors, such as living conditions and parental attitudes in the education of children, was crucial to their educational attainment. But it was believed that such attitudes were susceptible to alteration by persuasion, and that schools should thus seek the active cooperation of parents in the education of their children. The Southampton Project sought to do more than traditional lip-service had thus far done in achieving such active cooperation, fully aware that for some schools this was a 'taboo' area.

For this reason, and because it was clear to the team that parental participation must be taught, a second relevant area of research concerned with parent education was probed. Stern (1960) had observed that the very decision of a school to engage in parent education might lead to an important increment in cooperation between home and school, whilst Sharrock (1971), commenting on the cautious attitude to parent education to be found in Britain, had reported evidence suggesting that the majority of teachers might regard parent education to be partly the work of schools. This was a hopeful sign for the team; but on the other hand, Townsend (1967) had demonstrated the inadequate provision of in-service courses directly related to parent education and home-school relations. So the two main strands of the project design emerged in the form of parallel 'in-service' programmes for parents and teachers.

Additional background information was provided by the various surveys of home-school relations and descriptions of the strategies for their development and improvement. Work reported by Morton-Williams

(1967) surveyed such factors as parents' attitudes to the education which their children were receiving, and to their relationships with the teaching staff of their children's schools; whereas some other surveys had been restricted to more formal channels of parent/teacher contact, such as PTAs. Young and McGeeney (1968) described an experiment designed to improve home-school relations and to discover the influence of such improvement on the educational achievement of children; and Sharrock (*op.cit.*) gave an account of an action-research programme in which information gained from a survey of parents was fed back into the participating schools in order to stimulate change in parent-school contacts. This rapid feedback was also incorporated into the design, and hints on the methods to be adopted with the parents' groups were drawn from one early piece of experimental work which was reported in 1957 by Kellmer Pringle, and involved parent/staff group discussion at the Remedial Education Centre of the University of Birmingham.

Thus the aims and design of the project gradually took shape. However, we were also indebted to descriptive work in the area, two main sources of which may be cited. First, there were those writings, including several recent reports, which demonstrated the interrelationship of the educational and social services in developing greater equality of educational opportunity. The format and framework of the teacher groups owed much to this work. Writings such as those of Clegg and Megson (1970), and in a more systematic fashion the work of Birley and Dufton (1971), clearly exposed the bankruptcy of educational strategies alone in the pursuit of greater equality of opportunity, an assertion which was further reinforced by other national and international writings. Second, there were those descriptive accounts of work seeking to foster home-school relations through the development of community schools and particularly in deprived areas, stimulated and supported in the UK by a growing interest in compensatory education. Concern with the latter led to the development of relevant work in the five EPA research areas, aimed at improving educational opportunity for the socially disadvantaged; preparation of the findings of this large-scale action-research project had already commenced, and was followed later by the publication of the 'Halsey Report' (DES 1972), and Midwinter's book *Priority Education* (1973).

Such was the background work on which the project drew heavily, but there was also a tradition of concern for these areas at Southampton University. Over the three years, 1969-1972, the Southampton School of Education had been developing work in the area of the social aspects of education with practising teachers. In October 1971, for example, a part-time, in-service course, entitled 'Social Disadvantage and the Child' was initiated by a team of lecturers with the help of funding from the DES and the support and assistance of the LEAs in the region. The course sought through lectures and seminars, led by staff of the School of Education and personnel from local authority departments, to broaden the teachers' understanding of the social dimensions of their role and the interrelationship of the educational and social services in attempts to mitigate the worst aspects of social disadvantage. In the second phase of this course, small groups of teachers sought to develop empirical and descriptive studies into such areas as home-school relations, the pastoral role of the school, linguistic development, and the curriculum.

In the Southampton University Department of Extra-Mural Studies too, much experience existed of facilitating parental discussion groups. Such groups had been arranged in the 'disadvantaged' areas: one involving working-class housewives from a prewar council estate in one of the project schools' catchment areas, another in the old inner part of the city led by a tutor who had worked in the West Riding EPA project, and the third an ambitious piece of research, into ways of involving working-class people on large overspill council estates in forms of adult education aimed at helping the residents to generate community activities through self-help activities (see Fordham et al. 1979).

The aims of the project

The major aim of the project* was to study and, if possible, to improve the relationships of parents and teachers in a number of social and educational settings, in the first instance through the initiation of a series of investigations, giving rapid and confidential feedback to the schools involved, followed by action-research experiments. Thus, building on the widespread recognition of the need for parents to understand more about and to assist in the education of their children, the project aimed to involve parents in helping to further improve the educational service by developing understanding and tolerance of recognized contradictions in educational practice by finding ways to bridge them. It sought to foster community interest in educational values and objectives, including social services personnel and

*Described in detail in Lynch and Pimlott (1972).

members of voluntary organizations who worked with and alongside both groups. Finally, it attempted to add to the human efficiency of the process of formal education by seeking to clarify the objectives of this process for parents.

The project team was committed by these aims to seeking strategies which would help to secure parental involvement for all social groups, including those that were educationally and socially disadvantaged by criteria such as social class and ethnicity. Procedures were therefore aimed (a) at increasing parental concern, information, and interaction in educational matters, teacher interest in the parental involvement issue, parent-teacher understanding and communication, parent and teacher appreciation of the wider social dimensions of the education of children; and (b) at assessing the impact of improvement in these areas upon the educational and social welfare of the schoolchildren.

Research procedures

A pilot study was begun in October 1972 in three clusters of Southampton schools, balanced so as to contain substantial urban middle-class, urban working-class, and immigrant populations. Both *Enquiry I* (Morton-Williams and Finch 1968), and the N.F.E.R. Constructive Education Programme (1965-1971) had noted a marked decline of contact between home and school in the secondary compared with primary years of education, and so the clusters of schools each included a core secondary school. Prior to the commencement of the pilot study, monitoring activities were carried out to locate existing areas of parent/teacher cooperation and to secure the support of local authorities, schools, and parents' and teachers' associations. Because it was necessary to establish a theoretical and empirical base-line against which the action research part of the study could be developed, a sample of parents and teachers in each of the schools was surveyed by questionnaire for their views and perceptions of home-school relations, and this involved one other urban LEA in the south of England, three secondary comprehensive schools, and parents of children in up to sixteen schools. In addition, a smaller sample of respondents was surveyed through in-depth interviews.

Information from the pilot survey and interviews was rapidly processed and fed back to the schools concerned, and on the basis of this, the action part of the research was begun, first by involving parental and teacher discussion groups, and later, combined teacher-parent discussion groups which attempted to grow from provision of information, instruction, and guidance to self-programming work. The discussion groups were serviced in the first phase by project observers who drew up discussion records after each meeting, including summaries of discussions, inventories of educational and social relations issues, expressions of fear and uncertainty, and proposals for improvement. These were then discussed by the project team and were influential as the work proceeded. It seemed important from the beginning that, for confidence to be generated before major initiatives were taken, there should be a clear recognition of the human relations problems involved. Wherever possible, therefore, university staff were involved in working with these groups, as projections of currently existing or expanding in-service and/or adult education programmes. The major pedagogical philosophy was one of 'conscientization' on the part of the team (Freire 1972).

Research instruments and data

Survey questionnaires and interview schedules were developed on the basis of a theoretical framework covering potential social functions of the school. Responses were coded, first, to provide groups of variables from parents, including information concerning both parents, their education, occupation, family circumstances, and the age(s) of the child/children involved in schools concerned; second, to identify parents' perceptions of home-school relations and attitudes to them, the existing provision, desired extension of that provision, their confidence in contact with school and other educative agencies; and third, to define the parents' concept of the educative role of school. Subjective, objective, and intersubjective dimensions were drawn across factual, behavioural, and attitudinal data. Behaviour- and attitude-change dimensions were sought, as well as factual information on the grounds that recognition of an enlarged social function for the school on the part of the parents and teachers was involved. Because it was recognized that such extension had to be seen against the background of an increasingly 'privatized' society, with all the problems which that must entail for anyone seeking to develop and encourage 'involvement', particular attention had to be given to the motivation of groups and particularly 'those who never came'. This was achieved through contact with and support from local authority departments and such voluntary organizations as the local community relations council. For all of these reasons, it will be clear that a pluralist model of social change had to be adopted. Both consensus and structural conflict models were eschewed, though they were considered.

The initial collection of data aimed to provide a base-line for the work, and sought to monitor and evaluate the development of the work concurrently over a period of one academic year. The results of this first stage of the work were available in confidential form to the research schools by mid-1973, and they were used as a basis for the further development of the action-research method. Schools were offered consultancy advice on the interpretation of the initial results and their implications for the schools and their teachers. Financial and organizational assistance was also offered to the schools to arrange teacher in-service and adult education programmes. Where possible, arrangements were to be on a flexible self-programmed basis.

The aims and work of the parent groups

Parallel discussion groups were provided for parents and teachers in the three research schools, by the University Department of Adult Education and the School of Education. Looking first at the *parent* groups, their aim was to attract the 'average' parents who rarely, if ever, seek to actively understand and influence the way their children's schools operate. Indeed, the researchers deliberately sought to avoid those confident and articulate parents who tend to dominate parent-teacher organizations and parent evenings, and instead, to encourage the nonparticipators. It was intended that the parent groups should primarily discuss the importance of the home and the influences of both parents and the social environment on the education of their children. Furthermore, the informal and flexible programme of evening meetings included information about developments in the modern curriculum and teaching methods, and the changing structure and values of education. Practical discussions on existing methods of communication between home and school and ways in which parents could be more actively involved in the everyday life of the school were emphasized.

Whilst the teacher and parent groups were conducted separately in order to prevent professional domination, loss of confidence, and the exchange of initial prejudices and attitude-hardening dialogues, it was intended that the teacher and parent groups at each school should eventually be brought together at the end of their respective sessions. In this way, it was hoped that some permanent impact of a practical nature might be achieved which would help to improve home-school relations in all three schools.

After obtaining the active if not always enthusiastic cooperation of the three head teachers, informal notices giving information on the parent meetings were sent home with each child. In addition, posters and notices were displayed in post offices, shop windows, and launderettes in order to attract the normally nonparticipative mothers to the courses. In one area, a parent group leader used the highly effective though time-consuming practice of knocking on the doors of parents in order to encourage them to attend the meetings.

All three parent groups eventually attracted sufficient parents to establish worthwhile meetings. On the first evening, considerable efforts were made to encourage informality and remove anxieties and tensions. This was largely achieved by choosing skilled adult educators as group leaders who had no formal connections with the schools, and by holding the meetings in neutral premises near to the schools but not in them. While the general aims of the parent groups were agreed by all three tutors, they were left free to determine the content of their group discussions with the parents and to adjust their programme of meetings to satisfy the emerging parental interests and needs. Every effort was made to foster the parents' grasp of the educational and social significance of the home and social environment on their children's attitude to school, as well as the vital importance of deliberately structured home-school relationships.

The parent group leader was expected:

1 To develop personal relationships with parents and relevant parent social groups before the meetings commenced
2 To liaise closely with the heads and staffs of the schools concerned and to be sensitive to their problems
3 To devise a variety of ways of attracting parents from varied backgrounds into the discussion groups – this would require a high personal commitment and the use of unconventional approaches
4 To lead group discussions, arrange visits, introduce visiting speakers, arrange for films, and generally service the educational needs of the group
5 To evolve practical exercises for parents which would enable them to assist their child's home education, e.g., learning through play methods
6 To obtain teacher cooperation and involvement with the parent groups so that eventually parents could observe and take part, in a limited way, in the process of formal education

7 To draw up reports after each meeting of the events, deliberations, and issues raised
8 To attend coordination meetings at which reports could be read and discussed
9 To involve themselves with the overall project and its aims, and to be in a position to answer general questions about it and know where to refer more specific ones
10 To assist the group to develop initiative and organizing abilities so that parents could develop and sustain their own activities.

The social skill and sensitivity to establish and sustain a group of parents was considered to be an indispensable quality in the selection of group leaders. The group leader had to be prepared to involve himself/herself personally with the members of the group and their problems. In short, the level of commitment had to be high if the discussion groups were to succeed. The programme not only included talks, discussions, visits, films, and outside speakers, but also the involvement of parents in practical exercises and, if possible, experience in actual classroom situations. Where possible the group leader adhered to the prearranged programme, but if the continuation of the group was threatened he had to show considerable initiative, flexibility, and experimental capacity. The success and vigour of the parent groups was central to the success of the whole project. It was considered essential to find a meeting place which did not inhibit or intimidate parents.

Each parent group's programme included:

1 Preliminary meeting: aims and introductions
2 The organization of education in Southampton
3 The family and education – family rearing patterns/social class/language
4 How children learn
5 The importance of education in the distribution of life-chances
6 Curriculum and how it is developed
7 The training and work of the teacher
8 The social services and the school
9 The school and the community.

At the commencement of Phase II, no attempt was made to impose a detailed description of the work to be done in the second series of parent discussions. Much depended on the ground covered in the first term and the experience gained and evaluated by the group leaders. Different groups developed differently and so required individual assessment. Ideally, however, it was envisaged that the second term could deal with more abstract discussions on the values and aims of education, parents' and teachers' organizations, an outline of the major findings of educational research, visits to school and the Curriculum Development Centre, talks by teachers and other parents involved and interested in education, and the development of initiative and confidence in the parents so that they could develop schemes and programmes of their own.

The aims and work of the teacher groups

The objective of the *teachers'* groups was to develop increased awareness of the social dimensions of learning and of the teacher's role in its widest possible sense. To achieve this objective, the role of the teacher group leader was seen as:

1 To liaise closely with the head teacher and staff of the school concerned
2 To study the programme schedules and use these as guidance for the discussions
3 To initiate discussions within the teacher group and to be sensitive to its members' professional needs
4 To introduce visiting speakers and arrange for films to be shown
5 To arrange for relevant visits where necessary and generally to seek ways of fostering the professional development of participants
6 To draw up a report after each meeting of the events of the meeting, its deliberations and issues raised
7 To attend coordination meetings at which reports would be described and discussed
8 To acquaint himself in outline with the overall programme and its aims, to be in a position to answer general questions about it, and to know where to refer more specific ones
9 To assist the group to begin to take its own initiatives, to programme its own activities, and to begin to study the school and its social context.

The skill of the teacher group leader in achieving a sensitive balance between nondirective and programmed activity was crucial to the development of the project. It was important for teachers to feel that the sessions were worthwhile and that they were learning something, at the same time as appreciating that they had a very real role in deciding on and improving their own learning experiences. Thus, although it was desirable to set out and publish in advance a detailed yet flexible programme, on the other hand it was important that teachers realized the options open to them in the development of the work of the group. This included discussions, lectures by visiting speakers, syndicate-work visits, and later in the programme the possibility of T-group sessions. The meetings were not intended to provide information concerning the substantive or subject aspects of education; but rather to help teachers to study more closely the social dimensions of the teacher's role, and the interrelationship and interdependence of education, the social services, the home, school, and community.

Bearing this in mind, the following, set out in question form, was the proposed outline programme in Phase I:

1 What is the project? How is it organized and financed? What is it aiming to do and how does it expect to achieve this?
2 What is the role and responsibility of the teacher in education? Does the teacher transmit values and information? Whose values and what information?
3 What is the role of the home and family in learning? What evidence is there concerning relationships between family characteristics and educability?
4 What is the pastoral role and organization of schools? What is their social function?
5 How is the internal organization of schools related to other social services? How are the social services organized and under what circumstances can one expect to come into contact with them?
6 What are the roles of the school counsellor, a member of the social services department, a member of the police department, the education welfare officer, in the fostering of home-school relations?

At the commencement it was considered unwise to be too precise about the second phase programme, but it was thought that it should ideally include a session on educational research, on parents' associations and the role of parents and the wider community in formal education, a talk by a member of a parents' association, and an opportunity for one or more T-group sessions. Films and video-tapes were also used. Information could also begin to be fed across from one group to another and back from any surveys or interviews which had been carried out and processed, prior to the group taking on greater autonomy in programming its own activities.

The outcomes of the project

The value of the research described here is best measured by asking what the concrete and applicable results were for the money that was spent. Was it *effective*? Were the initiatives taken and the time and effort devoted to this modest, small-scale pilot project in attempting to identify and improve parent/teacher relationships worthwhile? With regard to the first cluster of questions it must be stated that the grant from the Schools Council was less than £1,000, although additional resources were obtained from elsewhere. But it was the unpaid commitment and enthusiasm of the research team who believed deeply that it needed doing which sustained the work and brought it to a successful conclusion. But there are a number of clearly identifiable items which could be said to have arisen directly from the project, both in the sense of provision of factual information and also, more importantly, in terms of behavioural and attitudinal change; although it is fair to say that tangible results specifically traceable to action-research projects are elusive. It is with all the usual provisos, therefore, that the following comments are made.

First, the improvement in staff information and morale, in two of the three clusters of schools, was quite noticeable. The way in which they felt able to develop new initiatives for the involvement of parents, even including the presence of some parents in classrooms while teaching was going on, was an achievement which the researchers felt to be extremely encouraging. This was believed to be the result of their increased knowledge and self-confidence, their greater knowledge of their own pupils' parents, and the frank examination of their own hopes and fears, concerns, and anxieties. They could identify gaps in information, provision, and understanding. Adjustments were made, for example in modes and styles of communication with parents and the channels through which they could communicate with the school.

Second, there were the insights gained by the project team into the strengths and failings of the strategies that they had proposed and developed. The opportunity to discuss and analyse with a group of parents and a group of teachers the programmes which had been arranged meant that it became possible to build on the research experience in the formulation and design of future projects.*

Third, specific initiatives, indicative of greater staff interest, confidence, and awareness, can be cited, such as that taken by one of the neighbourhood secondary schools in arranging a programme of in-service education on the theme of pastoral care and the social functions of the school jointly with its nearest neighbourhood comprehensive. It is fair to claim that this particular initiative arose directly from the project itself, though it seems apparent that such developments will only survive in the long term if, in each school, at least one member of staff is given the time and resources to prepare joint parent/teacher activities.

Fourth, there is the statistical evidence that became available through the surveys, questionnaires, and schedules which were developed and administered as a central part of the research project. Whilst caution is needed in interpreting these results because the project was on a small-scale and rather more akin to case studies than to a major social survey, there were, nonetheless, identifiable elements which seemed to reinforce either commonsense views current within the educational system at that time, or the results of research elsewhere. Full details of these are available in the Schools Council publication arising from the project (Lynch and Pimlott 1975). Reference should be made, however, to the attitude of immigrant parents to the education of their children as assessed through the questionnaire and interview schedules. There were strong indications that, contrary to the assumptions of many educationalists, these parents were more ambitious for their children to succeed than nonimmigrant parents, and that their nonparticipation in educational matters and school activities did not mean that these parents were uninterested in the education of their children. Ongoing social class and ethnic differentials in terms of parents' participation in schools were identified. Moreover, the social class distinction was the source of quite important cultural clashes within one institution, and could be said to be effectively excluding parents from the lower socio-economic groups from even wishing to be involved in school and particularly the middle-class-dominated parent-teacher association. Such clashes remain as yet unassessed for their impact on wider issues of parental

*Nothing in greater depth has been done in the interval since the end of the project in 1974, notwithstanding current N.F.E.R. work.

involvement and the development of a more participating society.

In general, there is no doubt that parents and teachers see the aims of schools differently, the amount of information which is provided, how it is provided, what opportunities exist and do not exist for involvement, and where improvements might commence. In other words, there is massive scope for breakdown in communication, misunderstanding, and professionalism which can often be damaging for children. One thing which clearly emerged from the teacher group evaluations was the desire of teachers for further courses in the ill-defined area of relationships between themselves and other members of social and professional groups such as educational welfare officers. Communication in the schools involved in the pilot project with parents and other professional groups, such as educational welfare officers and social workers, whilst varying in quality from school to school, was susceptible to very considerable improvement to the satisfaction of all parties. There is a clear need, as yet unsatisfied, for further in-service courses to focus on this area.

It is important to emphasize that the project did not, indeed could not within the brief time span involved, attempt to achieve long-term improvements in the quality and quantity of parental involvement. It was envisaged as a pilot project from which a future national study could grow. What it could do, and did try to do, was to develop strategies for the involvement of parents which could be tested for their effectiveness in the short term and assessed for their potential in the long term. In the event, due largely to political opposition, proposals for a national project were frustrated, and the work in this area remains largely at the same stage as when the pilot project was completed in 1974. In spite of much talk of parental involvement and information, in spite of revisions in the terms of reference of boards of governors and managers, in spite of the Taylor Report (DES 1977) and Circular 15/77 (DES 1977), for political and restrictive professional reasons, progress in the intervening years has been insubstantial and disappointing.

Issues arising from the project

From the very rich and wide-ranging investigations and activities which were part of the project, this section focusses on a number of points which were not referred to in the formal report which was published by the Schools Council. It attempts to link those points to current school problems, structures, and functions.

There is the central and relatively neglected role of parents in any effective pastoral care provision. Some participants in the project felt that there was a tendency to minimize if not to discredit parents, for example, by the encouragement of their participation from a position of weakness if not ignorance. Without knowledge, understanding, and cooperation between parents and teachers, pastoral care strategies adopted by professional agencies are crucially weakened, with consequent social and financial implications such as further fragmentation of the child's life and a waste of scarce resources.

At the same time, it is apparent that an effective home-school link-up is only one cornerstone of such an effective policy of intercommunication, and more specifically pastoral care. Cooperation and communication between existing agencies, both voluntary and statutory, needs to be deliberately examined and fostered if information flow and mutual understanding between schools, the home, and helping agencies is to be improved, and current administrative procedures and referral systems tested for their effectiveness and improved. Such improvement is indispensable to more effective support and intervention strategies, and it can only be achieved through sensitive analysis of the existing situation and by interprofessional team work. At the moment, this is inhibited by excessive concern for professional boundaries and by overrestrictive professionalism.

The current focus of pastoral care appears to be excessively school-based, in the sense that it implies a global but professionally and legally ill-defined commitment for teachers; a commitment for which little training is offered at either initial or in-service levels. Similarly, a prerequisite to effective diagnosis and timely referral is the identification of flexible, clear, and mutually understood task repertoires by the professionals concerned and the provision of adequate training. Parents are still often totally excluded from effective decisions in present procedures. Whilst the project began the process of tackling this cluster of issues, there was neither the political will, the professional support, nor the financial resources for a continuation, in spite of a proposal to this effect having been put forward.

Certain trends in social development and their educational implications are already clearly discernible. For example, the continuing fragmentation of social life and the rootlessness of many young people today is likely to increase the future importance of pastoral care in schools, as is the increasingly multiracial context of growing numbers of secondary schools. Identification of the emotional and intellectual needs of contemporary youth, and the development of appropriate organizational responses in schools, has lagged behind the mounting social crisis of youth and the legitimation crisis of schools. Conceptual and empirical work is urgently needed to provide a further basis for training for the professional needs implicit in this crisis, for it is evident that a short-term 'bolting of the stable door' can provide only a fragile response. A number of recent tragic cases illustrate this need (e.g., Southampton City Council 1974).

If sources of voluntary assistance could be identified, the strain on current resources could be eased. Initiatives such as the establishment of parental groups in this project, the transfer of funds from further to community education, the linking of professional efforts such as was attempted here, the support of a wide range of adult education activities in the community, and the pooling of the community human resources must be seen in the context of parallel evidence-gathering activity and the development and testing of all alternative strategies for the identification and forging of responses to currently unmet needs.

There can be no *one* answer or permanent solution. But the role of universities, polytechnics, and colleges in assisting educational systems to respond to social change cannot be overemphasized, although it must be seen against the background of the limited human and financial resources available. By and large, however, the neutral territory of such institutions provides a unique opportunity for seeding and experimental activities, for the provision of starter courses, and for the support and servicing of those who are in a position to act.

Existing departmental and professional structures, boundaries, and commitments need to be reviewed in the interest of a flexible and speedy response to identified problems. Indeed, organizational boundaries are already beginning to be challenged for their social relevance. This process needs to be systematized and institutionalized as social needs and problems emerge which are not susceptible to resolutions within existing structures. The slowing down of growth in educational budgets only makes more important continual reappraisal of the finance involved, according to explicit and socially sensitive priorities. Important long-term policy issues are at the base of any response, and these should be opened up for wider discussion, on the basis of deliberate decisions and informed judgement, rather than inspired drift. At the moment, and in spite of all the talk and writing, parents are very far from being recognized as partners by schools. But then, by and large, neither are other 'support' professionals either.

References

Birley, D. and Dufton, A. (1971), *An Equal Chance: equalities and inequalities of educational opportunity*, Routledge & Kegan Paul.

Central Advisory Council for Education (England) (1967), *Children and Their Primary Schools*, H.M.S.O.

Central Advisory Council for Education (England) (1959), *15 to 18*, H.M.S.O.

Central Advisory Council for Education (England) (1963), *Half our Future*, H.M.S.O.

Clegg, A. and Megson, B. (1970), *Children in Distress*, Penguin.

Committee on Higher Education (1963), *Higher Education*, H.M.S.O.

DES (1977), *A New Partnership for our Schools*, H.M.S.O.

DES (1972), *Educational priority: report of a research project sponsored by the DES and the S.S.R.C.*, (the 'Halsey Report'), H.M.S.O.

DES (1970), *In-service Training of Teachers in Primary and Secondary Schools, H.M.S.O.*

DES (1977), *Information for parents*, Circular 15/77. H.M.S.O.

Fordham, P., Poulton, G., and Randle, L. (1979), *Learning Networks in Adult Education: non-formal education on a housing estate*, Routledge & Kegan Paul.

Freire, P. (1972), *Pedagogy of the Oppressed*, Penguin.

Lynch, J. and Pimlott, J.A. (1975), *Parents and Teachers*, Schools Council Research Studies, Macmillan.

Midwinter, E. (1973), *Priority Education*, Penguin.

Morton-Williams, R. (1967), 'Survey among parents of primary school children', in C.A.C.E. (1967) *op.cit.*

Morton-Williams, R. and Finch, S. (1968), *Young School Leavers: report of a survey among young people, parents and teachers*, Schools Council Enquiry 1, H.M.S.O.

NFER, 'Constructive education project'. (Unpublished report sponsored by the DES and the Home Office, 1965-1971).

Pringle, M.L.K. (1957), 'An experiment in parent staff group discussion', *Educational Review*, Vol. 9., p.128-135.

Schools Council (1970), *Cross'd with Adversity*, (Working Paper 27), Methuen.

Sharrock, A. (1970), 'Aspects of communication between schools and parents', *Educational Research*, Vol. 12, p.194-201.

Sharrock, A. (1971), *Home/school Relations*, Macmillan.

Southampton City Council (1974), 'The Butter Rerport', Southampton.

Stern, H.H. (1960), *Parent Education*, Univeristy of Hull.

Young, M. and McGeeney, P.J. (1968), *Learning Begins at Home: a study of a junior school and its parents*, Routledge & Kegan Paul.

CHAPTER 6

RESEARCH ON HOME-SCHOOL RELATIONS

Anne Sharrock

*In this chapter, which concludes the theoretical contributions of Part Two, Anne Sharrock reviews a range of significant research and development studies which have attempted to explore and illuminate the relationships of homes and schools.**

Writing in 1964, Green, the author of an early study concerned with cooperation between parents and teachers, said 'there is very little literature on the question of home-school relations which originates in this country or is based on English experience.' The lack of any review of research in this field was very evident even at the end of that decade. Since then, increasing attention has been paid by educationalists, parents, and politicians to relations between schools and their pupils' homes. Whether that attention has been matched by an increase in relevant research will be one of the questions this chapter tries to answer.

Although the importance of home background for success in education had long been acknowledged, it was only after the Second World War that most of the major studies investigating the operation of this influence were undertaken. Such studies, some of which are discussed elsewhere in this book, have been concerned not only to show that children from certain social strata tend to do less well at school, but also to identify precisely those features of the home environment which are the most significant in influencing this success or failure. While a tripartite system of secondary education was still operating, interest in the home environment tended to be related to selection for the different types of secondary education. Educa-

*This is a revised version of a paper originally published in *Linking Home and School* (Longman, 1972).

tional research provided evidence that factors other than ability influenced selection, so supplying ammunition for the arguments in favour of comprehensive schools. Now that the comprehensive system is virtually nationwide the usefulness of such research has not declined, since it has become increasingly obvious that an unfavourable home background exerts its influence earlier and more extensively than was thought some years ago.*

Research into the relations between home and school can either be concerned with how the home influences attainment, length of schooling, and other aspects of education and occupational choice; or it can study the contacts and interaction between the two and their effects. In this chapter, research relating to both categories will be discussed but with more emphasis on the latter.

The relationship between home background and attainment

The past twenty years have seen the appearance of several major pieces of research which have contributed greatly to our understanding of the relationship between the child's home background and his attainment in school. Even before World War II, however, attention was beginning to be paid to this relationship (e.g., Hughes 1934), and its importance was underlined by Burt (1947) in the early postwar years. At that time, of course, the context was still that of selection for tripartite secondary education, but even then a more meaningful relationship between home and school was being advocated as an outcome of some of these researches. Campbell (1952) had shown that home environment affects secondary school achievement, and (though there was need for more research in this field) suggested that 'close cooperation between school and parents might enable use to be made of these findings in the most satisfactory manner'.

In 1959, Fraser described the position as still 'one where relatively little scientific research has been carried out to determine which aspects of the environment are most influential and which are relatively unimportant'. Fraser herself showed that home environment was more closely related to educational attainment than I.Q. was, and gave additional support to what was, by then, becoming very strong evidence for the importance of the child's home environment for his progress at school.

In the decade after Fraser's Aberdeen study, further evidence was pro-

*As, for example, in Floud, Halsey, and Martin's (1956) *Social Class and Educational Opportunity*, Heinemann.

duced of the relationship between progress at school and certain features of the home background. (Indeed, the home appeared to influence not only school attainment but also age of leaving school and other aspects of life related to education.) The importance of parental interest was emphasized in *The Home and the School* (Douglas 1964) and its sequel *All Our Future* (Douglas et al. 1968), reports initiated by the Population Investigation Committee. The 1964 report, concerned with primary school children, stated that the influence of parental interest on test performance was greater than that of any of the other three factors – size of family, standard of home, and academic record of the school – that were included in the analysis, and that it became increasingly important as the children grew older. *All Our Future*, which followed the same children through their secondary schooling, underlined the importance of the home.

Education and Environment (Wiseman 1964) had been planned as the first major project of the Manchester School of Education. Its second phase was 'an investigation of the relationship between educational attainment and social and environmental factors'. It was, however, the *school's* neighbourhood environment, of which the home is simply a part, that was under consideration in this northern survey, and no attempt was made to assess parental interest or to gather other data from individual children or parents. The results did, though, imply the necessity of looking further into the home to try to identify such aspects.

Perhaps the most important contribution during this period to the process of studying home background in relation to attainment was *Children and Their Primary Schools*, the report of the Plowden Committee (1967). The Government Social Survey carried out in 1964 the National Survey Among Parents of Primary School Children for the committee. Over 3000 parents were interviewed in their own homes about 'their attitudes towards the education their children were receiving and their relationships with the teaching staffs of their children's schools'. Interviewers also obtained information on the interest displayed by parents in their children's education, on the socio-economic status of the families, and on the physical conditions of the homes. The report echoed Douglas' findings in stressing the importance of parental attitudes: 'The variation in parental attitudes can account for more of the variation in children's school achievement than either the variation in home circumstances or the variation in schools.'

Although the report concluded that there was certainly an association between parental encouragement and educational performance, it felt that it was not then possible to say whether 'performance is better where parents encourage more' or whether 'parents encourage more where performance is better'. Not surprisingly, the committee offered the commonsense suggestion that each factor was related to the other and that homes and schools interact continuously. That it is an *interaction* we are concerned with here, and a complex one at that, has emerged since Plowden as both one of the essential features of any investigation into home-school relations and possibly the most inhibiting factor as far as the undertaking and completion of such research is concerned. (Cohen, 1979, for example, points out that more than a decade after Plowden there was still possibly insufficient investigation of the nature of the relationship between parental attitudes and children's social and academic progress at school; in her own study, parents described their own reactions to helping their children as being strongly influenced by the behaviour of their children.)

The Plowden Committee not only investigated features of primary school children's background which seemed likely to be related to performance in school, but made positive recommendations about action to be taken in the light of their findings to encourage a more fruitful partnership between home and school. The publication of the report was something of a watershed; much of what has happened in home-school relations, and other areas, in this country since then has developed in direct response to the initiatives of Plowden, or has to be seen in relation to the climate of opinion it created.

Thus, by the late 1960s educational research had been devoting an increasing amount of attention to the pupil's home environment in an effort to discover what environmental factors could account for variations in educational performance which were not the result of differences in innate ability, in so far as this can be measured (Craft 1970). For example, Cullen's (1969) survey in Ireland also substantiated existing evidence of a relationship between social class and educational performance. That differential performance could not be explained solely in terms of genetically determined ability – the nature *v.* nurture debate was to emerge again during the 1970s – was again underlined, and the usefulness of the concept of social class as 'a good indication of the probable educability of the child'.

A variety of environmental factors, such as social class and parental interest, had therefore been revealed as having an association with educational performance. Not only was there an association with more material features of the home environment, but also with less tangible aspects, such as parents' attitudes to education and other socio-cultural features such as 'language codes' (Bernstein 1961, and elsewhere). Bernstein's work indicated that there was a kind of culturally induced backwardness, transmitted and sustained through the effects of linguistic processes. The type of public language mode of speech ('restricted code') which the working-class child learned led to a low level of conceptualization; since the speech mode typical of the learning situation was formal and thus more akin to that of the middle-class pupil (who was more familiar with 'elaborated code'), the working-class pupil was, Bernstein hypothesized, inevitably at a disadvantage, and difficulties of communication would arise between teacher and working-class pupil.

The kind of socio-cultural variables which are needed to investigate which features of the home might be the most important for progress at school and for the interaction between home and school are not easy to isolate, and there are considerable problems involved in trying to measure, for example, 'parental attitudes', which do seem to be of the utmost importance.

If the process of investigating the relationship between home environment and school progress has shown an association between parental interest, encouragement, attitudes to education and achievement, then one might have expected parallel research into ways of fostering such interest and encouragement and supporting the 'right attitudes'; in short, research into the whole question of the relation between these two partners in the educational process – the home and the school. There has been an increase in research relevant to home-school relations in the decade since Plowden, but it has not been as great as might have been hoped for, and the emphasis has perhaps been on development rather than research.

Relations between two social institutions

The study of the relations between two social institutions, such as the home and the school, has comparatively few prototypes. Yet to try to increase contact and cooperation between the two without understanding the implications of their relationship may be inviting worse confusion. In 1968, William Taylor suggested four factors that need study as the theoretical basis for understanding the contacts between home and school: traditions of home-school relations in this country; the nature of the teacher's role and task in the school; the psychological factors in the relationships between teachers, pupils, and parents; and the interests of the family as an ongoing social unit.

The first of these has been considered in *The Family, Education and Society* (Musgrove 1966). Although he did not describe the actual contacts between parents and the staff of their children's schools, Musgrove considered the family as an educational agency, contrasting its influence with that of the school. The historical approach was also adopted in *Home-School Relations* (Sharrock, 1970b). Over the years the demands on the school have not only increased because of the more heterogenous nature of the pupil 'pool', but also because of social and political changes and the increasing impact of developments in psychology and human biology. Coombs and Lüschen (1976), in considering the evaluation of the performance of educational systems, suggest four constructs – effectiveness, efficiency, responsiveness, and fidelity – which can be used in examining the system output in relation to goals, cost, demands, and societal needs.

Responsiveness – whether the educational output has changed to reflect changes in the demands groups or individuals are making upon the system – is particularly relevant in the recent history of home-school relations: as Lynch and Pimlott (1976) point out, 'there was the marked tendency during the 1960s for people in this country to form pressure groups to seek solutions to particular problems'. This was especially so in the field of education, and several bodies (see below) were making demands for schools to be more responsive to the needs and wishes of parents. So far, however, there does not seem to have been any major work of social history devoted to the historical aspects of home-school relations in this country, and this is perhaps unfortunate since the insights it could afford might aid a clearer view of the way ahead.

To take Taylor's second point, many of the numerous studies of the teacher's role were reviewed by Westwood (1967a,b) in the journal, *Educational Research*. One of the classic studies of this kind was, in fact, written very much earlier – Willard Waller's *The Sociology of Teaching*, which first appeared in 1932. The ways in which the teaching and parental roles differ and overlap would appear to be a useful focus of attention for students of home-school relations; possible sources of conflict could be highlighted and possible areas for collaboration suggested. Waller noted that, 'in fact parents and teachers usually live in a condition of mutual distrust and enmity. . . . This fundamental conflict between the school and the parent is accentuated by the fact that parents and teachers are involved in different alignments of group life affecting the child.' Whether or not it is less true now that a 'condition of mutual distrust and enmity' exists between parents and teachers, the 'social/educational distance implicit in the role of teacher' (Lynch and Pimlott *op.cit.*), while not making failure inevitable, does necessitate close consideration of the mechanics not only of any home-visiting schemes but also in general strategies for bringing about closer parent-teacher relations.

The sociology of the school was described by Hoyle in an excellent article in 1965 as 'a rather neglected field of the sociology of education', and this is still perhaps broadly true. Recently, however, the 'Schools, Parents and Social Services Project' (quoted by Daphne Johnson in Chapter 21), in looking at the caring systems in secondary schools, has studied not only the different objectives and values of teachers in relationship to the contingent caring systems, but also the problems experienced by schools in 'crossing the boundaries' in order to work with other groups and institutions.

The third of Taylor's suggested areas of study would include teachers' and parents' expectations of each other's roles and their attitudes to each other. These are considered below. Lastly, the question of the interests of the family in relationship to the interests of the school and, by extension, to society, has apparently not been dealt with in any systematic way.

Parents' attitudes to education and to teachers

Mention was made earlier of the increasing emphasis on the importance of parental attitudes. One of the problems here is that of determining *which* attitudes to *what*. Sometimes 'attitude' is taken to be synonymous with 'opinion', or an expression of a preference for something, e.g., a particular form of education. Generally the term 'attitude' has been used fairly loosely in the literature, and a strict definition will not be adopted here since this would exclude some relevant work. The problem remains, however, of ascertaining whether it is parental attitudes to education, or to teachers, or to the school, or to children, or to life in general, or some mixture of all or some of these that is significant.

Investigation of parental attitudes as measured by the degree of interest expressed in the child's education and by preference for type of secondary school was the method used in some of the earlier studies of social factors related to success in education, (e.g., Floud, Halsey, and Martin 1956, Political and Economic Planning 1961, Donnison 1967). In *Children and Their Primary Schools*, the report of the survey among parents of primary school children shows that questions on preferred type of school were used here too, together with others on the responsibility and initiative taken by parents over the child's education, paternal interest and support, the parents' aspirations for the child, etc. (Several variables were classified as attitudes in this survey but were not all tested in the same way.)

The level of interest shown by parents figured too in Douglas' *The Home and the School*, assessed partly from the teachers' judgements and partly on the number of times each parent visited the schools to discuss their child's progress with the head or class teacher. This is not the only study in which parents' visits to the school have been used as an index of their interest (see also Rex and Tomlinson 1979), but this method has certain obvious disadvantages.

The use of more sophisticated attitude measures, such as attitude scales, was not so widespread, at least in this country, in the earlier studies of parental attitudes, although measurement of attitudes by such means was becoming increasingly important. Some of the problems associated with attitude measurement seem to be accentuated in the case of parental attitudes and this is perhaps why researchers have tended to avoid investigating them. Nevertheless, some attempts have been made to use attitude scales of various types in the study of the relationship between home background and attainment, and of relations between home and school.

As interest in home-school relations increased, it became more obvious that comparatively little was known about parental attitudes to education and related topics. Craft (1974) investigated participation in secondary education in Ireland, using questionnaires and Likert-type scales for parents which attempted to chart fathers' and mothers' attitudes to education and to teachers and to analyse more basic value orientations.

More traditional and direct methods have continued to be used and can provide useful information. In a Schools Council pilot study carried out in 1972-1973, parents' views on education and opportunities provided by their child's school were investigated by questionnaires and home interviews (Lynch and Pimlott 1976)* In fact, the aim of the study was 'to seek to improve home-school relations in three secondary schools'. One of the indications from the action-research side of the programme was that changes have a better chance of being instituted if accompanied by adequate explanation and understanding, i.e., that parental attitudes are susceptible

*See also Chapter 5.

to modification if the procedures for inducing change are sufficiently well thought out. As Fleming noted in 1959, 'it is more readily admitted that changes can be effected in the attitudes of even the most antagonistic'.

Elsey and Thomas (1976), in a small but valuable 'consumer survey' of the parents of children at a school in the Nottingham area, looked at parents' (and teachers') views about key aspects of school life in general. Among several topics studied were overall aims of education and the involvement of parents in different aspects of school life. (Items on school objectives and their expression were mostly borrowed from the Schools Council survey of young school-leavers.) One important conclusion drawn, which is obviously highly relevant for schools as informers and educators of parents, was that if parents were without sufficient knowledge to express opinions on certain matters studied, then this indicated a fairly serious breakdown between the school and the community it served.

A *change* in parental attitudes could improve home-school relations and, it is inferred, raise the level of attainment, but comparatively little research has been done in this country on schemes designed to change parental attitudes and assess any educational outcomes that could be directly linked to such changes (see below). Miller (1971) had suggested further research was needed to determine the effectiveness of different means of encouraging parental interest; and attempts to change parental attitudes abound in the numerous development schemes of the late 1960s and 1970s, particularly in educational priority areas, but they have perhaps not been adequately researched yet.

Whether attitudes to education and/or schools do in fact spring from more fundamental value orientations could be a question raised by a recent project of East Sussex LEA and the University of Sussex on 'Accountability in the Middle Years of Schooling'. As part of the research, interviews were carried out with seventy parents and, from these, five parent 'profiles' have been drawn up. The profiles were described as modes of apprehending and approaching educational matters '. . . a coherent position from which schools are judged'. The study as a whole, intended as a policy analysis in the area of accountability, was not concerned solely with parental attitudes but it obviously has implications for home-school relations (and is interesting moreover for its relevance to Coombs and Lüschen's (*op.cit.*) comments on policy-making and educational systems).

Parents' attitudes to teachers would be expected to colour their relations with them, and it is safe to assume that these attitudes will be affected by parents' conceptions of the teacher's role. An enquiry among teachers and parents by Musgrove and Taylor (1965) showed that parents agreed in substance with the ratings made by teachers, although it was interesting to note that there were some considerable discrepancies between what teachers thought parents regarded as important and what parents did in fact think.* *Enquiry 1* (Schools Council 1968) also showed considerable similarity between teachers' and parents' views on many school objectives; the greatest differences appeared to be on questions relating to careers and the vocational orientation of school work, with parents tending to give these relatively more importance. Substantial differences between parents and teachers about the importance of various school objectives could be a source of conflict between them.

Heads' and teachers' attitudes to parents and home-school contacts

In the field of home-school relations it is obviously essential to investigate not only parents' attitudes, but also those of teachers and heads. According to Green (1964), 'in selecting certain ways of communicating with parents and rejecting others, the teachers of any school are revealing quite fundamental attitudes to education.' Until fairly recently, however, there had been little systematic investigation of the attitudes of teachers, in this country at least, to contacts with parents on broader aspects of education. Yet if the types of home-school contacts chosen by teachers reveal attitudes to education, then perhaps these attitudes should be investigated more thoroughly, although possibly one should distinguish between heads and teachers, because the contacts chosen may well reflect the attitudes of the head rather than of the teachers.

For many years Wall's (1947) enquiry into head teachers' experience of parent-teacher cooperation was apparently the only survey devoted solely to heads'/teachers' opinions or attitudes on home and school contact. (In this study, the overwhelming majority of teachers felt the need for cooperation between home and school, but there was no such unanimity about the ways in which it might be achieved.) In the late 1960s and 1970s the picture began to change: Spencer (1969), for example, investigated one spcific form of

**Home, School and College*, a discussion paper prepared by the LEA Inspectorate (*op.cit.*), also notes the discrepancy between heads' perception of parents' views and what parents actually thought.

contact – PTAs – in an enquiry directed to heads. Later work with broader aims has included data on such opinions, on teachers' attitudes to parents in general, or on specific aspects of education. Studies such as those led by Douglas, the surveys of teachers for the Plowden Committee, and *Enquiry 1* have all been concerned, in one form or another, with the relations between home and school.

How teachers see their role, and the role of the parent, can indicate their attitude towards contact with the home. Cohen (1967) looked at 'the teacher as a liaison between school and neighbourhood', and compared expectations held by students, tutors, and head teachers. The responses to the question whether teachers should visit the homes of problem children to discuss their difficulties with their parents showed attitudes to contact with the home in a very direct way (see also the section on Types of contacts, below). Interestingly enough, although 64 percent of students expressed approval, only 18 percent of heads did so. In Lynch and Pimlott's Southampton study (*op.cit.*) teachers' attitudes to home visiting were similarly sought, and over 80 percent thought a school counsellor ('a teacher specially trained to help a child in difficulties') should do this, compared with 50 percent supporting the idea in the case of the child's teacher. In this particular study and in others, there is evidence that teachers feel extra training is perhaps needed to implement some aspects of closer home-school contact, and that this closer contact will also involve extra time and effort on their part and thus merit higher pay.

Differences between heads' and teachers' attitudes have emerged in various studies, as in the Plowden Report, which provided information on teachers' preferences about types of contact. Not surprisingly, heads preferred their own individual interviews with parents while teachers preferred theirs. Although surveys of this kind do not add much to our knowledge of the basic attitudes underlying such views, some attempts have been made to investigate teachers' attitudes to education and their views on its aims (Oliver and Butcher 1962, 1968, Taylor et al. 1974). Elsey and Thomas (*op.cit.*) also sought teachers' views on overall aims of education. In the Schools Council study which was in the broader context of an enquiry into the aims of primary education, it is interesting to note that Taylor et al. (1974) found that teachers thought parents were only of little influence on what is taught; but when asked to indicate whether or not they felt each of the twenty-eight influences listed could be reciprocated, the largest percentage of reciprocation (41.7 percent) was for parents. In general, it seemed that teachers are in receipt of influences to a much greater extent than they feel able to reciprocate them, i.e., a low general level of reciprocation – except for parents. In a different context, could this be taken to mean that in their contacts with parents teachers would see themselves as the dominant partners and less as 'functionaries'?

There does not as yet seem to have been much attempt to relate attitudes to education to preferred types of contacts with homes, and the study of the relation of schools with homes generally is only proceeding slowly. One thing that seemed to be clear, at least in *Children and Their Primary Schools* and in *Enquiry 1*, was that heads and teachers preferred informal contacts to formal ones. (The recent NFER project on *Parental Involvement in Primary Schools*, see Chapter 9, does report an increase in the number of PTAs, but there still seems to be some suspicion that they are counterproductive in some cases.) If this pronounced preference indicates fundamental attitudes, it may still be inappropriate to try to bring about greater parent-teacher cooperation by the formation on a large scale of organized bodies of parents.

Finally, another potential source of conflict arising out of discrepancies between heads'/teachers' and parents' views has been outlined by Tomlinson in a study of children moving into special education in Birmingham (see Chapter 12). Thirty heads were asked about their perceptions of the problems West Indian and Asian children in general presented in the school. Tomlinson notes, '. . . the immigrant parents' expectations of the schools and the definition of their children as a problem, both by educational policymakers and by teachers, produce a situation of misunderstanding at best and direct conflict at worst.'

Types of contacts between homes and schools

Whether attitudes to education or anything else do underlie the types of contacts which heads and teachers choose to have with their pupils' homes, we should at least know what contacts do exist, their extent and effectiveness. Until the Plowden Report this was a relatively unexplored field. It might seem simple to find out the numbers of formal associations of parents and teachers, such associations being one of the most obvious, though not necessarily most effective, ways of linking homes and schools. In any case, some PTAs are unaffiliated to the National Confederation of Parent-Teacher Associations.

It is now possible to get a clearer idea of the extent of these associations from data gathered in studies mentioned above. There would seem to have been a marked increase in the number of PTAs in the years since the Plowden Report, at least in primary schools. Seventeen percent of the national sample for the Plowden Committee had PTAs, whereas the national sample for NFER referred to above shows an incidence of 35 percent, which did not include less formal associations such as 'Friends of the School'. No recent national data exist for secondary schools, but 16 percent of fifteen-year-old leavers, 30 percent of sixteen-year-olds, and 46 percent of eighteen-year-old leavers were in schools with a PTA according to *Enquiry 1*. These averages concealed variations, between regions of the country for example. There is as yet no adequate data on the range of activities undertaken specifically by PTAs, and it is sometimes hard to distinguish between those carried out under the aegis of the PTA and those for which the school itself (or the head) is responsible.

Children and Their Primary Schools and *Enquiry 1* provided some valuable information on the opportunities provided for parents to visit the schools and the extent to which these opportunities were taken. As far as primary schools are concerned, the picture has now been brought up to date by the NFER project described in Chapter 9. Its aim was 'to establish the extent and nature of parental involvement in primary school life nationally, a decade after Plowden'. It shows a wide variety of ways in which schools attempt to involve parents, and discusses the factors influencing school-based and classroom-based involvement. Social class still seems to exert a strong influence, which calls into question the methods used to date to try to counteract this influence, but other factors should not be ignored. The two earlier studies had shown differences between primary and secondary schools, with far fewer parents of secondary school children having had any real talks with their child's head or class teacher. The more frequent presence of the parent through physically bringing the child to school in the younger age-groups seems related to the achievement of an easier day-to-day contact in the early years of school life, not to mention what have been described as progressive feelings of curricular incompetence as the child grows older.

The data from these surveys* give us some idea of the various types of contact between home and school, but they do not fill in all the detail nor do they tell us much about the effectiveness of these contacts in promoting

*And of others based on local initiatives, e.g., a county survey carried out by the Surrey LEA inspectorate in 1976 which included data from questionnaires sent to heads of all secondary schools and the views of about 400 'selected' parents.

cooperation between home and school. However, 55 percent of the heads in the NFER survey believed that parental involvement had increased over the last two years, and 63 percent of these believed parental attitudes had changed markedly as a result. The assumption is, of course, that the 'right' parental attitudes, and parental interest and encouragement, will help to raise the level of attainment, so this cooperation is presumably meant to foster the right attitudes, awaken and increase such interest, and support this encouragement. By so doing one hopes that not only will attainment levels be raised generally, but that this will happen in the very cases where it is most needed, which seem to be among the children in the semiskilled and unskilled working class. This desirable state, it is inferred, will be reached if parents are accepted as 'full partners in the educational system'.

There have, in fact, been very few attempts to assess carefully the effectiveness of different forms of contact between home and school, or to introduce changes in the contacts in a school and assess the results. (The introduction of changes have been legion and the literature is extensive, but assessment of the results is another matter.) Apart from Green's (*op.cit.*) study, that reported by Young and McGeeney (1968) was also concerned with the development of cooperation between school and parents. It described an 'attempt to introduce change into a school . . . to make new arrangements for communicating with parents and see what happened afterwards'. Statistically significant changes in test results were reported as a result, but these may have been, as the authors point out, due to practice, better teaching, *or* increased parental interest, and there should have been a longer interval between the test and retest.

Communication with parents is probably one of the most crucial aspects of home-school relations. Traditionally the most common form has been the school report, and there has been considerable dissatisfaction expressed in recent years with the traditional forms of written reports (Jackson 1971). Even earlier, the need for better methods of communication with parents was stressed in both the P.E.P. (1961) pamphlet and *Education and the Working Class* (Jackson and Marsden 1962), and also by Sharrock (1970a). Elsey and Thomas (*op.cit.*) point out that schools might still be failing to give parents information that was needed in order to be able to form opinions. A much larger-scale project now under way and due for completion in 1981 is the NFER 'School Reports to Parents' study. This aims to 'investigate current school policy and practice concerning reports to parents, examining in detail the operating procedures and the implications for teachers, parents and pupils in selected schools'. Evidence from this survey in secondary schools it is hoped will provide guidelines for schools seeking to make their reporting procedures more effective.

Reports are, of course, not the only method of communication. 'The written materials which schools produce, chiefly for their parents, are an important but often neglected feature of their contact with the outside world'; Bastiani (1978) in *Written Communication Between Home and School* looks at some functions of school brochures and describes four different models or types: the basic information model, the public relations model, the parental involvement model, and the developmental model. Again, one conclusion is that more hard work needs to be done if parents are to understand modern education in any meaningful way and to be involved effectively, for example, in subject choice.

Two other types of contact or involvement should be touched on here, although it will necessarily be briefly. Educational home-visiting schemes (see also Chapter 7 and 8), and the involvement of parents as managers/governors have both featured more frequently in discussion of home-school relations in the past decade. The National Children's Bureau has collated information about home-visiting schemes (Pugh 1977), which in this country appear to have originated in 1970 as part of an EPA action-research programme in the West Riding. The NCB points out that whereas earlier, American projects tended to be compensatory, 'the British schemes have aimed to help parents feel that they have an important part to play in their own child's development'. This emphasis on encouraging mothers to play their 'unique and irreplaceable part in promoting the educational development of their children' is firmly stated in Raven's project for the Scottish Council for Research in Education (report forthcoming). It does, however, raise some pertinent questions about possible undesirable effects, and whether or not it is possible to influence the sort of person a child will grow up to be. It also raises questions about the most effective type of approach by EHVs, and the difficulty which high socio-economic status researchers have in finding items which low socio-economic status informants will see as 'very important'.

Since the publication of the Taylor Report in 1977, and its recommendation that the governing body of schools should consist 'in equal numbers, of local education authority representatives, school staff . . ., elected parents (and eligible pupils) and representatives of the local community', more attention has been paid to the involvement of parents in school life as governors. Parent governors were not of course unknown before that date,* but although the Taylor Report pointed out that 'Parent governors are an important means of developing a closer relationship between homes and schools', there has not yet been any large-scale investigation in depth of parents as governors and of their effectiveness. It may still be the case, as Lynch and Pimlott (*op.cit.*) point out, that 'it is clear that innovations involving greater parental participation in school government have a weighty task of parent education to reckon with if they are to be successful.'

Parent education

Do schools have a responsibility, not only to educate children, but to undertake some form of parent education? An international survey by Stern (1960) was a major contribution to the understanding of what constitutes parent education, and what is its *raison d'être*. In *Parent Education*, the medical, psychological, and social reasons for parent education were explored. The report suggested that the importance of the parent-child relationship, for example, could be made more generally known through some form of parent education. Lynch and Pimlott, more than a decade later, felt that their work indicated that a majority of parents still believed the home's influence was minimal compared with that of the formal processes of education. If this belief is indeed widespread, and evidence of the need in other areas for greater attention to parent education has been quoted, then schools and probably also the organizations concerned with home-school links have so far failed to meet the demands which a real 'educational partnership' would necessitate.

Organizations concerned with home-school links

Perhaps the three principal organizations in this country that have been most concerned with the relations between home and school are the National Confederation of Parent-Teacher Associations, the Campaign (formerly Confederation) for the Advancement of State Education, known as CASE, and the Advisory Centre for Education (ACE). The NCPTA is the descendant of earlier bodies such as the Committee for Parent-Teacher Cooperation. The Home and School Council now exists mainly as a coor-

*A survey published by the National Association of Governors and Managers in 1975 showed that in 70 out of 82 LEAs provision was made for parents to be represented on governing and managing bodies.

dinating and publishing body, but it did carry out research work of its own at one time. The NCPTA, CASE, and ACE are each committed to the promotion of better links between home and school and each has been using a variety of methods and approaches to this problem. None of these organizations has so far been the object of or instigator of major research, although they have produced some local surveys and small-scale studies. Their emphasis has been, perhaps understandably, on development.

The need for further research

In this paper and elsewhere in this book some recent research in the field of, or relevant to, home-school relations is discussed. The boundary between research and development is not always clear and many of the projects that 'catch the headlines' are more properly forms of the latter. In considering research into the relations between home and school, I have looked at some of the mass of evidence which now exists to confirm the link between a child's home and his performance at school. Since there is little doubt that the two are related, it then seemed logical to look at research on the parent-teacher relationship, and at some of the factors which may determine the type and effectiveness of contacts in bringing about a closer, more harmonious, and more fruitful partnership between homes and schools in the education of children.

There are many obvious gaps in our knowledge still, particularly in research of the second kind. The present climate of opinion is, in some respects, favourable to the expansion of such research, in spite of the emergence of a renewed emphasis on an 'accounting' model of education. The current, unfavourable economic situation, however, may force a postponement of research programmes that could provide vital information, although obviously some important contributions have been made in this field in the past decade.

What research does seem most necessary? Some possibilities have already been mentioned. Other projects reported elsewhere in this book raise issues that need further examination: if it is true that schools 'constitute for parents part of their frame of reference in a way not found to be true of other caring agencies', then the school's significance is something that could be built on in a more purposeful way. Another interesting point raised by the work of Johnson et al. is that parents' perceptions of the school are conditioned by family dynamics in a way not generally understood by teachers. We still therefore need more sociological perspectives on the relation between the two social institutions – school and home – and more information on the attitudes of heads and teachers that are significant in their contacts with parents, and about the corresponding parental attitudes.

The existence of discrepancies between parents' and heads'/teachers' views was mentioned above. Lynch and Pimlott note divergencies not related to parental satisfaction or dissatisfaction with the school, and wonder whether 'the former cosy consensus between parents and teachers is gradually changing'. Is this related to an increasing trend towards consumerism and participation? To what extent are teachers' dissatisfactions and frustrations likely to prevent what they see as perhaps increasing ramifications of their role? One area that surely merits further attention is that of the forms of communication between school and home, particularly in view of the persistence in the findings of social class as an important variable. Then there are the views of pupils (Garvey 1977) which have received scant attention as yet.

In spite of the methodological complexities, more evaluative research on the effectiveness of home-school contacts in raising levels of attainment and in effecting attitude change would be welcome. The possibilities of further research in home-school relations are legion, and any research carried out is likely to be welcomed by teachers, educationalists – and parents – since it could suggest changes in actual practice.

References

Some relevant studies which are not referred to in this chapter are included.

Banfield, J., Bowyer, C., and Wilkie, E. (1966), 'Parents and education', *Educ. Res.* Vol.9, No.1, pp.63-66.

Bastiani, J. (ed.) (1978), *Written Communication Between Home and School.* University of Nottingham.

Bernstein, B. (1961), 'Social structure, language and learning', *Educ. Res.*, Vol.3, No.3, pp.163-176.

Burt, C. (1947), 'Symposium on the selection of pupils for different types of secondary schools', *Brit. J. Educ.Psychol.*, Vol.17, Pt.2.

Campbell, W.J. (1952), 'The influence of home environment on the educational progress of selective secondary school children', *Brit. J. Educ. Psychol.*, Vol.22, Pt.2.

Central Advisory Council for Education (England) (1954), *Early Leaving* ('Gurney-Dixon Report'), HMSO.

Central Advisory Council for Education (England) (1967), *Children and their Primary Schools* ('Plowden Report'), HMSO.

Cohen, J. (1979), 'Patterns of parental help', *Educ. Res.*, Vol.21, No.3, pp.186-193.

Cohen, L. (1967), 'The teacher's role and liaison between school and neighbourhood', in *Linking Home and School*, ed. M.Craft, J.Raynor, and L.Cohen (1st edition, 1967), Longman.

Coombs, F. and Lüschen, G. (1976), 'System performance and policymaking in West European education: effectiveness, efficiency, responsiveness and fidelity', *Int. Rev. of Educ.*, Vol.22, No.2, pp.133-153.

Craft, M. (ed.) (1970), *Family, Class and Education: A Reader*, Longman.

Craft, M. (1974), 'Talent, family values and education in Ireland', in Eggleston, S.J. (ed.), *Contemporary Research in the Sociology of Education*, Methuen.

Cullen, K. (1969), *School and Family*, Gill and Macmillan.

Department of Education and Science (1977), *A New Partnership for Our Schools* ('Taylor Report'), HMSO.

Donnison, D.V. (1967), 'Education and opinion', *New Society*, 26 October.

Douglas, J.W.B. (1964), *The Home and the School*, MacGibbon and Kee.

Douglas, J.W.B., Ross, J.M., and Simpson, H.R. (1968), *All Our Future*, Peter Davies.

Elsey, B. and Thomas, K. (1976), *The School in the Community: A Case Study in Community Education*, University of Nottingham.

Erault, M. 'Accountability in the Middle Years of Schooling', Joint Project of East Sussex L.E.A. and the University of Sussex (report forthcoming).

Fleming, C. (1959), *Teaching: A Psychological Analysis*, Methuen.

Floud, J. (1962), 'The sociology of education', in *Society: Problems and Methods of Study*, ed. T.D. Welford et al., Routledge & Kegan Paul.

Floud, J. and Halsey, A.H. (1961), 'Homes and schools: social determinants of educability', *Educ. Res.*, Vol.3, No.2, pp.83-88.

Floud, J., Halsey, A.H., and Martin, F.M. (1956), *Social Class and Educational Opportunity*, Heinemann.

Fraser, E. (1959), *Home Environment and the School*, University of London Press.

Garvey, A. (1977), 'Do children want parents in school?', *Where*, No.125.

Goodacre, E.J. (1968), *Teachers and their Pupils' Home Background*, NFER.

Goodacre, E.J. (1970), *School and Home*, NFER.

Green, L.J. (1964), 'The development of parent-teacher cooperation in a London junior school', unpublished M.A. thesis, University of London.

Green, L.J. (1968), *Parents and Teachers: Partners or Rivals?*, Allen & Unwin.

Hoyle, E. (1965), 'Organizational analysis in the field of education', *Educ. Res*, Vol.7., No.2, pp.97-114.

Hughes, A.G. (1934), 'Discrepancies between results of intelligence tests and entrance examinations to grammar schools', *Brit.J.Educ.Psychol.*, Vol.4, pp.221-236.

Jackson, B. and Marsden, D. (1962), *Education and the Working Class*, Routledge & Kegan Paul.

Jackson, S. (1971), 'Those bad school reports', *Where*, No.54.

Johnson, D. (ed.) et al. (forthcoming), *Secondary Schools and the Welfare Network*, Allen & Unwin.

Lindsay, C. (1970), *School and Community*, Pergamon.

Lynch, James and Pimlott, J. (1976), *Parents and Teachers*, Macmillan Education,

Schools Council Research Studies.
Miller, G.W. (1971), *Educational Opportunity and the Home*, Longman.
Musgrove, F. (1966), *The Family, Education and Society*, Routledge & Kegan Paul.
Musgrove, F. and Taylor, P. (1965), 'Teachers' and parents' conceptions of the teacher's role', *Brit. J.Educ. Psychol*. Vol.35.
Oliver, R.A.C. and Butcher, H.J. (1962), 'Teachers' attitudes to education', *Brit. J. Soc.Clin. Psychol*. Vol.1, pp.56-59.
Oliver, R.A.C. and Butcher, H.J. (1968), 'Teachers' attitudes to education', *Brit. J. Educ. Psychol*., Vol.38, Pt.1.
Political and Economic Planning (1961), *Parents' Views on Education*, P.E.P.
Pugh, G. (1977), 'Educational home visiting schemes', *Where*, No. 132.
Raven, J. (1979), 'Educational home visiting and the growth of competence and confidence in adults and children', Scottish Council for Research in Education, (report forthcoming).
Rex, J. and Tomlinson, S. (1979), *Colonial Immigrants in a British City*, Routledge & Kegan Paul.
Schools Council (1968), *Enquiry I*, HMSO.
Sharrock, A. (1970a), 'Aspects of communication between schools and parents', *Educ. Res*., Vol. 10, No.3.
Sharrock, A. (1970b), *Home/School Relations*, Macmillan.
Spencer, A.E.C.W. (1969), 'Parent-teacher associations in Catholic schools', *Catholic Education Today*, March/April.
Stern, H.H. (1960), *Parent Education: An International Survey*, University of Hull; Hamburg: Unesco Institute for Education.
Taylor, P.H. et al. (1974), *Purpose, Power and Constraint in the Primary School Curriculum*, Macmillan Education, Schools Council Research Studies.
Wall, W.D. (1947), 'The opinions of teachers on parent-teacher cooperation', *Brit. J.Educ. Psychol*., Vol. 17.
Waller, W. (1965), *The Sociology of Teaching*, 1st Science Editions, Wiley (first published 1932).
Westwood, L.J. (1967a), 'The role of the teacher–I', *Educ. Res*., Vol.9, No.2, pp.122-134.
Westwood, L.J. (1967b), 'The role of the teacher–II', *Educ.Res*., Vol.10, No.1, pp.21-37.
Wiseman, S. (1964), *Education and Environment*, Manchester University Press.
Young, M. and McGeeney, P.J. (1968), *Learning Begins at Home*, Routledge & Kegan Paul.

CHAPTER 7

COMPENSATORY EDUCATION AND SOCIAL POLICY

Jack Demaine

Many accompanying chapters take the view that schools or welfare agencies need to 'compensate' for deficiencies in children, homes, or broader social arrangements and priorities. In this chapter, Jack Demaine considers a variety of perspectives.

Introduction

The idea of 'compensatory education' is usually discussed with reference to Project Head Start in America[1] or to the educational priority area policy recommended by the Plowden Report.[2] In this chapter we will be concerned primarily with the latter and therefore with England, and with more general questions surrounding the notion of compensatory education.

The notion of compensatory education involves the idea of the 'lack' of something which has to be 'compensated' for and it invariably involves the idea of 'need'. Compensatory education is usually conceived in terms of 'positive discrimination' in favour of groups or individuals in need. Before we examine these ideas in detail, let us look at the classical formulation in paragraph 151 of the Plowden Report. Here we find the statement of what Plowden considered to be the problem and what it considered to be the solution:

> The many teachers who do so well in face of adversity cannot manage without cost to themselves. They carry the burdens of parents, probation officers and welfare officers on top of their classroom duties. It is time the nation came to their aid. The principle, already accepted, that special need calls for special help, should be given a new cutting edge. We ask for 'positive discrimination' in favour of such schools and the children in them, going well beyond an attempt to equalise resources. Schools in deprived areas should be given priority in many respects. The first step must be to raise the schools with low

> standards to the national average; the second, quite deliberately to make them better. The justification is that the homes and neighbourhoods from which many of their children come provide little support and stimulus for learning. The schools must supply a compensating environment. The attempts so far made within the educational system to do this have not been sufficiently generous or sustained, because the handicaps imposed by the environment have not been explicitly and sufficiently allowed for. They should be.

Plowden recommends that such positive discrimination should be administered through the mechanism of educational priority area (EPA) designation and financing. We will leave discussion of EPA policy implementation until later. For the moment we will examine some of the basic concepts involved in the conceptualization of what Plowden and others regard as the problem to be tackled.

Social policy and the politics of need

Educational provision is an aspect of welfare policy. The character of provision is the result of social policy (including educational policy) politics. The sphere of politics is never reducible to political parties but, in the determination of educational policy on provision, political parties (in Britain almost exclusively the Labour and Conservative Parties), their political ideologies, and the apparatuses of implementation of policy are crucial.

The apparatuses of implementation include the local education authorities (LEAs), the schools, the teachers, and other agencies within the schools. Any assessment of compensatory education policy will involve the problematization of political agencies and apparatuses of decision-making and policy implementation. It will be concerned in particular with ideologies and/or practices involved in decision-making and policy implementation. In this chapter we are concerned with pedagogic practices/ideologies, as well as with the practices/ideologies of public expenditure decision-making with respect to what Plowden (and others) refer to as 'special need'.

In most discussions of compensatory education, a conception of 'need' is posited in the context of the nonsatisfaction of such need; compensatory education is the remedy. An immediate problem arises when we seek the means of calculation of need, in order to calculate the forms and levels of compensation. Since compensatory education programmes are part of social policy, they are financed through public expenditure and are subject to public expenditure policy/politics. If the notion of needs is to be used in any significant sense, then that which is specified as 'need' in social policy//

political discourse must be taken in terms of a specific policy or political demand. It is true that in many such discourses need is expressed in either arbitrary or in absolute terms. Nevertheless, in terms of an analysis of policy, implementation, and practice we can treat 'need' as demand which may or may not be met in a particular case. With respect to the demands (expressed as needs) in the Plowden Report we will see that those demands/needs were not, in the event, met.

In a nonfunctionalist, nonevolutionary conceptualization,[3] whatever may be calculated as a need (or again a 'basic human need') by teachers, educational administrators, politicians, etc., has to vie with that which may be calculated as 'need' in other areas of expenditure. For example, at the level of central government, the 'need' in the social sphere (including education) vies with what is calculated as, for example, the 'military need'. At the level of local government, 'need' as calculated for educational programmes vies with what is calculated as, for example, the 'transport services need'. Whatever is expressed as a 'need' is a policy demand with respect to a specific area. Policy decisions are political and their political character cannot be disguised by speculative arbitrary references.

This is not to say, of course, that educationalists and their lobbyists cannot make claims in arenas of public expenditure decision-making in terms of 'human needs'. It means simply that such political formulation carries no guarantee of success. Another form of political discourse which might supplement a form in terms of need is that in terms of consequences. An example from another sphere of social welfare discourse is the argument that 'if increased infant mortality is to be the price for keeping within the forecast public sector borrowing requirement, it is preferable that the implication be openly recognised.'[4] The consequence of nonimplementation of compensatory education programmes is the persistence of conditions regarded by Plowden and others as amounting to the lack of provision of an adequate educational environment. As we shall see towards the end of this chapter the recommendations of the Plowden committee were not implemented in the form in which they appear in the report.

Material and cultural deprivation

The notion of compensatory education usually involves the term 'deprivation'. Compensatory education programmes are concerned with policy towards children who in their schools and neighbourhoods are said to be deprived of both cultural and material circumstances considered necessary for the provision of an adequate educational environment. Of course, as we have seen above, the designation of what is 'necessary' and 'adequate' is political in the sense that it involves policy and political ideology and the struggle for the conditions of implementation of policy.

The term 'cultural deprivation', which is often used in the discussion of compensatory education, is derived from the so called 'culture of poverty' thesis.[5] A characteristic of arguments associated with the idea of a 'culture of poverty' is the persistent stress on culture (shared norms, values, meanings, etc.), rather than on material and economic conditions of poverty and the problems of the poor. The popular ideology is that the poor are poor because they are lazy, apathetic, stupid, etc. The 'culture of poverty' thesis is the academic equivalent of that popular ideology and ignores or denigrates the structural aspects of poverty and its economic and material conditions. In the discussion of compensatory education, problems are often set up in terms of 'cultural deprivation' and the supposed 'culture of poverty'. The idea of cultural deprivation is taken up by Keddie in *Tinker, Tailor . . . The Myth of Cultural Deprivation.*[6]

Keddie sets out to question teachers' alleged[7] 'taken for granted assumption' or 'myth' of cultural deprivation. She argues that for educational actors (teachers, educational administrators, etc.)[8]

> . . . . the term becomes a euphemism for saying that working-class and ethnic groups have cultures which are at least dissonant with, if not inferior to, the 'mainstream' culture of the society at large. Culturally deprived children, then, come from homes where mainstream values do not prevail and are therefore less 'educable' than other children. The argument is that the school's function is to transmit the mainstream values of the society and the failure of children to acquire these values lies in their lack of educability. Thus their failure in school is located in the home, in the pre-school environment, and not within the nature and social organization of the school which 'processes' the children into achievement rates. (Keddie 1973, p.8)

Keddie argues that it is the *institutionalization* of the concept that 'has increasingly put these children at a disadvantage in terms of what is expected from them from the day they enter school', and when she declares that her concern is to 'raise problems about the appropriateness and consequences of the concept of cultural deprivation', it is not the *concept* of cultural deprivation that is to be investigated but the consequences of its institutionalization – the consequences of its alleged adoption by teachers as one of their assumptions. Keddie's critique is not directed at the concept of cultural deprivation, but at *teachers* and teachers' culture. Keddie's arguments merely urge teachers to change their subjective viewpoints. Teachers are urged towards a reorientation in which they will come to regard the culture of 'working-class and ethnic groups' as no less valid than the 'mainstream culture' that they as teachers are alleged to represent. This might lead to

> . . . a redirection of educational research away from attempting to formulate how to make children more like teachers. It would be more sensible to consider how to make teachers more bicultural, more like the children they teach, so that they can understand forms of English which they do not themselves use as native speakers. (Keddie 1973, p. 10)

In the 'taken for granted assumptions' of teachers, it is the culture of the children which is said to be regarded as deficient. Keddie merely changes the articulation of cultures, and the 'mainstream culture' of the teachers is now categorized as deficient in that it does not encompass that of the child.

In this 'redefinition' of the 'problem', the educational circumstances of certain groups of children remain largely the same. It is still the case that

> . . .children come from poor homes, often slums, live in overcrowded conditions which deny access to privacy, and lack variety in their surroundings which leads to stimulus-deprivation. (p. 11)

Keddie's 'solution' to educational problems, that is, her redefinition of the problems,[9] finds the source of the educational underachievement of children living in such conditions in the deficiency of teachers' mainstream culture. Her explanation of underachievement relies on *cultural* explanation, insisting that its source is in the dissonance of the child's and the teacher's culture. Furthermore, the insistence on the primacy of the everyday experiences of children involves an antagonism towards contemporary educational practice, and this position is clearly advocated in Keddie's discussion of Neil Postman's paper, *The Politics of Reading*.[10]

> In asking what reading is for, what literacy is about, Postman argues that school education as it is practised must be a form of social control with political implications (using both the narrower and wider meanings of power and coercion). This, together with his suggestions of how the mass media might become an integral, natural and meaningful part of school education, is the paper's strength. Not only is it clear that school education is historically and technologically stagnant but that the insistence on literacy is peculiar to school education and not to the life-worlds of learners (who would here include teachers) in most other contexts of their social lives. (Keddie 1973, p.16)

Keddie attempts to substantiate the 'radical' critique of contemporary educational practice through a number of other illustrations. It is argued that the everyday experiences of children are valid in themselves, in that everyday activity involves thinking and reasoning, which is at least as complex as that involved in mathematics, reading, or writing. She argues that papers by Labov and Gladwin[11]

> suggest that so-called minority-group cultures may be seen as not only adequate in their own right, but perfectly competent to conceptualize logically and imaginatively. The perception of these cultures as deficient seems to arise from the ignorance of those who belong to what they perceive as the dominant cultural tradition. (Keddie 1973, p.13)

Commenting on Gladwin's paper which includes an account of the Trukese[12] activity of navigating a sailing canoe, Keddie insists that

> We have, after reading his paper, to ask not only whether navigating a boat is not like driving a car, but whether either is really qualitatively different from doing a sum or reading a book. (Keddie 1973, p.17)

Keddie's enthusiasm for 'practical experience' obscures from her the particular utility of numeracy and literacy. It is *not* a question of whether navigating a boat is different from the skills of numeracy and literacy, but that the latter facilitates the capacity to learn not only to navigate but to engage in other activities. This is not to argue against practical experience but to argue that (in this example) whilst the child who can *only* navigate cannot, by definition, read and write, those who can read and write can *learn* not only to navigate but to engage in other activity – cultural *and* political.[13]

Keddie's romanticism[14] towards everyday experiences involves her in an explicit antagonism towards contemporary education and contemporary educational practice which is concerned with teaching children concepts and skills including those of literacy and numeracy. The consequences for educational practice of the implementation of her 'radical' pedagogy is the *deprivation* of children of their formal education.[15]

Bernstein's critique of the concept of compensatory education

Basil Bernstein's paper titled 'A Critique of the Concept of "Compensatory Education" '[16] is perhaps the most widely read discussion of the subject amongst practising teachers and teachers in training. Before examining that paper, a brief word on Bernstein's work.

Bernstein's work over the last twenty years, much of which has now been collected together in the volumes of his *Class, Codes and Control*, has been prominent in accounting for the importance of language in socialization and education. Bernstein has argued that linguistic 'codes' developed by children during their primary socialization, and specifically in relationships with the mother, differ between what he calls the 'working class' and the 'middle class'. We shall return to Bernstein's conception of 'class' presently.

Linguistic codes and 'educability'

Bernstein's studies are concerned with children's *forms* of speech; not with dialect nor with matters of underlying grammar or with slang but with the different *use* of vocabulary and the grammatical system. The differences arise from the 'social structure' and, specifically, out of different forms and techniques of socialization. Bernstein argues that working-class children develop forms of speech which are typified by a 'restricted code', as an effect of primary socialization in which the mother places (in comparison to the 'ideal type' middle-class mother) 'less emphasis upon language when she controls her child and deals with only the particular act and does not relate it to general principles and their reasoned basis and consequences' (*ibid*, p. 195). The forms of speech thus generated are typified by the *restricted* code in the sense that there is a 'restriction on the *contexts* and on the *conditions* which will orient the child to universalistic orders of meaning and to making those linguistic choices through which such meanings are realised and so made public' (*ibid*, p. 197). Middle-class children, on the other hand, are alleged to develop an 'elaborated code' which Bernstein designates as the conceptual opposite to the restricted code. The elaborated code is the product of forms and techniques of socialization which are in exact opposition to those used by working-class mothers.

The differences thus generated become crucial when the child enters school because the linguistic form adopted by the school is that of the elaborated code. Thus, the middle-class child is already familiar with the forms of language used in the school whilst the working-class child, Bernstein argues, has first to learn how to learn. That is, in order to learn he must first learn the elaborated code in which school work is expressed.

Bernstein's work has been used to account for social class differentials in educational achievement in terms of differences in 'educability'. Working-class children have been said to be linguistically and/or culturally deprived and, as such, (in comparison to middle-class children) less 'educable'. Bernstein has resisted such interpretations of his work as 'misinterpretations'. However, it is clear that his work, spreading as it does over two decades, does not constitute a unitary discourse governed by a principle of coherence. Appearing within it are positions which are contradictory and, in particular, earlier arguments which Bernstein, with good reason, wishes to displace. Thus, some of the interpretations of his work which he designates 'misinterpretations' may well be legitimate, even though they are representations of positions which he now rejects.

We will examine here a particular aspect of Bernstein's work on language and culture with which he too has been particularly concerned: the *consequences* of his work for educational policy and for pedagogic practice. This is an area in which Bernstein claims to have been misunderstood and in which he has been at pains to 'reinterpret' the meaning of his research findings.

Linguistic deprivation and compensatory education

In the paper 'A Critique of the Concept of "Compensatory Education" '[17] Bernstein gives a short account of his work on linguistic codes and is concerned to counter what he argues are misrepresentations of his position. The explicit aim of the paper is to attack the *concept* of 'compensatory education'. Referring to the evidence of the Newsom Report on the gross material inadequacy of certain schools Bernstein argues

> I do not understand how we can talk about offering compensatory education to children who in the first place have not, as yet, been offered an adequate educational environment. (*Education for Democracy*, p.111)

Bernstein is against the *concept* of compensatory education; against the *idea* that any provision of an adequate educational environment, where none had been provided before, could be considered as 'compensatory' whether it formed part of a compensatory programme or not. Bernstein is not against the provision furnished by educational programmes called 'compensatory'.

With respect to the concepts of culture and language, Bernstein rejects as a misinterpretation the equating of his concept of 'restricted code' with the notion of 'linguistic' or 'cultural deprivation'. He argues further that the notion of the teaching of the 'elaborated code' has become part of the concept of the provision of compensatory education, but that, contrary to such a notion, the teaching of children to use the elaborated code is not *compensatory* education; it *is* education. He suggests that

> we should stop thinking in terms of 'compensatory education' but consider instead, most seriously and systematically the conditions and the contexts of the educational environment. (*ibid*, p.114)

Bernstein is at pains to displace the concepts of 'compensatory education', and the related concepts of 'cultural deprivation', 'linguistic deprivation', and 'social disadvantage' because, as he says,

> the work I have been doing has inadvertently contributed towards their formulation. It might be, and has been said, that my research through focusing upon the subculture and forms of familial socialization has also distracted attention from the conditions and contexts of learning in schools. (*ibid*, p.144)

On the question of linguistic codes he recognizes that 'the concept "restricted code" has been equated with "linguistic deprivation" or even the non-verbal child' (*ibid*, p.144), but in terms of his research formulations he gives very little ground, maintaining that working-class mothers are not 'nonverbal' but nevertheless that they

> differ from the middle class mothers in the *contexts* which evoke universalistic meanings. They are *not* linguistically deprived, neither are their children. (*ibid*, p.177, emphasis in the original)

Bernstein thus attempts both to maintain his theoretical argument on the generation of linguistic codes (in particular, here, the argument that working-class socialization and culture generates the restricted code), and to align himself with left-wing progressives who do not regard linguistic and cultural differences as the *cause* of social and educational inequalities. Bernstein first unites with them in their insistence that social inequality and the lack of provision of an adequate *educational* environment for certain groups of children is largely responsible for their lack of educational achievement and the subsequent social class differentials. He agrees that his work on socialization has drawn attention away from these dominantly important issues only to then revert to his theory of socialization and linguistic codes. Bernstein wants to have it both ways or, as Harold Rosen has put it in his article 'Language and Class', 'as the Jewish proverb has it, he is trying to dance at two weddings at the same time'.[18]

What Bernstein argues, in effect, is that working-class children *are* deprived of the ability to use the elaborated code as a result of their socialization and that the teaching of children to be able to utilize the elaborated code is not compensatory education,

> The introduction of the child to the universalistic meanings of public forms of thought is not compensatory education; *it is* education. It is not making children middle class. . . . (*ibid*, p.120)

Bernstein correctly argues that the use of the elaborated code and the invoking of universalistic meanings is not a middle-class preserve (whatever that might mean). We could add that neither is literacy in general nor is numeracy. Nevertheless, he conceives of the working-class child as a deficit system, deprived of something (the elaborated code) that middle-class children are alleged to have as a result of their socialization.

However, Bernstein's concept of the restricted code is no concept at all; it represents merely an alleged *absence* of something alleged to be found in middle-class children. Hence the curiously exact opposites of the elaborated and the restricted codes.

The theory of linguistic codes apart, Bernstein's comments on educational provision are quite sound in that he arrives at a position in which he argues that the proper role of the educational system is to take whatever capacities children have as the starting point and to develop and extend them. Here, at least, the educational system rather than the family is the major social institution with responsibility for education. The creation of an adequate educational environment is the priority of *schools* and responsibility cannot be displaced onto the home.

Bernstein's position is distinct from that of the 'radicals'[19] who treat working-class culture as an end in itself, and it is also distinct from that of those traditionalists who treat the school as an agency with the hopeless task of combating the effects of working-class culture. Bernstein's adoption of a position in opposition to this latter position is clearly incompatible with his theory of codes.

Classes and linguistic codes

One of the main sources of the theoretical problems in Bernstein's work is in his conception of 'class' and in his attempts to associate forms of socialization, language, and codes with classes. Despite the appearance of the *word* class in many of his papers and in the title of his collection of papers *Class, Codes and Control*, Bernstein has no coherent, and certainly no elaborated, conception of 'class'. As Harold Rosen and others have pointed out, we are provided with a conception of class only by implication. Bernstein's class system consists merely of a 'working class' and a 'middle class'. The latter is populated by mothers who are articulate, skilled child-minders, whilst the former is not. The working class, like the middle class, has no internal differentiation in Bernstein's conception. The concepts of class, like the concepts of codes developed upon them, are nothing but dichotomous oppositions.

In his earlier research, on which the notion of restricted and elaborated codes is based, it is observed that certain groups of 'working-class' and of 'middle-class' mothers use child-rearing techniques which are different in the *use* of language and in the form of language used. No adequate means is provided to demonstrate that these groups were representative of the working class or the middle class in the generality of the concepts of class that Bernstein infers them to represent. There is, therefore, no means of determining that certain uses of language in socialization and certain forms of linguistic code are generated through such forms of socialization in specific classes in general in the way Bernstein infers. Thus, the 'restricted code' and the 'elaborated code' are designated as 'types' or 'ideal types' by Bernstein himself. Given the lack of theoretical and empirical rigour in which these 'ideal types' were formulated, there is little or no reason to treat them as anything but *stereotypes*. The theory of codes depends on stereotypes in a double sense. Stereotypes of linguistic codes are implied both from and to stereotypes of social classes. The consequences for educational policy and for pedagogic practice based on Bernstein's theory of codes are obvious. If 'working-class' children are essentially less 'educable' than their 'middle-class' opposites, then no amount of change in policy or practice could alter the patterns of social class differentials in educational achievement.

In his paper 'A Critique of the Concept of "Compensatory Education" ', Bernstein is unable to *combine* his theory of codes with the progressive comments he makes on educational provision except at a superficial level. On the contrary, there are two discrete levels of discourse: the theory of codes and the commentary on provision. Bernstein's comments on provision cannot be deduced from his theory of codes and there is no indication of the means of achieving the forms of provision he appears to favour.

Educational priority areas and educational expenditure

This chapter has, so far, been concerned with discourse on pedagogic practice with respect to concepts involved in the notion of compensatory education. That discourse has a particular significance in that teachers and teachers in training are involved in the implementation of educational policy. The importance of teacher education should never be underestimated.[20] The form in which compensatory education was implemented (through the EPA programme) in the late 1960s and early 1970s is not, of course, reducible to pedagogic practice. In this section we will examine some of the problems involved in the analysis of public expenditure decision-making with respect to educational provision.

In their book, *Poverty: The Forgotten Englishmen*, Coates and Silburn examine the Plowden recommendations in some detail. They conclude that Plowden's

> prescription was a bold and imaginative one, on the whole. But to be effectively applied it needed immediate and expensive action. Such action has not been forthcoming, on anything like the required scale. On 29 August 1967, it was announced by the Department of Education and Science that £16 million was to be allocated for school building in Educational Priority Areas. The Secretary of State declined to designate E.P.A.s himself, on the grounds that local education authorities 'are well placed to judge which districts suffer from the deficiencies which the Plowden Council had in mind'.[21] The allocation was to be made for both major and minor works, and to be spread over the two years 1968-70. On 19 November 1968, Mr Crosland's successor, Mr Short, announced that some 5,000 teachers in 500 schools were to get increments of £75 on their salaries, in consonance with the Plowden recommendations.[22] Plowden had recommended increments of £120 as a 'first step' and L.E.A.s had submitted a list of 1,500 schools which they felt to be qualified for such aid. (p.133)

As Coates and Silburn go on to say, the Plowden Committee itself was not satisfied with the subsequent actions of the DES and issued a statement saying that 'piecemeal progress' had been made but that the Department 'has not formulated a systematic policy' in response to its report.[23] If the response was not adequate in Plowden's terms in 1969, what of the 1970s and 1980s?

In the 1970s there were cuts in public expenditure as a response to national and international events. In Britain, the effects of the three-day week and the sterling crisis led to the loan terms negotiated with the IMF. On the international markets, the decline of the US dollar and the rise in the price of oil resulting respectively from the financing of the Vietnam and Yom Kippur wars has led to further decline in world trade and to inflation in the western economies. In Britain, in 1979, the election of a Tory Government which adopted stringent monetarist policies has led to further cuts in public expenditure. In these circumstances policies regarded by Plowden as necessary in 1967, but not financed adequately then, are not even on the political agenda in 1979-1980. Economic recession hits the most vulnerable the hardest, be they nations or children.[24]

The public expenditure cuts, coming as they do at the same time as tax cuts for the better off and policy for expenditure of £55 million per annum from public funds on private education,[25] bring public expenditure policy into the arena of public gaze. 'Gaze' is more appropriate than 'debate' although neither is accurate.

Educational expenditure and policy review

If policy for compensatory education is to be argued in terms of the politics of need, the 'need' has to be subject to review. However, there is evidence which suggests that such reviewing of 'need' has fallen into dereliction, or is simply beyond the ability of those charged with the responsibility of review. In his article 'Expenditure Decision-Making by English Local Education Authorities', W.F. Dennison argues that the power of review has been largely superseded by what he calls 'decision-making-incrementalism'.[26] At national level, public expenditure policy, including calculation of the public sector borrowing requirement and decision on levels of rate support grant to local authorities, which has direct relevance to education provision, goes on largely 'behind closed doors'.

In his article, Dennison argues that the 96 local education authorities are vital agencies of resource decision-making, responsible for about 85 percent of current educational expenditure (DES 1977, Table 2). They operate under constraint of central government (mainly through the DES) to ensure control of total spending, and to ensure that legal requirements are satisfied and that broad outline educational policy is developed. Dennison shows that a second level of constraint operates through the relationship of the LEA to the local authority, of which the LEA is only one part. As Dennison says,

> the education committee for each LEA . . . must justify its expenditure plans alongside those of the other services of the local authority, and ultimately it is the main Council of the authority, advised by the Policy and Resources committee, which agrees, and as a result sanctions, particular expenditure. (*ibid*, p.241)

Dennison goes on to show that the constraints on LEAs are considerable in that central government can manipulate the size of rate support grant which for an average authority amounts to around 60 percent of its total resources. Central government 'can powerfully influence total expenditure on all services, and therefore the detail of educational spending. Nevertheless, given all the restrictions the ultimate decision as to whether or not to spend, and items of expenditure, are local decisions made as part of a compromise between education and policy and resource committee members' (*ibid*, p.241).

Schools with children who might be regarded as in need of compensatory education are also schools in their own right. They are subject, like any other aspect of public service, to the effects of decisions made by both local and central government. The question of review of need applies to all aspects of public service and schools are no exception. The decision-making processes and in particular the processes of review at central and local government level must be crucial to educational provision.

Central government and public expenditure

The document titled *Behind Closed Doors: An Analysis of Public Expenditure Planning* (hereafter BCD), produced by the National Union of Teachers, the Association of University Teachers, NATFHE, other public service unions, and the NUS, argues that major decisions on spending on public services, including education, are made without sufficient public scrutiny and debate. BCD argues that, nationally:

> There is virtually no opportunity for the public, Parliament, or trade union representatives to be informed about, or to be consulted on, the decision-making process. No papers are published, no draft proposals are discussed with Parliament, no negotiations are held with unions representing the workers concerned. The 'public' services are governed in private – behind closed doors. (*ibid*, p.1)

The calculation of levels of rate support grant (RSG) to the local authorities (which is vital to education and to other public services) involves what are now effectively three systems. The Public Expenditure Survey Committee (PESC), the Cash Limits/Estimates systems (now telescoped together), and the Financial Information System (FIS) is used by Government to plan and monitor public expenditure.[27]

PESC involves annual review of all public expenditure programmes starting with *existing* policies, and after Cabinet decisions leads to the publication of the annual White Paper containing the stated expenditure plans over the next five years (at constant prices). The cash limits/estimates involve allowance for forecast inflation over the coming year and the results are then used as a ceiling for the actual money spent whatever price movements occur. Finally, FIS is a system for monitoring actual spending against spending plans and cash limits. Space prohibits more detailed discussion of the overall system.

None of the procedures prior to the publication of figures on RSG are subject to public scrutiny. BCD makes the point that the PESC, Cash Limits/Estimates, and FIS systems are not merely technical routes for calculating, collating, and recording the cost of Government programmes.

> These procedures generate real constraints on the theoretical ability of the Cabinet to increase public expenditure programmes, and its responsiveness to democratic pressures. (*ibid*, p.5)

The LEAs and expenditure review

Local authorities are charged with the responsibility of assessment and review of specific local need. For example, it was on the basis that local education authorities were 'well placed to judge which districts suffer from the deficiences which the Plowden Council had in mind' that the then Secretary of State declined to designate EPAs himself. The issue of local authority autonomy and the constraints on them cannot be discussed in any great detail here.[28] However, there are a number of important points concerning educational policy decision-making made in Dennison's paper.

The staff of the LEA has the task of preparing the budget document for approval each year. The budget document acts both as a decisional base and as an expenditure plan. It contains a large number of detailed items together with figures on proposed expenditure on each item for the forthcoming year, actual expenditure on items in the previous year, and actual expenditure for the year two years before the budget year. It is the budget document which goes before the education committee for discussion and approval. Dennison argues that

> there is a real chance that with this format those who make decisions will be overwhelmed both by the sheer volume of information upon which they must decide, and the manner in which this information is presented to them. It is extremely difficult, for instance, to extract from the plan the proposed cost of a particular function. It could well be that an education committee member wishes to know the suggested expenditure upon actual teaching in primary schools. At budget time he will have before him details of the whole of the primary education sector, but these details will include information about a range of peripheral activities in some way connected with primary education, and therefore the evidence he might wish to use to make, perhaps, an inter-institutional or inter-authority comparison of expenditure will be incalculable from the supplied information. (p.243)

Although there may be LEAs where committee members are skilful and industrious, for Dennison the format of the budget plan is most likely to lead to what he calls decision-making-incrementalism.[29] That is, expenditure decisions are made in terms of an increment (at a time of public expenditure cuts it may be a decrement) in relation to expenditure in previous years *rather than in relation to specific needs*.

If educational policies which involve consideration of need are to be implemented, then review of provision and assessment of need are crucial. We have seen that at both local and central government level there are limitations to the processes of review and assessment of need. BCD proposes a number of reforms including the publication of papers at all stages, which would certainly be a step towards more open government. The proposal BCD makes for a process of negotiation with unions concerned at all stages (National Union of Teachers, AUT, NATFE, other teaching and public service unions) would certainly be a step towards a more participatory mode of expenditure decision-making. The proposed parliamentary debate at all stages would bring the decision-making process into at least that arena of debate.

However, there is clearly an argument for reform at the local level of expenditure decision-making. There is also a strong case for implementation of the recommendations of the Taylor Report.[30] The latter would provide not only for the democratization of control of the individual school but would also provide a mechanism of review of provision and assessment of need of the individual school. Furthermore, it would strengthen (in some cases *provide*) the mechanism linking home and school.[31]

Conclusion

Education is part of social policy. A social policy for compensatory education involves assessment of specific need. It has been argued that the recommendations of the Plowden Report have not been implemented in the form in which they appeared in the report. Public expenditure decision-making at the levels of both local and central government is not structured so as to review provision and assess need adequately. Finally, national and world conditions have led to inflation and to decline in production.[32] Policies of cuts in public spending have led to decline in educational provision which has had greatest effect on the less well off and the poor.[33]

In addition to problems of its financing, the policy for compensatory education faced other obstacles. For example, the Jensenite ideology of the late 1960s and the argument that Project Head Start was doomed from the start.[34] The problem of the training of teachers who would be involved in EPAs in England was not helped, as we have seen, by the pedagogic ideologies of the late 1960s and early 1970s.[35]

Finally, we must ask what it was that compensatory education might have been expected to achieve. Implicit in the discussions of compensatory education is the idea that educational inequality is one of the main causes of economic inequality. Hussain points out that this leads to

> the belief that economic inequality can be, at least in part, reduced by widening access to educational institutions and taking positive measures (e.g., compensatory education) to reduce educational differences. However well intentioned and noble the belief may be it rests on a strange, but unstated, premise that somehow the provision of more education will lead to a disappearance of low paid occupations. (Hussain 1976, pp.419-420)

Society and social inequality[36] cannot be reduced to the effects of educational inequalities, and the phrase 'education cannot compensate for society', in that context, has some truth to it. However, the educational system is *part of society* and social policies in the educational sphere are clearly important. Any serious attack on social problems and inequalities would involve polices across a broad range[37] of areas including health, education, housing, child care,[38] employment, incomes, taxation, benefits, social welfare, etc. What is crucial is the politics of such an attack.

References

Bibliographic references follow this section.

This paper has benefited from seminar discussion and from helpful critical reading. I would like to thank all those who have made helpful comments, and to thank especially Lorraine Culley, Stephen Savage, and Mike Shuker.

1. Including the *Banneker Project* in St. Louis, an eight-year programme, the *Higher Horizons* programme in New York (five years), *More Effective Schools in New York* (three years), and others in Berkeley, Philadelphia, Seattle, Syracuse, Washington, and in many other cities in the USA. See *U.S. Commission on Civil Rights*, (1967).
2. A report of the Central Advisory Council for Education (England), Volume 1: The Report, *Children and their Primary Schools* (1967).
3. For discussion, see Stephen P. Savage, *Theories of Welfare and the Denial of Politics* (University of Bath, School of Humanities and Social Sciences, department research paper).
4. See the document *Behind Closed Doors* (1979).
5. See especially the works of Oscar Lewis. The notion of a 'culture of poverty' was first put forward by Lewis in 1959 in his book *Five Families: Mexican Case Studies in the Culture of Poverty*, and later used in his books *The Children of Sanchez* (1962) and *La Vida* (1968). Cf. Harrington *The Other America: Poverty*

in the United States. For a most effective critique of Lewis and the notion of 'culture of poverty' see C.A. Valentine (1968).

6. See the introduction to Keddie (1973) and her contribution to *Sorting Them Out: Two Essays on Social Differentation*, Open University, E282 Unit 10 (1972).
7. There is nothing in Keddie's writings to indicate that teachers do subscribe to the 'myth of cultural deprivation'. This is not a minor problem for a sociology of education concerned with analysis at the level of meanings, expectations, values, attitudes, etc. Keddie's notion that some teachers subscribe to the myth of cultural deprivation does not mean that it can be assumed that others do. She herself warns that such generalizations cannot be made. In her paper 'Classroom Knowledge' in Young (1971), for example, she warns that 'throughout this account references to teachers and pupils are specifically references to teachers and pupils *of this one school*', *ibid*, p.134.
8. The term 'actors' is used by Keddie following the terminology of 'phenomenological' sociology. Cf. Schutz (1967). See Demaine (1980b) for critique of 'phenomenological' sociology of education.
9. See Keddie (1973, p.11) for her account of the 'deficit theory'.
10. 'The Politics of Reading', *Harvard Educational Review*, Vol. 40, No. 2, May 1970, pp. 244-252 and reprinted in Keddie (1973).
11. William Labov, 'The Logic of Non-Standard English', *Georgetown Monographs on Language and Linguistics*, Vol. 22, 1969, and Thomas Gladwin, 'Culture and Logical Porcess' in Ward Goodenough (ed.), *Explorations in Cultural Anthropology*, both reprinted in Keddie (1973). Cf. Valentine (1968), especially chapters 1 and 3.
12. Melanesian islanders, see Gladwin above.
13. See Kingdom (1976) for a discussion of political education.
14. Keddie warns against romanticism herself.
15. Anthropological radicalism is not, of course, confined to Keddie. See, for example, Sir Edmund Leach's article 'Literacy be damned' and others. Leach (1969, 1974, 1977, and 1978).
16. The paper has been published in a number of books, collections, and journals. Versions of the paper have appeared under the different title 'Education Cannot Compensate For Society' in *New Society* 26 February 1970, pp. 344-347 and in the 2nd edition of Rubinstein and Stoneman (ed.) *Education For Democracy* (1972). In Bernstein *Class, Codes and Control*, Volume 1 (1971) and in Rubinstein and Stoneman (1970) the article is titled 'A critique of the concept of compensatory education'.
17. In the present paper the page numbers given refer to the first edition of Rubinstein and Stoneman, *Education for Democracy* (1970).
18. Rosen (1972).
19. Cf. Young (1971) and see Demaine (1977).
20. See Culley and Demaine (1978) for a discussion of teacher education and the importance of sociology of education in teacher education.
21. DES Press Release, 29 August 1967.
22. *The Times*, 19 November 1968.
23. *Daily Telegraph*, 10 January 1969.

24. See Field (1979), Townsend (1979), Robinson (1976), for example.
25. *Education (No.2): A Bill to amend the law relating to education* (Bill 57), 25 October 1979.
'The cost of the assisted places scheme (clauses 17 and 18) will be about £55 million a year when in full operation and will be met by central government.' (p. v, note 2). (This was amended to £25 million at Committee Stage.)
26. *Educational Studies*, Vol.5, No.3, October 1979.
27. See chapters 2 and 3 of *Behind Closed Doors: An Analysis of Public Expenditure Planning*.
28. For further discussion see Neve (1977). Also see Demaine (1980a).
29. One of the limitations of Dennison (1979) is the attempt to suggest a 'general theory' of expenditure decision-making.
30. *A New Partnership For Our Schools*.
31. See Demaine (1980b) for discussion.
32. The economy will decline by between 1 and 2 percent in 1980 with the impact of decline being concentrated on manufacturing industry. See *Bank of England Quarterly Review*, published 19 December 1979.
33. For an account of public expenditure cuts with reference to education see Lukes (1979).
34. See Jensen (1969). For a discussion and critique of the concept of I.Q. see Demaine (1979). For a discussion of the American Head Start programme and the benefits see the Washington report of the Consortium of Developmental Continuity.
35. See Demaine (1980b) for further discussion.
36. The notion of 'equality' is presently being widened by, for example, the Equal Opportunities Commission. With reference to education see their pamphlet *Do You Provide Equal Educational Opportunities?*
37. See *Higher Education into the 1990s*, February 1978, for an optimistic view on the effect of such policies.
38. Mottershead (1978) is interesting in this respect.

Bibliography

Bank of England Quarterly Review, (December 1979).

Behind Closed Doors: An Analysis of Public Expenditure Planning (1979). Published by the National Steering Committee Against the Cuts, Civic House, Aberdeen Terrace, London SE3 0QY.

Bernstein, B. (1970), 'A Critique of the Concept of "Compensatory Education" ', in Rubinstein and Stoneman (eds.).

Bernstein, B. (1971), *Class, Codes and Control*, Volume 1, London, Routledge & Kegan Paul.

Coates, K. & Silburn, R. (eds.) (1970), *Poverty: The Forgotten Englishmen*, Harmondsworth, Penguin.

Culley, L.A. and Demaine, J. (1978), 'Sociology of Education and the Education of Teachers: a critique of D.R. McNamara' *Educational Studies*, Vol.4, No.3.

Demaine, J. (1977), 'On the new sociology of education: a critique of M.F.D.

Young and the radical attack on the politics of educational knowledge', *Economy & Society*, Vol.6, No.2.

Demaine, J. (1979), 'IQism as Ideology and the Political Economy of Education', *Educational Studies*, Vol.5, No.3.

Demaine, J. (1980a), 'Sociology of Education, Politics and the Left in Britain', *British Journal of Sociology of Education*, Vol.1, No.1.

Demaine, J. (1980b), *Contemporary Theories in the Sociology of Education*, London, Macmillan.

Dennison, W.F. (1979), 'Expenditure Decision-making by English Local Education Authorities,' *Educational Studies*, Vol.5, No.3.

Department of Education and Science (1977), *Statistics of Education, 1975. Volume 5. Finance and Awards*, London, HMSO.

Department of Education and Science and the Scottish Education Department (1978), *Higher Education into the 1990s: A Discussion Document*, London, HMSO.

Equal Opportunities Commission (1979), *Do You Provide Equal Educational Opportunities?*, Manchester, EDC.

Field, F. (1979), 'Poverty and Inequality: The Facts', *Poverty, No.42*.

Goodenough, W. (ed.) (1970), *Explorations in Cultural Anthropology*, New York, McGraw-Hill.

Hussain, A. (1976), 'The economy and the educational system in capitalist societies', *Economy & Society* Vol.5, No.4.

Jensen, A.R. (1969), 'How Much Can We Boost IQ and Scholastic Achievement?', *Harvard Educational Review*, Vol.39, No.1.

Keddie, N. (ed.) (1973), *Tinker, Tailor . . . The Myth of Cultural Deprivation*, Harmondsworth, Penguin.

Kingdom, E.F. (1976), 'Political Education', *Research in Education*, November 1976.

Kogan, M. (1978), *The Politics of Educational Change*, London, Fontana.

Leach, E. (1969), 'Education for What?', Roscoe Lecture, Manchester University, April 1969.

Leach, E. (1974), 'Freedom and Social Conditioning', Raymond Priestley Lecture, University of Birmingham, October 1974.

Leach, E. (1977), 'Literacy be damned', *Observer*, 20 February 1977.

Leach, E. (1978), 'The Disutility of Literacy', Loughborough University, April 1978.

Lukes, J. (1979), 'The Missing Millions' and 'Off With Their Overheads', *Guardian*, 14 and 21 September 1979.

Mottershead, P. (1978), *A Survey of Child Care for Pre-School Children with Working Parents: Cost and Organisation*, Manchester, Equal Opportunities Commission.

Neve, B. (1977), 'Bureaucracy and Politics in Local Government: The Role of Local Authority Education Officers', *Public Administration*, Autumn, 1977.

Newsom, J. et.al (1963), *Half Our Future*, a report of the Central Advisory Council for Education (England), London, HMSO.

Open University (1972), *Sorting Them Out: Two Essays in Social Differentiation*, E282 Unit 10. Milton Keynes, The Open University Press.

Plowden, B. et al. (1967), *Children and Their Primary Schools*, A report of the Central Advisory Council for Education, Vol. 1, London, HMSO.
Rosen, H. (1972), *Language and Class: A Critical Look at the Theories of Basil Bernstein*, The Falling Wall Press.
Robinson, P. (1976), *Education and Poverty*, London, Methuen.
Savage, S.P. (1979), *Theories of Welfare and the Denial of Politics*, (unpublished paper, University of Bath).
Schutz, A. (1967), *The Phenomenology of the Social World*, Evanston, Northwestern University Press.
Taylor, T. et al. (1977), *A New Partnership for Our Schools*, London, DES/HMSO.
Townsend, P. (1979), *Poverty in the United Kingdom*, Harmondsworth, Penguin.
U.S. Commission on Civil Rights (1967), *Racial isolation in the public schools*, Vol.1. Washington, D.C., U.S. Government Printing Office.
Valentine, C.A. (1968), *Culture and Poverty: Critique and Counter-Proposals*, Chicago, Chicago University Press.
Young, M.F.D. (ed.) (1971), *Knowledge and Control: New Directions for the Sociology of Education*, London, Collier-Macmillan.

PART THREE

Home-School Relations in Practice

CHAPTER 8

THE INVOLVEMENT OF PARENTS

Patrick McGeeney

*This first chapter in Part Three consists of an extract from Patrick McGeeney's survey of primary and secondary schools who were pioneering imaginative home-school programmes in the years following the Plowden Report.**

> Few other social institutions have changed their attitudes and techniques as quickly and as fundamentally as the primary school. Sometimes there has been little short of a revolution, since the parents were at school themselves. They may hear about these changes in a garbled way from other parents or perhaps from the mass media, before they learn about them from the school. The school should explain them so that parents can take an informed interest in what their children are doing. Parents will not understand unless they are told.[1]

Implicit in this statement from the Plowden Report is the assumption that parents need to understand how their children are taught, so that help with school work can be given at home. Resistance to this proposal on the part of some teachers may arise from a fear that their professional status will be undermined if it is conceded that outsiders with no specialized training should assist in the teaching process. The argument is that most parents would object strongly if their children were to be taught at school by untrained teachers and that in effect this is what a parent becomes if he tries to educate his child at home. The weakness of this argument is twofold. First, it is not suggested that parents be asked to usurp the teacher's professional responsibility, but to support it. Help with reading, for instance. Ideally in the early stages of primary schooling, each child should have the opportunity of reading aloud to the teacher day by day, but with a

*Extracted from *Parents Are Welcome*, 1969, Longman Group Limited.

class of forty or more this is not always possible. Many parents already listen to their children reading and, given the right advice, could be encouraged in this respect to support the teachers more effectively. Second, it may well be that where parents do encourage reading, writing, and number work at home this can have an appreciable effect upon educational achievement. One study of a junior school[2] suggests that few parents managed to avoid getting involved in their children's efforts to learn. Though some managed to help unobtrusively and enjoyably, others failed to appreciate the need for patience and understanding in handling a child's difficulties. Those who have either a conviction or hunch that parental support can make a difference will not easily be persuaded by directions from the school that tuition should be left entirely to the teachers. Would it not be wiser to accept the parents' desire to help by channelling their enthusiasm in the right direction? This would necessitate telling them what *not* to do as well as what they might do in the way of home encouragement.

Innovation in schools

The principle that parents should be well informed about experimental changes in teaching techniques is already well established in many schools where i.t.a. (initial teaching alphabet) has been introduced – perhaps of necessity because of the publicity given to it through the mass media. The i.t.a. Reading Research Unit at the outset issued a booklet[3] explaining the new alphabet. The preamble unequivocally supports the view that parents should be invited to become partners in the experiment. 'Parents like to know how their children are being taught because they want to help the teachers give their children the best opportunity to learn reading and writing.'

The first section explains simply 'Why i.t.a. has been introduced', followed by 'How i.t.a. works'. In this latter section, the principle that parents need to learn in order that they may teach more effectively is further reinforced (in the i.t.a. script):

> Some parents may wish to learn i.t.a. so that they can understand how their children are progressing, or they may want to write words for their children to read. May we introduce the alphabet of i.t.a. to you parents who would like to have a try at it?[4]

The exposition of i.t.a. is simple, clear, and brief – a model for the kind of written communication required if parents are to be told how their children are being taught. Following the sound educational principle that theory should be reinforced by practice, the booklet ends with a few exercises for parents to try out themselves. The assumption is that parents more readily identify themselves with their children's learning when confronted with similar problems and difficulties.

If the assumption is valid[5] in the case of experimental teaching techniques which constitute an extremely radical departure from traditional teaching methods, why not in the case of less radical changes? 'Look and Say', for instance. Many of the mothers I have interviewed felt puzzled and helpless in their attempts to assist their children to read, because of the differences in approach compared with the method used when they were at school. 'They don't learn them the alphabet which I thought would have been better. They learn them more by looking at pictures. We had to teach the boy the alphabet ourselves.' The attempts on the part of this parent to teach the child capital letters conflicted with the school's policy of using only lower-case script in the early stages. Thus the child was left even more confused than his parents. Similarly with arithmetic where the differences between the old and new methods were so marked that parents would complain, 'I can't make head or tail of the way they do it nowadays, so I say to him, "You work it out your way and I'll do it mine, and see if we get the same answer." We generally do.'

Mistakenly, the emphasis was on getting the correct answer as against the school's encouragement of each child to arrive at its own short-cuts to the solution of a problem. Schooled in the traditional rote-learning, some parents complained at the lack of drilling in the three Rs, particularly spelling, punctuation, and tables. When, as sometimes happened, this was reiterated in front of the children, confidence in the teachers may have been undermined.

It is not pretended here that such out-of-date notions can easily be dislodged, but at least among these parents there is a measure of concern for the way their children are being taught. By very definition an interested but uninformed parent is in need of information. The attempt to impart it should be made.

Advice to parents

The head of an infants' school in North London, when questioned about what sort of advice he gave to parents who asked how they might help their children, replied:

> Just talk and listen to your child, as much as possible. This is the most

valuable thing you can do. Ask him to read signs at the bus stop and in shops and other places. Get him to count the change when shopping. Ensure that you read to him, particularly at bedtime. Give him immediate access to mud and tin cans to experiment with. Take him on journeys and visits. Introduce him to the local library and help him to find his way about and make a suitable choice. With regard to arithmetic, ask *him* how it is done. See that he gets plenty of sleep and fresh air. Control and discuss television programmes with him.

Sound advice though this may be, the likelihood is that those with sufficient initiative to ask may be the least in need of it; and some may hesitate to knock on the head's door in case they seem pushing or interfering. The same advice sent to all parents in a letter might ensure that a larger number receive it, with the additional advantage of economizing on the head's time.

Too often, however, letters from schools are delivered in a manner intended to convey more of a warning than a welcome.

The procedure to be adopted when visiting the school is first to see my secretary. She will deal with enquiries of a purely routine nature, and will arrange for you to see me if necessary. On no account should this procedure be by-passed and a teacher approached directly in or out of the classroom.

Those on the receiving end of this frosty communication from officialdom must be left in doubt as to whether they are bidden to bring their queries to the head or forbidden to do so. In sharp contrast is the following letter of welcome and advice sent to all parents by Miss Margaret Wright, head of the Hunters Bar Infant School, in Sheffield.

Dear Parents,

Very soon your child, with others, will be starting school, and in order that they may settle quickly and happily in the new environment, I hope you will not mind if I make a few suggestions, with most of which I am sure you are already familiar.

Talk often to your child about this new adventure – never threaten with school. Make sure that you tell them how you will miss them while they are away. Tell them the kind of things you will be busy doing in their absence – cooking, making beds, etc. Assure them that you will be missing them and awaiting their return, and that every care will be taken of their toys and things in their absence. It is dismaying if smaller brothers or sisters are allowed to spoil their toys whilst they are away at school.

Don't be alarmed if, during the first few weeks, there is a sudden breakdown, and your child becomes clinging and doesn't want to be left. Just talk in a reassuring manner and make your departure quickly. Tell the child at what time you will return. I can assure you that if the distress was very real and lasting I should get in touch with you. If you have said that you will be waiting at the gate, make sure you are there – a little child can feel that mother will never again appear if this promise is broken.

I shall probably suggest, if it is feasible, that your child comes in the morning only, or for an even shorter time. Some children find a full school day too much at first, and if we work together we can gradually lengthen this period. Not all children need this form of introduction to school life. If children have been used to leaving mother, and have had lots of contact with other children, they will settle much more quickly. I shall write to you suggesting times for a preschool visit – please try to come and stay with your child. Here is a chance for you to share their new experiences.

If children can cope with all their garments (these should be clearly marked) it helps to make the settling in process much more simple. Most children can, of course, cope with their own toilet needs, and can ask in recognisable terms when they need to visit the toilet.

Often parents ask what they can do about children reading and writing before they come to school. Rarely is a child ready to do any formal learning before starting school, but talking with them and having books available is of immense value. I know you will have all read to your children and allowed them to use pencils and crayons. Counting games are fun, and a great help to us when they begin to learn.

Now for a little about our school. I know many of you will be told by your children that 'we played all day'. Let me assure you that this is not really so. At this early stage the things we want them to learn are presented in a play fashion. To a small child play is work, and we know that you will find yourself surprised what a great deal of knowledge your child is absorbing and learning in this way.

We try to give each child the minimum time of eighteen months with his first teacher. We have found constant change of teacher, who at this stage must be the mother's substitute, is very harmful to the child's progress.

I also want to emphasize that I am here at any time to answer your queries. It helps the school and the child to know of any changes at home which may have disturbed them. Never feel that any problem is too small for you to consult us about. It is only by working together and knowing each other well that we can make sure that every child is a happy, confident, secure little individual, growing up to be a valued member of the community.

Yours faithfully,
MARGARET J. WRIGHT
Head Mistress

Not even the most anxiously diffident could fail to respond to such an invitation as this. How should it be followed up? It might be possible to make a personal interview more effective by suggesting that parents need to be shown as well as told how their children are taught. The most economical way to do this is obviously to explain to the parents collectively at an evening meeting. Here again, however, sometimes the criticism of such meetings is that the parents are unable to obtain the information they want. Take this reaction, for instance, reported in an article in the *Guardian*:

> We have to sit on little chairs and endure talks on things we have known for years, that Johnny will read better if he is read to at home, that Home and School is a good thing because it is a good thing. . . . Must I put up with another year of lost evenings, of stalking Johnny's teacher during the social hour and losing her in the crowd because she saw me first? Yet I know quite well that when it comes to the night of the first meeting, a child will come to me at 7.20 and say, 'Aren't you going? It's in our room. Miss Smith will be there. You'll see my drawing – third room on the left as you go in. All the other mothers will be there.'[6]

Though one might sympathize with the teacher's unwillingness to be confronted with so forthright and critical a parent as this, there is some substance in the view that parents' evenings can be a waste of time. This may happen even where teachers are convinced of the need to explain teaching methods to parents, as I was able to observe for myself at a number of meetings in one particular school.

Gerard Vane Junior School

Three meetings on reading were held in the autumn term. The attendance was reasonably good, nearly half the parents turning up on each occasion. The first two meetings, addressed by Mr. Roberts and Mrs. Germaine, concerned as they were with the parents of children, in the main, of average or above-average attainment, were very different in tone and atmosphere from the third (Mrs. Laurie's class) which involved parents of backward children, and for this reason will be considered separately.

The room had been made to appear welcoming with a large fire, daffodils on the table at the front, examples of good writing pinned up on the side, and bright lights shining on the walls. Tea had been prepared to give to the parents on arrival. But in spite of this the atmosphere was very sticky. The teachers were nervous and so were the parents, probably because it was difficult for either to know which role to adopt in relation to each other. If the teachers took the easiest course of behaving to the parents as they did to their children, then the parents would be bound to think them superior and standoffish. If they behaved as though they were parents themselves – on terms more or less of equality – they might have felt awkward and so might the parents, who probably did not quite expect to be treated as equals. After their unsuccessful attempts at a compromise of semiinformality over tea, the teachers retreated defensively behind a row of tables to begin the lesson.

Mr. Roberts and Mrs. Germaine chose a similar approach: a quick run-through of i.t.a. and the principles behind and objections to the phonetic method; an explanation of 'Look and Say', with examples of the way it was applied in their own lessons; twenty minutes for questions; and a few points of advice on what parents might do in the purchase and choice of books, the use of the local library, the value of play in child-learning, and ways of developing writing skills through letters and scrapbooks. The rest of the time was taken up with further questions and discussion.

Both teachers had prepared their material with care and presented it in logical and orderly sequence. The content was perhaps too compressed for their audience of working-class parents, and the vocabulary and syntax were too complex. The fact that one or two parents referred to the 'Look and See Method' suggests that the basic principle was not really understood by some of them. More detailed examples together with the recapitulation of the various points, with a pause between each for questions, would have been valuable. Not that there was a shortage of questions; but the answers given were too cryptic. For instance:

Parent: Do they sometimes read words without knowing their meaning?
Teacher: Yes, they do.
Parent: Aren't you relying too much on memory with the Look and See Method?
Teacher: A child has no analytic approach at all. It has to rely on memory.

The replies to these and other questions ought to have been illustrated specifically, possibly with the use of apparatus within the classroom. On the whole the teachers talked too much, the parents too little. Some of the questions should have been thrown back for general discussion. At the end, the parents were asked whether they had benefited from the meeting. There was general agreement among them that they had, the majority being in favour of further talks on teaching methods, particularly in arithmetic.

The value of allowing parents to take part in the discussion actively was demonstrated at the third meeting during Mrs. Laurie's talk to parents of backward children. These parents were more obviously concerned, even excited. Though the intention was to follow a similar procedure to the two previous meetings, Mrs. Laurie had not got very far before she was interrupted. At this point the meeting became alive and remained fairly so because the parents joined in – one in particular – and for the rest of the evening neither Mrs. Laurie nor Miss Curtis, the head, were able to talk for very long at a stretch. This time the parents led the discussion and not the teachers, by deciding for themselves the questions to be raised.

Mrs B.: When Merle is reading a book to me at home and she misses the capital letters I get so worked up that I make Merle read the whole passage over and over again. . . . I pull her hair when she doesn't read right, and say, 'What's that word?'
Mr. F.: There's one word in those books I don't agree with: it's 'can't'. You never see the word 'can't', do you? It's 'cannot'.

Though Mrs. Laurie made more than one brave attempt to go on with her lecture by talking about phonetics, she'd lost control by then and no one paid any attention, except to her answers to *their* questions. It is doubtful anyway whether any of the parents had the slightest idea what phonetics meant. However, at the end of the meeting when Miss Curtis asked 'Has the meeting been useful?' the reply given by the leader of the discussion, Mrs. B., was almost cheered by the other parents: 'I thought my Merle was the only one like it. It makes you more at ease to know that there's so many others in the same boat.' Another mother: 'I have never seen my son's teacher before. Now I've had the chance and really seen you tonight I feel better about it.'

Perhaps because the evening was such an extraordinary muddle and the parents talked a great deal, the atmosphere was better and, even if only to the extent that they were allowed to let the teachers know the strength of their feelings, it was more of a success than the earlier ones.

In all three of the meetings the teachers came along with the intention of presenting the parents with blocks of information that were conceived in terms of what the staff thought to be essential and not what the parents might want to know. The necessity for exploration of what the parents already knew about education was apparent from one of the questions asked: 'At what age does a child leave the primary school? They start at five, I know, but from five to when?'

The teachers talked too much, in the first two sessions at any rate. Though outnumbered, they commandeered three-quarters of the discussion. Too often when a parent was groping inarticulately towards the formulation of an idea the teachers would step in before anyone else had a chance to challenge it or develop it. Parents were not allowed to crystallize their own ideas and the general assumption was that the staff's opinions ought to prevail: a one-way traffic of instruction rather than a mutual exploration of a common problem. It was not that the teachers were intent on displaying themselves as experts versus the rest; rather they were used to providing the answers and couldn't get out of the habit. They had no notion how to conduct a discussion among adults. This reluctance to encourage the audience arose partly because the teachers were on the defensive. All four teachers were sitting at one end of the room, and whenever an implicit criticism was made they all rushed in to defend themselves. It was obviously difficult for teachers to take suggestions from parents about how things should be done; they feel that parents must have confidence in them. However, the comments of the parents at the end of the 'backward class' meeting suggested that, when parents were allowed to pursue the points they were interested in, regard for the teachers was increased rather than diminished. At these three meetings, what the parents ought to do and ought not to do wasn't clearly defined. The meetings were drawn to an end too hurriedly and haphazardly, before ascertaining the views of the parents. No attempt was made to find out what suggestions the audience might offer.

A further meeting on arithmetic was arranged, which was attended by twenty-five parents. It began with the head's attempt to explain principles: 'Before the mastery of techniques must come understanding of concepts, etc.' It was obviously too disjointed and abstract an exposition, so much so that one father broke in to ask:

> What I want to know is are you teaching long division in this school, and if so how are you teaching it? We carried the three down. How do you do it here?

This, as in the meeting of parents of backward children, could have opened up the meeting into a lively discussion based on the parents' own questions. But the father was rebuffed, and this set the tone for the whole of the meeting.

Mr. Carter, a first-year teacher who spoke after the head, was more successful because he demonstrated the use of coloured sticks and referred to sums written in advance on the blackboard; but he also tended to be too abstract, and the parents' questions were not used to the best advantage.

The most successful was Mrs. Furze, who based her talk on an explanation of the apparatus. 'Many parents say that maths nowadays is nothing but play. But children learn when they are not trying to do it.' She then paraded beads on rings, bingo cards, snakes and ladders, shove ha'penny, picking-up sticks to find how many different colours you could collect together, a wheel that clicked over the floor – one click equals one yard – to give the children an idea of distance, and an electric board where the light came on when the correct answers were given to a sum.

> There's a great field here for clever fathers, in making these kinds of educational toys. Try and create the right sort of apparatus at home and you might make some money as well. We should like any father to contribute something to this table.

In one respect the meeting was more successful than the ones on reading, because there was more demonstration through the use of apparatus. But the same criticisms levelled at the other meetings applied in some measure to this one: the teachers talked too much; the centre of interest started from the teachers' point of view rather than the parents'; too little interchange of opinion; a concentration on too many aspects of the subject; no recapitulation of the points made; and no attempt to ascertain precisely what information the parents had gained from the meeting. Asked whether the meeting had been any good, a general hum of 'Yes's' went around. One father thought there ought to be four meetings like this in the year, and a mother thought there could be one every month. Perhaps the most important and relevant observation was that offered by another father who said: 'You aren't getting the response you should, because this is the first year and this is the first time some of us have been to this school.'

A more fundamental criticism was that in spite of the insistence that pupils were no longer compelled to remain in their desks doing formal exercises, but instead were encouraged to learn through discovery and experience, the approach to the parents was at odds with everything that was expounded. They were seated in rows facing a group of teachers who delivered a formal lesson. The majority, unaccustomed to applying the sustained concentration required in listening to a lecture of this kind, were restless. Some were bored. Very few, if any, were persuaded to become involved imaginatively in the processes of teaching and learning. For all but a minority, interest in theory and principles was marginal – not likely to be understood or appreciated unless demonstrated to be effective in actual performance. When asked what problems they wished to discuss, invariably from time to time some parent would stand up to ask specifically a question related to his own child's difficulties in reading or arithmetic, only to be disappointed on being told that that was not the particular purpose of their being invited. Hence, this sort of comment: 'I agree with having these meetings to explain things . . . but after all, when you go up to the school it's really only your own child you're interested in, isn't it?'

In order to meet the demands of the parents, a more practical approach is needed, in line with modern teaching methods. The rest of the chapter describes some schools which have been more successful in this respect.

De Lucy Primary School

Roughly 11,000 people occupy the council houses on the Abbey Wood Estate, which, in spite of its proximity to London, is a lonely, isolated community, cut off to the north by a higher sewer bank, to the south by the railway, and on the other two sides by flat featureless marshland along the eastern reaches of the Thames. Hardly the sort of place to attract many visitors. What induced me to go was a brief notice in *The Times Educational Supplement* reporting a 'Maths for Parents' evening at the local primary school, De Lucy Juniors. Since then, on more than one occasion, television crews have been along to film the remarkable experiment in parental education tried out by the head, Peter Bensley, and his staff.

The school has a three-form entry, unstreamed throughout, and has a national reputation for successful new mathematics teaching. On the first evening I visited the school, there was to be a second mathematics class for parents. Whose idea was it to hold one?

> It was at a P.T.A. committee meeting. We were talking in one of the classrooms, and there was some Dienes apparatus on a table. One of the parents asked what its use was – we had been discussing that evening what sort of thing the P.T.A. might do – so I suggested they might like to come along one evening to discuss the teaching of maths.

How was it organized?

> I don't believe in planning a meeting of this kind to the *n*th degree. My conception of a P.T.A. meeting is that we meet to exchange views. The parents know what they want to find out, and my experience is that if the situation is relaxed and friendly the right questions emerge naturally out of group discussion, just as in teaching children and, if a particular issue does not emerge then, it means either it has not occurred to them or that they are not yet ready to deal with it. It is not our place to tell them what to discuss, but to present them with an educational situation which we hope will provoke them into thinking purposefully about the problems of learning.

Beyond that Mr. Bensley was not prepared to go in suggesting what might take place that evening.

Around 7.15 the parents began to drift in, and seated themselves in groups of four or five at tables on each of which was a pile of Dienes apparatus. Other than a greeting or welcome here and there, little was said by the teachers present. No introductory address from the head. Having decided where to sit, the parents played with the bricks, asking questions of a teacher whenever they chose to do so. They were, in fact, confronted with the same classroom situation as their children on first being introduced to the Dienes apparatus. Eventually, when the parents' curiosity was aroused sufficiently to ask to be told the purpose of the apparatus – and only then – the head was prepared to explain to them collectively.

For the next ten minutes, Mr. Bensley demonstrated the theories of Piaget by filling beakers and saucers with beads or with liquids and, by means of cards of different shapes, showed how difficult it is for children to grasp the concept of equivalent volumes and surface areas. He then presented an imaginary dialogue between a human being and a Martian with one arm and only three fingers, each endeavouring to explain to the other their respective bases for computations. This was intended to show the parents that the choice of a three or ten base was arbitrary. This of course gives only the bare bones of the head's exposition. His teaching technique was brilliant. Whenever a question was asked, it was thrown back in a different form, thus leading the parents to find their own answers.

After this, parents were invited to solve problems of the sort given to their children. For example:

With a 3 base or a 5 base:

1 Make a 'block' with a tunnel right through the middle, just big enough to put a 'long' through.
2 Make a 'block' with two tunnels right through the middle, each big enough to put a 'long' through.

In this way the parents found themselves working – as their children did – in small groups, learning through the experience of handling the apparatus, discussing difficulties together as they arose, and turning to the teacher when they encountered a problem they could not solve. (At one table there were two newly appointed young teachers also learning how to cope with the Dienes apparatus.)

For the last half hour or so, questions were thrown open for collective discussion.

Mrs A.: Do the children not think of these bricks more as a toy than something to learn?

With commendable restraint the teachers withheld the pedagogic impulse to answer the question, and instead asked the parents whether they felt they had learned anything. When they said they had – and enjoyably so – there was little need for the staff to amplify the principles of learning through play.

> *Mrs B.:* I get the feeling that my daughter seems to be guessing part of the time. I noticed she used to do that in reading.
> *Head:* Is there anything wrong with having a guess?

After much argument, the parents *themselves* concluded that most words are learned, not by consulting a dictionary, but by guessing their meaning in the context of different sentences.

Condensed and simplified thus, this evening's 'lesson' sounds as if the staff had discovered the formula for instant education. This was not so, any more than the lessons given to the children which the evening was intended to illustrate. Inevitably, not everyone was convinced by two hours of demonstration and practice. The parents' resistance, like that of some teachers in other schools, reflected a fear that so radical a departure from traditional methods might 'hold the children back when it comes to proper arithmetic sums'. A few, aware for the first time how different the new methods were, felt less confident of their ability to help their children at home than before they came. For most of them, the experience of being encouraged to air their views freely and openly was a new one. Discussion about how they might help was rambling and inconclusive, until one mother (cautiously tentative in case her proposal might be misconstrued as interference) suggested she might be in a better position to understand her role in relation to the teacher's if she had the chance to see the children at work during the day. The head, equally tentative but less cautious, put the question to his staff, 'Would you find it a nuisance if parents wandered into your classroom?'

Unbeknown to the parents, this was an invitation to resume an argument which had taken place in the local public house before the meeting began. One eager enthusiast in favour of parental support said he had no reservations whatsoever.

> As far as I am concerned, parents are welcome to come into my classroom. I have no objection to them sitting in and taking part. There are plenty of jobs parents could do that I'd like taken off my hands.

Another teacher just as strongly disagreed. 'If we assume that parents can teach the children, well then, what does our three years of teacher training amount to if anyone can do our job?'

After a long controversy the evening concluded with an invitation to the effect that, 'Next term the fourth-year children will be studying the Norman Conquest. You can come in and see what the children are doing if you wish. We'll leave the classrooms open for you.'

And the following term, week by week at certain times, classrooms were opened to parents, some of whom took an active part in the children's activities under the guidance of the teachers.

Further evening lessons were given in music, English, and art. The last was run by David Bennett, the deputy head. As the parents came in, they had a choice of rooms, where the materials were at hand for art and crafts: lino cutting, paste and paint combing, ink roller finger patterning, polystyrene block printing, and various kinds of drawing and painting equipment. As before, no introductory talk was given. The difference, however, on this occasion was that the children were present, continuing with the craftwork they had been engaged in during the day. Parents were simply asked to join in and to ask questions if they needed to do so.

Some two hours later, when the equipment had been cleared away the parents seated themselves in a semicircle to discuss the educational purpose of the evening's activities.

> *David Bennett:* I am sure you must have many questions. Fire away.
> *Parent:* About what?
> *David Bennett:* Well, for instance, do you think this kind of thing is a waste of time for your children?
> *Parent:* When I was at school we had to draw what we could see – say, a bowl of fruit. Can you really call this art?

In the ensuing argument, what convinced most of them that creativity is not synonymous with producing an exact likeness was the comparison of their own efforts with those of the children displayed on the walls. More difficult for the parents to accept were the implications of the Work List Day, when it was explained that children were offered a choice of reading, mathematics, art, or other subjects. They found it hard to believe that, given a genuine choice of activity, some of the children would not resist the temptation to play about idly. On this and many other issues raised, though not entirely convinced of the effectiveness of the new teaching, the parents were at least beginning to question their assumptions about the validity of the older methods. In any case, the teachers themselves were not seeking unqualified approval of what they were setting out to achieve.

This, I think, was the strength of these 'lessons' at De Lucy – their honesty. Indicative of this was the fact that the doubts about whether to open the classrooms were aired in front of the parents; and what took place really did reflect the day-to-day teaching within the school. Further, the 'lesson' at each stage started from what the parents felt they needed to know. The request to hold such meetings came from them; it was their questions which determined the pace and direction of the discussion (they talked as much as, probably more than, the teachers); and the proposal to be further involved also came from them. By focussing attention on learning through doing, the parents could identify themselves with their own children's problems, at the same time being presented with a situation which enabled them to appreciate the principles of modern teaching. Perhaps the most important principle they learned, applicable to them and their children, was that a truth arrived at for oneself carries far more conviction than a truth foisted upon an audience by others. An additional advantage of the practical approach was that it left the parents relaxed. Intensely preoccupied in their fumbling – sometimes hilarious – efforts to solve problems, much of the restraint and formality which attend so many parent-teacher functions disappeared. Of most significance perhaps was the parents' eagerness for further tuition. What more could any teacher require at the end of a lesson?

Participation by parents

The main concern so far has been to examine the problem of communicating to parents how their children are being taught and to illustrate how various schools have attempted to meet the problem. But is there anything the teachers can learn from the parents? How far should the latter be encouraged to involve themselves in the education of their children on the school premises? I put this question, somewhat hesitantly, to all the heads I visited. Only a minority were resistant to the suggestion; some were in the transitional stage of tentatively exploring ways in which parents might help on the premises; and in a few schools they were already being utilized as auxiliary helpers.

At Stillness Junior School in South London, for instance. According to the head mistress, Miss M.H. Stevens, arising out of a project, 'In the Steps of William the Conqueror', which involved the whole of the upper school, she decided to take the children by coach to Pevensey, Hastings, and Battle. A letter was sent out to the parents asking whether any of them would like to join the coach party. Those who did (eighteen of them) were brought up to the school beforehand to talk about the project and were shown the worksheets to be given to the children. On arrival at Pevensey, each of the six groups of pupils was left in the charge of a teacher who was able to call upon the parents to help in the exploration of the neighbourhood. The value of this kind of I-Spy expedition to the parents is that it enables them to see the possibility of adopting a similar constructively educational approach towards their own family outings to places of interest; to the teachers, a chance to talk to adults occasionally above the conversational level of Janet and John, and a relief from the strain of shepherding droves of children. As one teacher at another school said, *à propos* of a visit to the zoo accompanied by parents, 'This is the first time I have been on a school journey without returning utterly exhausted.'

There were not many teachers, however, who were prepared unreservedly to apply the same principle to parental participation within the classroom. Among those who had no qualms whatsoever was Mr. F.W. Wakeford, head of the Dame Tipping Primary, a village school in Essex.

> When parents come up to enrol their children, they are told they are welcome to come into the classroom whenever they wish – yes, at *any time*. They are also informed they may have copies of our schemes of work. Even parents of preschool age children may join us in classroom activities.

His 'open school' policy was prompted by an exchange visit to the United States. Taken aback at first to find so many parents helping in an auxiliary capacity in American schools, he was eventually convinced by the evidence of their informed interest in their children's education. Very few of the Dame Tipping parents have taken advantage of Mr. Wakeford's offer: 'I think this is because, when you say they can come into the school whenever they wish, they feel nothing is wrong, and this makes them less likely to press to come into the school.'

The idea of a *community school* was conceived and developed in practice in the interwar years by Henry Morris in the village colleges of Cambridgeshire. His work has inspired a number of teachers to apply his educational theories in urban areas. One of them is Cyril Poster, head of the Lawrence Weston School. The account given below is drawn largely from a report written by him of his educational aims and practice and from conversations during my visit to the school.[7]

Lawrence Weston school

Lawrence Weston is a well-planned postwar housing estate in northwest Bristol, hedged in on three sides respectively by National Trust land, a road, and the River Avon. On the fourth side are the docks, the main source of employment locally. The school is a comprehensive of 1,000 pupils, 80-85 percent of whom live on the estate (no more than fifty are owner occupiers). Their fathers are manual workers, lower level managers, or small shopkeepers. This homogeneity of social class is, in the head's opinion, a disadvantage. In a community where there are no professional middle-class members, there is less likely to be a demand for cultural and communal facilities supportive of education. 'What is the point of encouraging a child to read if he has to walk three miles to a library?' The head knew that the initiative would have to come from the school.

He was appointed in 1959 when the present buildings were still at the drawing-board stage. At the time there was no public library on the estate, and little likelihood of there being one for many years. Mr. Poster suggested that the proposed school library 'should be resited, enlarged and designed to meet the needs both of school and community', a proposal which was readily accepted by the chief education officer and the city librarian. One obvious question to be settled first was the usage of the library. It was decided that it should be 'used exclusively by the school during the morning session, but open to the public (as well) during the afternoons and evenings, on Saturdays and during school holidays'.

The library opened in May 1962, with the advantage to the school of a stock of volumes well above that in the average secondary school, first-rate reading and study conditions for the pupils, and the experience and expertise of a qualified librarian and two assistants who can use the resources of the National Library System. How about the calculated risk of opening the school in this way to the public?

> There were some early misgivings that the presence of adults on the school premises would be a distraction to the pupils, or that adults might be disinclined to use a library that required them to mix with large numbers of young people. In practice, from the outset, a strong sense of communal use rapidly developed, and in many cases there is a 'family' approach to the library . . .
>
> . . . But perhaps the greatest gain is in continuity: the library continues to serve the school's pupils at the weekends and during the holidays, school leavers continue as members of the library whose routine and facilities they have grown used to over the years; and, most important, many primary pupils already have a sense of community with the school through the library which makes transition at eleven very much easier.

This was the first major step towards a community school, so successful that there is considerable support for a policy of siting a swimming pool – and perhaps eventually a running track – on the school campus.

In the initial phase, like any other school of its kind, the after-school activities were run voluntarily by the staff. Inevitably, because of the isolation of the estate and the lack of social amenities, these activities began to attract outsiders wandering in with nothing to do. They were looking for leadership. Consequently, in order to meet this potentially much greater demand, it was decided to appoint an activities organizer, whose responsibilities were envisaged in wider terms than what is generally considered to be the function of a teacher youth leader. First, he was to be a vice-principal of the West Bristol Evening Institute, centred on the school. Second, he was to be responsible for all school activities which took place in the evening sessions. This was to be a managerial function. That is to say, not to lead the various clubs and groups, but to assess potential needs and to ensure that leadership would be carried out effectively by others.

> Finally, he was to teach five sessions in the school, partly to gain a real identification with staff and pupils, and partly so that his teaching commitment would in overall terms release five teachers each from one day session, in return for the voluntary running of one evening session.

The objection that this arrangement might weaken the voluntary principle was never accepted by the staff of Lawrence Weston School. My own experience of teaching and observation of many other schools suggests that responsibility for running after-school activities is more often than not unequally shared. Some teachers are disinclined to participate because of pressing domestic commitments, some because they are studying for further qualifications, and others because they have already undertaken evening teaching commitments elsewhere. The advantage of the system at Lawrence Weston is not only that it coordinates the expertise of the staff more effectively but that it actually extends the voluntary principle to include help from outsiders – parents in particular.

The staff are able to contribute in several ways. They may be employed in the evening institute, either in teaching or in youth work. In both capacities they may either be paid additionally for the extra commitment or take an evening session in lieu of a half-day session. Acceptance, which becomes a binding commitment for the year, is entirely a matter of choice. This does not of course preclude teachers from running clubs and groups in a voluntary unpaid capacity. The distinction between paid and unpaid service should be made clear. The latter is concerned with extracurricular associations, such as the chess club, which requires 'no greater supervision from the teacher who leads it than an occasional look in before he starts and after he finishes a completely different evening activity elsewhere in the school'. On the other hand, 'This "session in lieu" tends to be reserved for the most academic of the evening activities: extended day classes to "O" level in Art and Music, for example, or a Chemistry practical session for Fifth and Sixth year pupils.'

One reason for seeking leadership of various kinds among adults within the community is to provide the young people with a variety of social contacts. On three evenings a week, for example, the three art and craft rooms are open for practical work, supervised by 'parents who have some talent in puppetry or pottery or other branches of the subject. A printing club is run by the husband of a member of staff, a pigeon club by a local pigeon fancier, an aero-modelling club by a parent.' Where a pupil feels that his particular needs and interests are not being met, he is told by the activities organizer that, if he can muster enough support and find an adult to run it, provision will be made. In this way, a wine-making club and three 'pop groups' have been formed. A dozen or so adults act as unpaid supervisors of working groups.

None of the school's five youth clubs is directly in charge of a member of staff.

> There are two Upper School clubs, likely soon to merge now that the Sixth Form Centre is nearing completion, for present members of the Sixth, their contemporaries who have left school, and an assortment of boy and girl friends. The three Lower School clubs are run by student teachers from the Redland College of Education, or by Sixth Formers and former pupils, occasionally with the assistance of students on teaching practice from Bristol University.

Links with local secular and denominational youth groups are established through the area youth committee, the leaders of which meet once a month.

The main participation of other adults is through enrolment for classes at the evening institute. Additionally, the school encourages the development of more informal cultural activities – a TV study group, for example.

> In music, this had been done in a number of ways. There is an adult choir, which admits young people: in one family, grandparents, parents and child are all members. Parents and older pupils have joined in the formation of a dance band. The school orchestra is often strengthened for performances by adults – staff, friends, former pupils.
>
> Displays of the school's Art and Craft work make a considerable local impression. A bias towards three-dimensional and functional art forms – pottery, puppetry, design in particular – has, as with the music, led the community to a closer identification with what the school is aiming to do.

This identification has been strengthened further through drama. The plays produced are written for or by the school: there is a strong theatregoers' club, and a theatre workshop.

Similarly, outsiders are invited to share the school's recreational physical activities.

> The school recognises the decline in popularity among some older pupils of the team game, and sets out to provide a wide range of choice. Judo, fencing, climbing, camping and field crafts, canoeing, trampolining, skating, cycling, badminton, table tennis . . . and for most of these there is some form of continuity for school leavers.

Local sports clubs are welcome to use the school's training facilities. Two local football clubs and one major athletic club have taken advantage of this opportunity.

Links with the world outside the school are established in many ways; through general studies and careers guidance and through the development of social service. Lawrence Weston, incidentally, is one of the four schools selected nationally for a five-year pilot scheme to introduce an A-level course in business studies. This will necessitate contact with the wider community of industry and commerce in and beyond Bristol.

What is the impact of all this upon the community in general, the parents in particular, and, most important, the pupils? Though the effects are not easily measurable, the attempt to evaluate such an experiment as this ought to be undertaken by researchers. How does an estate such as Lawrence Weston compare with others of a similar kind with regard to juvenile delinquency rates, the use of the library, care of old people, relationships between the old and younger generations, the boredom of housebound housewives, and many other facets of community and social relations? Without the evidence, we have to rely on impressions.

The extensive programme of parents' year meetings (visiting speakers, demonstration lessons, mannequin parades, displays, coffee evenings, and the like) is well attended. It was estimated that 85 percent of the parents, from this predominantly manual working-class community, attended the meeting just before my visit to the school; and the theatre workshop's presentation played to an audience of well over a thousand. The proportion of pupils staying on in the sixth has increased over the last three years from 20 to 35 percent of the annual intake.

Once started – as we have seen in other schools – a venture of this kind gathers momentum. Already there are plans for further developments.

One obvious way in which to meet the needs of housebound mother up an afternoon crèche for preschool children, professionally staffed but assisted by girls of the school as part of their Home Economics course. This crèche would allow mothers to attend further education classes and courses which could be set up in school: in shorthand and typing, cookery, arts and crafts, woodwork, physical education, and even perhaps more academic pursuits to provide a challenge for lively minds. A large school can usually find reserve capacity in the afternoon without too much difficulty. A tentative beginning has been made with an afternoon cookery class for adults.

There is a more pressing need for a short stay children's home for about ten children attached to the school with a member of staff and his wife as house father and mother. The incidence of temporary family breakdown on the estate is alarmingly high, and in spite of an excellent network of welfare services in the city, situations deteriorate through delay. More important, any provision for children in families when there is sudden or serious illness, desertion or mental breakdown frequently results in the child's removal to another locality or another school. From the community which he knows and which could best cherish him he is abruptly cut off.

References

1. Plowden Report, Vol. I, p.42.
2. Young, M. and McGeeney, P. (1968), *Learning Begins at Home*, Routledge & Kegan Paul.
3. Downing J. (1964), 'How your children are being taught to read i.t.a.', *Reading Research Document No. 2*, Institute of Education, University of London.
4. *ibid.*, p.3.
5. I have come across some schools using i.t.a. which do not distribute the booklet to parents. Some had done so when the new alphabet was first introduced into the school, as it was felt necessary to allay fears that the children were being used as guinea pigs; but once the new alphabet was more generally accepted, the distribution was discontinued.
6. R. Wyatt, *Guardian*, January 1966.
7. Poster, C. (1968), 'The head and the community school', in *Headship in the '70s*, (ed. B. Allen), Blackwell.

CHAPTER 9

PARENTAL INVOLVEMENT IN PRIMARY SCHOOLS: THE NFER SURVEY

Richard Cyster & Phil Clift

Following Patrick McGeeney's survey of post-Plowden developments, described in the previous chapter, this paper reports the latest large-scale, national study of parental involvement in primary schools, which was recently completed by the NFER.

Background

With the publication of the Plowden Report in 1967,[1] the significance of the part which parents have to play in the education of their children was for the first time given official recognition and endorsement. A minimum programme for all primary schools was recommended, which included the welcoming of parents into school, regular meetings between teachers and parents, and the sending of written information on a regular basis to parents about their children's progress and the school's activities.

It was supposed that various benefits to the children might ensue from the closer links thus developed between home and school. In fact, little hard evidence existed to support this supposition at the time, nor has conclusive evidence emerged as a result of the various initiatives in this field of endeavour since then.[2] There remains, however, a common conviction amongst educationalists that the involvement of parents in their children's education can only be beneficial, although the forms which this involvement should take are not generally agreed. This conviction has been supplemented in recent times by the emergence of parent pressure groups (e.g., the Campaign for the Advancement of State Education) and by the publication of the report of the Taylor Committee[3] which recommended an increase in parental influence in the management of schools.

It was against this background of increasing interest, on the part of some parents at any rate, and the convictions of educationalists, that in September 1976, NFER undertook a two-year investigation of parental involvement in primary schools. The brief was to investigate the extent to which parents in England and Wales are currently being involved in their children's primary education, the various ways in which schools are attempting to bring this about, and the factors influencing the prevalance of this involvement.

The survey

The autumn and spring terms of 1976-1977 were spent in developing a questionnaire suitable for use in a postal survey. The development was carried out in consultation with the head teachers of a large number of primary schools, located throughout England and Wales, and with a variety of other interested bodies including teacher unions and parent pressure groups. By the middle of the spring term, the questionnaire was in a suitable state for piloting.

Concurrently with the development of the questionnaire, the sample of primary schools to which it would later be sent was drawn, and permission to approach the head teachers sought from their chief education officers. The visits to schools had strengthened the belief, held at the outset, that in respect of parental involvement the different types of primary school (nursery, infant, etc.) behave in somewhat different ways. It was therefore decided that each type should be sampled separately in order that the questionnaire data could be analysed by school type, as well as for primary schools as a whole. The results of analyses might then be reported by school type where differences amongst them reached statistical significance, as well as for all types combined.

The questionnaire was piloted with a 10 percent subsample of these schools, the responses being used to categorize the answers to the many open-ended questions included at this stage. The final version was despatched at the beginning of the summer term 1977, and an overall response rate of 83 percent was achieved. Table 9.1 gives the number of primary schools of each type receiving a questionnaire, and the number returning it completed.

The high response rate coupled with the size of the initial sample ensured good overall confidence limits. The confidence with which data from a sample may be extrapolated to the population which it represents is deter-

Table 9.1 Sample and Response Rate

	Questionnaires sent out		Questionaires returned		
School Type	% of population	number	% of population	number	response rate %
Nursery school	15	104	13.5	93	89
JMI, infant, or first school with nursery unit	15	348	14.6	339	97
Infant or first school without nursery unit	8	387	7.1	344	89
JMI or combined without nursery unit	4	458	2.9	332	73
Junior or middle school (deemed primary)	8	395	5.9	293	74
TOTAL		1692		1401	83%

mined by the absolute size of the sample. Thus, the total number of schools drawn was determined by the decision at the outset to maintain a 2 percent confidence limit, i.e., to be 95 percent confident that the sample data reflects that of the population within a range of plus or minus 2 percent of the reported (sample) figure. However, when each school type is treated separately, the limits vary from 5 to 10 percent.*

For easier and unambiguous interpretation of the results, the second type of primary school was subsequently split into infant or first school with nursery unit, and JMI with nursery unit. The information necessary to make this split had not been available at the time the sample was drawn and became available as a result of its being sought as question 1 of the questionnaire.

Parental involvement in schools

The survey yielded a rich harvest of data on parental involvement, all of which is included and discussed in the main report.[4] A selection only, of the parts considered to be most interesting and important, is presented here.

Surprisingly, only 35 percent of primary schools now have a parent-

*For a full discussion of these issues, see the notes to the Appendices of the full report.[4]

teacher association. Even when added to the 26 percent who claim a less formal parents' committee or 'Friends of the School', this leaves about 40 percent without any parent group recognizable as such. However, this represents a distinct increase on the survey reported in Plowden,[1] when only 17 percent of primary schools had a parent-teacher association. Evidence from the case studies suggests that many head teachers may feel that formal parent-teacher associations can scare parents away rather than encourage them to become involved. In certain case study schools they had been abolished for this reason.

In relation to the minimum programme recommended in Plowden, the data suggest that the other traditional forms of contact between home and school – parents' evenings and open days – occur in over 95 percent of primary schools, with an attendance level of over three-quarters of parents in half of these. Such formal contacts between parents and teachers are supplemented in over 90 percent of schools by contact of a more informal nature. Sixty-five percent of schools send written information about themselves to new parents, with 92 percent inviting new parents to visit them before their children start to attend. In marked contrast, less than half of all primary schools send written reports concerning children's work and/or behaviour to parents, those doing so being predominantly the schools for older children (i.e., seven to thirteen years). Home-visiting is carried out as a matter of policy in connection with about half of all primary schools by education welfare officers or home liaison workers of various kinds. In 22 percent of schools, predominantly nurseries and schools with nursery classes, such home-visiting is undertaken by the head or assistant teachers.

The extent and variety of school- or classroom-based parental involvement is shown in Table 9.2. Helping on school visits and outings and with sewing and minor repairs to equipment are by far the most popular methods by which parents become involved in school-based activities. In spite of widely expressed professional misgivings on the part of teachers and their unions, more than 25 percent of schools have parents in to hear children read.

In fact the debate over parents' involvement in classroom-based activities has most often been fought on the battle-ground of teachers' professionalism, with the teaching of reading emerging as the central issue. Though all heads to whom the team spoke agreed that parents should never be employed to teach reading to nonreaders, or to children who were having difficulty with their reading, they were divided on the question of parents

Table 9.2. Percentages of all primary schools involving parents in school- or classroom-based activities.

Type of Involvement	Percentage of Primary Schools
Parents help on school visits and outings.	78
Parents do sewing (e.g., costumes for Christmas play) and minor repairs to school equipment.	65
Parents provide transport for football, etc., matches at other schools.	54
Parents with specialist knowledge (e.g., local policeman, fireman, etc.) give talks to children.	45
Parents help with craft work, cooking, music, etc., under supervision of teacher.	36
Parents help in school library, covering books, etc.	29
Parents hear children read under supervision of teacher.	26
Parents help with football, after-school clubs, etc.	22
Parents help dress children after P.E. or swimming.	20
Parents help generally in classroom, putting out materials, cleaning up at end of day, etc.	19
Parents do major repairs and/or alterations to school buildings (e.g., turn cloakrooms into classrooms).	10
Parents run or help with holiday play scheme.	7
Parents run a library scheme for the school	4

working with fluent readers. Many felt that parents hearing children read, no matter how fluent they were, still amounted to teaching and called into question the three-year professional training of the class teacher. Others were more of the opinion held by the head of a primary school in an East Anglian market town:

> If we believe that a child needs a warm relationship with an adult to learn to read, then we should, if necessary, provide a surrogate mother. The bastions of tradition need undermining. Why is everyone so sensitive about the fanciful differences between the hearing and teaching of reading?

The wide variety of ways by which schools attempt to involve parents is complemented by an equally wide variety of associated problems. These are set out in Table 9.3.

Table 9.3 Percentages of all primary schools reporting various problems associated with parental involvement as significant or minor.

Type of Problem	Rating*	Percentage of Primary Schools
Lack of confidentiality on the part of some parents, e.g., parents gossiping between each other about some children's inability to read, their bad behaviour, etc.	S M	7 25
Presence of parents in classroom causes behaviour problems in children.	S M	4 14
Complaints from those parents not involved about those who are.	S M	3 10
Staff unwilling to allow parents into their classroom.	S M	8 15
Parents unreliable in the time and amount they turn up to help.	S M	5 13
Parents too eager, try to take over class from teachers or school from head.	S M	3 4
Parents more interested in their own child than the class as a whole.	S M	7 19
Parents do not fully understand the aims of the school, so tend to criticize what teachers do.	S M	3 15
Parents wish to help in the school for the wrong reasons, e.g., because they are bored at home.	S M	3 12
Parents apathetic, unwilling to take the least interest in school and its activities.	S M	9 21
Many of the mothers working so they cannot come into the school to help.	S M	25 28
Problems in attracting parents who either can't or don't want to visit the school.	S M	18 28
Problems of involving parents who have difficulty in speaking English.	S M	7 8

* S = Significant problem
M = Minor problem

It is interesting to note that despite parallels drawn with the US experience, relatively few schools find problems with parents who try to take over the class from the teacher or the school from the head: this is the least frequently encountered problem of all. Indeed, the main stumbling-block concerns parental apathy, the difficulty of involving working mothers and those parents who either cannot or do not want to visit the school.

Many head teachers appear to be looking to their parent body to alleviate shortages both in cash and in classroom help. The survey indicates that over half (59 percent) of primary head teachers would like to see a greater number of parents involved in school activities, 52 percent would like to see parents involved in a wider variety of activities, and only one-fifth consider that they already have so much parental involvement that it would not be practical to extend it any further. Fifty-five percent of primary heads believe that parental involvement has increased over the past two years, and 63 percent of heads believe that parental attitudes have changed markedly as a result. Perceived changes in specific parental attitudes are shown in Table 9.4.

The main reason for sampling by school type was to be able to test hypotheses about the relationship between parental involvement and the ages of children. There was insufficient evidence to support the hypothesis that the presence of a nursery unit in a school increases the general level of parental involvement. There is, however, some evidence that classroom-based involvement is generally greater and more frequently reported in schools catering for the lower age-range. The relative infrequency of formal contacts, such as newsletters and school reports, in nursery and infant schools, suggests that the general prevalance of daily informal contact renders these unnecessary.

In fact, a cluster analysis of the survey data suggested that there are two broad types of parental involvement in primary schools, the one associated with older (seven years and over), and the other with younger children. The characteristics making the most important contribution to distinguishing between these involvement types are those concerned with the casual day-to-day contact between parents and children made possible by *bringing* (as distinct from sending) the younger children to school. The prevalence of parental help in the classrooms of schools for the younger children contrasts with parental help in the schools (but not actually in the classrooms) of the older children. This contrast was further explored in the case studies, and seems to derive in part from progressive feelings of curricular incompetence

Table 9.4 Percentages of all primary schools reporting perceived changes in parental attitudes.

Change in Attitude	Percentage of Primary Schools
Parents find it easier to visit the school to talk to teachers or head.	61
Parent and teachers understand each other more easily.	59
Parents have a greater appreciation of the difficulties with which teachers have to contend.	58
Parents have a greater appreciation of the school's educational objectives.	54
Parents derive personal benefit from their involvement with school activities.	50
Parents take a greater interest in their children's education.	48
Parents give greater support to school functions, open days, etc.	47
Parents have a deeper understanding of modern educational methods in use in their children's school.	38

on the part of parents, and in part from an increasing organizational formality on the part of schools as children progress through the primary years. The problems encountered (Table 9.3) also differentiate: those characteristic of the *earlier* years involving disturbances to children's behaviour resulting directly from the presence of parents in the classroom, and virtually all the others tending to characterize the *later* primary years. (It must be realized of course that the way in which these characteristics discriminate between each type is one of emphasis only and is not absolute.)

The social service role played by primary schools was surprising in its prevalence. Over 80 percent of primary head teachers spend time advising parents on social or domestic problems not directly connected with their children's education, with over *90 percent* of nursery schools engaging in this practice. An interesting corollary to this new role for teachers is that higher levels of school-based involvement are consistently reported by heads who also attribute some of their pupils' in-school behaviour problems to home circumstances. A possible inference is that those heads conscious of the difficulties their pupils have to face at home are more willing to involve parents in school, using this involvement therapeutically for the parents as well as educationally for the children. This notion was supported by the case studies.

Factors influencing school-based parental involvement

The project brief specified an attempt be made to indicate the factors which influence school-based parental involvement as listed in Table 9.2. Of these, the strongest appears to be the social class of the parents.

Studies of educational achievement emphasize the importance of the child's social background, and the crucial role played by parents in fostering in their children positive attitudes towards school.[5] In the absence of direct data from parents, it was not possible to construct a measure of social class which would take into account the composite nature of that variable. For the purposes of this project three questionnaire items were deemed suitable as indicators of social class. These were housing categories and school location, type of parental employment, and the percentage of children receiving free school meals. This last has the merit of being the most objective of the measures available since head teachers would be in a position to provide accurate information. Wedge and Prosser (1973) used this in *Born to Fail*[6] as a measure of poverty. The analysis confirmed the expected relationships between these three items, all of them being significant beyond the .001 level. While no claims are made that these three items serve as a *complete* measure of the composite social class variable, the degree to which they interrelate suggests that they adequately represent it at least.

Analysis of the data revealed a strong relationship between all three measures of social class and most forms of school-based involvement. It would seem that membership of a particular social class exerts a definite influence on the likelihood of parents helping in their children's school. The more professional are parents' occupations, the more well-off they are, the better the area in which they live, the more likely they are to become actively involved in their children's schooling. What cannot be determined, of course, is whether the relative lack of involvement among working-class parents should be attributed to these parents' lack of interest, to the school's unwillingness to involve them, or perhaps to some other factor as yet untested. It is, however, a fact that parental involvement seems to add yet another string to the bow of middle-class educational advantage.

At the outset, it had been expected that the level of school and classroom-based parental involvement would also be directly related both to the architectural openness of a school and to the informality of its teaching approach. As expected, these two factors proved to be strongly interrelated and are best discussed together.

The experience of the project team during visits made to a variety of schools suggested that it is easier for any outsiders, whether researchers or parents, to gain access to a school with open teaching areas which they may enter without attracting undue attention. A closed classroom door, on the other hand, may be more than enough to deter parents who possibly remember their own school days with decidedly mixed feelings. It also seemed that teachers working in a cooperative or team-teaching situation appeared far more at ease working with, and being watched by other adults, than those working in a singular situation. Because design and organizational features are to some extent associated with different types of primary school, it was decided that each main age-group, (nursery, infant, junior) should be treated separately for the purpose of this analysis, in order that the results would not be confounded by a possible age-effect.

For the *nursery* age-group there is no significant relationship between level of school-based parental involvement and either school architecture or organization. This may possibly be accounted for by the relatively undifferentiated architecture and curriculum of most nursery schools and classes.

The relationship between level of parental involvement and school architecture for the *infant* age-group is statistically significant for five forms of involvement, and between parental involvement and curriculum organization also for five forms. As might be expected, these activities are almost exclusively the classroom-based ones, including parents hearing children read, helping with craft work, and helping generally in the classroom. Levels of parental involvement appear to be appreciably higher in infant schools with more open architecture and employing an integrated-day teaching approach.

The relationship between school- and classroom-based parental involvement and school architecture and organization for the *junior* age-group appears to be somewhat more tenuous. Thus, there is a statistically significant association between school architecture and four forms of parental involvement, and between curriculum organization and three forms of parental involvement. As for infant schools, the classroom-based types of involvement predominate, and again are more prevalent, in schools with more open architecture, and in schools organizing the curriculum on an *integrated* rather than a *collected* basis. Curriculum integration appears to be a more important influence on parental involvement than either vertical-versus-horizontal grouping, or team-versus-individual teaching.

In addition to these major influences, i.e., social class of parents and the design and organization of the schools, the involvement of parents is affected by a number of other factors. Chief in importance, as measured by the number of different types of involvement it influences, is staff/pupil ratio, to which it is inversely related: the less favourable the ratio, the more prevalent is parental involvement, suggesting that schools are willing to turn to parent volunteers where paid help is scarce. School size is also a significant factor, with the larger schools manifesting higher levels of involvement. The length of the present head teacher's incumbency, rate of staff turnover, and rate of pupil turnover, all influence parental involvement in curvilinear manner: the prevalence of various types of involvement increases as school stability (as measured by these factors) decreases, up to a point, beyond which it decreases again. Neither pupils' ethnic origins nor the prevalence of working mothers in a school seems to exert much influence.

The factors influencing parental involvement are, of course, interrelated to a greater or lesser degree, and the true extent of the influence of each in isolation is thus difficult to judge. However, when even the most strongly interrelated were examined in conjunction with each other, in three-way contingency analyses, there was still a substantial residual influence attributable to each, and it is thus legitimate to place the various factors in rank order in terms of number of aspects of school- and classroom-based parental involvement they each influence.

Case studies and conclusions

Case studies were made of ten schools selected from those replying to the questionnaire in an interesting and positive manner. Both teaching and nonteaching staff were included, and a random sample of parents were also contacted and interviewed in their own homes. The main points arising from interviews with *teachers* at the case study schools included the anxiety to defend the professional integrity of their teaching role from the wholesale intrusion of parental amateurs, and concern over a ramification of their

Table 9.5 Rank order of influence on parental involvement.

Factor	Number of types* significantly influenced (out of 13 possible)
Parental occupation	10
School location (type of neighbourhood)	7
Staff-pupil ratio (junior)	7
School architecture (infants)	5
Curriculum organization (infants)	5
Staff-pupil ratio (infants)	5
School size	5
Head teacher's incumbency	5
Staff turnover	4
School architecture (junior)	4
Pupil turnover	4
Free school meals	4
Behaviour problems	3
Curriculum organization (junior)	3
Connection with a church	3
Pupils' ethnic origin	2
Proportion of working mothers	1

* See Table 9.2 for a list of types of involvement.

teaching role (e.g., to include the counselling of parents on social and domestic issues).

The large majority of the 150 *parents* interviewed appeared to be far more concerned about whether their children were happy in school (as nearly all were), whether they ate their school dinners, and whether they fitted in with their classmates. There was little evidence of concern about the methods by which they were taught, methods that are so different now to when they themselves were at school.

What is evident from this study is that the involvement of parents to any significant degree in the life of their children's school is no easy matter. It is hindered by a lack of enthusiasm on the part of many, mainly working-class parents, and by many inherent architectural and organizational features of schools. For their part, teachers rightly perceive parents as an additional and avoidable complication in an already demanding professional life. They also fear that the broadening of their professional role evident in recent times, of which the counselling of parents is a particular example, may lead to its dilution, with their energies being expended in a variety of ways peripheral and debilitating to their main task of educating the children.

Parental involvement in primary schools is a topic, amongst many others in education, in respect of which teachers are under some pressure to make fairly radical changes in their ways of working, in the hope, rather than the certainty, that the outcome will justify the effort. The survey data suggests that primary schools have progressed cautiously towards a greater involvement of parents over the decade since Plowden; the case studies suggest reasons why the progress has been, and should continue to be, cautious.

References

1. Central Advisory Council for Education (1967), *Children and Their Primary Schools*, (The 'Plowden Report').
2. For example, Young, M. and McGeeney, P. (1968), *Learning Begins at Home*, London, Routledge & Kegan Paul.
3. Department of Education and Science (1977), *A New Partnership for our Schools*, (The 'Taylor Report'), HMSO.
4. *Report on Parental Involvement in Primary Schools*, (forthcoming), Windsor, NFER.
5. Peaker, G.F. (1971), *The Plowden Children Four Years Later*, Windsor, NFER.
6. Wedge, P. and Prosser, H. (1973), *Born to Fail*, London, Arrow Books.

CHAPTER 10

PARENT-TEACHER CONTACTS: A CASE STUDY

Roger Harris

In this more detailed case-study, Roger Harris, head of a new purpose-built middle school, reports on the implementation of a programme for maximizing parent-teacher contact, from the head teacher's point of view.

It has been the view of many authors that close contact between home and school is desirable, because it improves the effectiveness of each of these agencies in their role of socialization, by means of mutual reinforcement. In certain situations conflicts can arise between the aspirations of the school and the values of the home, but it is generally accepted that an increase in home-school understanding will bring benefits to the child.

The disparity between the middle-class attitudes of the school and the working-class values of some of its parents has been investigated by a number of studies, and provides a background of cultural dissonance upon which cooperation must be carefully etched. The extent of this disparity must vary enormously, not only from school to school and from family to family, but also *within* particular families.

Parents may hold precious certain working-class attitudes but not others. They regard the school from a gradually changing point of view. In most cases they may be persuaded to support the objectives of the school if they feel that genuine help is being offered to their children. A successful school will recognize the need to communicate its ideals to the parent body. If it can improve the parents' understanding, it will be more likely to have their support.

Within the context of home-school relations, there is another area of communication difficulty which originates in the inevitably different points of view of the communicants. Parents are necessarily examining the activities, attitudes, and aspirations of the school in the light of their effect upon their own child. The school evaluates them in terms of the overall effect on the whole population of children in the school, and on those who will follow them. Parents are rightly biased in favour of their offspring, whom they view in a sympathetic and highly subjective light. It is often difficult for a parent to accept the validity of an organizational procedure adopted by the school which acts against the interests of his child, even though it might be favourable to the school as a whole. Again, the remedy will be found in effective communication.

At this stage it may be of value to examine the various categories of parent-school interaction in terms of their function, in order to explore ways in which the quality of contact might be improved.

There are two possible origins of the interaction: they may be parent-initiated or school-initiated. *Parent-initiated* contacts can be classified according to the degree of involvement in school life which they generate. Some contacts are purely explanatory. The parent gives some reason for an irregularity with regard to the expectations of the school. For instance, a note is sent explaining why a child has been absent, or a telephone call request is made for a child to be excused P.E. Other contacts are enquiring, in the sense that the parent seeks an explanation of an aspect of the school's organization or the behaviour of a member of its staff. Some of these contacts may be challenging or even aggressive, but they nevertheless present an opportunity for a more personal involvement than explanatory contacts usually entail. A third group of parent-initiated interactions are those which might be termed supportive. Parents contact the school to offer to assist in some way. Help may be given in organizing and transporting sports teams, in laminating workcards, or in digging out a school pond.

School-initiated contacts fall into three categories according to the focal point of the activities concerned. Some of them are parent-orientated in the sense that they are designed to provide a service for the parents from which they will benefit directly. Examples of this type of contact include social events, concerts and plays, and open evenings during which children's work is displayed. Other school-initiated contacts focus on the children themselves. The school may communicate with particular parents in relation to a learning difficulty or a behaviour problem exhibited by their child. On some occasions, consultation evenings may be arranged so that a formalized platform is provided, upon which discussion might take place. A third group of school-initiated interactions comprises those which are intended to benefit the school as an organization. Fund-raising activities may be of this type, as are occasions when the school directly asks for help in relation to its various activities. Appeals for extra materials for practical craft work, requests for assistance with typing or with the building of an adventure playground will fall into this category. These various types of home-school contact are summarized in Figure 10.1.

Figure 10.1 Types of parent-school interaction

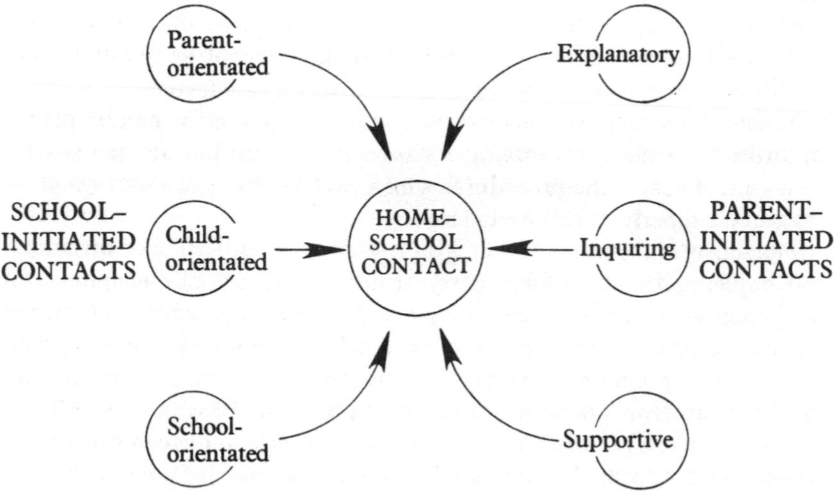

From the school's point of view, several points may be made in relation to this model. Firstly, it is desirable that school-initiated contacts should be effective and well supported by the parent body. The purpose of each activity should be communicated to parents so that they will see reasons for giving their support. Just as teaching is largely about motivating the children, so the organization of parent-school relations is about capturing the imagination and interest of the parent body. Explanations of relevance should be given when requests are made. What may be obvious from the school's point of view may be much less so from that of the parents.

Secondly, it is hoped that school-orientated contacts will be received with sufficient enthusiasm to bring about reciprocal supportive contacts by the parents. The school will encourage parents to initiate contact if it adopts a welcoming attitude. Many parents feel anxiety about contacting school, perhaps stemming in part from their own school experiences. For some, the head teacher may still be an authority figure, at least in the context of the school setting and in relation to school matters. Much good is done if parents are helped to feel at ease and made to realize that their view is respected.

Thirdly, the school should, in general, communicate its aims and organization sufficiently well so as to reduce the parent-initiated enquiries to manageable proportions. Some specific strategies for improving the school's communicative output are included in the final section of this chapter.

As the head of a new purpose-built middle school in Staffordshire, serving an area of private housing, I have been in a very favourable position to initiate a wide range of home-school contacts, untainted by precedents set by earlier head teachers. Certainly it has been a time to innovate, though the long-term effects of the procedures which have been established cannot be evaluated properly at this early stage.

The school is a semi-open plan, group six, 9–13 middle school, with some 380 pupils and a three-form entry. Prior to the school's opening, the catchment area had been served by two primary schools from which the children transferred to a comprehensive school at the age of eleven. The purpose-built premises of the new middle school were not available during the first two terms owing to a delay in the building programme, and the school was housed in mobile classrooms on the edge of the comprehensive school which it feeds. I was appointed at the beginning of the term before the school opened. This initial term was one in which staff were appointed, and books, furniture, and equipment were ordered.

Right from the start, I placed a premium on communicating my intentions to the parent body. During the initial term, evening meetings of parents were held in the feeder schools which the children attended. The parents were given an outline of the main reasons for reorganization, reassured about the quality of the temporary accommodation, and given opportunities to question the principles on which the organizational decisions had been based. In addition, newsletters were sent out, informing parents about staff appointments, homework demands to be made, protective clothing to be worn, and the like. It had been my intention to hold an open evening at the end of this initial term, to enable parents and incoming pupils to inspect the temporary accommodation and new equipment.

Delays in the redecorating of the mobiles meant that this had to be deferred until three weeks after the start of our first term, but the parents were sent written details together with a plan. In all these early communications with the parents, it was stressed that they would be welcome to contact me at any stage to resolve any queries which they might have.

During our first two terms in temporary premises three further newsletters were sent out, written reports of the children's progress were given to parents, and parent-teacher consultation evenings were carried out. Soon after moving to our new building, all parents were invited to an open evening during which I talked to them about what we were aiming to do, and about the developing patterns of organization which we were to employ. The parents were encouraged to explore the school, and to examine the wide range of books, facilities, and equipment which we were using.

By means of further newsletters, parents were encouraged to participate more actively in the life of the school. An evening was spent by three members of staff, together with about thirty parents, papering display boards with hessian. A group of forty parents and two members of staff planned and organized, by means of weekly meetings at the school, a Saturday summer fête and sports day for the children. Stalls, side-shows, and refreshments complemented a sports occasion in which more than 90 percent of the children took part, and a very reasonable profit was made for the school fund. Mothers were involved in the production of typed programmes for a school play, a school newspaper was initiated and made available to parents and pupils alike, and two ladies visited regularly to help in the school library.

At the time of writing (November 1979), the school is in its fourth term. Eight mothers now help in our rapidly expanding library – laminating posters and worksheets, typing index cards, covering books, and so on. Eleven parents turned out to transport teams to a recent netball fixture. Evening visits have been made by teaching staff to the homes of two children with special problems, where it was not possible for both parents to visit school during the working day. Many other avenues of contact have now been opened up, some by the year leaders (senior teachers who have pastoral responsibility for a year group). If there are persistent behaviour difficulties, continual failure to complete homework, or the like, then the year leader will write to arrange a meeting with the parents concerned. This meeting will aim entirely at solving the problem involved, to the satisfaction of all interested parties. Attempts will be made to isolate the problems and to discuss their consequences. Parents' views will be carefully monitored and various possible alternative solutions will be evaluated. Failures by children to keep to a homework schedule have resulted in the institution of a homework record book to be checked and signed by parents and teachers alike. In other cases, parents have undertaken to regularly review their child's work at home; and in yet others, parents have requested that the school take a firmer line on their behalf. Sometimes more junior teachers are also involved in the discussions, but the emphasis is still placed on a sharing of viewpoints and the generation of a cooperative solution.

General information about the school is now available to parents in the form of a school booklet. This document details the aims and the organizational features of the school. It provides lists of both members of staff and school governors, and briefly describes the changing curriculum throughout the four years. There is a specific section devoted to parents which emphasizes the value which the staff place on contact with parents, and reiterates the willingness of the staff to meet them to discuss any anxieties which they might have.

As a supplement to this booklet, year leaders have also prepared and distributed documents which give more precise details concerning the organization within their respective years. Parents of first-year children, for example, have been sent a document describing the first-year curriculum. There are sections on reading skills, on research work, on class organization, on reading, and on homework. These last two sections are formulated as follows:

Homework

Your children may already have brought some work home to do after school, and you may wish to know what we would require of them in this respect. We do not have a formal homework timetable, and therefore on many nights your child may have no homework to do. When homework is set, it will be more than likely to take one of the following forms:

1. Finishing work – for example a story or exercise started in class.
2. Learning spellings, tables, and particular facts.
3. Researching and finding out information.
4. Handwriting practice.

Usually children are given more than one night in which to accomplish a task, and they are then advised not to leave the work until the last night in case homework is given by another teacher and they find themselves with too much work to do in one night. We realize that we are expecting quite a lot of the children and that it will take a little time for them to learn to spread their work load in a sensible way. However, I know from experience that children of this age-range can and do enjoy being responsible for organizing their work in this way. They also feel better prepared for the slightly fuller homework commitment of the second year, and for a homework timetable by the third and fourth years.

Obviously there will be occasions when domestic arrangement make the completing of homework impossible. Some children have brought a note to school from their parents explaining the situation. This has been much appreciated, and of course the children concerned have been given the opportunity to do the work at break-times.

Reading

Your child should be bringing home a reading book each evening, together with a marker. It is desirable that even our most fluent readers have the opportunity of reading to an adult as often as possible. Children who still find reading difficult would benefit greatly from reading daily to an adult. If you were able to find a moment to hear your child read each evening, this would greatly help him. We hope that you will write the date, the pages heard, and any words which have caused difficulty on the marker card which accompanies the book. Many primary and middle schools operate this system very successfully. You can easily appreciate how a teacher with a class of thirty children would find it impossible to find the five hours it would take to hear each child read for ten minutes day.

In the middle school we are able to offer your child a much broader and more demanding curriculum, but we do not intend to neglect areas which are still important to your child's basic education. For this reason, we hope that you will be able to help us with reading practice at home. With your support in this way, we will be able to continue to give important time to formal skills, which we regard as essential if the children are to learn successfully in other lessons.

These extracts clearly illustrate several principles. The school is not setting itself up as an aloof academy, like some private club from which the uninitiated are excluded; but rather as a supporting socializing agency which endeavours to do the best for the children in its care, within the context of their whole lives. Inherent in the discussion is a commitment to the value of cooperation between home and school, and clearly there are areas of negotiation left open to both sides.

I believe that it is important that parents are provided with regular, and, where possible, objective, assessments of their children's attitudes and attainments.

Parent-teacher consultation evenings and written reports were mentioned earlier in this chapter. Parents have received a calendar of these categories of interaction and it may be as well for us to examine these elements of contact in more detail. (See Figure 10.2.).

Figure 10.2 Yearly calendar of parent-teacher interaction

	Year 1	Year 2	Year 3	Year 4
October 1979	Consultation Evening	Consultation Evening		
December 1979				Written Report
January 1980			Written Report	Consultation Evening
February 1980	Written Report	Written Report	Consultation Evening	
June 1980			Consultation Evening	
July 1980	Written Report	Written Report		Written Report

At an early stage of the academic year, consultation evenings give parents an opportunity to meet the teachers and to discuss how well their children have settled down. Even as early as October various measures of attainment will have been made, but the teacher will not be in a position to discuss the rate of a child's progress with any degree of reliability. By mid-year, consultation evenings provide an opportunity to look more closely at each individual child's progress. The teachers concerned will have several sets of measurements to compare, together with records passed on to them, and the approach will be prescriptive as well as descriptive.

The term 'written report' does not refer to some all-embracing generalized document, vaguely appropriate for most occasions but not precisely designed for any. A report relevant to the secure, home-based, nonspecialist environment of the first year would be quite inappropriate in the subject-tutor atmosphere of the fourth year, so several different forms of report are sent home to parents. Some are entirely verbal descriptions of the effort, attitudes, and progress of the child concerned. Others are codified comparisons between each particular child and his peers. Specific distributions are worked out for the various criteria described, and these are included in the information sent to parents. For instance, one form of report used in the upper school includes grades of the type illustrated in Figure 10.3. The derivation of these grades is based on the approximate distributions shown in Figure 10.4.

Another type of parent-teacher contact commonly implemented by schools is the formal association. This may be a parent-teacher association, a parents' association, or something similar. There are important differences between these forms of organization. The views of a parent-teacher association can be thought of as relating closely to the views of the school,

Figure 10.3 An example of an upper school report form

ATTAINMENT

A – Progressing with great ease.
B – Little difficulty encountered.
C – Making steady progress.
D – Has problems mastering skills required.
E – Consistently encounters difficulty.

ATTITUDE

1 – Exemplary.
2 – Generally pleasing.
3 – Usually satisfactory.
4 – Very difficult to motivate.
5 – Consistently poor.

	Attainment	Attitude	Exam Results/ Average
English			
Maths			
Science			
French			
Art			No Exam
Technical Studies			No Exam

Figure 10.4 Grading distribution in the upper school

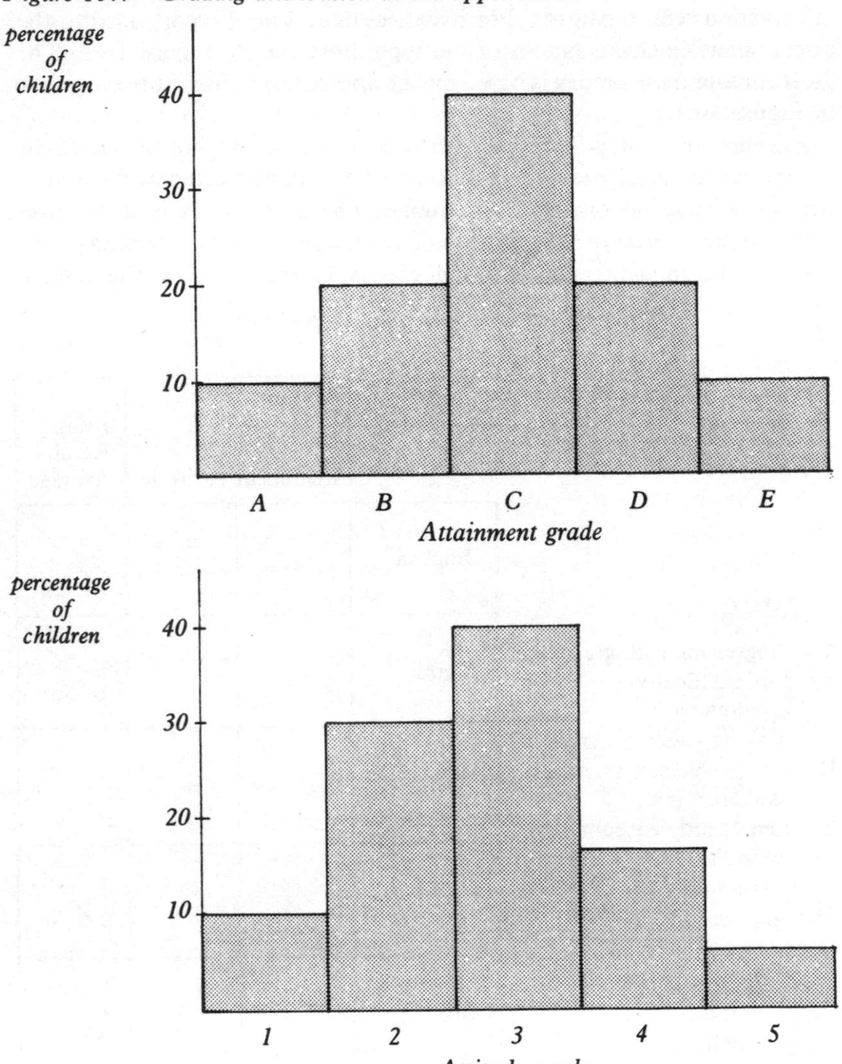

Note: The skewing to the left of the attitude distribution was based on a general feeling of the staff that the attitude of the children in the school was generally very good.

especially if the head teacher holds a key position in the organizational structure as chairman, president, or the like. A parents' association is a rather more independent body, involving the teaching staff on a voluntary and perhaps a casual basis. The head teacher will certainly need to monitor its activities, and ought really to be in a position to strictly limit them if necessary, or to dissociate himself from the views of the association if need be. His responsibility as an employee is to the education authority, and if the views of an association which he heads come into conflict with county policy then he could be in a difficult position.

Many advantages are to be gained by having a formal association. Parents may well take more responsibility in the organization of events and functions designed for their members if they have specific roles to play. Some of them will undoubtedly have more points of contact with the school. Many of these contacts will be more relaxed in a social setting. Formal associations also provide an opportunity for the school to approach parents by means of other parents, and this will supplement other forms of more direct interaction. But above all, school associations must be supportive organizations, and it is only within that context that they can perform effectively in a way which will benefit the children. In my view, their role will not include planning curriculum or commenting on teaching methods. An effective head teacher will need to respect parental opinion about such matters as sex education; he may recognize a need to talk to parents about new approaches to learning which have evolved in his school; but in those matters involving the professional skills of the teaching staff, parental involvement is necessarily passive.

It is inevitable that within the membership of a formal association, there will always be one or two parents who will wish to bring pressures on the school to come into line with their particular expectations. Indeed, some head teachers have been discouraged from extensive contact with parents for this reason. But it is a fundamental part of the head teacher's brief to ensure that the control of the education of the children remains in his hands, and it is not necessary to keep the entire parent body at arm's length to achieve this.

Above all, it seems that careful planning of the programme of parent-teacher interaction is essential. Consultations must take place with staff as to the nature, the implementation, and the timing of the various forms of contact engineered by the school. Adequate information about the school must be communicated to the parents so that they gain a full understanding of its aims and philosophy, as well as its organizational structure. More detailed information concerning the activities in which the children are engaged may serve to stimulate the interest and the support of the parents. The school has a responsibility to ensure that there is adequate feedback to the parents about the attitudes and attainments of their children. A school which encourages the cooperation of its parents will be more effective as a consequence; it must achieve the active and supportive participation of the parent body if it is to maximize the opportunities which are available to it.

CHAPTER 11

PARENTS' PERCEPTIONS OF SECONDARY SCHOOLS

Daphne Johnson & Elizabeth Ransom

The advocacy of closer home-school links is normally associated with teachers, researchers, and administrators, but this important chapter reports the findings of a recent major study in which the views of parents were canvassed.

The stereotype of the apathetic and uninterested parent is often used by teachers to people the background of those pupils about whose home life they know little or nothing. Comprehensive school teachers contacted during a three-year research study* referred to a small minority of enthusiastic parents, who were members of the parent-teacher or other similar association, and were highly supportive of every activity of the school. Teachers also reported fairly frequent contact with a minority of 'problem' parents, who were often in touch with the school regarding one crisis or another. In between lay the silent majority of unknown and invisible parents who were presumed to be apathetic and uninterested.

This chapter claims that parents are *not* apathetic about their children or about how they get on at school. It is based on 109 home interviews with parents of children attending comprehensive schools in two outer-London boroughs. Our research sample (Johnson 1980) led us to three or four families who came into each of the visible categories of enthusiastic or problem parents. But the great majority of the home interviews were with

*The *Schools, Parents and Social Services Project*, funded by the DES from 1974-1977. This research study examined the relationships between home and secondary school, and between secondary school and a number of welfare and control agencies (Johnson 1980, also Ransom 1980).

'unknown' parents who had little contact with the school. Their views form the main substance of this paper.

The home interviews and the nature of the interview data

The interviews were carried out during 1976 and 1977. The parents interviewed lived in modest circumstances, mostly on public housing estates. In most of the families both father and mother went to work. Many parents were on shift work. The schools which their children attended were neighbourhood comprehensive schools close to London Airport.

During the open-ended home interviews, parents were encouraged to describe and discuss a number of aspects of family practice and experience. These included primary school life and the choice of secondary school, expectations of and interaction with the secondary school, and the relationships of parent and child during the secondary school years.

Data from the interviews are qualitative, and no attempt is made here to collate the data in quantified form. Study of all the interview accounts nevertheless conveys certain overall impressions, some of which are reported here. For the most part, however, the data are used to demonstrate the variety and range of parental ideas and attitudes encountered in the research.

The home-secondary school relationship from the parents' point of view

Over the last twenty years, a great deal has been written about the ways in which a close relationship between home and school can benefit children's educational progress.* Television and the popular press have further promoted the findings of research-based books and reports on this subject. The idea of the desirability of a home-school relationship had by the 1970s achieved such public currency that parents interviewed who had little contact with the school seemed to feel apologetic about this.

However, they had their own good reasons for keeping themselves to themselves. Researchers were made aware that, from the point of view of the parent, school is not a central focus of family life, though it is an important aspect of it. Nor are the skills which children acquire at secondary school the only important ones. Parents appraise their children across a wider range of skills than the schools can be aware of.

*See, for example, Fraser 1959, Halsey 1961, Mays 1962, Douglas 1964.

For parents, their children's secondary school years are a sequel to the earlier years of primary school. During those earlier years some parents have gone through a laborious process of weaning their children away from the shelter of home into school. Having got children to accept the idea that school life and home life are separate and different, parents find it only sensible to 'let well alone', and not attempt to keep too close an eye on what goes on at school.

Moreover, during the secondary school years parents are conscious of their children's rapid physical and emotional development. The teenage years, from the family point of view, are a time when young people can begin to learn to stand on their own feet. According to each family's style and circumstances, standing on their own feet will imply different things. For some parents and their sons and daughters, it becomes particularly important for the secondary school pupil to achieve some degree of financial independence, through part-time work. In other families, emotional independence has higher priority. Both the younger and the older generation feel the need of emotional breathing space. In some cases young people hanker for, and parents encourage, a degree of independence in their personal life style, so that family members' activities become less intimate and more open to outside influences. Parents do not always find it appropriate to curtail their own and their children's growing independence of one another by keeping in close touch with other important adults in the child's life, whether these are employers or teachers. The secondary school provides a kind of sheltered workshop for the young people to try out their personal capacities.

The factors so far described which, for parents, limit the desirability of a close home-school relationship have been family-based. There are others which derive from parents' perceptions of the school and the teachers.

Some parents consider that teachers' expectations about parents' responsibilities for their children are based on a model appropriate for the parent of the primary school child, but not the secondary school child. Even though teachers themselves find adolescent pupils hard to handle, they take the line that parents at any rate should wield undiminished authority over their children. Yet, while the legal responsibilities of the parent remain the same throughout the school years, in practice the growing autonomy of the adolescent should, some parents feel, be accompanied by growing responsibility for his own actions.

Parents recognize many influences at work on their secondary school-age children. Parent-teacher encounters are sometimes experienced as occasions when parents are called to account for their child-rearing performance. This is not acceptable to many parents, who consider that many other influences including the teachers' are also at work on their child.

Parents tend to see the parent-teacher relationship as of low priority compared with the pupil-teacher relationship. Whether or not parent and teacher can work out a relationship which is satisfactory for them both is far less important than that teacher and pupil learn to get on together.

Many parents accept that it is, in principle, a good thing for home and school to be in touch. But at the secondary school stage the home-school relationship, they feel, must be mediated by the pupil as a young person. The pupil himself is the link between home and school. Parents only reinforce that link by going to the school themselves if their child wants them to do so.*

Ways in which parents give support to their children's secondary schooling

Even though the parents interviewed were not regular visitors to the school, they considered they did give support to their children's secondary schooling. The home-based, rather than school-linked, support which they gave was in terms rarely touched on by teachers, in their appraisal of appropriate home-school relations.

One source of support parents referred to was their home-making. Despite the demands of employment, and in particular the exigencies of shift-working, parents considered they succeeded in providing an affectionate and caring background for their children. Moreover, husbands and wives often reduced their own free time together by alternating working hours, so that one parent was available when the children were at home.

Some parents described ways in which they supplemented the perceived educational deficiencies of the school by giving some kind of home teaching. This was a minority activity, usually offered to those family members who were perceived as backward compared to their siblings. But many more parents felt that they *should* have been able to help their children by explaining homework difficulties or testing children's knowledge. It was a

*Recent research interviews by Johnson with third- and fourth-year pupils indicate that some young people of this age like to keep home and school in separate compartments of their life. (Disaffected Pupils Project, Educational Studies Unit, Brunel University, in progress.)

source of some frustration to many of the parents interviewed that changes in teaching methods, and their own limited secondary education, meant that much of their children's school work was incomprehensible to them.

Although not many parents taught their children themselves, a number of them referred to the supplementary educational resources which they provided. These ranged from television to private tuition, and included a great deal of transport to and from a variety of extramural activities. Some of the children were heavily involved outside school in sporting activities, associations, or classes through which they pursued hobbies and acquired skills. The school, however, often knew nothing of these children's spare-time skill training or education.

Parents were often concerned to emphasize that they were interested in everything their children did, not just their school activities. Going to a dancing display or a club sporting event was just as important as turning up for school functions. (It can in fact be postulated that in supporting and facilitating the child's spare-time, voluntary activities, the parent is giving the child, and himself getting, more satisfaction than by attendance at school events. The compulsoriness of education is an ineluctable factor in the home-school relationship and may influence the relatively higher value which some families place on voluntary 'free-time' activities.)

Another source of family support for their children's secondary education to which some parents referred was the guidance and advice of the pupil's brothers and sisters. This could be more relevant and helpful to the secondary school child than guidance from mother and father, some parents felt. This was not only because siblings were more closely in touch with what was entailed in secondary education, but also because adolescent children found the advice of contemporaries more acceptable than guidance by an older generation.

The different kinds of support which parents were giving their children during the secondary school years did not confirm the school's idea of them as apathetic parents. But teachers' appraisals were based only on the extent to which parents responded to invitations to visit the school, whereas the interviews took place in the children's homes, giving access to a wider range of information about family practice.

However, family aspirations were not entirely privatized. The question of choice of secondary school and what parents expected children to get out of their secondary education proved to be subjects about which parents had a wide range of aspirations which were not always being satisfied.

Expectations and choice of secondary school

The possibility of parental choice of secondary school is a perennial issue. Whatever the feasibility and reality of such choice, in terms of outcome for particular families, it is of interest to note the factors on which expressed preference have been based.

Throughout the 1970s, it was the practice of the local authority in each of the outer-London boroughs studied to ask parents to list a number of secondary schools, in order of preference, when their children were of an age to transfer from primary to secondary school. Our home interviews were with parents whose children had already been at secondary school for from one to six years. Given the lapse of time, parents could not always remember which actual schools they had named in their list of preferences. However, they were less hesitant about stating what the reasons for their preferences had been. The time of transfer from primary to secondary school had been a time of real appraisal, although the focus of appraisal was not the same in all cases.

Some parents had made a child-focussed choice, based on their appraisal of their child's health, ability, and temperament. Others had appraised the secondary schools, so far as they were able, and made a school-focussed choice, based on such criteria as size, whether mixed or single-sex in pupil intake, their amenities, and the degree of proximity to airport flight paths.

A very few parents had appraised the educational system and made a system-focussed choice. For example, some parents living outside the boroughs studied, in local authorities where secondary education had not yet been reorganized on comprehensive lines, had expressed a preference for their child to attend a comprehensive school.* Another type of system-focussed choice has an historical element, in that parents had expressed a preference for their child to attend a comprehensive school which had previously been a grammar school rather than comprehensives which had secondary modern antecedents.

Most parental preferences regarding secondary schools seemed to have been based on circumstances prevailing at the time of transfer, rather than with an eye to the ensuing five or seven years. Details of family organization and convenience which prevailed at the time were often referred to, and any

*The fact that these families were among those approached in our research indicates that their preference had been granted, and the children were now pupils at one of the four comprehensive schools studied.

child-focussed appraisal was usually in terms of the eleven-year-old's capacity and development rather than the pupil's forthcoming adolescent years.

The time of transfer from primary to secondary school is the stage at which the home-school connection is temporarily supplanted by direct dealings between family and education office. For their part, in allocating children to secondary school, the education offices in the two boroughs studied were using criteria of nearness to the home and sibling attendance. In the majority of cases these criteria were congruent with those being used by parents who, appraising their sons and daughters as eleven-year-olds, did not want them to travel far, and who found it convenient to have all their children attend the same secondary school. However, for those parents who had attempted to make a knowledgeable choice based on other criteria (for example, those parents who had visited a number of schools to examine the facilities and in some cases question the head teacher), considerable bitterness against the education office was engendered if their preferences were not granted. The idea of parental choice was felt by such parents to be a mockery. Strong feelings were expressed, and sharp exchanges with education officers recalled, even several years after the event, when the child in question might be nearing the end of his secondary school life. Promotion of the idea of parental choice of secondary schools may be politically counterproductive, unless the administrative reality of choice is congruent with the range of parental aspirations.

We conclude this summary of some aspects of parents' perspectives on their children's secondary education by noting some of the expectations which the parents interviewed had of what secondary school might mean for their child. The wide variety of expectations which parents severally expressed are a salutary reminder of the difficult task which teachers in each school face if they aspire to satisfy the expectations of *all* the parents with children at the school.

For some parents, *social and welfare* expectations are paramount in their thoughts about secondary schooling. They hope that the secondary school years will be an enjoyable and happy experience for their children; that the school will be a place of safety for them while they are maturing; that it will provide them with an opportunity for social education, in learning to get on with other people.

Other parents see the secondary school years as a *transitional educational phase*. These were the parents who were conscious of the existence of an educational 'system' of which primary and secondary education were only a part. Further and higher education were part of these families' social reality, even though their children would not necessarily stay on to take advantage of such education.

An alternative interpretation of what secondary school had to offer was that it would provide a *phased introduction to the outside world*. During the secondary school years, it was hoped children would acquire a variety of job experience and job knowledge, learn the rights and duties of citizenship, and learn generally how to cope with life.

For some parents, a major expectation was that their children would benefit from *counselling* through the secondary school. Vocational guidance, advice, and help, they considered, should be forthcoming during the secondary school years.

Other parents hoped that their children would acquire specifically *'employable' skills*. This seemed to be especially so for girls. The range of parental opinion about appropriate sex-roles and life-styles cannot be gone into here. But it can be noted that, in discussing the probable futures of sons and daughters, parents frequently implied that boys had longer both to acquire and use such skills than their sisters, who might be better advised to leave school ready equipped for the labour market. And some parents set store by some kind of passing-out certificate or 'piece of paper' to show what had been achieved, even though the attainments listed might only infer employable attributes rather than describe marketable skills.

A number of parents were hopeful that the secondary school would offer *an experience individually tailored to their child's needs*. They considered that the child's potential could be individually studied by the school, and his educational experience be structured so as to fulfil his revealed potential.

For other parents, their children's secondary school years simply extended the time span during which *basic education* could be acquired. Literacy and numeracy were the hoped-for outcomes. For yet others, the years at secondary school were seen as *time-serving*. Secondary schooling was a required experience, from which their children would be 'let out' at the end. While not necessarily an unhappy time, the secondary school years were largely irrelevant to the real business of life.

All these categories of expectation about secondary education were mentioned with roughly equal frequency during the parent interviews. Some parents' expectations extended across more than one category. But since our aim is to cover the full range of parent outlooks expressed, rather than to evaluate which are the most commonly encountered, some less consistently mentioned expectations should also be noted.

A few parents looked to secondary education to work as a *change agent*. During the secondary school years the child's horizons could be broadened, he could be encouraged or 'pushed' to fulfil his potential. Another expectation to which a few parents referred was the *opportunity for the accumulation of knowledge* which the secondary school years could provide. This tended to be defined as knowledge which 'might come in useful', rather than 'learning for learning's sake'. Finally, some parents hoped simply that their children would get a '*good education*', an expression which seemed to imply the opportunity to follow a range of subjects.

Talking with mothers and fathers in the privacy and individuality of their family homes is an experience which reveals the inadequacy of stereotyping. Expectations and attitudes vary widely among families in roughly equivalent economic circumstances. The idea of a relationship between home and school receives lip service from teachers and parents alike, so much a part of conventional wisdom has it become. But the idea is not based on universally held assumptions about what is fruitful and appropriate. Unvociferous parents have well worked-out views of their own about the scope of a relationship between home and secondary school, which teachers need to understand and take account of.

References

Douglas, J.W.B. (1964), *The Home and the School*, MacGibbon & Kee.
Fraser, E. (1959), *Home Environment and the School*, University of London Press.
Halsey, A.H., Floud, J., and Anderson, C. (1961), *Education, Economy and Society*, The Free Press.
Johnson, D., Ransom, E., Packwood, T., Bowden, K., and Kogan, M. (1980), *Secondary Schools and the Welfare Network*, Allen & Unwin.
Mays, J.B. (1962), *Education and the Urban Child*, University of Liverpool Press.
Ransom, E. and Johnson D., with Bowden, K. (1980), *Family and School*, (in preparation).

CHAPTER 12

ETHNIC MINORITY PARENTS AND EDUCATION

Sally Tomlinson

One of the few published accounts of its kind, this chapter reports on the particular needs and opportunities for linking home and school in a society where multicultural classrooms are coming to exist in most regions.

In a society in which racial hostility rather than harmony is all too often evident, good home-school relations between teachers and ethnic minority parents are crucially important. An essential part of the preparation of all teachers who intend to work in multiracial schools is that they should have some knowledge of the culture, traditions, and backgrounds of minority group parents; and particularly that they should understand the expectations that parents who were immigrants into Britain have about the education system on behalf of their children. This poses something of a problem for teachers, who are mainly white, middle class, themselves educated into an ethnocentric view of the world, and who, as a number of research studies have indicated, often have difficulty in understanding white working-class homes with different values, attitudes, and life-styles to their own. Teachers have, by and large, been left to pick up information themselves about the backgrounds of the ethnic minority children they teach. They have been given little guidance as to whether the parents of the children have come from India, Pakistan, Bangladesh, Cyprus, Kenya, Jamaica, Guyana, or any other of the countries once included in the British Empire; whether they are Sikh, Muslim, Hindu, Catholic, Baptist, or Pentacostal; whether they speak Urdu, Punjabi, Bengali, Gujerati, Hindi, or any of the West Indian creole languages; and they have largely been left to interpret this information themselves, and to guess how the home backgrounds might affect the children they teach. One inevitable consequence of this random process has been that teachers have tended to react to minority group parents as 'problems', and myths and stereotypes have been too readily accepted.

While there is an increasing amount of descriptive literature now available to teachers to help them understand the cultures and home backgrounds of ethnic minorities,[1] there is a paucity of information as to how the parents themselves actually regard schools, teachers, and the education of their children. We do know that the majority of ethnic minority parents had their own beliefs and expectations about education shaped partly by their own experiences in colonial education systems; and that school systems set up in colonies were often distorted to meet the needs of the colonizing country.[2] The education system set up in the Indian subcontinent, the West Indies, and East Africa, in which many of the present parents were educated, were all colonial education systems, but differed in important respects. In India, for example, a western-style education system began to be seen as a means to status and mobility as early as 1844, when government job preference was given to those with an 'English' education, and there was a concentration on urban élite education and a neglect of primary and rural education. Thus, an Indian immigrant from an urban area might well have different expectations of the English education system for his children compared to a rural immigrant. In the West Indies, there was a concentration on primary education to produce a plantation work-force, and a neglect of secondary education. Thus, it is not surprising that many West Indian immigrants into England did not complete a secondary education, but have expectations that their children will do better educationally than they were able to.

The Handsworth Study

In order to provide some information on the educational backgrounds of ethnic minority parents, their contacts with, and satisfaction or dissatisfaction with the schools their children attended, and their career aspirations for their children, questions were included in a wider survey of West Indian, Asian (mainly Indian), and a comparative 'British' group of householders in Handsworth, Birmingham, in 1976.[3] The views of the 'British' sample who had children at schools provided a useful yardstick to assess how different or how similar the views held by the West Indian and Asian parents about schools and education actually were.

Of the 700 ethnic minority adults interviewed (of whom those with children had 1300 children currently living with them), most had received their education overseas and thus had no first-hand experience of English education. The majority of West Indians had left school by the age of fifteen, indeed 56 percent had left school by fourteen, and thus they had little secondary schooling. Only 30 of the West Indian parents had any kind of school-leaving qualification. Thus, West Indian parents educated overseas would seem to have a basic schooling appropriate to the skilled, or semi- and unskilled occupations they were currently working in. In this they were somewhat similar to the 400 'British' interviewed, the majority of whom had left school at fifteen and were primarily employed in skilled or semiskilled manual occupations. The educational backgrounds of the Asians were more diverse. Nearly 20 percent had had no schooling whatsoever. As one Indian father put it, 'my rural primary school was six miles away and I wasn't going to walk twelve miles a day just to get an education.'

On the other hand, half the Asians interviewed had stayed at school until fifteen or over, and had more school, higher education, and work qualifications. It was more likely that some Asian parents would be working in occupations for which they were educationally 'overqualified'. For example, the Indian parent with a philosophy degree who was working as a waiter, and the Indian-born teacher from Uganda working as a bus driver.

Contacts with schools

By and large, migrating to Britain had not increased the education or skill levels of the West Indian and Asian parents to any degree, and they were eager for their children to take advantage of the educational opportunities they did not themselves have. They also rightly perceived the English education system as a major means for acquiring job security and social mobility. However, any immigrant parent is disadvantaged in trying to understand the complex English education system, with its stop-go policy of comprehensivization, its curriculum innovations, and its mysterious streaming and setting processes. These things are difficult enough for indigenous parents, and doubly so for immigrant parents, some of whom are also handicapped by language difficulties. Nevertheless, contrary to widespread beliefs that some minority group parents do not take much interest in their children's education, our study indicated that not only do they take great interest, but both West Indian and Asian parents have made particular efforts to try to understand a complex and unfamiliar system, and they have high expectations of school.

In a multiracial area such as Handsworth, the schools are likely to contain a majority of children of immigrant parentage, although in the mid-1970s the majority of these children would be British-born. Certainly the West Indian and Asian children in our study mostly attended 'majority immigrant' schools.[4] The white people in the area were mainly older people whose children had grown up and left, and out of the 400 'British' householders interviewed, only 92 had children at school. Thus, schools are currently a matter of great concern to the ethnic minority communities. It is worth noting that the school may be the one compulsory 'white' institution that many minority parents have to deal with. It is possible for an Asian worker who has lived fifteen years or more in England to work in an ethnic group, and to shop and to socialize wholly within his ethnic community – his major contact with the majority society being the school. This situation makes it even more important that schools should understand and assist parents.

In the Handsworth study, parents were asked whether they had visited their children's schools recently. We considered that actually visiting a school constituted a good measure of parental interest. Various reasons have been put forward for ethnic minority parents failing to visit schools – 'parental apathy' being one of the most common. We found little evidence of apathy, even among parents who had not visited the schools. One Indian parent discussed the question seriously with us, but felt that teachers should be left to educate his children 'without my interference'. Other parents felt their command of the English language was not good enough to communicate meaningfully with teachers. Long working hours and shift work have also been offered as reasons for parents failing to visit schools, and indeed our study showed that West Indian and Asian parents, including mothers, worked longer, more 'unsocial' hours, and did more shift work, than whites living in the same district.

Table 12.1 shows that while the 'British' were the *most* likely to have visited their child's school in the last six months, the majority of West Indian and Asian parents had attended; it was interesting, in the light of the view sometimes expressed that Asian parents are more interested in their children's education, to see that West Indian parents were rather more likely to have visited their children's school than Asians.

Table 12.2 shows that just over half the parents had been to a parents' evening or open day, which, as most hard-pressed teachers will admit, is not the ideal time to fully discuss a child's progress, or for parents to get to know

Table 12.1 Parental visit to school in last six months

	West Indian %	Asian %	British %
Haven't been	21	31	11
Saw teacher	47	50	48
Saw head	22	15	20
Saw both	9	4	20
Saw careers officer	1	0	1
	100.00 (285)	100.00 (202)	100.00 (92)

Table 12.2 Reason for school visit (those who had been)

	West Indian %	Asian %	British %
Parents' evening/ open day	54	56	53
See child's work	10	13	3
General progress	21	21	29
Academic problem	1	2	3
Discipline problem	6	–	4
Attendance/illness	2	1	2
Can't remember/ other	6	6	6
	100.00 (225)	100.00 (140)	100.00 (92)

the options open within a school. However, many of the West Indian and Asian parents had made a special visit to talk to the head or teachers about their children's progress. Only six West Indian parents had visited the school about a discipline problem; and in the light of a commonly held stereotype that 'all' West Indian parents want schools to use corporal punishment, it was interesting that when both West Indian and Asian parents talked about discipline, they were referring to a firm, controlled environment within which it was possible for children to get on with the business of learning, rather than to punishment.

We asked the parents whether they were satisfied or dissatisfied with the education their children were receiving, and initiated discussions as to why they answered as they did. Asian parents were rather more likely to say they were satisfied with their children's education, but almost as many West Indian and British parents expressed satisfaction. Thus, in a multiracial area, it is encouraging that a majority of all parents are satisfied with their children's schools.

Table 12.3 Parental satisfaction with schools

	West Indian	*Asian*	*British*
	%	%	%
Children doing well/ good reports	77	56	64
Good teachers	11	11	22
Regular schooling	5	16	6
Happy at school	4	8	–
Not held back by coloured children	–	–	4
Other	3	9	4
	100.00 (212)	100.00 (165)	100.00 (63)

Table 12.3 gives some indication as to why parents say they are satisfied. If children get good reports, appear to be doing well, and have good teachers, the parents express satisfaction. However, some of the comments by the parents indicate that ethnic minority parents do depend very much on teachers' reports and opinions. For example:

> I follow the opinion of the teacher, the reports show my children are doing well at hard work (West Indian parent).
>
> The teachers are very good, I'm happy there's no trouble at school at all for my children (Indian parent).
>
> My daughter is getting on well – teachers seem to take more interest in children here and push them if they do well (West Indian parent).
>
> I'm satisfied, my children can read and write and speak English (Pakistani parent).

There is the possibility, illustrated by these comments, of misunderstanding between parents and teachers. Teachers may be able to give good reports about children and encourage basic literacy and English language, and yet the children are not necessarily gaining the skills and qualifications the parents ultimately hope the school will equip them with.

Table 12.4 Parental dissatisfaction with schools

	West Indian	*Asian*	*British*
	%	%	%
Held back by coloured children	4	14	48
Teachers no good	16	19	4
Low standard of education	22	14	19
Poor teaching methods	22	11	15
Poor discipline	4	18	7
No encouragement to slow learners	16	3	–
Didn't get secondary school of choice	4	4	–
Other	12	17	7
	100.00 (50)	100.00 (28)	100.00 (27)

As Table 12.4 indicates, a small number of ethnic minority parents were dissatisfied with their children's schooling. But this is an important group, for the dissatisfaction stemmed both from peceived differences between the English education system and the overseas education of the parent, and from a genuine feeling that the English education offered to their children was deficient. For example, differences between teaching methods, discipline, and curriculum content often worry parents:

> The teaching here is different, in India children are made to learn, here the teachers are not strict enough (Indian parent).
> They don't teach him enough about Britain, when I was at school I learned the history and geography of Britain (West Indian parent).

Parents are also critical of what they perceive to be wrong teaching methods, and low standards:

> My children have only learned to draw pictures, they can't read or write yet (Pakistani parent).
> The children don't get homework, the teachers don't seem to have standards, and are disinterested in his progress (West Indian parent).

Even some of the parents who said they were satisfied with their children's education did occasionally add somewhat fatalistic comments such as, 'Well, we have to be satisfied, don't we.' And there was some tendency on the part of West Indian parents, in particular, to blame their own children for educational failure, rather than the school:

> If he doesn't learn its his own fault isn't it? The teachers are there to teach him.

When we compared the educational and occupational backgrounds of the parents with their satisfaction or dissatisfaction with schools, we found that Asian parents who were 'underemployed' considering their own educational qualifications were more likely to be critical of the education their children were receiving and to expect more from schools. Amongst West Indians, those who were dissatisfied with their own jobs and had made efforts to acquire more skills themselves were more likely to be dissatisfied.

Amongst parents with children at secondary school there was some confusion about differences between CSE and O-level courses, and the appropriate age to begin studying for these courses; and there was not sufficient appreciation of the necessity for the two-year sixth-form course leading to A-level as the normal route to higher education and professional training. Again, some minority parents were putting an inordinate, and sometimes misplaced, faith in teachers to make sure their children took the right course of study at the right time, to achieve particular ambitions.

One major course of dissatisfaction with schools on the part of white parents, and curiously, on the part of a few West Indian and Asian parents, was that children were 'held back' by coloured children. This of course has been one of the most commonly expressed fears of white parents since children of ethnic minority parents first came into schools, but there is no research evidence to support the suggestion.[5]

When the West Indian and Asian parents referred to 'good' teachers they had in mind teachers who got down to the business of teaching literacy and numeracy in the primary schools, and 'subjects' leading to examination qualifications in the secondary schools. They also preferred teachers who were strict, 'pushed' the children, but were kind and were 'nonracist'. Parents are very much aware that schools are not insulated from the wider society and that teachers can reflect or condone racist attitudes. They very much appreciate teachers who, while being aware of racial tensions and hostilities, manage to teach black and white children together successfully, without being conciliatory or patronizing. As one West Indian mother remarked:

> At *X* school they treated my children like pigs, but now they're moved to *Y* school the teachers are real nice and don't look down on black or white.

Career aspirations

There has been a certain amount of literature devoted to discussing the proposition that immigrant parents have 'unrealistic' ambitions for their children,[6] particularly in view of their children's level of performance and achievement in school. We therefore asked parents whether they would like their children to stay on in education after the minimum leaving age, and what kind of jobs they envisaged for their children. Overwhelmingly, ethnic minority parents wanted their children to stay on in education after the minimum leaving age, girls as well as boys. This enthusiasm for education could well be exploited and encouraged by schools. Indeed, teachers in multiracial schools do frequently comment on the numbers of ethnic minority pupils, particularly Asians, who stay on into the sixth-form. But, as noted previously, it becomes crucial to explain to parents exactly what the children are studying at sixth-form level, and what qualifications or further training this can lead to. Ethnic minority parents are very much aware of the discrimination their children face in seeking employment after school, and place great faith in the acquisition of educational qualifications to overcome this. They are, however, not always informed of the relative usefulness of, say, acquiring O-levels at eighteen instead of sixteen. For example, the Indian father who was confident that his daughter, studying O-levels at the age of nineteen at a further education college, would be accepted on a radiographer's course might illustrate this educational naivete.

When employment opportunities for all school-leavers are low, of course, encouraging children to stay at school may also be a very practical adjustment to the situation on the part of ethnic minority parents.

When asked about their career aspirations for their children, the most interesting factor to emerge was that there was no difference between the numbers of West Indian, Asian, and 'British' parents (about a third of each group) who declined to choose a career for their children, and replied that it was 'up to him/her'. This freedom of choice applied to girls as well as boys, and there was little evidence of Asian fathers curtailing their daughters' educational or job opportunities. Only eight Asian fathers specifically said they did not want their daughters to work.

The parents who did specify a particular career for their children mentioned a wide variety of jobs, although more variety for boys than for girls. For boys, professional jobs such as doctor, solicitor, or engineer were mentioned slightly more by Asian parents, but certainly not enough to justify the stereotype that 'all Asians' want their children to be professionals. Like the West Indian and 'British' parents, some Asians aspire for professional and white-collar jobs for their children, others for skilled manual jobs. The one thing common to all groups is that they want their children to obtain jobs with skills, security, and the prospect of long-term employment and they look to the schools to equip their children for entry to such jobs. Ethnic minority parents do not see themselves or their children as part of a 'disadvantaged' group in British society. As one Indian parent said, 'I come here to work, I've worked hard, and I don't want to see my son unemployed here.'

Technician, draughtsman, mechanic, computer-operator, clerical officer, builder, policeman, armed forces, and industrial apprenticeships were mentioned by ethnic minority parents. Interestingly, they did not seem to want their sons to be teachers; this was an occupation mentioned for their daughters, along with nursing, doctoring, banking, accountancy, clerical work, commercial and shop work, hairdressing, and entertainment.

Language and culture

The major focus of policies directed towards the children of immigrant parentage from the 1960s has been concerned with language acquisition. Lack of English and poor English has always been perceived as a problem by teachers who, even in the mid-1970s, are likely to note minority group children arriving in school (as immigrants or born in Britain) with little or no English. Teachers also express concern that the creole languages spoken in many West Indian homes impede the learning process for West Indian children.[7] In the Handsworth study we decided to ask parents their views on their children's language difficulties. A quarter of the Asian parents interviewed thought that their children had had difficulty in using the English language when they first attended school, and most of these parents were aware that efforts had been made to help their children, either in school or by attendance at a language centre. These parents thought their children would be at a disadvantage if they did not acquire fluency in the English language and that for older children this can pose special problems. For example, one Indian father, arriving to work in Britain in 1967, had only managed to bring his wife and sons in 1975, as the immigration procedures had taken a number of years to complete. Thus, his children were aged fourteen, twelve, and nine on arrival and had been sent to an immigrant language centre. Neither parent had any experience of the English education system; the mother did not speak much English herself, and both were worried at the handicap their sons faced in accommodating both to a new language and to a different education system.

However, three-quarters of the Asian parents and all but three of the West Indian parents thought that their children had no difficulty with the English language at school. This may indicate a source of some considerable misunderstanding between home and school, particularly West Indian homes. West Indian parents who speak creole in the home use it as any regular linguistic system. They do not regard creole as a deficient or inadequate system in the way that teachers are reported to perceive it.[8] They think that their children can use standard English, which is the language medium used in schools, and they expect schools to improve their children's use of standard English.

Similarly, there appears to be a greater possibility of misunderstanding between West Indian schools and homes over the question of cultural traditions. The early idea that the children of ethnic minority parents would assimilate into British society and submerge their ethnic identity gave way during the 1970s to a recognition that cultural diversity was something that should be both tolerated and encouraged. The Asian communities have certainly retained and even strengthened their religious and cultural traditions in Britain, and most multiracial schools not only respect but capitalize on these different cultural traditions. By contrast, teachers often perceive West Indian children as having no cultural traditions, and are wary of groups that seek to promote a black cultural identity outside schools, or colleagues who encourage the teaching of black studies within schools.

We were interested to find out how many parents supported educating their children in their own cultural traditions outside schools, and, in the case of West Indian parents, how far they supported black studies. Table 12.5 shows the 'extra school' to which the parents in our Handsworth study sent their children.

Nearly a quarter of Asian parents sent their children to mosque or temple school outside English school hours, for instruction in religion or mother tongue. No less than 65 percent of West Indian parents reported sending their children to Sunday school, including Sunday schools belonging to a variety of pentacostal sects; but few parents reported sending their children to the black holiday schools run by a group of black community workers in Handsworth. West Indian parents were distinctly ambivalent about their children studying black studies or cultural programmes. They themselves were educated in a system which stressed European achievement and

Table 12.5 'School' attended other than ordinary school

	West Indian	*Asian*
%	%	
School at mosque or temple	–	24
Black holiday/Saturday school	3	2
Sunday school	65	5
Other (ballet, piano, etc.)	1	2
None of these	31	67
	100.00 (285)	100.00 (202)

England as the 'mother country', and as the previously quoted comment from the West Indian parent who wanted her son to 'learn about Britain' indicated, they found it difficult to appreciate a different curriculum for their children. Indeed, some of the parents were suspicious of attempts to promote a 'black consciousness' in their children[9] They were also aware that time spent doing black studies might well be time taken away from acquiring the credentials necessary to succeed in British society. In this, the West Indian parents were expressing views much nearer to the teachers' than the teachers themselves realized, and we felt there was much scope for active discussion between home and school.

Conclusions

Schools and their children's education are a matter of great concern to ethnic minority parents, and understanding between home and school would seem to be a crucial factor in promoting the educational and subsequent occupational success which, ideally, both teachers and parents aim for on behalf of the children.

Despite the different colonial educational backgrounds from which minority group parents come, we concluded in the Handsworth study that the parents do expect from the English educational system broadly what indigenous parents expect. That is, they expect schools to teach their children in a controlled, orderly, nonracist environment; and to equip the children with skills and qualifications which will enable them to obtain, at the very least, respectable manual working-class jobs, and not slip into unemployment and 'disadvantage'. Some, but by no means all, ethnic minority parents aspire for these children to be socially mobile into white-collar and professional jobs, and they certainly expect their children to be offered opportunity for mobility and success by taking public examinations.

However, ethnic minority parents are at a disadvantage on several counts when dealing with schools and education. They have not experienced the education system their children are passing through, and their own overseas educational experiences may lead them to have diverse and sometimes inappropriate expectations of the English education system. These parents depend far more on teachers than do indigenous parents, for information about what goes on in schools, what courses are available and appropriate, and how their children are progressing, and it seems that schools have been slow to realize the extent of this dependency, and to make special efforts to help and inform the parents.

Although it was encouraging to note the extent of satisfaction with schools on the part of all parents in a multiracial area, many ethnic minority parents were somewhat overoptimistic about their children's educational chances. There was certainly a gulf between the way parents perceived schools and the way schools perceived their children, particularly the children of West Indian parentage, that could produce (at best) situations of misunderstanding.

We concluded that one way of improving home-school relations with ethnic minority parents would be the introduction of much more structured links, both to inform parents about the education system in general, and thus help make discussions of their own children's education more meaningful, and also to encourage teachers to listen to the views of ethnic minority parents without preconceived stereotyping.

References

1. For example, James, A.C. (1974), *Sikh Children in Britain*, Oxford University Press, for the Institute of Race Relations.
   Watson, J.L. (ed.) (1977), *Between Two Cultures*, Oxford University Press.
2. See Altback, P. and Kelly, E.P. (eds.) (1978), *Education and Colonialism*, Longman.
3. This study, carried out between 1974-1978, is reported in Rex, J. and Tomlinson, S. (1979), *Colonial Immigrants in a British City – a class analysis*, Routledge & Kegan Paul.
4. i.e., schools with over 50 percent of the enrolment having parents born in the New Commonwealth.

5. See McEwan, E.C., Gipps, C.V., and Sumner, R. (1975), *Language Proficiency in the Multi-racial School*, NFER.
6. See Fuller, M. (1974), *Experiences of Adolescents from Ethnic Minorities in the British State Education System*, Mouton, Paris.
7. See Edwards, V.K. (1979), *The West Indian Language Issue in British Schools*, Routledge & Kegan Paul.
8. *ibid.*, p.42.
9. In Rex, J. and Tomlinson, S. (*op.cit.*), chapter 7. The problems relating to the ethnic consciousness which may emerge among young people who have different expectations or expectations not shared by their parents is discussed.

CHAPTER 13

COMMUNITY EDUCATION

Eric Midwinter

To conclude Part Three, Eric Midwinter's chapter on community education places home-school relations in a broader context, and argues a case for the restructuring of assumptions about parental participation and the nature of schooling.

Community school or community education?

It was very early morning in the chilly depths of the 1978-1979 winter, and snowflakes hurried over the station platform. Two cold young commuters tried to hearten one another. 'Look Robin,' said one, 'I do believe there's a train approaching.' 'Wait a minute, Adrian,' said his less optimistic companion, 'every now and then they send through a cardboard replica to keep us on our toes!' Over the last ten or fifteen years a few cardboard replicas of community schools have been sent along to keep us on our toes, and maybe it is time to tighten up the definitions. Of course there is no patent or copyright taken out for the use of the title, but some confusion is abroad in the land as people vie for the benefits of a splendid-sounding label. It is particularly galling to draw attention to this, because the schools in question are so obviously attractive and progressive in manner. Indeed, what they represent is an aspect, sometimes a significant aspect, of community schooling, but they rarely, if ever, encompass the whole of what community schooling should mean.

The chief offenders, if that is not too pejorative a word, are the dual-purpose schools, where, for very proper reasons of economy and to provide districts with a secure social focus, facilities are available for adults. There are now several secondary schools of this type, some of them purpose-built, up and down the country, and they are all very welcome. They are in the tradition of Henry Morris' Cambridgeshire Village Colleges,[1] and it is a tradition that has travelled well, especially into new towns, like Milton Keynes, with its Stantonbury campus, or Telford, with its Madeley Court.[2] At their best, they meet one of the requirements of the community school, namely, the provision of a service to the catchment area as a whole and some feeling of the need for coherence in fresh or fragmented neighbourhoods.

That is very much the 'community' convention for secondary schools. On the other hand, primary schools, especially in the post-Plowden era, have sought to improve relations with the home, and that has been seen as their kind of 'community schooling'. It is certainly a step towards it, but, once more, it is the prerequisite rather than the objective. The point here is that many schools have settled for a general and social relationship with parents. Witness the National Consumer Council survey of parental views in 1977,[3] carried out by Gallup Polls. Many parents feel they do not know enough about what goes on in their children's schools. The survey found that 28 percent of all parents questioned felt that they were not told enough about their children's progress, and 39 percent that they were not told enough about the teaching methods used and the choice of subjects offered by their children's schools. Although 83 percent of parents were either 'very satisfied' or 'fairly satisfied' with the way in which their children were being educated, it is still disturbing that such a substantial minority should feel so ill-informed about these specific aspects of their children's education. This bore out the findings of the National Parental Survey, undertaken as part of the Educational Priority Area Projects in 1969.[4] A great majority of parents were delighted with the way the school treated their children and themselves; an equal number had no notion of what methods and so on were utilized in the schools. It seems churlish to complain. By dint of hard and dedicated endeavour, lots of primary schools enjoy the friendship and confidence of the parents, and this puts them light-years ahead of those which don't. It is an essential, an indispensable, part of the community school that this is so; of itself, it does not make for a community school.

Both at secondary and primary level, then, in what are often supposed to be the superior models, there is a fatal gap. In the former, it is the separation of provision, frequently and illuminatingly revealed in structural divisions as between 'head teacher' and 'adult principal'. In the latter, it is the chasm between a happy social relation and an effective working relation with parents. In a word, the gap is an educational one. While seeking to offer a humane and civic-minded service to the community, the direct effects of that community on *educational attainment* are often ignored. Further, the political role of the school in its community is seldom considered, by which is meant the profound issue of the nature of control. This question was touched on, without too much elaboration, by the Taylor Report on the government of schools, but it needs fuller analysis; it should certainly be central to the development of the community school.

These sorts of questions, and one or two tentative answers, were raised in the action-research programmes of the Educational Priority Area Projects, most notably in the West Riding of Yorkshire (Denaby Main) and the Liverpool legs of that enterprise.[5] Such initiatives have been pursued, sporadically, elsewhere – the Bellefield Community Primary School in Rochdale is an excellent illustration. But it is probably only in Coventry that an overall concept and sense of process has evolved. No other authority has, cradle to grave, attempted quite so much to probe the fabric of its education service from professional and political angles. Under the influence of John Rennie, Coventry's leading community educator and an important official in that city's education service, and in an atmosphere where both officers and members are sympathetically disposed towards such ideas, policies about the educative weight of home and community and about the thorough-going place of both in the management of schools have been adopted and practised.[6]

Possibly we are discussing the difference between community *education* and community *school*. Certainly the tauter version stems from basic propositions about how the educational process takes place, and what its place should be in the social scheme of things. These two premisses are, by and large, complementary sides of the community education medallion. The former relates to the effect of the community on education, and the latter to the influence of education on the community. It is proposed to discuss the two separately, although, obviously enough, the intrinsic linkage between them should not be forgotten.

The effect of community on education

This analysis begins with the well-rehearsed findings of the last quarter of a century about the effects of home and neighbourhood on educational attainment. These do not claim baldly that society produces the school, and that the school has, of itself, no weight to throw into the breach. They do, however, force teachers and others to moderate very substantially the old-fashioned view of the school as a change-agent, able to realize the potential of children without reference to their social background, indeed – in the most naïve versions – in spite of deplorable social conditions. Taking the Wiseman research in the Plowden Report as but one example, and then crudely summarizing, it would appear that, on a 100-point score affecting primary school achievement, home and neighbourhood amasses 82 points, and the school a frail 18. It is significant that, in the recent and deservedly applauded Rutter Report,[7] it was shown that, while schools, as expected, differed greatly, they differed uniformly. In other words, a splendid school treated *all* children with equal splendour, and a terrible school was just as impartial in visiting its horrors on *all* children; the one did not compensate for, nor the other further penalize, children from difficult home circumstances.

In a recent study, included in the National Consumer Council's publication, *Why the Poor Pay More*, I delved into the phenomenon over a widespread area, exploring the relation of the following three factors for each of England and Wales' 104 local education authorities.[8]

a Social composition, using the distinction between manual and nonmanual families, and an educational index for the population, using the percentage of that population with a degree or its equivalent – this to erect a socio-cultural signpost for each LEA.
b The pupil-teacher ratio, the number of pupils per thousand population, and the annual per capita expenditure on education – this to give some clue to the input of resources in each LEA.
c The percentage of the age-range currently in attendance on higher education courses – this as an indicator of output, of how successful the treatment has been.

Space is insufficient for all but three instances – all taken from the London area, a high, a medium, and a low illustration.

Table 13.1

Local education authority	Nonmanual % of population	% of pop. with degrees	pupil/ teacher ratio	% of pop. on school registers	expenditure £ per pupil	% of age-range at university
Bromley	63.1	13.4	21.2	16.0	295	14.1
Hounslow	43.6	7.4	19.3	17.2	320	7.8
Barking	26.6	2.0	21.6	18.5	294	2.4

Predictably, a knowledge of social and cultural background is a safer guide to eventual performance than a knowledge of the technical fabric of the service.

I am indebted to Adrian Leaman of the Geography Departmenn of the North London Polytechnic who analysed a random sample of thirty LEAs from these tables. The correlation between the two outer variables – percentage of nonmanual population and percentage of age-range at university – is $r = +0.81$, and a test of significance shows this result to indicate a strong association. Alternatively, there is no significant relationship to be found between expenditure per pupil and percentage of age-range at university.

There is little doubt that, in relative terms, the nation is not too far removed from a technical commonalty of provision. By dint of teacher quotas, rate support grants, and the like, equality of opportunity, in that concrete and material sense, has nearly been achieved. The heftier imbalance is in the social and cultural features of the children's background. Those *cris de coeur* for more teachers and more books may, from the angle of the socially disadvantaged, be misplaced. The way ahead would seem to lie in improving the ability of the community, crucially the home, to support children educationally. The lesson of the successful suburban school is that the language, the values, and the aspirations in its catchment area are more appropriate for schooling as presently defined than in the inner-city school. A solution would entail alterations on both sides: in making schooling more apposite for the subculture in question and in drawing parents more readily into the actual educational process. The effect of what has come to be called the 'educative community' – that totality of experiences which the child assembles from home, environment, and peer-group – so forcefully dictates how or whether a child will respond to educational stimuli that teachers ignore it at their peril. Home and school relations are no longer a matter of choice, a sentimental feeling among some teachers that it is somehow more decent to have pleasurable client relationships; they are a matter of acute professional concern. The teacher or school which refuses to consider the concept that the child plus the parents, rather than the child minus the parents, is the proper unit of treatment is, to that extent, acting unprofessionally. This goes, in short, beyond the 'happy family' syndrome of the primary school with its gracious open evening and wine and cheese-oriented PTA, or the secondary school with its badminton courts generously thrown open to the public. It is about a methodology for educating children and adults in concert.

The major thrust of the Liverpool EPA Project was to test, at preschool, at primary, less at secondary, but certainly at adult education levels the issue of interest. It was frequently argued that lack of parental interest was the fault to be rectified. A shallow reading of J.W.B. Douglas' (1964) research could be interpreted as having this inference, and it was assuredly the explanation most often heard in staff rooms.[9] The Liverpool EPA Project was, basically, an action-research exploration of whether parents lacked interest, or whether – the hypothesis ran – their latent interest had not been efficiently stimulated. Teachers, finding that conventional modes of home-school relations failed miserably in inner-city and other deprived districts, assumed that parents were constitutionally lethargic. The project was eager to ponder the alternative explanation that the conventional models operated well in a middle-class area because their cultural attributes suited the bourgeois cast of mind and temperament, and that other kinds of culture (in primitive terms, a metropolitan working-class one) might respond more briskly to more appropriate welcomes.

This in fact proved to be the case. By utilizing devices of a colourful and vibrant character in keeping with the norms of the parent body, and by seeking out nonformal foci (the shop, the factory, the pub) for the educational dialogue, one was able, time and again, to attract or spur the interest of parents. By reducing the formidable institutional air of the school, and by representing 'education' as a humdrum part rather than an esoteric aberration of everyday life, teachers demonstrated this truth many times; and so much so that it might be stated, of the primary school in the most appalling circumstances, that with a little energy, wit, and invention, some 90 percent of parents may be guaranteed to show interest. The project 'exorcised that persistent hobgoblin of teacher demonology, the feckless, apathetic working-class parent'.[10]

It was chiefly arithmetic. Although one suspected the consequences were beneficial in a scholastic sense, it was never claimed that the project improved educational achievement through parental engagement. That was to come later, and small-scale experiments in Coventry and elsewhere are now bearing fruit of this kind. What had to be demonstrated first was that the interest *could* be mobilized.

The moral was, in part, negative. The unremarkable discovery that the majority of parents care fervently about their children's education and encourage them all they can knocked on the head the comfortable and roseate view that, so long as parents provide a secure, cosy, and sympathetic hearth, all will, educationally, be well. It was a common impression (especially, it sometimes seemed, among socially mobile working-class teachers) that such was the case. But interest, like patriotism, is not enough. The other trait to be considered was what might be called 'know-how'. In the homes of children whose parents had themselves negotiated the educational system more or less successfully there is, often fortuitously, a background of knowledge and day-by-day deportment which is helpful to the child. One might even present the polarized caricature of the happy, safe 'disadvantaged' home, and the arid, riven 'advantaged' home, with the children in the latter, whatever their other encumbrances and sufferings, remaining the more favoured ones educationally. In some part by accident, the know-how is provided: the *Daily Telegraph* bounces through the letter-box daily; the conversation in the house and the avenue are in tune with the mores of the schools; and so on. Even the marital rows are carried on in the elaborated code.

But this only served to underpin the need for parental involvement, that this 'knowing of the ropes' might be spread. Put plainly, community education should and must embrace a reversion of the equation that the school educates, and that the community, via parents' meetings, its governors, or whatever, makes occasional connections with that process. The truth must be accepted that, whether teachers like it or not, the community at large 'educates'; and community education rejects the Victorian heritage whereby the school – as was the case with most nineteenth-century social institutions – withdraws the child from his or her host community and offers a treatment *in vacuo*.[11] It is worth noting, in passing, that 'community' in this sense is definable as the child's commonwealth of experiences. It does not refer to a geographic pale, although, necessarily, the child's locale will figure vitally. It must also include universalisms, of which television, the pop culture, advertising, and football are but four random examples. It is, and rightly, an expanding term, not least because it is the task of those engaged in community education to push out the frontiers of that educative dimension as fully as possible. However, the critical feature for the individual pupil within the confines of his own little educative world is normally the parent. Mothers and fathers determine much of the shape of the child in terms of his capacity to benefit, or not, from his schooling.

Not unnaturally, there is some argument about how most effectively an improvement in parental performance might be obtained. The contending viewpoints, put simply, entertain either a direct or an indirect approach.

The one leaps straight for the jugular of parental participation, insisting that parents should, by whatever means, be inducted into the actual processes their children are undergoing. They might, for instance, be taught about the reading schemes their youngsters are using, and told how they might most advantageously offer assistance. The other takes a more leisurely or detached view, claiming that, through broad-based adult education, the levels of awareness and the general confidence of the parents are heightened, and, all round, they become more efficient parents in relation to their offspring's education. Both sides accept, however, that in many cases unorthodox approaches are to be preferred, and that conventional devices (whether it be the course of lectures on how reading is taught, or the course of lectures on the Victorian novel) are of little avail. For instance, as was demonstrated by the Priority Everyman Theatre-in-Education team in Liverpool (1972-1975), the intricacies of infant reading or number work may be vividly communicated to mothers through colourful socio-dramatic techniques. The work of Tom Lovett in Liverpool (1969-1974) also illustrated this point admirably, combining as it did unorthodoxies of location, subject matter, and teaching method.[12]

Nonetheless, whichever approach, direct or indirect, is preferred, the necessity for teachers able to encompass adults within the day-by-day teaching process is paramount, and is at once the severest practical challenge facing community educators.

The effect of education on community

In turning to the effects of education on community, one might do worse than begin with a quotation from Professor Halsey's Reith Lectures of 1977-1978: 'a heroic age of universalist political controversy has ended. Freedom, the truly previous inheritance, has been preserved. Equality has been displaced by a political search for economic growth: and the problem of fraternity is still with us.'[13]

The question of considering the parent as part of the educational set-up is a professional one. Whatever one's political or moral commitment, it is indisputably of this order and, one hopes, should be an unavoidable issue for each and every teacher. This second consideration – education's role vis à vis its catchment area – is more avowedly ideological, and, whereas a parent-oriented teaching methodology would be part and parcel of its implementation, it does and would reflect a value-judgement about the character of society now and in the future.

In the main, it relates to that critique of what Michael Young has called 'giantism', whether this be represented by the anonymous state bureaucracy or the massive private corporation. It concerns the alienation of clientèle from institutions, indeed of citizens from the State, and advances the notion that people should much more frequently find themselves involved in human-faced, small-scale dealings, about which they can make their own decisions and invent their own destiny. It goes further. It yearns for a more cooperative and less competitive style of society, and one in which popular democracy begins to replace representative democracy. In that visionary longing, it drives a vertical line across the artificial right/left horizontal in which politics are usually defined. For instance, the tradition draws from the ideals centred both on the cooperative and utopian socialist ideas, and on that warming, benevolent aspect of mutual assistance which is part of conservative thinking. One might summarize this as Schumacher's 'small is beautiful' applied to social rather than economic agencies.[14]

How might this affect schools? It is perhaps most helpful to erect a circular model, with the school servicing and equipping the community to pursue that cooperative regeneration more successfully; and the community, in turn, overseeing and evaluating the school: a circular model, for improvements on the one side would generate improvements on the other in an upward spiral. The ability of schools to prepare and support citizens in this general role as constructive and compassionate mutualists and popular democrats raises questions about curriculum not appropriate for examination here. But the other turn of the wheel – the civic oversight of the community's school – is more properly a home-school issue, since it is the consumers of education, the pupils, and those surrogate-consumers, the parents, who would be chiefly concerned.

The parent-governor movement, in one particular sense, is then a step in this direction, and with approximately 20,000 parent-governors now in the field, it is a growth-point of some consequence. Of course, it is no more than one angle of this new phenomenon, for no one would pretend that each of these 20,000 stalwarts is a miniature Fourier or Saint-Simon on each board of governors. But it is fair to claim that, by representing the user constituency on each governing body, the way is prepared for substantial popular and local control. The Taylor Report, historically, is a decentralizing document, emphasizing that, in the mundane, everyday business of the school, and once the overall decisions have been registered at state or LEA level, those with the abiding interest – parents and pupils as appropriate, teachers, local councillors, and interested individuals from the immediate locality – should join together in the decision-making process. After the utilitarian tenet of Jeremy Bentham, effective governing should arise from as close an identification as possible of the interests of the governed and the interests of the governors.[15]

The notion of the parent governor may be justified on moral and democratic grounds as surely as it may be argued on professional grounds. The parent is responsible for his child's education and, as rate- and tax-payer, he foots the bill. It is fair to say that, of itself, a Taylor-made governing body is of little value: only when the school has fully-fledged linkages with home and community, with that ambience pervading the entirety of the school's life, is Taylorite management of beneficial avail. At best, the celebrated consensus quartet of Taylorism is no more – and no less – than the politico-administrative expression or methodology of an ongoing community school.

In this tighter definition of the community school, the title might be interchangeable with that of the fraternal school. But pessimistically, the other two prongs – liberty and equality – of the famed revolutionary trident have been tried and, not least in their jarring and warring the one with the other, have been found lamentably wanting. At its gloomiest, our society sees free opportunity deteriorating into selfishness, and egalitarian devices becoming uniform sterilities. Perhaps the time is ripe to 'try fraternity', so that, in the recent words of Michael Young, 'instead of shuffling off responsibilities on to any impersonal entity, people need to accept their responsibilities to each other, face to face, as human beings. If all this can only be achieved by small organisations, or by a devolution of power within larger organisations, and if sometimes this can only happen if people are ready to put up with a simpler life, then so be it.'[16]

This envisions a move from representative democracy, with each citizen's deposit of political sovereignty banked for a number of years with an increasingly aloof central and local system of government, to popular democracy, with citizens retaining much closer temporal and spatial oversight of their political working capital. Not only schools but other institutions – health centres, hospitals, police stations, housing estates, social security offices, parks, leisure centres, libraries, old people's homes – would necessarily be arranged in this manner. Indeed this would be imperative. The difficulties of running a comprehensive schools system in a 'selective' society would pale beside the problems of organizing a cooperative schools system in a 'competitive' society. Moreover, and in the private sector, there would be a parallel activity by way of working and consumer cooperatives, the whole perhaps most effectively presaged in Europe by the Mondragon cooperative enterprise in Northern Spain.[17]

It would be the Anglo-Saxon jury principle applied to most other areas of life, with what is, technically, the people's largesse being more practically so. The schools would, in that upward spiral toward a more stable and cooperative society, be valuable in helping to create what Professor Halsey called 'social collective consciousness'.[18]

Community education and the community

Now it must be emphasized that the two preceding sections – the one professional, the other polemical – are, of course, different in character. The former can scarcely be gainsaid as an element in the straightforward business of running schools day by day, while the latter is unashamedly ideological and concerned with a moral opinion of how the world should be. There are, however, two or three connecting points.

In the first place, for a fully-run scheme of community education there needs must be both that professional acceptance of the might of the 'educative community', and some ideological rationale (not necessarily the one defended above) about the political and moral responsibility owed by the school to the community. Without one or both features, a so-called 'community school' is probably no more than a traditional school with either avant-garde architecture or social trimmings. Community education rests on the dual agreement that some renaissance, however defined, of community life should be the end of education agencies which regard communal determinism as the crucial consideration in deciding means.

In the second place, it is the achievement of teachers, parents, and pupils in the first, the professional, stage of this commentary which enlivens hopes about the chances of success at the second, the ideological level. The massive demonstrations of parental goodwill, if properly mobilized, and the serious and diligent endeavours of many hundreds in the thankless task of parent governorship are testimony to this. A specific dramatic illustration of this groundswell has been in the voluntary preschool field, with the huge advance of preschool play groups, now estimated at some 30,000 in number, and certainly, since World War II, the most vigorous instance of social internal combustion of a cooperative brand. With more thoroughgoing cooperatives for young mothers, including important adult education and other components (one thinks particularly of the Home-Link venture on the Netherly housing estate, Liverpool, or the Scope groups in the Southampton area), this is proving an especially inventive vein.[19]

In the third place, and this is almost a corollary of the second point, the critical question for teachers (given some resolution of the prior political and administrative issues) is whether or not they can 'reprofessionalize' themselves to cope with a radically changed job-remit. This must in no way be tempered: it would be misleading to pretend that the revision would be other than profound. The traditional teacher role is turned on its head by fully-run community education, and, what is important to realize, the new skills required are the same both for the 'professional' and the 'political' wings of community education. Put simply, where, in the Victorian tradition, the conventional teacher withdraws his charges from the hurly-burly of everyday existence into some institutionalized cocoon, the community education teacher recognizes that his work and the school's initiatives must be totally encompassed by that everyday existence. The community school cannot be a secluding school. Whether one is concerned just with the aim of improving the educational awareness of the neighbourhood or also with some dedication to community improvement or rehabilitation, the school, in providing outgoing, deinstitutionalized services, calls upon its teachers to be of that ilk. The community education teacher, therefore, must become the steward or convenor of the 'educative community' in the round. He must perforce be social critic and social explorer, rather than, as in the past, social custodian, for community education's basic tenet is the need for change rather than preservation. Equally, he must be an adult educator, and then of an imaginative and nonformal kind, as well as a children's tutor, for his clientèle are properly so defined. In essence, all this requires a change in style, from the image of the academic, his charges clustered around him in cloistered privacy, to that of a more ebullient, a more colourful, and above all, a more public craftsman.

The repercussions for much of this on teacher recruitment, preservice and in-service training, the disposition of resources, and the levels of educational control within and without the school are endless. Unluckily, the time-span for their negotiation might not be, for the campaign for community education is, eventually, a piece of that general hypothesis which argues for fundamental restructuring of British society that it might survive in dignity, in stability, and in some degree of social well-being. That may seem an arrogantly far cry from the issue of organizing a successful open evening one summer's night in a pleasant primary school, but no apology need be offered for attempting to find a link, however tenuous and drawn-out, between daily practice and overall, long-term objectives. A health education poster in a West Midlands nursery school bore the compelling text: 'the first three minutes of life may be vital'. Underneath had been scribbled: 'the last three can be a bit dodgy as well'. In national terms, community education may well have a significant contribution to make in combatting that dodginess.

References

1. H. Rée (1973), *Educator Extraordinary: The Life and Achievement of Henry Morris,* Longman.
2. E.C. Midwinter (1973), *Patterns of Community Education*, Ward Lock.
3. National Consumer Council (1977), *Survey of Parental Views.*
4. A.H. Halsey (1972), *Educational Priority,* HMSO.
5. E.C. Midwinter (1972), *Priority Education*, Penguin, and (1974) *Educational Priority* Vol. IV, HMSO.
6. The Coventry Community Education Centre, Southfields School, Coventry, will provide a list of publications arising from these ventures.
7. M. Rutter (1979), *Fifteen Thousand Hours*, Open Books.
8. F. Williams (ed.) (1977), *Why the Poor Pay More*, Macmillan.
9. J.W.B. Douglas (1964), *The Home and the School*, MacGibbon & Kee.
10. E.C. Midwinter (1972), *Priority Education, op.cit.*; (1972) *Projections: An Educational Priority Area at Work*, Ward Lock Educational, and (1977) *Education for Sale*, Allen & Unwin.
11. E.C. Midwinter (1968), *Victorian Social Reform*, Longman, and (1975), *Education and the Community*, Allen & Unwin.
12. T. Lovett (1975), *Adult Education, Community Development and the Working Classes*, Ward Lock Educational.
13. A.H. Halsey (1978), Reith Lectures; *Change in British Society*, No. 4 'The Rise of Party'.
14. E.F. Schumacher (1973), *Small is Beautiful*, Blond & Briggs.
15. DES (1977), *A New Partnership for Our Schools*, ('Taylor Report), HMSO, and J. Sallis (1977), *School, Managers and Governors: Taylor and After*, Ward Lock Educational.
16. M. Young (1979), *Mutual Aid in a Selfish Society*, Mutual Aid Centre.
17. *Worker-Owners: The Mondragon Achievement*, Anglo-German Foundation, 1977.
18. For further analysis of cooperativeness in the public sector see E.C. Midwinter, 'The Professional Lay Relationship: A Victorian Legacy', *Journal of Child Psychology* Vol. 18, 1977, 'Teachers: Organized Labour Force of a Nationalised Industry', *Journal of Further and Higher Education* (1) 1977, 'The New Democracy: A Formula for Consumer Representation in the Public Services', *Journal*

of Consumer Studies and Home Economics 1, 1977, 'The New Democracy: A Structure for Consumer Representation in the Public Services', *ibid.*, 1, 1977, 'Public Provision: the Consumer Dilemma', *ibid.*, 3, 1979.

19. Both groups produce descriptive reports: Home Link, 54 Brittage Brow, Netherley, Liverpool 27. SCOPE, Kaleidscope Centre, 29 Teme Crescent, Millbrook, Southampton.

PART FOUR

Welfare and Liaison Roles

CHAPTER 14

THE EDUCATION WELFARE OFFICER: PAST, PRESENT, AND FUTURE

Keith MacMillan

Part Four begins with an authoritative review of the longest-established and most well-known of the welfare and liaison roles which operate in linking home and school – that of the education welfare officer.

The task of linking home and school is not the exclusive right of any one professional group. On occasion, teachers, social workers, doctors, nurses, policemen, and clergymen will all become involved. But there is one professional group, education welfare officers, whose role is to do *nothing else* but to link home and school. Established over a hundred years ago, their main task is to investigate reasons for children being absent from school and then to do what they can, depending upon the circumstances, to ensure that the child continues his or her education and receives the maximum possible benefit from it. This is clearly a highly complex and difficult task and requires a variety of skills, knowledge, abilities, and resources to accomplish it successfully.

It is only within the last decade, however, that this role has begun to receive increased public attention. For the previous hundred years, education welfare officers were left to develop their own expertise with neither public recognition nor support. Then came a flurry of government reports on education and the social services, which began to mention the education welfare service and its potential for further development. Working parties were set up and national research on the role was undertaken. It seemed that official recognition, better training, and career prospects were on the way. Yet to date this has not happened, except on a very modest scale and at the initiative of a few local authorities.

What went wrong? Was further development deemed to be of such low priority that it easily fell victim to public expenditure cuts? Was it a consequence of the apparent reluctance of the present (Thatcher) Government to dictate policy to local authorities? Were there too many vested interests opposing change? Was it that the education welfare officers themselves could not make up their minds about whether their primary professional allegiance lay with the teaching profession and hence within education departments of local authorities, or with the profession of social work and hence within the newly created social service departments? Or was it simply that the pattern of provision was so different between each local authority in the country that the task of streamlining and imposing uniformity seemed too formidable a task?

In this chapter some possible answers to these questions will be proposed. It is first of all necessary, however, to trace the origins of the education welfare service, and briefly to review the debate which led to the current stalemate concerning its future.

Origins

It has taken over one hundred years for the role and responsibilities of the education welfare service to evolve as needs were identified and public attitudes changed. Forster's Education Act of 1870 empowered local authorities to make school attendance compulsory and to appoint officers to enforce this. These officers became known as school attendance officers, although as they became well known in local communities they also received less official names such as 'kid catchers' or 'whippers in' or, more neutrally, simply 'school board men'. As the last term indicates, they were literally the representatives of the school board or education department, as they might be observed in local neighbourhoods visiting the homes of school children. The first officers were usually ex-policemen or servicemen, some even wore official uniform so that they could be easily recognized as authority figures. But these officers soon realized that the reasons for absence from school varied considerably between the extremes of, on the one hand, outright truancy, which was unlawful and could lead to the prosecution of parents, and on the other, serious illness. In between these extremes might lie a wide variety of factors which could inhibit regular attendance at school.

For example, poor school attendance could be due to the illness of the mother in a home with very young children to look after; to poverty, which tempted parents to put their child to work rather than attend school, in order to increase the family income; to a lack of appreciation of the benefits which schooling might bring to the life-chances of the child; to the embarrassment of a poor child ridiculed at school for wearing raggy or malodorous clothing; to the fear of a child being bullied by other children in the school yard; or to fear of a very authoritarian school teacher. All these could be explanations for the child's absence, and some of the reasons may not even have been fully known by the parents themselves. But a sensitive and alert attendance officer soon learned what to look for, and came to realize that even in some cases of persistent truancy prosecution would by no means provide the remedy. Where poverty seemed to be the problem, perhaps the officer could help by obtaining some relief from local charities or from the local authority; where the illness of a parent was the problem, perhaps the officer might arrange some assistance from a neighbour or a more distant relative; where anxieties at school were the reason, liaison with teaching staff might be the solution; and in other cases, the officer might need to do no more than to provide some effective counselling to the child or indeed to the parents.

In 1884, a national association of school attendance officers was formed which published its own journal to exchange experience. The pages of the early issues indicate widespread learning on the job, increasing understanding of many of the basic social problems in communities, and the establishment of something approaching standards of practice among officers. Stories of how officers were able to help particular families in many different situations, establish close liaison with local charitable organizations, or interpret the law in certain complex circumstances, all helped to create a feeling of identity and professionalism among the officers.

As the early foundations for the welfare state were laid in the first decades of this century, new laws were passed to protect children, for example, from neglect or from exploitation in work; and local authorities were given new powers to provide welfare benefits such as free school meals, free milk, clothing allowances, and transport to school. Some of these benefits were to be provided to all children, some only to those in greatest need. But how was this need to be identified? It made sense to call upon the representative of the local education authority who had most knowledge of social conditions in particular neighbourhoods, i.e., the school attendance officer. It is interesting to note in passing that Seebohm Rowntree in his pioneering surveys of conditions in York and London relied very heavily on the local knowledge of these officers. They therefore took on the responsibilities of administering the new welfare benefits, for in their hands these resources could be utilized most selectively and effectively for the benefit of the child and his family, and in order to further the objective of ensuring that children got as much advantage as possible out of the education provision which was theirs by right. When special educational provision was extended for handicapped children, sometimes involving residential accommodation or attendance at special schools many miles away from home (or indeed, in the provision of tuition in the home), these officers naturally became involved in liaison between special schools and the parental home. They usually accompanied the children on their journeys between home and school, and also provided greater liaison with other specialist medical, educational, or social work agencies.

As these responsibilities were extended, some local authorities began to change the title of these officers. They became school attendance and *welfare* officers, and later, education welfare officers. They would operate from the local offices of the education authority, but spent most of their time visiting schools and the homes of children of school age. In some extensive rural areas, the officer would not get back to his office more than once a week. The stock-in-trade of the officers was the knowledge of the catchment areas of particular schools. For many years in some authorities, the EWOs were expected to visit the home of every schoolchild in their allocated area, primarily for school census purposes; but in the process, the local knowledge gained was both immense and invaluable. They would build up a picture of the social and economic conditions in each home, which parents were at home during the day, whether there were elderly or infirm relatives there, as well as simply noting the ages of any children for official record purposes. Later, most authorities gained their statistical information for forecasting school populations from the normal population census, and so this blanket visiting was discontinued. But the basic, detailed knowledge of the local community and particular problem families was often retained, as conditions were not subject to rapid change from one year to the next. In addition, some education welfare services became responsible for administering the allocation of pupils to particular schools when they came of primary school or secondary school age, or when they moved into the area. This involved considerable first-hand contact with parents, and once again required detailed local knowledge, not only of the neighbourhood, but often also of particular schools.

By the 1950s, the role and responsibilities of the education welfare service, with obvious variations from one authority to another, was basically set. The unusual feature of this situation was that the service did not officially exist! There was no piece of legislation, other than the 1870 Act, which established or recognized the service in its contemporary role. Yet in the meantime, the youth service (1939), the youth employment service (1948), the children's service (1948), the local authority welfare service (1948), health visitors (1946), and home helps (1946) were all given statutory recognition in the legislation which established the services. The number of school psychologists, psychiatric social workers, therapists and other personnel of the school health service, and the number of social workers attached to local authority housing, health, and welfare services grew during the 1950s; and there was a proliferation of reports on the working of the social services. Among these were the Ingleby Report on Children and Young Persons (1956), the Underwood Report on Child Guidance Services (1955), the Jameson Report on Health Visiting (1956), the Younghusband Report on Social Workers (1959), and the Albemarle Report on the Youth Service (1960). None of these looked at the work of the education welfare officers, or considered how it related to the services which were the subject of the reports. There were no established qualifications for entry to the education welfare service; nor were there any training courses, academic support, or research services to create and disseminate new knowledge, other than the informal and voluntary work of the education welfare professional associations.

The Cinderella syndrome

During the 1960s, there was an intense and continuing debate in education policy on the subject of equality of educational opportunity, and this had profound implications for the education welfare service. The 1944 Education Act and immediate postwar legislation was intended to extend the opportunities available to children in school and, through the associated welfare benefits, to make it easier for children to attend school regularly. Stated crudely, the belief was that once children could get to school then it would be innate ability which would determine their life-chances. The education system was intended to produce a meritocracy which would ensure that the most able intellectually, rather than just the pupils from richer families, got the top jobs. But by the early 1960s, research was beginning to appear which indicated that the pupil's performance in school was related as much, if not more, to social background as it was to anything that could be identified as innate ability (e.g., Coleman et al. 1966, Jackson and Marsden 1962, Douglas 1964, Westergaard and Little 1967). The implication, as far as education welfare was concerned, was that attendance at school was not enough. If the home background was not conducive to a child's educational career, that is, if it did not have the appropriate parental attitudes and supportive facilities, then the child would not do as well at school as a child from a richer home, and hence would have a poorer life-chance.

Education welfare officers have been well aware, since the end of the nineteenth century, that social conditions and the home environment could have an important influence on the child's chances in life; indeed the motto of one of the professional associations is 'for every child a chance'. But they had perhaps believed, like most other people in education, that once in school every child stood an equal chance, and therefore their main task was to ensure that the child attended school as much as possible without undue anxiety, disruption, or real cost to his family. The implication of the new policy thinking was that this was not good enough. To have real equality of opportunity it would be necessary to provide extra resources to the home environment of disadvantaged children, together with the necessary support services, in order to *compensate* for their relative disadvantage.

It might have been thought that the education welfare service was well placed to make the best use of any extra resources which were directed at this objective. In earlier decades of the century, local authorities had chosen to channel what extra resources were then available through the service, as it was thought that EWOs probably had the best idea of where educational deprivation might exist and where, therefore, the resources could be most effectively deployed. Throughout most of the 1960s, however, the researchers and main policy-makers consistently ignored the education welfare service. It was not until 1967, with the publication of the Plowden Report, that any significant reference was made to them at all.

The Plowden Committee commissioned research on the role of the education welfare service in only three areas of the country, and seemed somewhat unimpressed by what they found. They concluded that the bulk of EWO time was spent on school attendance work and routine enquiries, with the rest primarily taken up with free meals and clothing, keeping track of changes in the child population of their areas, and following up children with verminous conditions. They noted that the EWOs tended to have been recruited into the service after ten years or more experience in other occupations, and tended to have relatively poor educational qualifications and to have received no college-based training in social work. The committee therefore argued that what was required was a 'school social worker' who would be professionally trained for the task, and would have a caseload no greater than that of other professional social workers. It was not envisaged that all current education welfare officers could be trained for this role, and the committee thought that those who were able to take on this new mantle would have to shed

> . . . duties which could be carried out more effectively by staff with responsibilities for social work. . . . Routine investigations of attendance could often be carried out more selectively and with less waste of time; they should probably be associated with social work since serious attendance problems often proved very complex, although different grades of workers, including that of welfare assistants, may be required for different types of cases. It is not satisfactory that the service mainly responsible for welfare work in connection with the schools should be largely untrained. (*op.cit.*, p.89)

This posed a difficult dilemma for education welfare officers. On the one hand, the committee had at least recognized their existence; but on the other, had indicated that they were unable to carry out the tasks that most of them were already doing. The service had a hundred years of experience on which it could draw to conclude that 'serious attendance problems often prove very complex' – without the Plowden Committee telling them so. Most of them had learned their skills on the job; they knew that they had not been formally trained at a college or university, but they had been asking for proper professional recognition and support for training for at least fifty years. Now the committee was recommending to the Government that a more prestigious professional role based on social work should be given the main responsibility for linking home and school, without making it explicit what would happen to the existing education welfare officers. The implication, however, was that some of the more able, who were eligible for and willing to undergo formal social work training, might be acceptable in this new role of school social worker; while perhaps the vast majority would simply become 'welfare assistants', but would *still* be investigating school absence and providing welfare benefits where needed. Many of the existing EWOs would, no doubt, have regarded the latter as a downgrading of their already poor status while retaining most of their existing responsibilities. Many of the officers began calling theirs the 'Cinderella Service'. The analogy is not altogether inappropriate. The Plowden Committee were saying what the Ugly Sisters might have said to a long overworked and exploited Cinderella, 'she does her best, poor thing, but she is only a maid after all. What we really need is a chef and a butler to tell her what to do.'

The Plowden Report was followed in 1968 by the Seebohm Report on the personal social services. Plowden had recommended a thorough review of all social services and had suggested organizing them on school catchment areas. The Seebohm Committee was unenthusiastic about this idea, but did take a similar line on the need to replace education welfare officers with qualified social workers. In their view, however, the social workers should not confine themselves only to providing the link between home and school, but should also act as generic case workers, taking on responsibility for other social problems that a family might face as well as those affecting the child's education. The Seebohm Committee also argued that such social workers would become responsible to, and work within, the proposed new social services departments of each local authority. This was going too far for most EWOs, who were strongly opposed both to becoming generic social case workers and to being transferred to the social services departments, whether as subsequently qualified social workers or as lesser welfare assistants. As a result of their opposition (and indeed that of the education authorities), EWOs in most localities remained within education departments when the new social services departments were formed.

An attempt was made to upgrade the training of EWOs by establishing a local government training board working party on this subject, under the chairmanship of Sir Lincoln Ralphs. They too perceived the future role of the education welfare officer as being more like a social case worker, although in the working party's report in 1973, they recommended that they should be based on schools, more like the Plowden concept.

What does the education welfare service actually do?

The reports and recommendations noted above about the future role of EWOs or about who should replace them were based on very limited research in only a few areas. This provided an incomplete picture of what the education welfare service actually consisted of or what it did. The reports carried only basic facts about the numbers of EWOs and about their level of training, age, turnover, etc., and most of this information was provided by the professional associations themselves. The author has tried elsewhere to provide more detailed evidence by undertaking a national survey of education welfare departments within local authorities, and by examining hundreds of case reports drawn from various parts of the country (MacMillan 1977).

In this national survey, it was found that the average number of school pupils per EWO was 3400. This is high, and in most circumstances tends to preclude detailed therapeutic social casework. On the other hand, the main core responsibilities of the education welfare service may be categorized broadly as *allocation and support duties* in the fields of nursery education, handicapped children, and school placement; *provision duties* in respect of clothing and free meals; and *regulation duties* in relation to school attendance, court procedures, child employment, and neglect. While this extensive range of responsibilities may preclude detailed casework, it does provide for frequent contacts between EWOs, parents, children, and schools, based on a diverse range of issues relating to these responsibilities. Analysis of EWO case experience provided considerable evidence of work which involved dealing with socially disadvantaged children and their families. Case outlines illustrated how officers' activities could be roughly classified as *discovery, first aid, counselling*, and *progress chasing* rather than lengthy social casework.

It is therefore mainly a liaison, support, and preventative role, rather than one that is specifically remedial. Where the cause of a child's absence or underfunctioning at school is found to stem from highly complex and deep-seated problems within the home, and requires further resources than the EWO could himself provide in the form of first aid or counselling, then he would normally call in the more specialized social services, including family case workers from the social services department, to work with the family. The EWO would tend to keep track of progress with the family, however, and provide liaison between the school, the home, and the more specialized social agencies. The research also indicated a widespread preference among EWOs themselves to remain allied to education departments, rather than to transfer to social services departments.

There is, however, considerable variation from one authority to another in the activities of education welfare officers. This is as one might expect, given the piecemeal development of the service over the last hundred years. The way the service is used will depend upon the emphasis placed on each function, the organization of each authority, the number of education welfare officers employed, the extent to which other services are involved in education welfare responsibilities, and also on the amount of administrative and clerical support available. Despite the recommendations in certain of the reports mentioned above, local authorities have not chosen generally to relieve EWOs of all their routine clerical and administrative duties. They appear to regard this work as an important source of intelligence relevant to the formulation and implementation of authority-wide policies, and also as a means of making contact with parents which could prove useful in the accomplishment of some of the less routine responsibilities.

What is significant, however, is the *similarity* in function and activities between authorities rather than the differences. On average, for example, something over 70 percent of EWO time is spent on visiting either homes or schools. The education welfare officer is much more than the school board man who knocks on doors, fills in forms, and prosecutes recalcitrant truants. The discovery role derives from the fact that *all* children of school age must receive education, usually in schools. This means that a teacher is often the first person to realize when something is wrong either with the child or at home. It may start with absence from school, or disruptive behaviour, and it is when the EWO follows this up with the home that deeper social problems may be discovered. At this stage, the EWO may decide that the problems are so deep-seated that referral to the social services department or other specialist therapeutic case workers may be appropriate; but given the general shortage of resources in these specialist services, the EWO may be able to give some first-aid support or counselling, drawing on the collective experience within the education welfare service and on close liaison with the schoolteachers. Indeed, in cases where sufficient resources from the social services department cannot be brought to bear upon the problems of a particular family, the EWO may himself become somewhat more involved in helping the family if his own time allocation and priorities allow. Where referral has been made to a more specialist social work agency, then the EWO will keep in touch with progress and provide liaison with the school on each child's case.

From education welfare to social work?

Following the recommendations of the Plowden and Seebohm Reports, and indeed of the Ralphs Report which recommended that the appropriate professional qualification for education welfare officers should be the Certificate of Qualification in Social Work, there has been a gradual tendency for EWOs to see themselves becoming social workers within the education service of local authorities. This appeared to them to be the most promising means by which they might gain more resources to provide for better status, pay, and conditions of work and training. Indeed, both the education welfare professional associations have now changed their names to include the title 'education social worker', rather than 'education welfare officer', although perhaps the majority of officers at local authority level are still known by the education welfare nomenclature.

There has been more provision of training courses for education welfare officers, although less than half still possess the required qualification. There is now much greater awareness among all professional groups involved with linking home and school of the value of the education welfare officer's role. The irony of the situation is, however, that the more education welfare officers think and talk of themselves as social workers, albeit operating from the education departments rather than from the social services departments in local authorities, the more they are seen as *under-qualified* to take full responsibility for the provision of the link between home and school, and the less their role is seen as distinctive from other social workers in the local authority. The greater their allegiance to the *profession* of social work, the weaker the arguments seem for keeping them organizationally separate from other social workers who are members of the social services departments rather than the education departments. It is therefore likely that their special identity and role (i.e., of discovery, first aid, counselling, and progress chasing,) will disappear – or will have to be reinvented.

The experience of those local authorities which transferred education welfare officers to the social services department after 1970 is most instructive in this respect. Only a very small minority of authorities chose to do this, notably Chesire, Coventry, Devon, and Somerset. The legislation which followed the Seebohm Report left it to the discretion of each local authority whether they wished to arrange for education welfare services to be provided by their social services departments on an agency basis on behalf of the education departments. Several other local authorities experimented in this way but in the majority of cases, apart from those noted above, experiments have been discontinued. The fact that responsibility has reverted back to education departments might be interpreted *a priori* as an indication that social services departments cannot adequately perform this function. This would, however, be an oversimplified interpretation of the problems that were encountered.

In some of these authorities, not all of the responsibilities of education welfare services were transferred to the social services departments. Many of the so-called 'routine and clerical duties' were left with the education department. Moreover, not all the education welfare staff transferred. More senior education welfare officers tended to remain within the education departments. Furthermore, those EWOs who did transfer did not automatically gain recognition as social workers unless they held the CQSW, which few had. The rest were asked to take courses leading to this qualification before they could be given professional status. Neither did they all remain primarily on liaison work between home and school. In Coventry, for example, the senior EWO became Courts and Police Liaison Officer. It was therefore a very difficult administrative task to absorb one group of officers with quite different traditions, customary working methods, and relationships into an entirely different culture where status, pay, and grading were all dependent upon qualifications and experience in professional social work rather than in education.

Head teachers in these authorities complained that their problems were not receiving the attention and resources that they had previously received from the education welfare service. Indeed, this was probably inevitable. Hardly any extra resources had been made available to the social services departments, and indeed many of the former EWOs were now on either part- or full-time training courses; others had left and new recruits had not the same experience of contact with schools. The social services departments ordered heir own priorities in the allocation of cases, tasks, and resources according to their own criteria of urgency. Education problems became just another responsibility among the very diverse social and community problems with which social service departments had to deal. While social services departments were trying to cope with these problems, they were subjected to local authority reorganization in 1974. This further complicated the pattern of provision. The absorption of certain borough councils into county councils, and the redrawing of boundaries of responsibility, meant that the above county councils inherited more groups of education welfare officers whose role had been highly developed in the *urban* context rather than in the county areas.

In the face of mounting opposition from head teachers to these units being broken up, a hybrid pattern tended to emerge with education welfare officers operating as before in one part of the new authority, while elsewhere the service was based on social services departments. Some schools, who had become disenchanted with the service they were receiving from the social services departments, put extra effort into developing their own pastoral staff. Before long these teachers were visiting the homes of absentees or of problem children in a manner which previously would have been undertaken by EWOs. While some of the new arrangements brought more experienced social workers into contact with the staff of the schools, some of them resented the expectation of the head teachers that their primary duty was to serve the educational objectives of the school rather than the individual needs of their clients.

The response of social service departments in the above counties to such problems varied from authority to authority, but usually involved the drawing up of quite elaborate plans to develop a group of social workers who would work in the catchment areas of particular schools. In most cases, these plans envisaged the appointment of additional staff working in a 'team' based on one or more schools. A team would normally include schoolteachers with pastoral responsibilities; professionally qualified social workers from the social services department who would deal with protracted casework problems with particular families; and usually one or more roles designated as 'education visitors', 'home/school counsellors', 'school liaison officers', or 'welfare assistants'. The task of these latter staff was to 'deal with simple truancy and administer the schemes, relating to necessities, clothing, welfare benefits etc.', or was regarded as 'an initial enquiry service for children absenting themselves from school . . . administering education welfare grants, and acting as a filtering service referring to their social worker colleagues for those children and families who need both the support of a social worker relationship and the broad range of services available through the social services department', (ADSS 1978, p.32 and p.41). It was thus explicitly recognized that there was a need for someone acting between the school on the one hand, and the specialist social case worker in the social services department on the other. In other words, the role of the education welfare officer was being reinvented.

In the event, with the severe restrictions on public expenditure which have been imposed over the last few years, none of the plans in these counties have received the extra resources for which they asked. As a result, in Coventry for example, the education department has instituted a new service comprising officers who will deal with truancy problems. It is therefore difficult to resist the temptation to conclude that where the education welfare service has been absorbed into social service departments, it has so changed its character that it has proved necessary to start again from scratch. Hopefully it will not take another hundred years to evolve a second time.

The present situation

Most authorities did not transfer the education welfare service to the social services department. But the future of the service is still plagued with uncertainty. As was noted at the beginning of this chapter, EWOs are not the only group of professionals who are involved in the home-school link, but they are unique in having as their *only* purpose the forging and maintaining of such links. All the duties, responsibilities, and activities of the education welfare service may be included under this heading. Yet their professional status has never been officially recognized, either by central government or by the other professional groups with whom they interact. How, therefore, may EWOs gain this status? Do they all have to gain the CQSW first? If so, who is going to pay for this? It is difficult to see how extra resources can be made available to the service, particularly at this time of severe constraint on public edpenditure. And even if this were possible, would they then regard their primary professional allegiance as being to colleagues within the social services departments, within education departments, or in the schools?

At the moment, it would appear that EWOs are regarded as being of lower professional status by both social workers on the one hand and teachers on the other. If they are willing to accept this situation, they may be able to preserve their independence and identity as a distinctive service somewhere in between. This can lead to communication difficulties and may have severe social costs as, for example, is shown by the case of Maria Colwell.

> In the 'welfare link' between the school and social services the role of the education welfare officer is of considerable importance in many cases, as it was with Maria . . . it is clear and somewhat disturbing that, in Maria's case, the division between education welfare services and the social services department made it more difficult for the education welfare officer's concern about Maria to reach the proper person (the social worker) with sufficient urgency and promptness. . . . We learnt that the local education department considered that the task of the education welfare officer should go beyond concern for regular school attendance and extend to more general issues of welfare. We understand that this is generally accepted. If this is so, then, at the least, liaison and coordination between the workers with substantial areas of mutual interest is indispensible. (Colwell Enquiry 1974, paras. 184-185)

But who is to provide this coordination? Can individuals with lower professional status command sufficient respect on professional matters to ensure the cooperation of both social workers and teachers? How can one be sure that this communication and coordination would be more propitiously achieved if EWOs were all to be incorporated in social service departments? The experience where this has happened would appear to suggest otherwise. There would still be the problem of communication between the schools and the social services department.

Quo vadis?

The conclusion would appear to be that such coordination would have to come from a senior position within the education department acting on behalf of the local authority as a whole. If it were to be within the social services department, then the teaching profession in schools or elsewhere would most probably not recognize the professional allegiance to social workers. In the areas where the education welfare service seems to be most developed and successful, it appears that there is such a senior person within the education department – sometimes it may be an assistant director of education or he may bear the title of 'chief education welfare officer.'

In large urban areas such as Birmingham and Manchester, the education welfare service seems to have this top-level commitment, which can provide an environment in which further experimentation may take place so that the role can continue to evolve and strengthen. In both Birmingham and Manchester, there has been significant expansion in the staffing of the education welfare service over recent years as well as major investment in in-service training, not just for the officers themselves but also jointly with teachers and with other social workers. Some of these in-service workshops and seminars have included staff from many other local authorities, so that the lessons from experimentation may be more widely disseminated. It is also interesting to observe that the new recruits into the education welfare service have increasingly among their number qualified and experienced schoolteachers. This may well be an appropriate pattern for the future. As the school population falls, more teachers may be willing to transfer to an enhanced education welfare service which may offer the best hope yet for strategies intended to mitigate some of the social handicaps which many children have in relation to their education. Since increasingly both teachers and social workers are tending to be trained in the same universities and colleges, it is to be hoped that over time they will develop a greater mutual understanding of their respective professional roles in relation to these issues.

For many years, the education welfare associations have been asking central government to issue guidelines to local authorities on how they might most effectively organize and develop their own education welfare service. There has been reluctance to do this not only because few, if any, extra resources can be made available to support any policy recommendations which might emerge; and not only because central government is increasingly reluctant to dictate to local authorities how they should conduct their affairs; but also because there is sensitivity to somewhat conflicting expectations on the part of the social work and teaching professions. It would therefore seem to be up to the education welfare service itself, at least in the first instance, to clarify where their primary professional allegiance should lie in the future. This ultimately will involve a choice between social work and teaching. The further they go along the path to social work, the weaker the links with education departments and schools may become. It would indeed be a bitter irony if, in the process, the education welfare service became lost from everyone's view.

References

Association of Directors of Social Services (1978), *Social Work Services for Children in Schools*.

Coleman, J. et al. (1966), *Equality of Educational Opportunity*, US Department of Health and Welfare.

Colwell Enquiry (1974), *Report of the Committee of Enquiry into the care and supervision provided in relation to Maria Colwell*, HMSO.

Douglas, J.W.B. (1964), *The Home and the School*, MacGibbon & Kee.

Jackson, B. and Marsden, D. (1962), *Education and the Working Class*, Routledge & Kegan Paul.

MacMillan, K. (1977), *Education Welfare: Strategy and Structure*, Longman.

Central Advisory Council for Education (England) (1967), *Children and their Primary Schools*, ('Plowden Report'), HMSO.

'Seebohm Report' (1968), *Report of the Committee on Local Authority and Allied Personal Social Services*, HMSO, Cmnd 3703.

Westergaard, J. and Little, A. (1967), 'Educational Opportunity and Social Selection in England and Wales: Trends and Policy Implications', in *Social Objectives and Educational Planning*, OECD.

CHAPTER 15

SCHOOL SOCIAL WORK

Karen Lyons

This chapter considers the nature of social work in an educational setting, whether carried out by the EWO under the aegis of an LEA, or by education social workers based in a social services department.

Introduction

This chapter sets out to summarize some points arising from my experiences as the education social worker on the London Education Priority Area Project,[1] and confirmed in subsequent practice in a local authority education welfare service. The term *education social worker* is used to denote those workers whose primary task and professional identification is with social work, but within the context of the education setting, whether they are employed by education departments (and then usually designated 'education welfare officers'[2]), or social service departments (in which case they may be designated 'school social workers'). It should also be noted that while the term 'social worker' is concurrently used to describe some workers employed by local authority social service departments, it does, of course, cover a much wider and more varied group, including probation officers and workers employed by voluntary social welfare agencies, such as the NSPCC and family service units.

A major change was occurring in the organization of social workers at the time when the London Education Priority Area Project was taking place, namely the implementation of the Seebohm proposals.[3] Debate continues about the extent to which social workers should be organized as part of a 'generic service' (as in social services departments), or should retain and develop specializations in relation to particular client groups. In practice, specializations remain, as in the probation service, hospital social work, and psychiatric social work in child guidance clinics and mental hospitals. I consider that education social work should be further developed as a recognized specialization, and I had begun to explore the implications of this view in the context of the EPA project, and in the resulting report (Lyons 1973). Further consideration of the subject has taken place subsequently, by the social work profession[4] as well as by individual contributors to this book, or those referred to subsequently. Over a similar period of time, developments have been taking place in the welfare and counselling aspects of the teacher's role as is also described elsewhere in this book.

It is the intention of this chapter to illustrate ways in which an education-orientated social worker, based outside the school (as distinct from welfare-orientated *teachers*), can make a particular contribution to those children and families who may be presenting or experiencing difficulties in relation to school, as well as a more general contribution to the welfare of the school as a whole. Prerequisites for undertaking this role include well-established working relationships with school staff, and a good knowledge of school routines and educational resources and procedures.

The London Education Priority Area Project

To illustrate different aspects of the work undertaken on the project and subsequently reported conclusions, I have selected three case studies not previously summarized for description.[5] By way of introduction, I should state that I was working in three primary schools only, in an inner-city area. This opportunity to concentrate on intervention at an early stage in a child's school career was a welcome change from the stress usually laid on, and resources given to, children of secondary school age. Such provisions are, of course, no less necessary at this later stage; but some opportunities for preventive work may have been lost through lack of appreciation of, and responses to, the particular problems that may be experienced by younger children at an earlier stage in the life-cycle.[6] A particular limitation of the project was the social worker's lack of statutory position with its accompanying responsibilities. This resulted in relatively fewer referrals of non-attendance problems and, in consequence, little consideration of the implications for working methods and relationships with clients and colleagues of an explicit authority role.

Case study 1

The first case I shall describe was referred early on in the project. It was an extreme example, with regard to the degree of disturbance of the child; though it was not untypical of a small group of cases which provoked strong feelings in the head and other teachers that certain children were 'unfit for ordinary education' and that the social worker's role should be to expedite transfer to some alternative. John was in his second term in the infant school and not yet six years old. On referral, he was described by the head teacher as mostly quiet in school, and tending to be solitary, but given to occasional bursts of disturbed behaviour in the form of aggression to other children if frustrated and, in one instance, of fire-raising. John's parents were apparently also concerned about his behaviour at home, and in fact the head teacher's referral was partly prompted by the mother's stated anxiety, as well as the child's obvious unhappiness and his effects on other children. John had already been seen by an educational psychologist soon after entering school and had been referred to a local child-guidance clinic and for part-time help of an educational/therapeutic nature at a special class which he attended from ordinary school.

The initial social work task was to collate information – from school medical records, the educational psychologist, the child-guidance clinic social worker, and the special class teacher – about assessments that had been made, current progress with, and involvement in the case, and the recommendations that were likely to result. It was also established that both the education welfare service and the social services department held records on the child/family, but that no worker from either agency was currently in contact with them. It was then discussed and agreed with the clinic staff that since attendance there was irregular, and primarily for the purposes of assessment, the education social worker should visit the home and offer support to John's mother in what was likely to be an interim period prior to John's placement in a special school for maladjusted children. At this latter stage, a special school social worker would work directly with the family and the school.

I subsequently visited Mrs. A., usually fortnightly, over a seven-month period including the long and stressful summer holidays. John was the elder of two children in an English family where father worked full-time, and traditional roles, that is, father as provider, mother as homemaker and child-rearer, were observed, roles incidentally with which the partners seemed relatively satisfied. Mrs. A. had experienced problems with John from birth and felt guilt and resentment about her lack of love for him, compounded by anger at his attention-seeking and bad behaviour, and she used the visits as an opportunity to talk about John's behaviour and the difficulties in her relationship with him.

Over time, John's progress and behaviour in school improved to a limited extent, due no doubt in part to the special educational help he was receiving, and Mrs. A. became less anxious about him and her own feelings. There were various issues to be discussed as they arose: the family was awaiting rehousing and was periodically frustrated about this; the special class teacher left; and the family made a temporary move to John's grandmother's home, because of her illness. This latter event, following soon on the departure of his special class teacher, resulted in a further period of disturbed behaviour on John's part; and Mrs. A's ambivalence about John going to a special school was overridden by a reawakened sense of need for help with and for John. It was timely that an offer of a special school place became available at this stage, and both Mrs. A. and the ordinary school head teacher were relieved at John's placement. A concluding visit was made to Mrs. A. at which she was introduced to the special school social worker. (She had previously been told that this would happen when John was transferred.) The new social worker subsequently confirmed that John was settling well, and that there was every likelihood that his stay at maladjusted school would be relatively short term, probably a year or two, rather than permanent.

Overall it had taken nearly a year from the time of referral to the social worker to the time of John's school transfer and the handing on of the case to another social worker. However, that year had been less stressful than it might have been for John and his family, both through the provision of a special class place for him, and also through supportive work with John's mother, helping her to modify her own expectations and treatment of the boy. Additionally, the school staff had been relieved of coping with the mother's anxiety, had been kept informed of the progress of the special school placement, and had been able to avoid suspending John knowing that relief was in sight.

Case study 2

The next case I shall describe was, in some respects, a more typical example of the sort of task traditionally referred to education social workers and certainly to EWOs, since one aspect of the problem was poor attendance. In this instance, the poor attendance, which was erratic rather than extreme, was linked to a generally low standard of physical care. The referral was partly made at the suggestion of the social worker, following an occasion on which the child's inadequate clothing had been particularly noticeable. Again, enquiries were made of interested parties: the class teacher, who described Shirley (aged five years) as 'no problem when she was there'; the health visitor (there were four children under five years and a fifth expected); the EWO, who had visited soon after Shirley's admission to school, but who had found the family unresponsive, and who regarded Shirley's lapses in attendance as insignificant relative to other pupils on his caseload; and the social services department. The last named had received a referral within the past year on the basis of concern expressed by a neighbour about the care of the children, but had assessed the family as not being negligent or uncaring, and had therefore not taken on the case.

I began visiting and maintained contact with the family over one year, on average monthly, but with most visits concentrated in the winter months when the family had most difficulty managing financially and meeting the children's physical needs for adequate warmth, clothing, and nourishment. In contrast to the previous case, this family seemed to be a united, loyal, and affectionate group, whose main problem was in relation to the rest of society; that is, their failure to match up to society's norms and standards and to cope with the external demands of work and school. Shirley, as the eldest of five (and within the year six) children, was already being included in taking some responsibility in the family; and one of the tasks of the social worker was to raise the level of the parents' awareness of the wider social and intellectual needs of their children, and of the positive benefits which school could offer to Shirley, and later to the second child for whom a priority place was made available in the oversubscribed nursery class, and who subsequently thrived in the school environment.

Other activities included giving advice and assistance with welfare claims; helping to arrange a retraining programme for Mr. B., an immigrant, with limited English and lacking work skills; and giving continuous encouragement to Mrs. B., an overworked but cheerful and warm mother. I was complemented in this work by an agreed arrangement of alternate visiting by the local health visitor, who paid specific attention to the needs and care of the under-fives. She further took up the issue of family planning, and oversight of the family's new baby. In this way some general improvement was affected in the family's circumstances, and a child who might easily have become a chronic poor attender, either through genuine minor ailments or because of domestic demands, was helped to establish a more settled pattern of school attendance with concomitant opportunities for educational and social development. Simultaneously, the anxiety of the school staff over Shirley's attendance and care was ameliorated, and a more sympathetic relationship was fostered between Shirley's teacher and her father, who primarily took responsibility for school contacts.

Case study 3

The third example concerns a single-parent family with one child, Richard, aged nearly six years. Richard was not a major problem in school, although he was inclined to be boisterous and lacking in concentration. The main concern expressed by the head teacher was the health and social circumstances of Richard's mother, and the consequent effects upon the child. Discussion with a social worker in the social services department revealed that Richard had been born relatively late in life to Mrs. C., as the result of a short-lived affair, following the death of her husband and two previous children in tragic circumstances. Mrs. C. had suffered from mental illness, requiring hospitalization and the placing of Richard in care when he was about three years old. The social worker had withdrawn from the case about a year before my inquiry when Mrs. C.'s health and her ability to cope with Richard at home had stabilized.

At the time of my visits, again extending over a year and averaging slightly more than once a month, Mrs. C. was in varying physical and mental health. She had mild depression, and some obsessional tendencies about securing a more regular income from Richard's father. The father now lived overseas and maintained only tenuous contact with them, sending occasional small money payments. She also expressed an acute desire to earn her own living and not to be dependent on state benefits. In practice, this proved difficult to achieve in view of her poor health (she suffered from bronchitis) and her sole responsibility for Richard. Mrs. C. frequently expressed both guilt and a strong sense of responsibility in relation to Richard. Sometimes she was unrealistic both about her own mothering capacities and about what could reasonably be expected by way of Richard's behaviour and educational progress. She also expressed feelings of loneliness and isolation. Her attitude to the school varied from being appreciative of the staff's efforts with Richard, to being critical about their lack of discipline and standards. Likewise, she sometimes showed pleasure at the social worker's visits and used them to share some of her pride in Richard's achievements, as well as her anxieties. At other times she proved highly elusive, failing to keep appointments or respond to visits.

Social work intervention in this case was aimed mainly at helping Mrs. C. maintain her independent status and caring role, and at helping her modify her more unrealistic plans and expectations. Information and advice were given about resources, both those available to meet material needs and those in the community (for example, a local mother's group, which might provide outside interests and social support). On occasion, the need also arose to act as a mediator between home and school, for example, when lack of direct communication or misunderstandings threatened the tenuous relationship which Mrs. C. maintained with school staff. In the event, some degree of improvement occurred during the course of the year; Mrs. C. had taken on a housekeeping and child-minding job for a neighbour in paid employment, and Richard had acquired reading skills and a greater ability to amuse himself. But it seemed likely that this mother and child would continue to lead a relatively isolated and mutually dependent life, with school being both an important outlet and stimulus for Richard's further development, as well as the agency most likely to become aware of any deterioration in Mrs. C.'s health or circumstances.

Discussion

Between them, these examples give the reader some indication of the type of cases referred to, and the methods of intervention used by, an educational social worker. It may be useful now to put these three cases into the context of the total caseload of the project social workers, and then to make some general comments about the role of an education social worker in relation to the three cases described. During an eighteen-month period (approximately), 184 referrals were made on 177 children in 170 families.[7] This averaged 27 *percent* of the total population of the three schools. This figure can be compared to estimates made of the need for social work help for schoolchildren by the Plowden Report (3-15 percent) and Clegg and Megson (10-20 percent).[8]

The cases themselves were not typical of all cases referred, since only 20 percent of the cases were assessed as requiring social work intervention on an ongoing basis (defined at the time as more than three contacts over more than three months), although 58 percent of cases were visited at least once. In another 23 percent of cases another social worker from the education or social services department, or a voluntary organization, was already involved to the extent that additional contact with the family by the education social worker would not have been appropriate.

The three cases are, however, representative in terms of the major reasons given for referral. Those reasons were, first, *social problems*, defined as relationship problems within the family, and/or concern about the care of the child (children), and including material needs. Twenty-nine percent of the reasons given for referrals fell into this category. Second, there were *behaviour problems*, for example, aggression, unhappiness, or withdrawn behaviour in school. These constituted 29 percent of the reasons given for referral. They also represented, to a lesser extent, educational problems, ranging from the need for special education through general lack of progress, to lack of contact between home and school, though this latter was not a major feature of these three cases. There were only minimal medical and attendance problems, given as reasons for referral in 19, 13, and 10 percent of cases respectively.

The cases also illustrate some aspects of how the education social worker spent her time. It should be noted that only approximately one-third of the time spent on work in relation to ongoing cases involved direct contact with the families concerned, and that a considerable amount of time (24 percent in relation to all cases) was spent liaising with other colleagues; these latter were primarily in the education and social work professions, but also in some instances in the medical and legal professions, and in some cases were officials in the Department of Health and Social Security, the electricity and gas boards, and the housing department. Time was also spent writing up records and reports and consulting with a senior social work colleague on the progress of particular cases. In addition, a relatively high proportion of time (18 percent) was spent in direct contact with school staff, usually in school, reflecting the emphasis given to availability and access to school staff.

It is partly this aspect of how and where the education social worker spends her time, combined with the fact that the *school* is the major source of referrals (76 percent in this study), that differentiates the role of an education social worker from a social worker in a social services department or other setting. While the style of intervention in individual cases is unlikely to be very different from that of other social workers, a main distinguishing feature would seem to be the general attempt made to link and relate what is happening to the child at home to that other part of his life, in school, and to make much greater use of educational resources of all kinds than might be usual or appropriate for other social workers. The other significant feature is the nature and extent of social breakdown apparent in these cases.[9] In none of these examples, or indeed in the majority of other referrals received, would it have been likely or possible for another social worker to have given the same degree of priority and attention, relative to other cases on their caseload. Indeed, two had been explicitly assessed as not requiring further social work intervention.

While it may be argued that the EPA social worker was an extra resource and, in that sense, able to be more selective about appropriate cases for intervention, I would suggest that this variation in what constitutes an appropriate case for referral to a social worker illustrates the potential of a well-developed education social work service for preventive work with children and their families.[10] What these cases do not illustrate, however, is the nature of the education social worker's contact with school staff, and participation in other aspects of school life geared to the needs of all schoolchildren. These contacts are not just to do with social problems, but with class outings, school open days, availability at medical inspections and in the staff room, and the opportunities these offer for early detection; for consultations with school staff instead of referral; and for meeting a wider cross-section of children and families than those defined as 'having problems'.

These cases demonstrate a variety of roles which an education social worker, in common with other social workers, may carry. Among these can be listed assessment, liaison, mediation, support, modification, negotiation, matching resources to needs, advising about procedures and advocacy. They also suggest some of the areas of knowledge and skill which an education social worker requires. In my original report, I suggested that in addition to the usual theory and skills which social workers need, education social workers also require some basic knowledge of the sociology and philosophy of education, of the structure, functions, and provisions of specific education authorities, and of the current organization, practices, and terminology employed in school.

These three cases also illustrate some aspects of the way a social worker works. From what I have written, it can be seen that there were no quick solutions to the problems identified. Indeed, in some respects there were no solutions at all. It is also apparent from these examples that the social worker's main relationship was usually with the adults in the family situation, rather than with particular children. This might not have been the case, however, with older children, or with children experiencing different types of problems (e.g., separation from parents). While the social worker came to know and be known quite well to Shirley and Richard, direct social work with the children was not a stated aim or method used. The children's needs would, for the most part, be met quite adequately by parents and teachers, particularly where each party's appreciation of the other's role and contribution could be enhanced.

It is less apparent from these examples that the social worker's assessment of the problems may differ from those originally giving rise to the referral, and that her aims and methods of work may not conform to the teacher's expectations of what should be done in a particular case. While this may, and sometimes does, give rise to tensions between teachers and social workers, regular dialogue can help clarify reasons for different approaches, and make more realistic the expectations of both professions. Neither illustrated nor tested in the context of this particular project, but increasingly a feature of education social work in practice, is the use of group work[11] as an appropriate method of social work intervention with, for instance, isolated mothers or children with school difficulties.

Finally, one further point arising from the project, which has both practical and organizational implications, was the question of the physical base for an education social worker. I concluded that part-time use of a designated room in a school could be invaluable in terms of availability to teaching staff, parents, and even pupils on a regular basis; but also that, overall, the education social worker should remain essentially based in the community, probably either in an education or social services department office. This would be mainly for the purpose of ready access to the social worker's own professional reference group and resources, but also to avoid an overidentification with school which could militate against social work intervention with some families.

My conclusion remains now, as it was in 1973, that social workers, with their different training, objectives, and methods, can provide a useful and supportive, if not always uncritical, service to teachers in their role of meeting the educational and social needs of all children. And I also conclude that education social workers, with their particular orientation and (hopefully) training and/or experience, can provide a more specialized service to that minority of families with school-aged children who may be experiencing stress at different points in the child's school life.

References

1. Lyons, K.H. (1973), *Social Work and the School*, HMSO; and for a fuller description of the context in which this work took place, and other aspects of the project nationally, Halsey, A.H. (1972), *Educational Priority*, (Volume 1), HMSO.
2. It may be useful to compare and contrast my experiences and ideas with regard to education welfare with those of Macmillan, K. (1977), *Education Welfare: Strategy and Structure*, Longman.
3. Report of the Committee on Local Authority and Allied Personal Social Services, HMSO 1968; see particularly paragraph 226.
4. B.A.S.W. Discussion Paper: 'Social Work in relation to Schools', *Social Work Today*, March 1974; Association of Directors of Social Services Report, 'Social Work Services for Children in School' 6/78; B.A.S.W. Social Work in Education Special Interst Group, Discussion Document: 'Social Work and the Education Services' summarized in *Social Work Today*, June 1979.
5. Three other case studies are described in an appendix to Lyons (1973), *op.cit.*; and for another example of a case which illustrated a wide range of family needs and required prolonged and periodically intensive social work intervention see K.H. Lyons, 'Tracey, Mary, Elizabeth and the E.W.O.', *N.U.T. Primary Education Review*, No. 2, August 1976.
6. Robinson, M. (1978), *Schools and Social Work*, Routledge & Kegan Paul, chapter 1, gives a useful summary of the family life-cycle, and the particular stress points at which social work intervention may be necessary. In general 'transition periods' from one phase or place to another (e.g., admission of child to infant school), particularly if role and relationship changes are necessitated, are points of vulnerability for children and their families.
7. For full details of 'Findings' see Lyons (1973), *op.cit.*, chapter 5.
8. C.A.C.E. (1967), *Children and their Primary Schools*, HMSO Volume II, app. 8, p. 137. Clegg, A. & Megson, B. (1973), *Children in Distress*, Penguin.
9. For a fuller discussion of the concept of social breakdown in the context of education and social work see Robinson (1978), *op.cit.*, chapter 1.
10. See also the chapter by K. Fitzherbert in this book.
11. See for instance, Rose, G. and Marshall, T. (1974), *Counselling and School Social Work*, Wiley, (appendix B).

CHAPTER 16

THE SCHOOL COUNSELLOR

Peter Daws

In this chapter, Peter Daws considers the rapid development of counselling in British schools since the mid-1960s; and he goes on to describe the role of the school counsellor, his aims, and his methods.

Beginnings

School counselling appeared rather abruptly in the mid-1960s and has become a very vigorous movement in the fifteen years since, having spread with equal enthusiasm and viability to the colleges and universities around 1970. Its appearance was something of a surprise, for in the early 1960s teachers had reacted unfavourably to the notion of counselling which they saw as an undesirable American practice our schools could well do without. One important factor which was to bring about a change in teacher attitudes was the emergence at that time of the comprehensive schools whose size magnified greatly the tasks of controlling pupils and of getting to know them with any degree of intimacy. Traditional modes of guidance and pastoral care proved unequal to what was expected of them in the new schools, and many head teachers turned hopefully to counselling as a more professional and fresh approach to pastoral care responsibilities to supplement the school's resources. Another factor was the growing aspiration evident in many secondary schools to adopt more ambitious approaches to the development of personal and social competences in children. The Newsom Report, which had appeared in 1963, had advocated the introduction of counselling.

That training programmes in counselling for experienced teachers were begun at the same time, 1965, in the Universities of Keele and Reading was fortuitous in both timing and content. They were initially conceived as courses in guidance, with an emphasis on educational and vocational guidance of the more traditional sort that was based on good recordkeeping, interviews and psychological tests, to gain further information, and other assessment skills. That they were changed to *counselling* courses right from the start we owe to the generosity of the Fulbright Commission, an American organization which offers the services of American scholars to help new ventures in other countries get off to a good start. The first two of what was to prove a fertile stream of Fulbright scholars who came to these and later courses persuaded us that counselling rather than traditional interviewing and assessment skills was what our secondary schools needed. The teachers who were recruited to these courses were unprepared for the strange unfamiliarity of their content, but they acquired the skills and absorbed the values of counselling and returned to their schools with messianic fervour.

Today, in 1980, around twenty courses of training are available on either a one-year full-time or two-year part-time basis. As well as providing the interpersonal relationship skills of counselling, they aim to develop a diagnostic eye and sensitivity in reading the behaviour of people and to give the groundwork of adolescent development, mental health, and the essential components of guidance. The annual output, therefore, of teachers trained in counselling is around two hundred, though in the present economic climate one may expect that recruitment to full-time courses will decline. However, there is no sign yet that the boom in demand for teachers trained in counselling is waning, and the movement remains a vigorous one.

What is counselling?

The central purpose of counselling is to help individual people to help themselves, to stand on their own feet, use their own resources, their own judgement, and to find the initiative to resolve their own difficulties and make their own decisions. In the pursuit of these ends counselling may also have to help them face themselves, and to decide the selves they wish to be and the lives they wish to lead, and the values that have primacy for them in making such decisions. The meaning of this *description* of counselling (it doesn't mention enough of the major things about counselling to be acceptable as a *definition*) may be sharpened by noting two major implications – for the nature of the process and for the kinds of personal problems for which it is appropriate.

First, the counsellor offers neither solutions, opinions, nor advice; nor does he present himself as an expert from whom such guides to action may be expected and which the client would be foolish to ignore. As a teacher, he or she may usefully do these things often, but the process in which they occur is not counselling. Second, there are two kinds of problem about which people consult other people: those that are separable from themselves and those that aren't. Separable problems remain the same whoever has them – a pain or illness, a legal tangle, a need to insure against risk, faulty plumbing. One takes such problems to an expert, and an answer will be given that does not require the nature of the person who has the problem to be taken account of. But problems that are inseparable from the persons who experience them cannot be usefully taken to experts; no one can offer definitive solutions to such problems: whether to marry and whom, whether to take a particular course or job, to terminate a pregnancy, to take in an aged relative, to leave a spouse. If we choose not to wrestle with such problems alone, we take them to people who are 'experts' in their understanding of us (that is, to friends or other intimates), because we know that they will listen with some understanding, that their attachment to us will not be threatened by the feelings and uncertainties that we disclose, and that they will be able more accurately and fully to share in a compassionate way our own view of the difficulties that face us. We may hope that they will help us to see our situation in alternative, more hopeful ways, and perhaps even offer for our consideration lines of action that had not occurred to us. We do not usually expect definitive solutions whose basis in specialist knowledge brooks no argument, for the problems we take to them are not of that kind. Where we cannot resolve such a problem alone, nor through having discussed it with a close friend or intimate, it is appropriate to seek counselling.

The basic ideas of the counselling process, what it is for, and how its ends are achieved were developed by the American, Carl Rogers, and called 'client-centred' therapy. In Britain, it was first practised in the context of marriage guidance in the 1940s. The soundness of Rogers' conceptualization of the therapeutic process has now been confirmed by a considerable body of research into the differences between effective and ineffective counsellors. Three necessary counsellor qualities have been identified: warmth, genuineness, and empathy.

If good outcomes are to be achieved in counselling, the client must sense that the counsellor genuinely cares about him and his predicament, and that this caring exists unconditionally and cannot be threatened by anything the client may reveal about himself and his feelings and the way he has behaved. To express a detached professional interest is not enough. Separateness there must be, but human involvement too. This quality of *warmth* has also been described as respect, nonpossessive love, and unconditional positive regard.

Genuineness refers to the counsellor's inclination and capacity to be open and spontaneous with his client, suppressing none of his feelings and not expressing out of a sense of politeness feelings that he does not genuinely have. Such openness and noncensorship of genuine feeling comes close to the customary behaviours of friendship and of spouses, and contrasts with the maintenance of a façade of professional mannerisms, such as a doctor's bedside manner, in which the possibility of real human contact is avoided. When the client experiences a real and genuine human encounter with his counsellor, he is able to relax, feel safe and trust him, and finds it much easier to be open and sincere in expressing what he feels about himself and his problem. Genuineness is sometimes referred to as congruence: there is no mismatch or incongruence between one's feelings, one's awareness of them, and one's expression of them. In a relationship, congruence in one person facilitates congruence in the other, and congruence is an essential element in therapeutic progress.

Empathy, the third quality, is the state of entering into another person's world and seeing it through his eyes, of sharing his feelings, his fears, joys, needs, confusions, and beliefs. In this way, one attains an appreciation of another's problem as he experiences it and makes compassion possible. Through empathy, the counsellor attains an inside view – the client's view – and not the outside view of the detached onlooker. Such an empathic awareness is essential if one is to help the client help himself, rather than engineer a solution for him.

The counsellor's first task is to establish with the client a relationship in which he feels accepted unconditionally, safe, and sufficiently relaxed to begin talking about his difficulties; and as the relationship deepens, he will do so with increasing confidence and decreasing reticence. The counsellor's task at this point is to concentrate on observing and listening so that he may grasp all the meanings conveyed by the client, not only through the meaning of the words he uses, but also through his hesitancies, the feelings he expresses, his facial expressions, body postures and fidgets. He is careful not to divert the course of the interchange, leaving the client free to decide his own pace and manner of unfolding and exploring his predicament – the 'nondirective' principle. Counsellor interjections in this phase will be few, and concerned either with checking or clarifying his understanding of what the client is saying, or with facilitating the client's expression of his own feelings about the things he is relating. When he grasps meanings that seem central to an understanding of the client's difficulties, notably strong feelings, ambivalences, uncertainties, and contradictions, he will restate them, reflecting them back to the client in a paraphrased way. This not only helps the counsellor to attain a clearer understanding, but the client as well.

When the client has gained a fuller appreciation of his difficulties and of how he feels about them (and he will often come to see that the real nub of his difficulties is not what he had supposed), this may prove all that is needed for him to decide with confidence what he should do about them; the counselling process need go no further. There is often, however, a second stage in which counsellor and client increasingly survey possible strategies of action, the options open to the client and the feelings he has about them and their possible outcomes. This phase will finish when the client comes to feel some confidence about what he should do and some resolution about doing it. Often, the real gains from counselling occur between interviews rather than during them, as the client reflects upon the insights he has gained or that counselling has made more readily accessible to him.

The following case illustrates well the value of counsellor perceptiveness and counselling in enabling young people to mature and resolve their difficulties through self-confrontation, self-examination, and even self-acceptance. These are frequently necessary factors in the counselling process if a satisfactory outcome is to be achieved.

> Peter was fifteen years old, but looked less. Slight of stature, with facial hair hardly discernible as yet, adolescence had begun rather late for him. To his careers teacher he expressed an enthusiasm for entering the navy, but his preference was met with strong argument against its suitability. Peter returned to the careers teacher, this time with a strong preference for joining the police. He was told he would not be considered tall enough. Another teacher, who had learned something of counselling, perceived the likely connection between Peter's unathletic build and the attractiveness to him of jobs that carried a strong masculine image. Noticing that Peter was becoming depressed by his vocational frustrations, he sought an opportunity to let him talk freely about his feelings and ambitions. Peter confided his disappointment in his lack of physical impressiveness, and came to recognize that his interests in 'manly' occupations did not go very deep and were essentially compensatory ways of denying his perception of his physical shortcomings.

Peter then found the courage to confess his serious doubts about his sexuality. His acute sense of his slight, unmuscular build and some humiliating encounters with girls had brought deep doubts about his masculinity, which he had struggled to avoid facing. He then admitted that his strongest vocational interest was in cookery, which served only to deepen his doubt that he was a real man. Through counselling, Peter found the strength to explore and evaluate his fears. The depression lifted. He embarked upon a catering course in a college of further education, maturation remedied his overyouthful appearance and an increasing maturity came through his finding the conventional adolescent experiences. At twenty-five, he is occupationally and personally succesful in an unspectacular, ordinary way.

Counselling in secondary schools

Counselling contrasts with the traditional mode of interviewing in schools. In this, the teacher decides that an interview shall take place, not the pupil. The teacher defines the problem, not the pupil, who may indeed not have one. The teacher directs the course of the interview, not the pupil; and he does most of the talking, usually conducting an interrogation designed to expose the pupil's faults and shortcomings. The teacher decides what shall be done about 'the problem', and tells the pupil, along with threats of what will befall him if his requirements are not met. He/she may conduct the interview in a sympathetic and kindly manner, but morally evaluatory overtones are usually present. Such interviewing has its place among the procedures that define pastoral care and it is often helpful, if only as a means of pupil control. However, it is not counselling.

Counselling and its associated skills are a small part of the total repertoire of competences harnessed by schools to meet children's developmental needs, to help them overcome the stresses and challenges of life and to mature through meeting them, rather than be emotionally crippled by being overwhelmed by them. The generic term that covers all that the school undertakes to protect and promote the personal and social growth of children is *guidance*. Psychological tests, vocational interest scales, emotional malfunctioning assessment schedules, the diagnosis of learning difficulties and associated remedial education, pupil record systems, pastoral care structures such as year and house systems or tutor groups, constructive disciplinary procedures, personal and social education programmes, careers education, case conferences, liaison with specialist outside agencies and with parents, counselling – all of these are important means whereby a school addresses the task of guidance.

Through guidance, schools express their active, caring, quasi-parental responsibilities, which go considerably beyond what counselling implies. It would not be sufficient, for example, to appoint a counsellor who was content merely to wait for individual children to consult him about their problems; nor, in the majority of cases, is it enough simply to help pupils work out their own salvation, for many children (like many adults, and with better reason) are insufficiently intelligent or mature to shoulder alone the awful burdens that life sometimes places upon them. Counsellors, just like any other teacher, have three main caring (as distinct from counselling) responsibilities: firstly, to exercise a sensitive and unremitting *vigilance* in order to identify promptly children in difficulties; secondly, to establish a close *relationship* with such children, so that what is troubling a child or causing his deviant behaviour may be identified; and thirdly, to undertake *remedial action*, which may require not only the cooperation of the child and other teachers, but also that of the parents and perhaps one or more of the specialist outside agencies.

There will often be an important role for counselling in this three-stage process, perhaps in helping to determine the nature of the problem from within the child's own perspective; perhaps in helping him to play an active role in resolving his difficulties through his own decisions and endeavours, as well as through helping the child acquire greater maturity and 'ego-strength' so as to become the better equipped to confront any future challenges and crises that may arise. Counselling is not only a remedial or problem-solving strategy, nor merely a means of helping young people to make decisions wisely; it is also an ego-strengthening, educative process.

So far, we have considered counselling primarily as it is used to help troubled or maladjusted children, and this emphasis has been deliberate; for in practice, because counselling is still a relatively scarce resource, it is usually made available where the need is greatest and most urgent. However, the primary purpose of school counselling is to enhance the development and well-being of *all* children, not merely to rescue the troubled and the disturbed. It aims to be a prophylactic and educational service first, and only secondarily a remedial and clinical service. If there were sufficient counselling expertise in our schools, and time enough to deploy it to serve all the needs that are apparent, it could contribute to answering all the naturally arising developmental needs of all children, as well as the transient and normal problems that most children experience from time to time; the special needs of particular categories of vulnerable children (e.g., those from immigrant minorities); the often quite severe difficulties that occasionally afflict and threaten to damage children who are in basically sound mental health (e.g., bereavement and grief); and, in cooperation with the psycho-medical services, to play a supportive role in the treatment of children who are severely emotionally disturbed. This spectrum of need that counselling can serve within guidance is set out in Figure 16.1.

Today (in 1980) there are about one hundred schools in England and Wales that have a designated full-time counsellor (usually but not invariably trained in counselling), who devotes the bulk of his/her time to guidance responsibilities. This may include some time spent in the classroom teaching aspects of personal and social education or providing remedial education. But there are upward of one thousand teachers, trained in counselling, in part-time guidance roles who might be labelled careers teacher, remedial teacher, head of middle school, coordinator of pastoral care, head of guidance, tutor to the sixth form, head of R.E., or head of house or year systems. Some are also to be found in the most senior administrative roles, such as deputy head; and there are a number of former school counsellors who are now heads of school. Yet others have been recruited to the ranks of school social workers, particularly within those local authorities that prefer this approach to maladjustment among pupils (see Chapters 14 and 15). And there are of course two or three times this number of teachers who have acquired some skill and understanding of guidance and counselling from short courses made available by the DES, local authorities, and many institutions of higher education.

What is of primary importance is not the title of *counsellor*, but the availability of counselling skill in schools to serve children and to help organize the guidance and pastoral care effort of teams of teachers, so that counsellors may share with them their own skills, purposes, and values. The tasks most commonly undertaken by trained counsellors, whatever their designated role in the school, are: (1) counselling normal children who are temporarily suffering anxiety, distress, or indecision; what have been termed the walking wounded; (2) counselling children who have to make educational or vocational choices, and working closely with the careers service; (3) interviewing children referred by other teachers as having 'behaviour problems', i.e., those who bully, pilfer, truant, are unduly aggressive, disruptive in class, inattentive – in short, troublesome children; attempting to identify the basic problem or cause and undertaking constructive action, which may or may not involve counselling; (4) identifying children with severe emotional disturbance, arranging their referral to a psycho-medical centre, and supporting such children in school before, during, and following the conclusion of their treatment; (5) liaising with all the outside specialist agencies that have responsibility for the welfare of children: the social services department, the school psychological service, the child guidance clinic, the careers service, the probation service and the juvenile court, the drug addiction unit, and the adolescent psychiatric unit where there is one; and (6) seeing parents when it is in the interests of the child, or when approached by parents who are concerned about their child. No counsellor, of course, could do all these things unaided.

Most counsellors also develop a special interest and area of expertise that may reflect a particular need of the pupils they serve or of the posts of special responsibility they fill: the process of decision-making, drug abuse, sex education, depression, delinquency, bereavement and grief, marital relationships, disciplinary techniques, study skills, behaviour-modification techniques, drama or art as diagnostic and therapeutic activities, the development of moral feeling, the special problems of particular ethnic minorities – these are but a sample.

Misconceptions about what counselling is and what school counsellors do are still widely held even among teachers. Some bald assertions in the context of this chapter may help to dispel them. For example, not every conversation undertaken with kindly intention is counselling. Counsellors do not pry into the private lives of children and their families; it is the children who decide what they wish to take about, and even whether they wish to approach a counsellor at all. Children's rights to privacy are respected, and if a counsellor agrees to listen to a child in confidence that confidence is respected. Counsellors do not coerce or even persuade children to do anything, nor do they try to impose solutions and decisions upon them. Counsellors do not take away from other teachers their right or their professional responsibility to respond to children who choose to take their problems to them rather than to the counsellor; but they do make themselves available as consultants when a perplexed teacher chooses to seek guidance on what he might do. Counselling is not a technique of social control; it is not a mode of discipline except in the very broadest (and correct) sense of that term. Counsellors are not mini-psychiatrists: they are concerned with growth, development, and the promotion of sound mental health, not with treating sickness. Counsellors do not make work for themselves, nor create problems where none existed; they do help bring to

Figure 16.1 Guidance and the spectrum of need

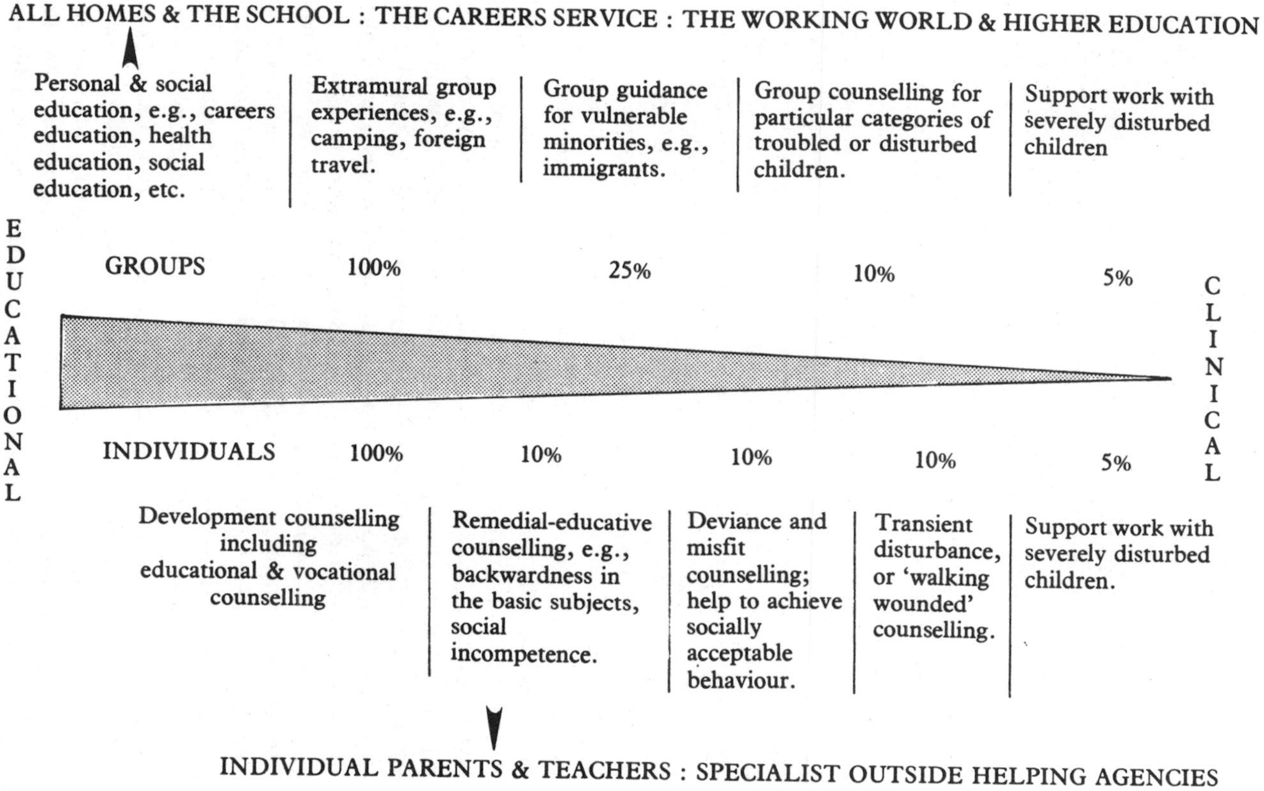

ALL HOMES & THE SCHOOL : THE CAREERS SERVICE : THE WORKING WORLD & HIGHER EDUCATION

Personal & social education, e.g., careers education, health education, social education, etc.	Extramural group experiences, e.g., camping, foreign travel.	Group guidance for vulnerable minorities, e.g., immigrants.	Group counselling for particular categories of troubled or disturbed children.	Support work with severely disturbed children

EDUCATIONAL

GROUPS	100%	25%	10%	5%
INDIVIDUALS	100%	10%	10%	10%	5%

CLINICAL

Development counselling including educational & vocational counselling	Remedial-educative counselling, e.g., backwardness in the basic subjects, social incompetence.	Deviance and misfit counselling; help to achieve socially acceptable behaviour.	Transient disturbance, or 'walking wounded' counselling.	Support work with severely disturbed children.

INDIVIDUAL PARENTS & TEACHERS : SPECIALIST OUTSIDE HELPING AGENCIES light what is there and hidden. Counsellors are not failed teachers fleeing from the classroom; all have earned their spurs as teachers before being accepted for counsellor training. It may appear less demanding, as one teacher put it, to meet the enemy one at a time. It isn't; counselling is an emotionally demanding business, and counsellors are relieved to escape back to the less charged atmosphere of the classroom from time to time for a welcome and necessary breather.

Values and influences

Counselling is not only a technique for relating to, understanding, and helping individual pupils. It operates within a framework of values and beliefs about the educational process, the nature of man, and criteria of growth and maturity. Three values in particular have strongly influenced the philosophies of many secondary schools, and are reflected in a variety of school activities. The first is that children are individuals, each unique in his/her way; and that this uniqueness should be nurtured and protected, and its expression encouraged within acceptable social limits, against unjustifiable pressures towards uniformity and conformity. The second is that a primary responsibility of all child-rearing institutions, particularly homes and schools, is to help children progressively to become independent and autonomous; and to assume responsibility for their own decisions, their own moral commitments, and their own behaviour, as contrasted with shaping their lives and their selves in obedience to the recommendations of acknowledged sources of authority. The third is that the development of the capacity for autonomous functioning follows from cultivating the habits of openness and empathy in the relationships that adults offer to the young, including teacher-pupil relationships, and this has added a new dimension to the long familiar concept of child-centredness in education.

Changes are evident in many secondary schools that can be ascribed in part to the influence of counselling. One is a much more widespread appreciation of the difference between a child's problem and an institutional problem. Formerly, when teachers were asked to provide a list of children's problems, they would offer a taxonomy of forms of behaviour deemed undesirable: truancy, disruptiveness, pilfering, declining school achievement, failure to complete homework, unpunctuality, etc. Admittedly, teachers must try to correct such behaviours, but they are not children's problems, they are the school's. Admittedly too, they may be symptomatic of a child's problem, but even this is not invariably true. In correcting such behaviours one may never identify a single child's problem. Furthermore, the more exemplary children who never give a teacher cause for reproach may have serious personal anxieties and distress that do not come to light in school, or only, in the case of suicides, when it is too late. This distinction between institutional and personal problems is now more widely appreciated by teachers.

A further change that counselling has brought is an appreciation that knowing a child from the inside and knowing him from the outside are two quite different kinds of knowledge, requiring different kinds of information obtained in quite distinct ways. School record cards tend to be filled with external facts about the child – his IQ, school achievements and scholastic progress, teachers' observations on his behaviour, character and motivation, details of his family circumstances, bereavements, and so on. It is illusory to hope that detailed pupil record systems can satisfactorily replace the kind of understanding that an empathic teacher acquires through years of sustained daily intimacy, and a good relationship of the kind achieved, for example, by the good parent. An external view of a child and an internal view acquired through intimacy of relationship may usefully complement one another, but they may be startlingly different. Certainly, they are never equivalent guides for school decisions and action.

Finally, counselling has brought back into education an enhanced awareness of the importance of the relationship that a teacher establishes with his pupils, collectively and individually, in determining his teaching effectiveness, that is, the pupils' learning achievements. Teachers have for long been aware of the importance of such factors as class control, lesson organization, blackboard technique, feedback, and logical presentation, to name but a few relatively impersonal factors; but little importance has been attached to teacher-pupil relationships as facilitators or inhibitors of learning. Relationship is a crucial factor in counselling, which is also a learning experience; and many counsellors have increased their effectiveness as teachers by adapting appropriately for the classroom what they have learned about the use of relationship in individual counselling. Classroom styles are becoming much less rigid and stereotyped, more flexible, more open and empathic than formerly.

It looks certain that the 1980s will see the continued development of these trends, and perhaps even the spread of counselling in an appropriately adapted form to primary schools, in which counselling is offered to anxious parents rather than to pupils. Counselling has brought a new dimension to the eternal challenge of building effective bridges between the generations. Its emphasis on respect for individuality and on guiding children towards successful independence is a welcome one. But arguably this has resulted in a relative neglect of the obligation to alert children to their social responsibilities, so that they may understand that 'no man is an island'. This challenge remains for counsellors and for schools in the decade ahead.

References

(Including recommended further reading)

Daws, P.P. (1976), *Early Days: a personal review of the beginnings of counselling in English education, 1964-1974*, Cambridge: Hobson's Press.

Halmos, P. (1965), *The Faith of the Counsellors*, London: Constable.

Hamblin, D.H. (1974), *The Teacher and Counselling*, Oxford: Blackwell.

Hughes, P.M. (1971), *Guidance & Counselling in Schools*, London: Pergamon.

Jones, Anne (1970), *School Counselling in Practice*, London: Ward Lock.

Morris, B. (1955), 'Guidance as a concept in educational philosophy' in *Year Book of Education, 1955*, London: Evans (reprinted in, *Objectives & Perspectives in Education*, London: Routledge & Kegan Paul).

Rogers, C.R. (1961), *On Becoming a Person*, London: Constable.

Truax, C.B. and Carkhuff, R.R. (1967), *Towards Effective Counselling & Psychotherapy*, Chicago: Aldine.

Wrenn, C.G. (1962), *The Counsellor in a Changing World*, Washington: APGA.

CHAPTER 17

THE HOME-SCHOOL LIAISON TEACHER

Robert Bailey

The appointment of home-school liaison teachers, particularly in areas of special difficulty, is a recent development in a number of LEAs. In this chapter, Robert Bailey discusses some of the central principles, skills, and strategies.

The appointment of home-school liaison teachers to a number of schools in several local education authorities in England, Wales, Scotland, and Northern Ireland has been an exciting and fruitful innovation in education in the 1970s. The appointments have come in the wake of that wave of research and reporting which, in the previous decade, cast up so much evidence of the importance of parents, the home, and the world outside the school for the education and development of the child. As is evident throughout this present volume, how education and social science has perceived these findings, interpreted them, and developed strategies of response has varied immensely.

It is important to recognize that the varied and hesitant development of the role of the liaison teacher and the rationale for liaison have reflected this wide range of interpretations. Sponsoring bodies like the Van Leer Foundation, the DES and SSRC, and Urban Aid; appointing authorities like Birmingham, Middlesborough, Bradford, ILEA, and Coventry (along with others like Nottinghamshire where the function if not the title of community teachers has had many common features); headteachers, and liaison teachers themselves, have held varied views of parents, the home and the school, and of the essential nature of the relationships between them – even within the same authority and the same school.

Liaison and innovation

This diversity of views is nothing new to education or to innovation; it can be the seed-bed for growth, and it can offer a creative tension rather than a destructive conflict. But there are frustrations and anxieties. Hidden curricula and often unconscious ideologies play their part. There is a need for support systems and safety valves which unfortunately are not always there. Yet for all the diversity of objectives and practice, despite the deliberate avoidance of settled aims in the name of sensitivity and flexibility, and with all the determination to create a role suitable to the unique situation of a particular neighbourhood, its school and parents, accounts by liaison teachers of the work they do and the training they are seeking or would like to receive, all show a marked *similarity* of process and skill. And it does seem that, over time, a core of aims and functions is emerging, far clearer and more sharp-edged than vague notions of 'enabling' or 'being a catalyst'.

Much of what follows tries to trace and delineate the essential aims, processes, and skills of liaison of the teachers thus far, looking at development over time and by argument and experience. What is still required, and this the teachers recognize and would welcome, is prolonged and extensive evaluation; the lack of this has been in part due to the short-term nature of some appointments, and in part due to a lack of research support in other situations. Some teachers have found themselves isolated, the only appointment of their kind, or attached to several schools but a member of none. Lack of supervision and specific training, and of some kind of career structure, has made growth and development hard for nearly all – and evaluation in such circumstances is of very limited value. Nonetheless, self-criticism and analysis and openness to change is a marked feature of the liaison teacher, and there are many examples of the way these same qualities have grown within the institutions and people with whom the teachers interact.

Liaison and participation

The ground for liaison teaching, as for so many other aspects of home-school links, was prepared by the Plowden Report (1967). A key passage at the end of the chapter entitled 'Participation by Parents' concluded:

> Much depends on the teachers. . . . Teachers are already hard-pressed, and nowhere more so than in the very districts where the co-operation of parents is most needed and hardest to win. We are aware that in asking them to take on new burdens we are asking what will sometimes be next to impossible. Forty

children will seem enough to many, without adding 80 fathers and mothers. Yet we are convinced that to make the effort will not only add depth to their understanding of their children, but will also bring out that support from the home which is still often latent. It has long been recognized that education is concerned with the whole man; henceforth it must be concerned with the whole family.

So described, engaging the participation of parents pointed clearly to the need for someone to share the burden with the teacher, even though, as many liaison teachers have discovered, support from the home is latent and can be utilized. What this passage also pointed to is the need to clarify certain bland terms before one can put liaison into practice with any confidence; 'participation' and 'cooperation' are neither synonymous nor necessarily compatible terms. Sociologists and community theorists have long looked with scepticism upon the former; and the most elementary linguist can recognize a deal of difference between 'cooperation of' and 'cooperation between'.

One of the most exciting features of some liaison teachers' work has been the establishment of a more than 'token' participation by parents in the ongoing education of their school child; and this on at least two levels. Firstly, by involving a number of those parents who do not normally take an active part, along with teachers, in their child's education, either because they are fearful of or hostile to teachers and schools, or because they fail to see its potential and relevance (which may indeed be hard to discern). Secondly, by negotiating a more direct and powerful influence for parents upon school education (even as, often, the liaison teacher secures greater influence for teachers upon home education); this has been achieved by the gradual introduction of parental assistance, and even some control, in the classroom and curriculum (which itself is being constantly rewritten because of this very participation), and by the formation of new consultation and management structures which give parents greater degrees of experience in exercising control, even before or in addition to the implementation of the Taylor Committee recommendations.

Even such a brief and partial resumé of some possible liaison activities as this raises three very important and fundamental questions. First, is it yet clear what the special processes of interaction and change are for which the home-school liaison teacher is responsible, and can these processes be taught and learned? That is, do such terms as 'involving' and 'negotiating', used in the previous paragraph, and 'liaison' (and all its vocabulary of enabling functions), which presumably are part of the process, refer to actual and acquirable skills? Or are they merely tautologies and redundant euphemisms for 'meeting' and 'talking', etc.? Secondly, if it can be decided what it is that constitutes 'liaison', is this something which requires another expert and specialist in the field (and some liaison teachers may be either, neither, or both)? Or is this something which most teachers should and could do, at least if given a little more time and insight? Thirdly, if a common element in liaison is securing greater participation by parents and 'family-centred' education, does this constitute a threat to existing notions of education in schools as a professional and institutional activity? And this final question draws one back to a very practical issue to which many home-school liaison teachers have had to address themselves in working out their roles: i.e., the extent to which liaison is dependent upon the willingness of head teachers to relinquish initiative and control, whilst at the same time having to retain responsibility. The following description of some aspects of the development of the role may help to answer these questions, and to explore the most urgent issues.

Liaison, social understanding, and educational understanding

The appointment in January 1970 of two home-school liaison teachers to two Birmingham primary schools, as part of the Educational Priority Area Project in that city, was based on an analysis of need which was described to the project schools in these terms:

> In general, all teachers are expected to develop good home-school links and this is a fairly easy task in a good area where parents come to the teacher. In E.P.A.s, the school can be overwhelmed by the social problems to the neglect of the educational problems, and one cannot expect all members of staff to have the time, or indeed the motivation to attempt to find out about the background of each child. Nevertheless, it must be clear that to make any headway educationally in EPAs, a real understanding of the home problems a child faces is quite vital. (Halsey 1972)

The brief went on to describe three specific duties as part of his major commitment to liaising between the class-based teacher and the home (the rest of his commitment being to a part-time teaching programme): first, to visit homes, at times normally inconvenient to staff; second, to substitute for a class teacher if a parent calls during school hours; and third, to foster and organize activities both during and after school hours, involving groups of parents and occasionally parents with children.

This description of an apparently simple, and clearly undeveloped, role identified the three activities which still are a feature of part of the work of the majority of liaison teachers. More importantly, it also identified two of the main aims: firstly, to increase the social understanding of the teacher; secondly, to increase the educational understanding of the parent.

Increasing social understanding

Conveying an increased understanding of the home problems a child faces might consist merely of transmitting information regarding home circumstances handicapping (or benefiting!) the child. But of course, knowledge is not necessarily understanding. Liaison teachers have found themselves needing to interpret the information and, even more importantly perhaps, to encourage the teacher to come into more direct contact with the social environment of the child and his family. They have sought to foster at least an occasional visit to homes, a greater and more frequent effort to meet parents face-to-face (if only by the simple rearrangement of interview times to suit the availability of parents), and the invitation to staff meetings of local social workers, community workers and policemen, etc., to convey greater knowledge of the stresses of life in the neighbourhood. These are opportunities liaison teachers can organize and introduce gradually from their own experience.

Yet when they have done this, the question remains, for what purpose? Is the social understanding merely to be filed away in the now, admittedly, more complete school records; or will it marginally modify the teacher's attitudes and emotive responses, or, worse, lower her expectations of the child? Or, worst of all, is this an exercise in academic voyeurism? This is an issue of the kind faced by education in recent years in the field of assessment. Peter Mittler (1969) has maintained that '. . . psychological assessment is at a turning point in its evolution. . . . The forging of an organic link between assessment and treatment is one of the most consistent themes . . . diagnosis divorced from treatment is a mere intellectual exercise and sometimes hardly that.' With regard to liaison, it seems essential that a link must be forged between the understanding gained of the social environment of the child, and the response and provision it is both necessary and possible for the school to make as a result of that understanding.

This conclusion is a very crucial one for the role of the liaison teacher, in any particular appointment, and it has had considerable implications for development or stagnation (or even atrophy) in particular situations. Significantly and rather inconsistently, but presumably intentionally, the Halsey

Report records that the practice of the liaison teachers took in a whole range of investigations, assessments, and treatments, which seemed to follow inevitably from the broad and open-ended stated objective of the Birmingham project; whilst the report's own policy definition of the liaison teacher's job is far more specific, restricted, and restrictive.

The profile provided at the time of the appointment to the Birmingham posts links liaison firmly with the community school (albeit the narrow and largely inappropriate Plowden model) and with a 'helping' function which is potentially infinite.

> At this stage within the development of what the Plowden Report calls a community school, it would not be helpful to try to define narrowly what the home-school liaison teacher's function should be, but the objective is clear: to enlarge the mutual understanding between the school and the families and the neighbourhood which it serves, and *to strengthen the help which they can give to each other,* bearing in mind *especially those children who need most help, and whose parents sometimes seek it least.* (italics added) (Halsey 1972)

Described in this way, the brief for the liaison teacher may involve working at both macro- and micro- levels in the context of community/neighbourhood, home, and school. And, from the experimental period in Birmingham to the more recent developments in Belfast and Manchester, this range of functioning has usually been the experience. Often the work of liaison has been an integral part of a larger community schooling or community education programme, as in the Coventry Community Education Project or the Birmingham Experiment in Community Education. Indeed, it could be argued that, without the support of a general policy of community schooling and community education, the social understanding which the liaison teacher generates will serve no purpose; whether or not that schooling and education is in the form conceived by Halsey (1972), Midwinter (1975), Smith (1974), Robbins and Williams (1976), Betty (1971), or any other post-Plowden theorists and practitioners, and whatever modifications are made according to such criticisms as those of Bernstein (1971), Merson and Campbell (1974), or Byrne and Williamson (1972).

Certainly, success in terms of a shift in the educational experience and success of the child as a result of liaison work depends upon a willingness in the schools affected to examine all aspects of their life, in the light of the new knowledge and understanding of the families and community with which they are partnered. This is so because, at the micro-level alone, in terms of identifying and interpreting the social experience of children and their families, liaison teachers have brought forward such aspects as:

a A more accurate picture of preschool experience (through pre-entry home visits), in terms of intellectual, physical, social, and emotional experience. Such a picture may be provided by an educational visitor (see later) or a health visitor. In which case it may be the liaison teacher's job, at least, to ensure that:

b Information available from other agencies is available and kept up to date.

c Records of progress and development and experience during school years are kept up to date and referred to by staff as needed, (where this is not already the case). (The whole of this work must be carried out in the light of policies on recordkeeping, confidentiality, and labelling, which means that the liaison teacher may also have to take an initiative in the organization of meetings of staff on such policies. At very least, the liaison process should never proceed without such policies being clearly laid down. The Warnock Report has some helpful words here.)

d Knowledge of the constraints on parents which prevent or hinder attendance at clinics, interviews with teachers, or school events. The response here has often been a greater flexibility by the health and education services; the liaison teachers are otherwise drawn into providing transport or child-minding, a problematic use of their time and skills.

e An understanding (gained from a home visit or persuasion into school of parents with whom a good relationship is established) that at some point in the school years of the child certain stressful home circumstances are causing learning difficulties, to which teachers may be able to respond by modification of the learning environment.

f The calling of a case-conference, or referral to other agencies, when the liaison teacher exposes the need for help outside the abilities and responsibilities of the class teacher.

Already it is possible to see that there are elements here of work which, even whilst being described as mere identification and assessment of social factors leading to greater social understanding, have an apparent overlap with the work of the education social worker and social caseworker. This is an issue which must be dealt with shortly.

The macro-level of identification and interpretation of social experience has involved the liaison teacher in becoming aware of those general environmental factors such as housing, poverty, unemployment, cultural differences, etc. which militate for or against the progress of the child. Here again, whether the liaison teacher initially simply locates a problem in overcrowding or the language of the mother in the home, her work very quickly moves towards the organization of a system of housing advice or the provision of second language classes. And then her work has an apparent overlap with that of the community worker. This must also be dealt with shortly. But first it is necessary to look at a narrower concept of home-school liaison.

Increasing educational understanding

When the Halsey Report reached for conclusions to the action-research of the various EPA projects, it defined the role of the liaison teacher very much in terms of 'increasing the educational understanding of the parents':

> The job of the home-school liaison teacher . . . is essentially educational. It is concerned partly with explaining the aims and methods of the schools so that parents can better understand the nature of the experience their children receive within them; and partly with encouraging parents to recognize and have confidence in their own capacity to teach.

The implication appears to be that the aims and methods which the teacher will explain are firmly established by the school, whilst the teaching which the parent might do will fit largely within those given aims and methods. Certainly, whatever the responsiveness and flexibility of the content and methods of the education, the liaison teachers are given the duty of explaining it and engaging the parent in the task; that is clearly an 'essentially educational' duty. But the experience and understanding of liaison teachers has usually taken them far outside such confines.

This is so, not because these teachers are particularly wilful or obtuse, nor especially because they have not had clear enough guidelines, but rather, experience seems to suggest, because with growing social understanding liaison teachers experience the need to redefine what is 'essentially educational'. Liaison teachers are usually qualified teachers. Many have a social science background. Some have even been social workers. Teaching is a prerequisite of the great majority of appointments because (a) their function is, indeed, seen as essentially educational; (b) for a variety of reasons, including the teachers' own preference, they are often required to teach part-time; and (c) they need to establish credibility with their colleagues in school. The liaison function can be interpreted, especially in the light of the Halsey definition, as being very much like that of the *educational visitor*, pioneered in the West Riding project, taking education out into the home, though in the case of the visitor concentrating upon the preschool child. Indeed, many liaison teachers begin their contacts with families at the preschool stage, and see the best aspects of their preventive work developing through introducing (like the visitors) educational materials and encouraging language and social development in the home. And they continue this work through the school life of the child. The education shops in markets and stores, the workshop sessions on maths and reading in classrooms and community rooms, the publication of lively and digestible school handbooks, newsletters and broadsheets, all may be the responsibility, in part at least, of the liaison teacher at primary and secondary level. And often the most fruitful centres of communication and interchange about educational matters have been the 'chat sessions' liaison teachers have set up in some suitably comfortable room in the school (even the staff room) on one or every afternoon of the week, perhaps an hour or so before the mothers take their children home.

All this can be seen as 'essentially educational'. Yet even in these 'pedagogical contexts' it can be recognized that the liaison teacher has, inevitably, to use skills not normally required of and not usually available to teachers, of however many years' experience, trained to teach children and spending by far the greatest proportion of their time in classrooms. It may be argued that nursery and infant teachers have always insisted upon meeting and entering into an educational dialogue with parents; that the best training courses in colleges and departments of education include parent-teacher relations in their syllabuses; and that, anyway, teachers are adults who meet adults when they are not teaching. But, of course, it is not only teachers who need to be taught the skills of adult interpersonal relationships and adult education; the current development of educational methods units in higher education reflects a need even at the centres of adult learning.

Making contact with families and gaining their cooperation in the education of their children has, then, required skills of adult education; and this can mean skills of publicity, to convey messages in attractive and clear, concise ways, and skills of group work, to secure interaction and learning in meetings and workshops on play and the curriculum and apparatus-making in school, etc. It has required a very good understanding of child development and curriculum theory, of learning processes and educational administration, in order to give a clear account to parents of what is going on in education and where they can and do play their part. And this same understanding has been needed in order that the liaison teacher can play her part in the development of a curriculum in the school which uses the neighbourhood as a resource, and the school as a resource for the neighbourhood. For if the community school is a hope for the future in priority areas (not to say that it is not, perhaps, the hope for the future in all sectors of education), then the liaison teacher has a very important part to play in ensuring the success of such a school's understanding of its community. And this has already proved the case in those authorities where these innovations have gone hand in hand.

The full consequences of social understanding

Description and discussion of the aims and methods of home-school liaison have so far identified some possible parameters of the work. This will vary in size and quality according to the established aims and resources available. But it will also vary according to the processes being used. We have already noted the way that, in setting out to gain social understanding, and even before any response to that understanding is entered into, the liaison teacher seems to be intruding upon the social worker's field of activity and responsibility.

Now, once again, the Halsey Report has something to say about this:

> Of course, sometimes the social services are inadequate and the liaison teacher will try to deal with emergencies . . . and sometimes the statutory services are so incomprehensible or difficult of access that poorer families need help in applying to them. Nevertheless the liaison teacher's job should be clearly distinguished from social work and his relation to social workers clarified.

Liaison teachers in practice have made a point of clarifying their relationship to social workers, psychiatric social workers, education welfare officers, and community workers. Their own emphasis, in some places, upon 'prevention' rather than 'crisis' work has controlled this. Clarification has, perhaps, been most successful where the teachers have established formal and informal means of consultation and coordination, by lunch-time meetings to discuss current activities, for example. But, very crucially, this has not necessarily meant that the liaison teacher has 'kept out of social work'. *For the facts of home-school liaison and the development of the liaison relationship as a process are that, once a link has been made with a person, a degree of interaction is established which cannot and should not be confined to some narrow delimited areas of discussion termed 'educational matters'.*

On the other hand, the liaison teacher has to establish, in her relationship with any person in liaison, parent, head teacher, class teacher, social worker, health visitor, caretaker, educational psychologist, education officer, policeman, etc., what is the range of her own abilities and responsibilities in relating to this person. This may appear to be begging too many questions and to be open to further narrow delimitations, according to how the teacher defines her abilities and responsibilities. Well, this may indeed be the case. What it seems wrong (and in the experience of practising liaison teachers) impossible to do is to set limits which are not related to the circumstances of the relationship. When two or more people meet they present to each other a unique set of perceptions. A harassed parent may fling open the door and say, 'Am I glad you came; I've got no gas.' The liaison teacher may read this as a 'social work' problem, and decide that referral is essential. But at very least, she must know how to continue the conversation, make the referral, and maintain, if possible, a continuing relationship for the good of the child.

Alternatively, the liaison teacher may have met this parent before, know the social worker is 'working on' the problem of arrears, and may see the need as one of calming and support for the mother, which she believes she can or cannot give; but again she must do her best to maintain the link for the good of the child. If some degree of counselling or social work is necessary and her experience and training has qualified her, the teacher might choose to give it. Such skills and provision are not so thick on the ground that the mother should be denied it.

If this is a correct analysis of the liaison relationship, then at very least, liaison teachers need skills of self-perception, communication, and empathy, together with a knowledge of interpersonal behaviour, and of agencies and patterns of care. So Rogerian theories and practice of counselling, and models of communication as provided by such writers as Litwak and Meyer (1965), will have great relevance to the practice and training of liaison teachers. But, as this present analysis indicates, there is a need for a far greater range of skills and knowledge, not only in the teachers themselves but in their colleagues also, if liaison is to be effective in promoting social and educational understanding and change. The disciplines of psychology, sociology, politics, economics, and management are all involved. The National Home-School Liaison Association is currently assessing the needs for local and national courses of training for staffs and specialists.

I have left many issues undiscussed: the problems of dual teacher/liaison roles for many teachers; the relative merits of area/school-based work; the differing aims and functioning of liaison teachers in primary and secondary schools; the resolution of the demands for prevention and crisis intervention. The discussion has reflected the fact that liaison teachers are analysts, catalysts, and activists. What this means in terms of work in any given situation varies with the nature of the need; clearly they cannot be and should not try to be all things to all men. But if linking home and school and providing cooperative care (Watkins and Derrick 1977) is taken seriously, there is a place for a person with the skills and the responsibility for providing knowledge, developing understanding, and forging links.

It is only necessary to listen to a head teacher enthusiastically recounting the benefits a liaison teacher has brought to recognize what a real asset such an appointment can be. And this is not just the relief of someone who has had some of his more direct responsibilities lifted from his shoulders, nor the satisfaction of someone who sees certain long-felt needs being met because he has an extra pair of hands in the school (though this may indeed be a part of the truth). This enthusiasm is likely to be related most importantly to the part the liaison teacher has played in breaking new ground in those intractable areas of education where need has been recognized for years, but progress has been minimal, and where, when success has been experienced, it has bred yet further development and growth throughout the life of the school. That is, where liaison teachers have gained the active cooperation for the good of the child, of parents, other schools, and outside agencies in such a way and to such an extent that education, rather than trying to compensate for society, has actually succeeded in joining forces with society to secure advance. And this has resulted not just from extra time devoted to the problems, but from *particular skills* and *new methods* being put into operation.

To arrive at the point where a multifarious group of parents – timid, hostile, bemused – enters into a cooperative arrangement with a multifarious group of teachers – timid, hostile, bemused – backed up by a multifarious group of other agencies for the education of their children, in a multifarious number of ways to suit the individuals concerned, it is necessary to have a knowledge of the pressures, weaknesses, and strengths experienced by each participant. It is also necessary to negotiate, a little at a time, meeting points for the participants, allowing confidence and ability to grow with the experience of small successes. Such knowledge and such negotiation is *not* the prerogative of the liaison teacher; nor is he or she omniscient and omnipotent. But there appears to be a place in educational development for a person who takes this field of knowledge and operation upon herself.

Some of the clearest and most impressive descriptions of this are in those authorities where programmes of liaison have been set up; programmes which do not prescribe the work in any rigid form within the various schools, but where at least some continuity of innovation within and between schools has been painstakingly developed, to allow preschool education, remedial and psychological support, area health and social services and special education provision to be used by and to make full use of the work of the liaison teacher. In such circumstances it has also been possible to establish a support service of resource materials and at least a basic in-service training programme. In these circumstances patterns of screening and assessment, educational guidance and referral, parental involvement in preschool, school, and postschool education of the child, and general community regeneration have begun to emerge as key areas of activity for the liaison teacher.

References

Bernstein, B. (1971), 'A critique of the concept of compensatory education', in B. Bernstein, *Class, Codes and Control*, Vol.1, London: Routledge & Kegan Paul.

Betty, C. (1971), *Focus on the Community School* – a booklet in a series edited by Jack Hames, for the London EPA Project.

Byrne, D. and Williamson, W. (1972), *The Myth of the Restricted Code*, University of Durham Department of Sociology.

Halsey, A.H. (ed.) (1972), *Educational Priority*, Vol.1, HMSO.

Litwak, E. and Meyer, H.J. (1965), 'Administrative styles and community linkages of public schools', in A.J. Reiss (ed.), *Schools in a Changing Society*, New York: The Free Press.

Merson, M.W. and Campbell, R.J. (1974), 'Community Education: Instruction for Inequality' in *Education for Teaching*, Spring, 1974.

Midwinter, E. (1975), *Education and the Community*, London: George Allen & Unwin.

Mittler, P. (ed.), (1969), *Psychological Assessment of Mental and Physical Handicaps*, Methuen.

Central Advisory Council for Education (1967), *Children and their Primary Schools*, ('Plowden Report'), HMSO.

Robbins, W.R. and Williams, W. (1976), 'Community Education', in J. Raynor and E. Harris, (eds.) *Schooling in the City*, Ward Lock Educational.

Smith, G. and Smith, T. (1974), 'The community school – a base for community development?' in D. Jones and M. Mayo (eds.), *Community Work One*, Routledge & Kegan Paul

'Warnock Report' (1978), (Report of the Committee of Enquiry into the Education of Handicapped Children and Young People), *Special Educational Needs*, HMSO.

Watkins, R. and Derrick, D. (eds.) (1977), *Co-operative Care*, Centre for Information and Advice on Educational Disadvantage.

CHAPTER 18

THE EDUCATIONAL HOME VISITOR

Geoff Poulton

Like home-school liaison teachers, educational home visitors are a recent innovation. In this final chapter in Part Four, Geoff Poulton offers an authoritative account of this significant development in home-school relations and community development.

The strategy of educational home visiting is still in its early stages of development. An experimental programme, which started in 1970, has contributed to the growth of two distinct patterns of organization within the United Kingdom – school-based and independent. This chapter traces the origins of educational home visiting and the subsequent developments which have occurred, from school bases and independent bases, in various parts of the country. Because educational home visiting schemes tend to be strongly influenced by local environmental conditions, their aims and operations cover a fairly wide spectrum. All the schemes, however, are concerned, in one way or another, with children under the age of five years. In general they are complementary to other educational and care facilities for families with young children.

Although differences in emphasis become clear when the schemes are compared, some dominant and commonly shared aims can be identified:

to help parents to feel that they have an important part to play in their own children's development

to help parents to feel that they have an important part to play in supporting each other in their neighbourhoods

to meet isolated parents on a regular basis, establishing school and neighbourhood links with them to foster closer liaison and understanding between health, education, and social services related to families

to enable children to start school confidently in the knowledge that some people and experiences will be familiar to them

to help develop language, manipulative, and cognitive skills in young children.

The *school-based* schemes aim to build up a sense of confidence and trust between teachers and parents. In the process they provide parents with opportunities to understand the functions of a school, and to act confidently in their relationships with the staff. The *independent* schemes probably place greater reliance on the resources of the families involved. From their ranks new visitors, convenors, activists emerge. Self-help is a key concept in the work of the independent schemes and they aim to encourage networks of family support where there is most need. They also aim to provide alternative models of service for administrators, policy-makers, and practitioners to examine and experience. All the schemes, both school-based and independent, are concerned for the quality of life open to the children and their parents.

The techniques used within a scheme depend heavily upon initial visits to families, when a relationship of trust and understanding must be established between the educational home visitor, the parent (usually the mother), and the child. The first visits usually enable a 'contract' to be drawn up, defining the identified limits of the visitor's work, and the level of commitment which the parents are prepared to give to the scheme. This usually means that the visitor will come regularly to the family's home, normally for one hour per week during a stated period of time. She will probably leave a kit of play materials with the family. Other books and toys may be left by her for short periods. The parents determine convenient times and dates for the visits, and their right to withdraw from the scheme is maintained.

During the visits the educational visitor usually concentrates initially on the child, introducing activities to stimulate and interest him. She then discusses what she has been doing with the child's mother. As the visits develop, the mother may become more involved in the direct teaching of her child during the sessions and between visits. Most schemes now encourage mothers to meet together to generate mutual support and activities, and so reduce the isolation experienced by some families.

It is difficult for the schemes to include families where parents work on a full-time basis, but a high proportion of those visited work part-time. In a number of areas, the weekly visits to homes frequently include more than one child at a time, as relatives and neighbours join the activities. As a result, educational visitors are often under pressure from other families in their areas to receive the same service. Selection of criteria to join visiting schemes therefore is an important issue for organizers to consider. This, and other issues, have been met in a variety of ways by the schemes and they will receive more attention in the pages which follow.

Origins

The concept of home and school being brought together in a partnership of learning has been well rehearsed in recent years. Since the early 1960s, political trends in the United States and in the United Kingdom have accelerated its promotion. Movements leading towards greater equality of opportunity included educational programmes for children under school age, in the hope that their performance levels would be permanently raised and with a consequent improvement in their life-chances. By the late 1960s, research studies which examined the effectiveness of early intervention programmes were being published in the USA. Their results influenced similar programmes being established in the United Kingdom.

During the initial stage of the West Riding Educational Priority Area (EPA) Project, much of the action-research team's attention was focussed on classroom-based programmes for children aged three years and above. The published results (Smith 1975, Smith and James 1975) compare a number of different curricular approaches used with children. While later stages in the project concentrated much more on ways of stimulating the educational role of parents (Poulton and James 1975), time limits excluded this work from the research programme, with one notable exception.

A home-visiting programme was set up by the project in September 1970. Its aim was, first, 'to study the educational environment of young children, particularly the mother-child relationship; second, to examine the stages in development in children's play and learning in the home; third, to try to discover, in cooperation with the mother, any problems or difficulties in the child's progress; and fourth, to work out a programme acceptable to individuals and families in the community whereby these problems could be overcome.'* These aims reflect the influence of home-visiting programmes carried out in the USA which were strongly child-orientated. These programmes were designed for children who lacked educational and emotional stimulus at home. Some used visiting tutors who concentrated entirely on the child's learning (Schaefer 1972). Others concentrated on improving the teaching skills of mothers, so that they could carry out a structured syllabus with their children (Levenstein 1972). Most programmes selected children from 'culturally deprived' homes, and were the subject of carefully monitored research studies (Bronfenbrenner 1972). The results of follow-up studies showed encouragingly low 'wash out' effects on the children, in contrast to the results of other methods of early education (Cicerelli 1969).

The home-visiting programme in the West Riding EPA Project seemed to be a logical development from the first year's work in a nursery setting with groups of children. Even at the age of three years, many of the children possessed language and small motor skills which were below national norms. By selecting a much younger age-group, eighteen- to twenty-four-months old, the causes of diminished performances in the children might be identified and remedied. In contrast with the US programmes, however, all children of a specific age-group, living in one school catchment area, were invited to take part. We expected that a wide range of families and children of different abilities would be found in the area selected, even though it was designated as an EPA.

The children were visited regularly each week by the same person, who was given the responsibility of establishing and developing the programme (Armstrong 1975). The first part of each visit was directed towards the child and consisted of introducing a toy or creative material, and encouraging him to play and talk. The second part concentrated on the mother's understanding of the child's actions and responses. One of the most important features to emerge from these discussions was the belief, held by many of the parents, that young children are only able to assimilate a very limited vocabulary. Few mothers thought that the children had to *learn* concepts of colour, shape, size, number and time, etc., but felt, in any case, that such matters were the prerogative of teachers, once full-time schooling began.

The programme was continued for a two-year period with twenty children before they joined a nursery class at the age of three years six months. Children in the experimental group, together with a control group in a

*Extract from Smith, G.A.N. (ed.) (1975), *Educational Priority*, Vol.4, HMSO, p. 138.

neighbouring town, were tested at the start of the programme and twice more – after the first and second years. Not only were the average scores of the experimental group higher than those of the control (Merrill Palmer, group average – experimental 113.0, control 99.3, year 1), but they were also assessed as more vocal, sociable, and imaginative.

By the end of the first year, the parents were more confident about the part they played in their children's education and they were keen to continue the programme. At this time a new home visitor was appointed to continue the work of the pioneer, Gina Armstrong.* In spite of some misgivings, the families accepted the new worker and the programme was maintained. Since the children were by now old enough and had developed some skills, a more structured approach was introduced in which cognitive and motor development was encouraged through programmes matched to the performances of individual children. We designed and used a simple indicator which enabled the home visitor to identify crude levels of skill and language development before constructing a programme for each child. By the end of the second year, the earlier gains made by the children had been maintained.

Although our attention had been focussed on the child and the educational potential of the parents in each family, a regular visit by an outsider who projected a desire to listen and help resulted in another important development. All the mothers used the opportunity to raise matters of immediate concern to them. Housing, money, family relationships, education, employment, and health were topics regularly discussed with both home visitors. In a number of cases they were able to provide help with social problems facing the parents, either by becoming directly involved or by referring the matter to other agencies. It became necessary for the home visitors to try to establish a balance between their educational task and other concerns of the families.

Sometimes disturbances within family life forced the educational programmes into a very low priority for the parents. A strike at the local pit, for example, generated anxieties and conflict in many families and they were much less inclined to maintain active participation in the programme. Although it was possible to demonstrate the efficacy of mothers as sustain-

*The EPA Project had reached the end of its three-year term, and the team disbanded. A new group of workers continued under the auspices of West Riding County Council and the Social Science Research Council, based at Red House Education Centre in Denaby Main.

ing agents during their children's early education, they were still vulnerable to the problems which generally face parents raising young children. As a result, both home visitors developed a great respect for the achievements of the mothers, many of whom daily faced very considerable difficulties with little help or support.

Social factors within the families had a marked effect upon the educational programme, compelling the home visitors to respond with forms of care more easily identified as *social work* than education. Yet care and education are closely interrelated. By conveying a profound respect for the mothers' abilities to bring up their families in the face of difficulties, the home visitors were reinforcing the parents' self-concept in parenting. This was an essential first step towards further learning and confidence-raising for the parents, but the home visitors, too, had much to learn, at first hand, of the social conditions experienced by the families.

The combination of a highly specific educational programme and a caring, supportive service demanded a high level of commitment and involvement from the visitors. Although members of a closely knit project team, both home visitors often felt isolated in their work. The intensity and volume of interaction between themselves and twenty families each week inhibited communication about their work with colleagues. We were beginning to realize some of the dilemmas and operational problems, as well as some of the advantages, which could arise in educational home-visiting programmes.

The strategy is extended

Central government and local authority hopes for an expansion in nursery provision were very high in 1972. The publication of the national EPA Project report* at this time supported recommendations contained in the White Paper, *A Framework for Expansion*. Interest in the EPA home-visiting experiment was expressed by a number of organizations, and in the summer of 1973 at least thirteen posts had been established to develop similar work in various parts of the country. I was able to monitor most of the original schemes during their first year of operation (September 1973 – August 1974), and to record the experience gained using the strategy in a number of different settings (Poulton 1975). It seemed important to focus

*The report *Educationl Priority*, Vol. 1, Halsey, A.H. (ed.) (1972), HMSO, summarized the main findings of the five EPA Project teams, and preceded most of their own published reports by two or three years.

the eye of research on the embryonic growth of a new movement and, if necessary, help to sustain it. In consequence, I carried out a survey of parents and educational home visitors involved in the schemes, while acting as a communication link between them in Birmingham, Lincoln, Batley, Grimethorpe, Fitzwilliam, South Elmsall, and Liverpool.

All thirteen appointees visited Red House Education Centre in preparation for setting up their own schemes. There were considerable social and demographic differences between their areas which required specific approaches. In Batley, for instance, a large proportion of the families to be visited were Gujerati-speaking. In some areas many families had experienced the trauma of moving from an agrarian society to an industrial, urban society. They contrasted sharply with the Denaby Main families who had grown up in an industrialized, stable community. The Red House model of home visiting therefore was not necessarily apposite elsewhere.

Further differences occurred within the agencies employing the home visitors. The West Riding LEA appointed six teachers, each to be based on an infant school. Priority Area Playgroups in Birmingham formed a team of visitors, each of whom worked in a particular part of the city, in liaison with statutory agencies. The Home-Link Project* in Liverpool had been developed by the EPA Project, funded by the Bernard Van Leer Foundation, to establish a neighbourhood-run visiting scheme. In Lincoln, a well-established nursery school appointed a teacher to visit families living on a large housing estate lying within its catchment area.

The *school-based* schemes followed the Red House model most closely. Although the ages of the children covered a much wider range, from nineteen to fifty-one months, at the commencement of visiting, they were selected by age within school catchment areas. Home visits were made on a weekly basis for one hour's duration over periods lasting up to three school terms. While all the schemes were concerned to improve cognitive, language, and social skills of the children through the joint efforts of parents and visitors, those based on schools were consciously attempting to smooth the path of entry to full-time education, both for parents and children.

The project-based *independent* schemes placed a greater emphasis on supporting parents with social problems, and maintaining visits until the children started to attend playgroups, nursery, or infant classes. Their

*The Home-Link Project moved from the Bronte area to Netherley on the outskirts of Liverpool during 1973-1974 and could not be included in the survey as planned. Only one home visitor from Liverpool eventually took part.

selection of families was often based upon referrals by social workers or health visitors. Such emphasis is reflected in a statment by Joan Jones, director of Priority Area Playgroups in 1973.

> Daily we have been assailed with stories of the inhuman treatment of young children, the plight of desperate parents, the frustration of social and health workers wanting to refer children, and teachers confronted by school children unable to communicate or manage basic skills.

The survey of parents included all who were on the initial visiting lists of eleven visitors in September 1973. Interviews were carried out with 129 parents at the start of the schemes, and again nine months later. The questionnaire closely followed one used during the West Riding EPA preschool follow-up studies. It was therefore possible to make comparisons between the attitudes to education of parents in the original scheme, its control group, and those obtained in quite different geographical areas. Many of the items produced quite inconclusive results, however. Few differences occurred between the pretest and posttest stages which could be ascribed to the influence of the educational home visitors. There was also a very even response to most items from the areas with very little difference between them.

Perhaps the most important result shown by the survey was that the majority of the parents interviewed were prepared to accept a considerable part of the responsibility for educating their children.* Over 70 percent said that they would be willing to help in school, if allowed. Further detailed questions asking parents to rate the importance of specific ways in which they might help the infant school, if asked, showed gains at posttest where children were involved in the help parents may give. Items such as 'supervising children in the playground', 'acting as an assistant during lessons', 'taking groups of children for lessons', all showed gains which could be linked to the work of visitors encouraging parents to see their role as educators.

A major area of interest contained in the survey was concerned with speech and language, and it was in these items that the greatest differences between pretest and posttest emerged. Children in the visiting schemes more frequently asked their parents for the meanings of words than in the control group. Closed schedules (Brandis 1970, Henderson 1969) were used to measure the parents' knowledge of the meanings of words. They yielded

*This finding confirms the earlier experience of all the EPA Projects since the majority of families visited were from social classes 4 and 5.

some evidence that parents were becoming more aware of the need to use words carefully with their children.

The survey was designed to record what was happening to the educational home visitors as well as the families during the first operational year. A semistructured interview was carried out with each visitor towards the end of this period. Question areas included: reaction of parents to the scheme; intrusion of family life; methods of dealing with social problems; reactions of children to the schemes; children's abilities to learn at home; curriculum content; use of school and home resources; reactions of school staffs; demands placed on visitors by schools and parents; developments in the schemes; balance obtained between educational and social tasks.

The results of the interviews largely reinforced the evidence obtained from the parents' questionnaires. All the visitors noted changes in the ways that parents talked to their children, provided books and toys, and adopted a more overt educational role. One visitor was disturbed by the apparent unwillingness of nursery staff in her school to recognize the formal educational work she had already carried out with incoming children. This is, of course, a familiar phenomenon at other stages in the educational system, extending from nursery classes to university classes, but the problem seemed particularly poignant in a supposedly integrated scheme.

In some schemes parents began to come into school to meet other mothers and fathers, or to help run playgroups. Visitors who left kits of materials in homes found that they were well used. The types of materials preferred most varied between areas. Asian families, for instance, did not like using clay and paint which they felt were messy. In some schemes for very young children, it was difficult to provide suitable toys and equipment; consequently, visitors built up their own banks of homemade items and domestic materials.

Liaison with other agencies varied considerably. We coined the term 'educational home visitor' very early in the West Riding schemes, to help allay possible misunderstanding by other field workers. In these areas, the schemes were set up with little interdepartmental discussion, just prior to local government reorganization. Much of the early liaison was left to the home visitors to establish with colleagues in other social agencies. In most cases, however, social workers, educational welfare officers, and health visitors soon adopted a good working relationship with them. The Birmingham schemes were set up in collaboration with social work and health agencies. As a result, the team of visitors were seen from the start as a complementary resource for families living under considerable social pressure.

The most disturbing response during the interviews with school-based visitors centred around the reactions of class teacher colleagues. Predictably there was initial suspicion about the merits of working with young children in their homes. Comparisons were made between the numbers of children to be taught in class and the 'one-to-one' ratio enjoyed by the visitors.* However, some of the visitors found greatest difficulty when they were confronted by the attitudes of colleagues to the families being visited. The visitors were all newly appointed, and were unaware of the heritage of relationships between their schools and some families. They sometimes found themselves defending the values of families in the face of those projected by the staff. Perceptions of families based on hearsay evidence and classroom behaviour had to be challenged by the visitors' first-hand knowledge of the people with whom they were working. This sometimes caused an uneasy alliance in the staff room between the visitors and their colleagues, and it also raised the ethical problem of confidentiality. Not only were they having to develop operational skills in work which was not very clearly defined, but they were also trying to promote an untried strategy amongst their colleagues.

It was clear from the interviews that visitors gained great support from the families they visited. They were warmly accepted by the families who often identified them as friends offering a special service. Only two families withdrew during the initial period of the schemes from September 1973 – June 1974. Many of the families looked forward to their weekly sessions with the visitors. Towards the end of the first year parents were organizing their own resources through toy libraries, book and clothing exchanges, and group meetings in their homes or at school.

The survey underlined some of the operational dilemmas raised in the EPA experimental programme. How could an educational home visitor best obtain professional support or supervision? What qualities and training should be required for the work? How many families should a visitor be expected to include on her list? Who should establish new schemes and by what process? How necessary are kits of materials and toys to the schemes? What criteria for selecting families should be used? Many of these questions

*During the first year, ten home visitors regularly met 377 children in the families. In addition many neighbours' and relatives' children 'dropped in' during home-visiting sessions.

were considered in detail by later schemes and a number of solutions have been established.

The question which emerged with compelling insistence from the survey was, 'What are the schemes trying to do?' The concept which permeated most schemes was associated with compensating for subcultural deficiencies, in order to provide the children with skills to function adequately in a wider society. The school-based schemes were in a strong position to exert influences and expectations on families. In the words of one head mistress who was considering appointing an educational home visitor, 'If we can catch the children young enough, then we have a chance of moulding them into our ways successfully.' Fortunately, this rationale was not evident in any of the original schemes or in those which were subsequently established.

Critics of home-visiting schemes have emphasized the intrusive nature of the strategy. Clearly, it does offer great potential for exerting cultural influences which may be unfamiliar to the families, and simultaneously projecting control mechanisms into working-class populations. The survey provided much evidence that, by working with the parents, the visitors were able to affect the cultural norms of the families. There is no doubt, however, that they were equally influenced by the families and were able to think in terms of a learning partnership between the families and themselves. Many of the visitors realized that they were trying to blend the expert knowledge of parents about their own children with their professional skills, not only for the benefit of the families, but also to stimulate the schools. In schools where understanding and support for the work of the visitors existed, changes began to occur in their relationships with local communities.

Further developments

In November 1976, the sixth conference for educational home visitors recorded an expansion both in school-based and independent schemes.* A number of LEAs had appointed visitors, mainly through urban programme grants. The appointments were usually to school staffs but the work of the visitors varied, as the following examples show:†

*The conferences began in 1973 as a means of reducing isolation experienced by the first group of visitors and to inform others interested in home-visiting schemes.
†Extract from the report on the sixth national conference held at Waltham Forest, 1976 (Mimeo.).

educational visitor visits each family weekly for one term, (lists range from 12 – 25 families), educational objectives;

educational visitor visits entire intake group of families weekly for one year prior to nursery or infant class, educational objectives;

educational visitor makes visits to all families on intake list, but phases out visits to homes where parents have taken up the idea of working with their children; she then concentrates on one-parent or isolated families;

educational visitor encourages parents to come into school with their children after visits which introduce the school to the family;

educational visitor works with class teachers who refer children presenting difficulty (learning or behavioural) in school;

educational visitor works with individual families, but also organizes group meetings for mothers and children, toy libraries, etc.;

educational visitor works with a small group of schools and visits families within their respective catchment areas, mainly in response to requests by teachers. Often involved in promoting the school to parents who previously appear to have shown little interest.

The Inner London Education Authority established the Deptford Educational Home Visiting Project in September 1974. This project combined the resources of a nursery school, an adult education institute, and a team of educational visitors. In common with earlier schemes, it aimed to develop the teaching triangle of parent, child, and teacher. Considerable emphasis was placed on helping parents to develop their skills as educators in order to help children achieve their full potential. In contrast to other schemes, the ILEA project provided an introductory training programme and regular support meetings for the visitors. It also included a monitoring and evaluation programme (Jayne, E. 1976, 1977). A further development was the establishment of volunteer visitors, mainly recruited from mothers who previously had been receiving visits from the professional team. Supportive training and back-up has played a vital part in the ILEA project, both for the volunteers and the professional visitors. This probably reflects the influence of the adult education input to the work.

By the 1976 conference, however, there was general agreement that educational home visitors were concerned equally with adult and child education. They required the necessary skills to work with both age-groups in a variety of settings. Most visitors had established regular meetings for parents in community halls or schools, and many had helped to set up playgroup and other facilities for young children and their mothers. Although the school-based schemes continued to reach out into their catchment areas promoting education, some began to build on the resources of local people to foster community initiatives.

Independent projects such as Home Link (Bell, S. and Burn, C. 1976), Home Start (Harrison, M. 1976) and SCOPE (Poulton, G. 1977) had all begun to influence the provision of family services. They, too, were community-based, but from the outset of their work they utilized the skills of local people to provide the main force for change and development in service for families with young children. While these projects aimed to reach the children by raising the parents' consciousness of their own educational and social capabilities, they all emphasized membership of an organization which was locally controlled. Their emphasis was on family support and growth, rather than on the child- or parent-orientated approaches of earlier schemes. They all included a major element of home visiting in their work but other activities and services have grown out of needs expressed by the families involved. Similarly, the Lothian Region Home Visitor Programme (Raven et al. 1979) was centrally concerned to provide family support, and to assist parents realize their own ability to influence the qualities of their children's intellect and character.

In the case of SCOPE, which was formally established in 1976 by a group of people involved in an *ad hoc* visiting scheme* and some interested professionals from social agencies, rapid growth has occurred during the past three years. From the outset, it seemed important to the founder members that three elements should be built into the work: first, the concept of care and support for everyone involved; second, the concept of education, stemming initially from the environments of families and neighbourhood groups; and third, the concept of autonomy for individuals and groups. These three concepts were seen to be interdependent in the work (Poulton, G. 1978, 1979).

Many of the mothers who joined SCOPE had been subjected to prolonged stress. As a result, some had succumbed to quite intense states of depression, which effectively reduced their self-concept in a number of roles. In consequence, their children often were not able to experience a consistent, loving relationship with an adult at crucial times during their

*This work was pioneered by Lin Poulton with limited backing from the Department of Adult Education, University of Southampton.

early years of development. In some families stress arose from complex and conflicting relationship patterns. More frequently, however, environmental factors appeared to have induced states of stress and depression. Factors included insufficient income to meet high electricity bills, rent or hire-purchase repayments – usually following occupation of a new house, unemployment, or loneliness experienced by young mothers distanced from relatives and friends on large housing estates. For some mothers, a combination of these factors made them feel unable to cope with the demands of family life at times. A visit to the doctor might bring respite through prescribed drugs, but such treatment could only ameliorate the symptoms and could not remove the cause of the anxiety state. SCOPE attempts to offer a supportive network of care during times when families are functioning at a low ebb.

By learning to establish relationships within a group of mothers it was possible for individuals to regain autonomy in their actions and thinking. So within local groups, each with its crèche for the children, the three elements of care, education, and autonomy can be combined. The convenors of each group have responsibility for encouraging a group consciousness to emerge, but they are also expected to visit the members in their homes if necessary.

Although the work of SCOPE's thirteen groups is its central function, an organizational structure has been devised to allow each group to retain its autonomy while also receiving support from the federated efforts of all the groups. The coordinator has overall responsibility for bringing this about. In other words, one full-time professional acts as a sustaining agent, through a constellation of groups, for roughly five hundred families. The work has diversified to include fathers in social functions and group sessions. Secondary school pupils take part in discussions at group meetings and help in the crèches. Residential accommodation is now available for families who require a break during periods of extreme tension and stress.

The organization has remained an independent agency controlled by its members. They determine the policy, administer funds, and maintain its activities through a management committee, to whom the coordinator is accountable. In consequence, a very wide range of educational tasks has to be faced by the members, from child development within families to group and management functions. Many of these functions cross the boundaries of statutory services for families, and continue the year round without interruptions for school holidays, etc.

SCOPE may seem to be only distantly related to the work of the pioneer educational home visitors. It recognizes the family as the most effective and economical system for fostering the development of the child. In common with other programmes, it tries to convey through home visits and group sessions a belief in the potential of parents as the child's first educators. Where social pressures block this message, most schemes attempt to find ways of alleviating such stress. SCOPE places much emphasis on parents having the confidence to make their own decisions, to value themselves, to feel valued, and to encourage the same feelings in others. The starting point is the family's view of life. All SCOPE can do is to bring into focus a wider range of possibilities and futures than the family previously had been able to recognize. The eventual route taken by the family must be its own conscious choice. It can make that choice, however, in the knowledge that a wider universe of friends is available to offer support, should it be required.

Summary

Home-visiting schemes operate in a variety of ways, as the previous pages indicate. Their development has been closely linked to the influences and changes which have occurred in early education during the past decade. Emphasis on early intervention to compensate for cultural deficiencies experienced by some children has given way to programmes which offer families social as well as educational resources. For many years there has been 'progressive fragmentation and isolation of the family in its child rearing role' (Bronfenbrenner 1978). Not surprisingly, therefore, agencies working with young children have turned their attention to the needs, aspirations, and resources of the whole family.

Most educational visitors have experienced conditions of work in homes where standards of hygiene and cleanliness contrast sharply with those found in schools. In spite of the differences in working conditions, all the educational visitors have accepted the challenge of their job and have effectively conveyed their commitment to the families through a very high and consistent standard of work. It is now recognized that they require regular professional support, possibly following the social work model of supervision. They also require a form of training which equips them to work with very young children as well as adults, both individually and in groups. Current information on the work of other social agencies and procedures used to cope with family problems is essential (Poulton, G. and Campbell, G. 1979). In addition, meetings which allow the exchange of information, sharing of experience, consideration of theories, and reflection on achievements are most important if the strategy is to develop.

The experimental nature of the EPA work provided an expectation that further development of educational home visiting could be measured in quantifiable terms, to support the premise that long-term gains in children's performances would result from the strategy. Parents have become involved in their children's education and children have started school confidently as a result of the schemes, but no longitudinal studies have been made, so far, to test the long-term effects of the work. For many families, the immediate effects of receiving a series of regular visits from a sympathetic, friendly person have adequately justified the establishment and running of the schemes. By taking educational services to people in neighbourhoods, they have added an extra dimension to the work of schools and playgroups.

References

Armstrong, G. (1975), 'An experiment in early learning', *Concern* 18.

Bell, S. and Burn, C. (1976), *A Kind of Challenge: The Story of Home Link*.

Brandis, W. (1970), 'The relationship between social class and mothers, orientation towards communication and control', Appendix III, *Social Class Language and Communication*.

Bronfenbrenner, U. (1974), 'Is early intervention effective?' in Clarke, A.M. and Clarke, A.D.B. (eds.), *Early Experience: Myth and Evidence*, Open Books.

Bronfenbrenner, U. (1978), 'Who needs parent education?', *Teachers Record*, Vol.79, 4.

Cicirelli, V.G. et al. (1969), *The Impact of Head Start on Children's Cognitive and Affective Development*, Westinghouse Learning Corporation.

Harrison, M. (1979), *Home Start*: Report on its development from November 1977 – March 1979, Leicester Council of Voluntary Service.

Henderson, D. and Bernstein, B. (1969), 'Social class differences in the relevance of language to socialisation', *Sociology*, 3, pp. 1-20.

Jayne, E. (1976, 1977), *Deptford Educational Home Visiting Project*, Inner London Education Authority.

Levenstein, P. (1972), 'Verbal interaction project: aiding cognitive growth in disadvantaged pre-schools through the Mother – Child Home Program, 1 July 1967 – 31 August 1970', *Research in Education*.

Poulton, G. and James, T. (1975), *Pre-school learning in the Community*, Routledge & Kegan Paul.

Poulton, G. (1975), *Educational Visiting in England*, unpublished M.A.(Ed) dissertation, Southampton University.

Poulton, G. (1977, 1978, 1979), *SCOPE for parents and children*, annual reports, Dept. of Sociology & Social Administration, Southampton University.

Poulton, G. and Campbell, G. (1979), *Families With Young Children*, report on a Hampshire-based study project, Southampton University/Hampshire County

Council/Hampshire Area Health Authority.

Raven, J. et al. (1979), 'Evaluation of the Lothian Region Educational Home Visitor Programme', *Scottish Council for Research in Education*, 51st Annual Report.

Schaefer, E. (1969), 'Children under three – finding ways to stimulate development', *Children*, Vol.16, 2, pp. 59-61, March-April 1969.

Smith, G. (ed.) (1975), *Educational Priority*, Vol.4, The West Riding EPA Project, HMSO.

Smith, G. and James, T. (1975), 'The effects of preschool education: some American and British evidence', *Oxford Review of Education*, Vol.1, 3, pp 223-240.

PART FIVE

Aspects of Organization

CHAPTER 19

ETHICAL AND POLITICAL ASPECTS OF COUNSELLING AND SOCIAL WORK IN SCHOOLS

Tony Marshall

Part Five is devoted to organizational aspects of home-school relations, and begins with a perceptive account of some of the less obvious features of counselling and school social work, based on a significant recent study.

Welcoming resented intrusions

In 1975, the late Professor Gordon Rose and I published an account of a seven-year study of an experimental school social work scheme in Lancashire. That research concentrated on two problems: what was the effect of the school social worker on the children who were clients, and what difficulties were there in implementing social work within an educational organization? The first question addressed the issue of whether school social work was a worthwhile innovation, the second, the issue of how best to initiate and organize such a scheme.

The answer to the first question took the form of empirical results showing reductions in delinquency rates for the four experimental schools compared with two control schools, and improvements both in behaviour (as perceived by others) and in test-based scores of social adjustment for children dealt with by the social workers. The size of the differences was sufficiently great to justify more extensive adoption of the programme, especially as measures of possible side-effects revealed no disadvantages.

Further details of the findings, however, revealed some results which might have appeared surprising to professional social workers. First, despite substantial differences between the four workers involved in terms of the extent of their social work training and their previous experience, there were no differences between them in the measured success rates.

Second, efforts of the local police juvenile liaison officers supervising similar children apparently produced even *better* results, despite minimal training in casework. And third, test scores of children's self-reported 'personal adjustment' (basically indices of self-esteem or lack of anxiety) were not worsened, but neither were they improved, by social work intervention.

Although these findings are discussed in the book and elsewhere (Rose and Marshall 1975), further consideration leads me to believe that we failed to draw out their full implications. The reliance we then placed on measured individual effects I now think was misplaced, not only on account of the technical problems of measurement and of experimental control in the social sciences, but because evaluation of the worth of a proposed policy involves more than just a consideration of its possible effects. Moreover, these other considerations are of greater importance in decision-making. (These arguments have been presented more fully in Marshall et al., 1978, which deals with the general problems of evaluation.)

In the present chapter I intend to explore the wider issues raised by school social work. These are essentially of an ethical and political nature and not readily amenable to quantitative research. The book by Gordon Rose and myself was largely written from the point of view of the two professions involved – social work and teaching. Comparatively neglected were the viewpoints of the pupils and their families, whose preferences and needs one might have thought to be salient to a scheme ostensibly introduced to serve them.

Any community scheme like this is inevitably a pluralistic one, involving many different interested parties, each with their own perspectives, needs, and resources, and such a situation cannot be adequately analysed from a single point of view. This emerges particularly clearly in the present case, in the appendix to Rose and Marshall (*op.cit.*) which was contributed by two of the social workers involved (Bob Adamson and Pauline Avery), although again, quite naturally, the perspective of the social worker – the 'faith of the counsellors' (Halmos 1966) – is the dominant one.

In this plural situation, not all groups, or interests, have the same degree of power to represent their views. The neglect we have already noted of the pupil's perspective in most discussions of school social work reflects the fact that the pupil is the lowest of the interested parties in the hierarchy of power. Parental views are more likely to be considered, but even these often carry little weight against the power of the professional educationalists, the teachers. Such power differentials operate subtly, and in such a way as to lead to unconscious bias in the evaluation of the scheme, even among researchers who believe in their own neutrality. By focussing on measures of child misbehaviour, or maladjustment to adult, more especially teacher, demands as criteria for our research, we were essentially adopting the viewpoint of the school, with its need to maintain control over the activity of its pupils. A successful scheme from such a point of view could be antagonistic to, say, the real interests of the children. A fair evaluation must consider the viewpoints of all interested parties, and most of all of the group who constitute the 'target' for the attempts to change people, for they are the most crucially affected.

Kelman and Warwick (1978) list four major ethical issues for the assessment of a scheme: the choice of goals, the definition of the target, the choice of means, and the assessment of consequences. All may involve value-judgements and different perspectives associated with different groups, although the more powerful ones may find their best interests are served by pretending otherwise. Warwick writes:

> Very often, in an effort to get on with practical action, the values underlying both the definition of the problem and the terminal state are treated as obvious or are glossed over as matters of science. Closer analysis usually shows that from an ethical and political standpoint these questions are considerably less obvious and neutral than they are made out to be.

Typically the goals of social intervention are amorphous. Commenting on the definition of goals for organizational development practices, such as 'organizational health', Warwick points out that these

> are amenable to widely varying conceptual and operational definitions. This ambiguity gives rise to serious ethical dilemmas. What is health for the manager or owner may well be disease for the worker. These definitional problems are compounded by disparities in power within the organisation. In the typical organisation development intervention, some parties, especially management, are in a much better position than others to impose or sell their own interpretations of these polymorphous end-states.

Speaking more generally, Bermant and Warwick argue that social interventions, ostensibly aimed at correcting some unsatisfactory state of affairs, may serve only to maintain the status quo in various ways. For example, they may

a reinforce management's image of responsibility and concern
b accept unquestioningly dominant definitions of targets and problems
c redirect protest into symbolic activity (e.g., into emotional expression

rather than practical action)

d encourage efforts to adjust to the established system (pragmatism)

e gather information on dissent or deviance which will help management to assert social control.

Any social intervention must, by definition, constitute an alteration to the current pattern of resource distribution and is thereby a political act. It may be introduced with various degrees of compulsion, which Kelman and Warwick rank along a dimension from coercion, through manipulation and persuasion to mere facilitation, i.e., the provision of a service or resources which people will be free to use or not as they choose. This dimension is used as a basic evaluative criterion by the contributors to the volume edited by Bermant, Kelman, and Warwick (1978), two of whose key questions are, 'In setting goals, who speaks for the person, group, or community that is the target of the change effort?'; and, 'In selecting the means, how does one assure genuine participation to the people who are its targets?'

Once a scheme has been initiated, however, its characteristics do not remain static. In the given context, it will become the focus of a competitive political struggle between interested parties, each intent on making use of this new resource for its own purposes, or at least limiting the degree to which the intervention will interfere with its usual practices. This struggle may be far from apparent, proceeding in such a subtle way that some parties may not even become aware of the availability of this new potential resource for some time, and often proceeding without any overt conscious effort on the part of the groups concerned. To the intervention agents themselves, however, subject to multiple cross-pressures and influences, the reality of this situation will usually be only too apparent, for it is they who are forced to make the accommodations which represent the ultimate balance of conflicting interests that will be served. Moreover, it is during this process that the intervenors find themselves faced with the most crucial ethical problems, juggling professional values with the demands of other groups.

The social workers in the Lancashire experiment were undoubtedly subjected to just such an experience. As representatives of a profession stressing sympathy and personal support, they constituted a resented intrusion into an organization structured around very different ends (though not necessarily incompatible ones). Interviews with teachers before the arrival of the social workers indicated quite a high level of criticism of the idea and much concern. Nevertheless, the experience of the workers once in post was not one of antagonism or general uncooperativeness, as Adamson and Avery point out, but one of ready acceptance 'on a personal level at least'. Once the resented intrusion became a reality it was necessary to welcome it with open arms, if this resource was not to become a threat to the status quo.

The rest of this paper will be concerned with some of the key incidents and issues which illustrate the ethical dilemmas the school social worker faces, and the constellation of political influences which determined what sort of intervention it turned out to be, and whose ends it really served, in the case studied.

Whose problems are yours?

The goals of the Lancashire school social work experiment were ambiguous in their origin. Primarily an attempt by various groups, including the church and the police, to introduce measures which would reduce juvenile misbehaviour of all kinds, its focus was blurred by the addition of the 'social work' component. Ostensibly a service to youngsters and their families, social work is at the same time moulded in its practices, values, and aims by a professional ethic which does not derive from the groups it is meant to serve. To some extent, too, it is opposed (in its encouragement of self-expression and self-assertion) to the increase in social control that others expect from it.

Thus, the existence of various demands and intentions can be perceived in the very origin of the idea. Focussing on schools as a way of facilitating contact with the necessary age-group introduced further aims and interests unrepresented in the original plans.

The following discussion is orientated around the principal interest groups involved with the experiment – the pupils, families, teachers, other bodies, and school social worker – although of course they are interrelated and it is in the interaction between them that the crucial problems emerge.

The pupils

Although pupils were always the main targets of the scheme and provided its rationale, being the lowest group in terms of resources and social power they were not consulted about the services they needed or the form the intervention should take. There are, to be sure, problems of explaining such issues to individuals below a certain level of understanding and of obtaining responsible decisions from them. Nevertheless, these were secondary school children, and the scheme would directly affect them. They were thought capable (and indeed were) of answering long, written questionnaires about themselves and of doing this conscientiously, so that some degree of consultation was certainly feasible. Although, if asked, they might not have opposed the existence in school of a person they could consult in order to talk over personal problems, they would undoubtedly have put greater stress, as a response to their own needs, on the provision of other kinds of facilities, particularly recreational ones, or on a reform of the school system making syllabuses more relevant and providing greater freedom of choice. Such measures would have been of general benefit, however, and one can make out a case for provision aimed at the more disadvantaged pupils. Nevertheless, such provision may increase their problems if it becomes associated with social stigma.

Given that the scheme was to take the form of the introduction of a school social worker, we can see in practice how this resource was employed by the children, and use this observation as an index of how valuable they themselves found it. The origin of the scheme, without consultation and in some cases without any general announcement of the social worker's arrival, meant that for a long time there was little knowledge in any of the schools among the children that such person existed, yet alone any realization that this was someone who could be approached at will and be asked for help. Even when the workers were more established, staff use of them as a means of referring 'difficult', 'odd', or poor children inevitably gave the impression that this person was not one the normal child should approach. Adamson and Avery (*op.cit.*) state that the avoidance of this kind of stigma was difficult, and that they sought to overcome it by clarifying their role among the children. This raises ethical problems of possible misrepresentation. While the social workers genuinely wanted to provide help and support to all kinds of children, they were inevitably used by teachers to deal with a more selected group, and therefore to perform a rather different function. The children perceived this, and realized that being seen to consult with the social worker would lead to themselves possibly being labelled by fellow pupils and by teachers as 'having something wrong with them'. For the social worker to encourage them to come by representing the situation otherwise might inspire false confidence which would later be regretted.

Another problem was that of confidentiality. Although this was always preserved in essential matters (apart from the high visibility of the child who was visiting, or being visited by, the social worker), Adamson and Avery report that they were subjected to pressure from teachers to divulge what they discovered. They perceived this pressure as having some legitimacy:

> Clearly if a social worker based in a school is going to expect teachers to pass on information quite freely to her about their charges, then it would be quite unrealistic and unfair to hope that they will not want information about the same children in return . . . on many occasions also, it will clearly be to the child's own benefit for his teachers to be made aware of his difficulties, so that they can seek to help in their own work with him. (*op.cit.*)

I do not think, however, that this could justify a breach of confidentiality in any circumstance. There is yet again a failure to conceive of consulting with the central party to the affair – the children themselves. Does a particular client want a certain teacher to know some fact or other he/she has revealed to the social worker? This surely should be the sole criterion; nor should the child be subject to any pressure to agree to such a revelation.

Although the numbers of children consulting the social worker of their own accord were always small (an important fact in itself when judging the scheme), the reasons for the few that did were very different from those applying when children were referred by others. The great bulk of the latter were selected for their long-standing behaviour, whether criminal, disruptive, infrequently attending school, or whatever. The children who came for their own reasons, according to Adamson and Avery, were either lonely or craving adult attention; or else they were normal children faced with crises (at home, school, or with boy/girl friends, for instance) or faced with difficult decisions (career problems, etc.) at that particular time. They came, then, for advice, discussion, support, or just company. The school-based social worker, as Adamson and Avery note, is well placed to provide this kind of service, being 'more likely to be available to listen to the child's problems in private at the time when the child is feeling distressed and looking for this kind of help' than the teacher or external social worker. This is true, and it is perhaps unfortunate that so little of their time was used in this way, for the children's interests, as we shall see, were only one part, and a relatively small part, of the set of demands on the social worker.

The families

The experiment was conceived as providing a home-school link, and the social worker was expected to spend a good deal of time liaising with families or pupils. There is some conflict of functions here, as casework duties stemming from referrals were likely to lead to a concentration on a few problem families, while the home-school link would imply contacts across the board. Again, there is a conflict between the interests of the whole group and those of the more disadvantaged members. In actual fact, all contact with families, although deemed important by most parties, was very limited because of time constraints which followed from in-school demands on the worker. Like the pupils, families were not given a great deal of information about the experiment. Typically, an announcement was made at the parent-teacher association which would reach only a few, and only those families which already had strong connections with school; or a circular was sent home with each child, which in most cases would make little impression. Few families sought out the social worker. The latter's day-to-day contacts were dominated by those who, by force of circumstances, were seen most often – the teachers. This gave teachers the power to represent their needs as the most compelling.

Parents' needs are likely to be very different from their children's. The latter's self-perceived problems, particularly at secondary school age, are likely to be related in some way to difficulties in relations with parents. Parental concern, on the other hand, is likely to be with what they see as their children's misbehaviour and waywardness as they attempt to cope with growing demands for independence. Parents seeking the social worker's aid are likely to expect help with controlling the child, not with supporting his/her demands. The social worker is thus caught up in a situation of conflicting needs. In helping untangle such problems does he/she take the child's or parent's side, or attempt to remain somewhere in between, conciliatory towards both? Although most would generally adopt the last course, this could be the least satisfactory to both parties, attempting to foster a mutual adjustment which is incompatible with the need for increased mutual independence. Adamson and Avery recognize the problem that stems from the fact that one party to a conflict-relationship may approach the social worker for help, that is, to reinforce their own position, only to regret later the revelations they have made, as, for example, when a parent requests help to cope with a misbehaving child, only to find that the social worker begins to delve into the causes for this behaviour and represents it as the result of parental deficiencies or mismanagement. The social worker appears to be representing a service to individuals, but is found in practice to act as a mediator, eschewing advocacy for any particular point of view.

Relations between schools and parents tend to be competitive ones. In the Lancashire experiment, schools remained firmly in control and parents had little effective say in how the schools were run. In other parts of the country, and perhaps increasingly nowadays, parents may have much more influence over teachers' behaviour. In such areas, one could expect parental pressures on a school social work scheme to be much more in evidence.

The teachers

Although ostensibly a service to children and their parents, social work located in a particular organization becomes a servant of the purpose of that organization, or of those who work in it. From the beginning, the marriage of education and social work was an uneasy one. It was imposed without any felt need on the part of the schools for such a service. To them the move represented a maldistribution of resources: any extra money injected into the schools would be better spent on providing more teachers and lowering pupil-teacher ratios. As Adamson and Avery say,

> It is very difficult with classes as large as they still are in ordinary schools for even the most sympathetic teachers to maintain a wholly positive relationship with all their pupils. . . . Even those members of staff who accept that what we are seeking to do as social workers is worthwhile, may sometimes find a little precious our insistence that we need time and privacy to conduct relaxed interviews with individual children, considering their own profession's lack of success in winning for them the conditions really ideal for teaching. (*op.cit.*)

Nevertheless, given that the intrusion was a *fait accompli*, it was ultimately welcomed for the advantages that it could procure. It was, after all, an addition to the schools' potential resources, even if not of the kind they sought. In our interviews with the teachers, we discovered that their major concern was with *control*. Children must limit their freedom of self-expression to make group teaching feasible, to bring order to the organization. Those who upset these expectations frustrate teachers' attempts to educate, increase the proportion of their time that will be, from their point of view, wasted, and increase the psychological pressure they are under. Loss of control is one of the teacher's basic fears. It is hardly surprising, then, that they tried to recruit the social worker's help in this vital process. The misbehaving children are the ones with social or personal problems, it is reasoned, and if the social worker is going to deal with them, perhaps some good could come of it after all.

This theme even pervaded the introduction of the social worker to the school. The worker was there, one head master announced in assembly, to help children with their problems, and help the staff with their problems too! That statement had a beautiful ambiguity. One could hardly believe he expected his teachers to become clients of the school social worker, however. *Their* problems, in other words, were the children with problems. Another head announced that 'from henceforward the truants had better watch out because someone was watching them'. Such an image is not calculated to persuade truants to consult with the social worker as a friendly confidant. The schools obviously had a great deal of power over the way that the experiment would be represented, and made use of this to ensure that their needs would be served. It was not unknown, indeed, for a class teacher to *threaten* a miscreant with referral!

The process of incorporation had thus begun. New to schools and their pupils, the social workers also depended on the staff for their initial workloads, which were overwhelmingly composed of children whose behaviour disrupted the orderly system. Even several years later this would still hold, and most referrals would still come from the staff, whether formally or picked up by the social worker in more casual conversation with teachers. In one school, for a while, the social worker's room was situated in a corridor out of bounds to the children. There was thus no doubt where the dominant power lay or the force of the pressures exerted. One social worker was adamant that he would not take on a teaching load at all – although this was accepted in the original plans – because of the necessary conflict between controlling a class and providing support to individual children. Nevertheless, within a short time, he was teaching several periods a week. If the staff were to accept a social worker, the social worker had to be one of them, sharing their problems.

Not all a teacher's time is taken up with controlling children. Once a system of order and mutual expectations is established, control issues recede into the background and only erupt from time to time. Many teachers establish good personal relations with their pupils and perform what they term a 'pastoral care' role. This is possible, however, only insofar as it does not conflict with the need to maintain order; that is, only as long as the child does not break the established rules. Similarly, it can be accepted that the pastoral care aspect of the school be enlarged by means of the appointment of a social worker, as long as this does not begin to threaten the maintenance of order. Whereas the teacher knows just how far to go, he/she cannot be so confident that the social worker will not prove to constitute, even unintentionally, such a threat. If sympathetic and supportive towards delinquents, is the social worker thereby rewarding them for their bad behaviour? Adamson and Avery report a case where some teachers objected to delinquent children being allowed to join an after-school group organized by one social worker for some of her clients, because they conceived a referral as a punishment that should lead to withdrawal of privileges rather than their extension. In the secondary school especially, teachers will not always be grateful for the shy introvert encouraged to be less docile and to have greater self-confidence, who subsequently becomes more of a classroom problem, nor for the uncongenial and difficult truant who is persuaded to attend school more regularly. Despite the fuss made about low attendance rates, little encouragement is given to the disruptive child to want to come to school. His or her reappearance may even be the occasion for punishment for earlier failure to attend!

One great fear among school staff is that of the 'underground movement':

> Some teachers seem to feel that their lot is difficult enough without their pupils being allowed to leave lessons to have 'cosy chats' with the social worker . . . it is strongly felt in some quarters that this kind of facility will allow the known malingerers amongst the pupils to find a very ready excuse for missing the lessons they least enjoy. . . .
>
> Teachers unfamiliar with casework methods must be tempted, it seems to us, to feel that behind the closed doors of the interview room there is a sort of conspiracy going on between social worker and child. . . . He does not know what an individual child is saying about him, or what response these comments are getting from the social worker, and he realizes that he can only learn what in fact does take place to the extent that the social worker is prepared to take him into her confidence. (Adamson and Avery, 1975)

Other bodies

Various groups beyond the school may be affected by, or attempt to influence, a school social work scheme. In the present case, an obvious instance is the group of people representing various bodies responsible for initiating the venture. Beyond the point of initial conception, however, these bodies had little direct contact with the scheme and never interfered. The practical shape of the intervention only took place, as we have seen, much later on. These bodies, all with a stake in the established status quo, would no doubt have stressed the controlling functions of such an intervention, so that their influence, if felt, would have been little different from that of the teaching staff.

Social work agencies in the community were also potential interest groups, and problems of increased caseloads following referral from the school social workers and problems of interdepartmental rivalry did occur, especially in relation to the educational welfare service whose main attention was directed towards nonattendance. In other sorts of schemes, such external interests may be powerful obstructive or facilitative forces. In the Lancashire experience, they were relatively of less importance than some of the other parties discussed in this chapter.

The school social worker

Not the least of the influences on a school social work scheme is the orientation of the worker himself. Apart from a wide range of personal attitudes, the professional backgrounds or training of such workers promotes certain tendencies. Three of the chief ones may be characterized as:

a an orientation towards personal relationships in the analysis and the solution of social problems, as reflected in the individual casework approach rather than concern for the socio-structural aspects

b an uncritical, accepting stance towards the attitudes and behaviour of others manifested in the assumption of a supportive role towards clients

c encouragement of mutual accommodation between parties to a conflict

Worthy and relevant as these values may be, they do predispose social workers away from the political and wider social implications of the issues with which they deal. Where organizational deficiencies, structural constraints, and questions of rights may be concerned, the social worker will tend to seek out *individuals*' faults as those he/she is trained to operate upon. There is no absolute necessity for social work to assume such a restricted orientation, nor are social workers unaware of the sociological causes of many of the problems they confront. There is, moreover, a minority radical movement within social work which is critical of its traditional political neutrality. Given the individual casework bias to their training, in a hierarchical situation such as a school there will be substantial inhibitions imposed on any tendency to raise political or ethical issues, and encouragement only to be concerned with the personal deficiencies of those individuals defined as problems.

Given that referrals come overwhelmingly from higher power groups in the organization and are of lower power persons, there tends to be an unexamined assumption that the social worker's job is to help or to persuade such clients to adjust their personal behaviour or attitudes to the prevalent norms. Clients have 'gone wrong somewhere' and 'need to be reformed'. Adamson and Avery affirm their faith in the 'possibilities for change that each person carries within himself'. But as one client herself remarked very perceptively, 'You won't ask her [a teacher picking on her] to change, but you expect me to.' One does at least have to raise the question whether it is reasonable or ultimately useful to demand readjustment of the child kicking against an unjust or inadequate system, against unreasonable actions on the part of parents, teachers, or others. What would happen to a school social worker who became an advocate of children's rights, a critic of the school's streaming arrangements, or an opponent of an organization that tended to maximize the freedom and convenience of teachers at the expense of their service to the pupils or their families? (This is not to say that teachers should not have a certain degree of control over their work situation, if only to keep their sanity in what can be extremely trying situations; but one should question whether the social worker should serve such ends alone.)

Despite the apolitical, uncritical stance of most social workers, their assumption of supportive attitudes towards clients may bring them into conflict with the school's need to exert social control, by, for instance, making it more difficult to justify punitive measures against delinquents known to be suffering from traumatic home problems. While the school must adapt itself to some extent to the new professional values and the stress on nonpunitive methods, it is likely that the pressures for adjustment in attitudes and practices will be much greater on the lone alien social worker than on the established staff. Such adjustments they were, indeed, forced to make in the Lancashire scheme, although Adamson and Avery point out that 'Social workers in other settings, in probation and child care, for example, have had to make a similar adjustment between the use of the authority inherent in their roles and accepting, non-judgemental principles taught in their casework textbooks.' At times they felt obliged to go out of their way to demonstrate they were not overly 'soft-hearted'; and the atmosphere of the school, types of children referred, and restrictions of time available for casework, all combined to put a greater stress on behaviour modification and less on underlying problems than they would have liked.

Social work on a tight leash

We have seen, then, that neither the aims nor the methods of school social work can be regarded as clear-cut, and that the definition of these is dependent on one's point of view. In operation, such a scheme is beset by a plurality of group and individual interests which exert pressure for social work practice to be moulded in particular ways. We have seen that the child's need for a reliable, nondirective confidant conflicts both with parental desires for increased control at home and teachers' needs to maintain control at school. Within these major interest groupings, subgroups occur pulling in different directions. Adamson and Avery noted, for instance, the problem of separate cliques of teachers with different styles of work and attitudes, who competed for the social worker's support. In the course of this 'cold war', in which the methods of work of the school social worker are the battle ground, differences in the power of separate interest groups to secure their own ends are readily apparent. While the worker's own values play a role, pressures from school staff are certainly just as important, probably more so. Especially conducive to the success of the schools in shaping social work to their own interests is the virtual monopoly they have in presenting the new scheme to pupils and their families, in running the organization into which the new role must be fitted, and in selecting the children for particular attention. This influence was so pervasive in the Lancashire experiment as not only to set limits on the social workers' freedom of action but also to affect their attitudes to their job and their methods of working.

The introduction of a social worker was originally predicated – at least in their own minds – on the desirability of providing service to youngsters faced with social and personal difficulties, the complexity or severity of which might prevent them successfully being resolved without help and advice or active support. The school was merely to be the facilitative context. In the event, the scheme became primarily a service to the school staff, and a force for the maintenance of the status quo. It did this by representing, symbolically, the concern of the school for its pupils' problems without requiring any alteration in teachers' behaviour or school organization; by accepting goals of school management as primary; by emphasizing adjustment on the part of pupils (or families) rather than teachers or the school structure; and by representing behaviour which, to some extent, might be a reasonable protest against unfair or inadequate educational conditions as merely symptomatic of personal inadequacies or social background.

The bias in the evolution of these schemes was also reflected in the lack of consultation with pupils or their parents, and the resultant 'voting with their feet' of these two parties, who rarely initiated contacts with the social worker. It is plain that the social workers were regarded by potential clients not as a service, but as persons one had to deal with if unfortunate enough to be in trouble. While representing themselves as potential supportive agents, the social workers actually operated as mediators between conflicting interests, thus misleading themselves and others about their real role.

The outcomes recorded by our research are explicable in terms of this rationale. Success predominated in terms of behaviour control; there were no improvements in levels of personal adjustment, i.e., in terms of happiness or self-confidence or freedom from anxiety. Moreover, these successes were not dependent on social casework skills, as shown by the lack of differences between workers with vastly different experience, and by even greater apparent gains in terms of behaviour control achieved by police juvenile liaison officers.

This kind of situation poses substantial ethical problems. One could look for a resolution of such problems only in a situation where groups share a certain degree of consensus. The conflicts of interest outlined above, however, were more basic than that. Accepting this conflict, Laue and Cormick (1978) argue that the only excuse for intervention would be that one party is disadvantaged with respect to the ability to represent its interests, and that the only acceptable intention is to redress that balance. It would seem that the school social worker is not provided with the resources and power to carry out such a task. Nevertheless, a person has the responsibility in acting out such a role, as does any kind of practitioner, to 'remain alert to the possibility that he is imposing his own values on the client; that in the course of helping the client he is actually shaping his behaviour in directions that he, the practitioner, has set for him' (Kelman 1968); and, one might add, not only his own values but those also of the employing or containing organization.

I do not want to be unfair to school social workers who perform as honest, helpful, and worthwhile a task as difficult circumstances allow. I merely advocate that more thorough awareness of these ethical and political problems should inform those choices they *are* free to make, in particular in their dealings with children. The latter should be in no doubt about social workers' mediatory role and the limitations on their support, and they should encourage greater representation in the school itself of the pupil's needs and points of view.

References

Adamson, R. and Avery, P. (1975), 'School Social Work in Practice', in Rose and Marshall (1975), *op.cit.*

Bermant, G., Kelman, H., and Warwick, D. (eds.) (1978), *The Ethics of Social Intervention*, Wiley.

Bermant, G. and Warwick, D. (1978), 'The ethics of social intervention: power, freedom, and accountability', in Bermant et al. (1978), *op.cit.*

Halmos, P. (1966), *The Faith of the Counsellors*, Constable.

Kelman, H. (1968), *A Time to Speak: on human values and social research*, Jossey-Bass.

Kelman, H. and Warwick, D. (1978), 'The ethics of social intervention: goals, means and consequences, in Bermant et al. (1978), *op.cit.*

Laue, J. and Cormick, G. (1978), 'The ethics of intervention in community disputes', in Bermant et al. (1978), *op.cit.*

Marshall, T., Fairhead, S., Murphy, D., and Iles, S. (1978), 'Evaluation for Democracy', in *Social Research in the Public Sector*, European Society for Opinion and Marketing Research.

Marshall, T. and Rose, G. (1975), 'An experimental evaluation of school social work', *British Journal of Guidance and Counselling.*

Rose, G. and Marshall, T. (1975), *Counselling and School Social Work: an experimental study*, Wiley.

Warwick, D. (1978), 'Moral dilemmas in organisation development', in Bermant et al. (1978), *op.cit.*

CHAPTER 20

THE SOCIAL EDUCATION TEAM

Derek Birley

*Moving on to modes of interdepartmental cooperation in school welfare provision, this chapter reports the development of one of the earliest innovations – the area-based social education team – which was pioneered in Liverpool.**

Social education teams were not conceived as an organizational device. They were created because of an organizational problem, but one that we saw as a symptom and not as the disease itself. The problem that sparked off the development was, in fact, a familiar one: to which department should certain additional staff belong if appointed? It happened to arise in Liverpool and the year happened to be 1966, but it could well have been anywhere else and any time in recent years. So, too, could the situation revealed by the more detailed study that followed. There was tremendous activity amongst those educationalists and social workers concerned about children with handicaps. An ever-growing range of problems was being tackled by many different agencies, each with its own traditions and techniques. Some owed administrative allegiance to education, some to other services; some were statutory, some voluntary. Most had been set up in earlier days to meet specific needs as they had emerged. Their paths crossed frequently, but more by accident or impromptu effort than design. There were, for example, remedial teachers assigned to schools for short periods on an *ad hoc* basis; education welfare officers concerned mainly with attendance; doctors largely involved with medical inspection and the process of 'ascertainment' for special education; school nurses engaged on their own

*This is a revised version of a paper originally published in *Linking Home and School* (Longman 1972).

inspections and visiting homes as health visitors; a few psychologists and social workers dealing with child guidance by withdrawing children from school to attend clinics. Communication among them, and with the schools they served, was erratic.

All these were specialists disciplined to look at people from a particular angle, belonging to an administrative set-up that encouraged selection or rejection of 'cases' according to narrow terms of reference. Add to them the child-care officers, housing officials, probation officers, police, and various family casework agencies, all of whom might be concerned with a particular child, and there was every chance of confusion. A more fundamental weakness, though, was that this welter of specialisms tended to conceal the need to look at children's problems in the round. Children are human beings, not cases. They are also, of course, members of families and residents of particular districts. Here we could see another weakness. Certain areas of Liverpool had more than their share of social problems. The same districts came highest on the problem lists of several departments – in, for example, educational standards, housing, child care, health, social and psychological adjustment, school attendance, and observation of the law. Yet the logic of this had not been followed: the weight of tradition and compartmentalism sanctified prevailing practices with little regard for their relevance.

Most field workers saw the need for closer links with other agencies and many took the trouble to make personal contact with opposite numbers. But goodwill and individual effort were nowhere near enough to surmount the enormous obstacles: different allegiances, different methods, different objectives (or assumed objectives), different professional attitudes. And sometimes, since the people concerned were human, these attitudes seemed to conceal vested interests. More was needed than tinkering with the organization. It was not enough to ensure that educational psychologists were attached to the 'right' department: it had to cease to matter which had nominal responsibility for them. The most serious problems and the areas affected most had to have concerted, skilled attention. Children needed help early enough for it to do some good. In short, there had to be cooperation, not merely coordination, and this meant turning sterile inter-professional tensions to constructive ends. For we were not only dealing with a multiplicity of separate problems; there was an interrelationship between them that added a new dimension to the task. Social and psychological factors, emotional and behaviour difficulties led to educational mishaps, and vice versa. For many children there was a vicious circle of deprivation and performance, with the human and physical environment of home and school interacting to their increasing disadvantage. Any expert involved had to see particular handicaps as indicators, facets of a whole.

The social education team tried to meet this exacting requirement. A pilot exercise in a small part of the area in greatest need brought together a school doctor, a school nurse, an educational psychologist, a psychiatric social worker, a remedial teacher, and a group of education welfare officers. Initially, they worked with fourteen schools in a concerted attempt to seek out handicaps of every kind that came between children and their education. Their brief was to discover the source of trouble rather than clear up particular symptoms, to do so, if they could, at the incipient stage, and then collectively to decide what action to take. We tried as far as possible to use existing resources. (We had, as it happened, little choice, but in any event an unrealistic level of staffing would have reduced the experiment's predictive value.) Nor did we wish to threaten traditional allegiances. So the team members were part-time, spending much of their week on their usual duties. However, there had to be someone whose first allegiance was to the team, to see that it operated smoothly and to see that its purposes were kept before the members. It so happened that a long-felt need of the education service in Liverpool was for expert attention to the effect of social influences on educational performance; so the opportunity was taken to appoint a full-time education guidance officer for this work, and to ask him to act as leader of the social education team.

The team then began meeting once a week to discuss certain children from families thought to need special attention, to decide on lines of approach, and, if necessary, to call on other agencies. The children's officer, probation officer, chief welfare officer, director of housing, and chief constable were informed of the venture and asked to send representatives to join in the work. Once a month the team enlarged itself to meet these colleagues. This, as well as forming a simple, organized link between social work departments, also offered a much easier channel of communication between schools and the various agencies; instead of wondering which one to approach they need only turn to the education guidance officer. He was also a permanent link between meetings for all participants.

Aside from his function as team leader the education guidance officer's role was an extension of that of the education welfare officer. Poor school attendance is at once a handicap and an indicator, often the first, of something more seriously wrong; something that could stem from trouble at home, at school, in the child himself, or all three. Legal sanctions, even if effectively applied (and they rarely are), are usually irrelevant to this sort of situation. For these children it is much more important to find out the cause of the trouble. Many EWOs had long accepted this, but had to reconcile it with the traditional duty of keeping up a high average attendance at schools. The social education team could not, of course, resolve this dilemma, but by showing the importance of attendance as an indicator it helped make the EWOs' role a coherent one rather than an uneasy amalgam of police and welfare functions. Thereafter it tried to make systematic use of their considerable skill and experience in identifying and treating the small proportion in greatest need.

Apart from detection, the EWO also had a key role in linking home and school which the team saw as the first practical step to be taken. The EWO tried to build up a good relationship with the parents of a child in trouble, to create an atmosphere in the home in which parents would at least talk about the difficulties. Then, if possible, he tried to bring home and school closer together. He and the education guidance officer were the main means of communication in this: they tried to make contact not only with heads but with class teachers, not always a simple matter, particularly in primary schools. They were not, it must be emphasized, forging these links as an end in themselves. They were acting as essential links in a chain.

Because this contact had a specific purpose it seemed more likely to succeed (and more likely to happen) than generalized attempts to improve communcations. This principle was applied in all team-working, internal and external. Thus the connection regularly being demonstrated between learning and emotional or behaviour problems constantly reminded psychologists and their social workers of the importance of providing schools with reports on the progress of children receiving treatment. Children still had to be brought out of school to attend child-guidance clinics and psychologists were rarely able to get into schools; but the remedial teacher made regular visits, which, programmed by the team, were a useful link between psychologist and class teacher. (This worked so well that when a much enlarged remedial service was later set up it was organized in district teams corresponding with the social education teams, with which they were linked through the psychologist members.) It was naturally hoped that when more psychologists and social workers could be appointed they would visit schools themselves, but this would not lessen the specific value of the remedial teacher in demonstrating practically how intellectual, emotional, and social factors were interrelated.

The role in the team of the school doctor was naturally related basically to the effect of physical factors. Medical knowledge can sometimes put an entirely new complexion on a problem, and the doctor was often able to give valuable guidance. But most doctors learned a good deal of the families in their areas, about other than medical matters, and the pilot team were fortunate in having a doctor member who contributed substantially in this way. Similarly, the school nurse's visits to schools (for eye and cleanliness inspections, for instance) and her quasi-health-visitor relationship with many homes in the area made her an important contributor. These medical colleagues helped to enlist the aid of general practitioners and hospital services on many occasions.

There were no formal procedures of referral: it was left to the discretion of individual team members to decide what they could handle alone in conventional fashion and what to refer to the team. Nor were full team meetings the only means of operation. The education guidance officer could pass on a problem to an individual member or to an agency outside the team. Within the first few weeks, for instance, he consulted voluntary agencies such as the Family Service Units, the Young Volunteers of Merseyside, the Liverpool Personal Services Society, and such obvious sources of help as the hospital service and the Ministry of Social Security. In short this was not another new agency, competing for custom, but a cooperative association supporting and strengthening what existed.

A team is not a committee. This one did not demand that all problems be brought before the whole group and wait a week for the privilege. Nor, conversely, was it thought necessary for meetings to be held if there was nothing to discuss. Its terms of reference related to objectives rather than administrative frontiers. Of course, it was hoped that there would be operational advantages. Less time might be wasted passing pieces of paper or telephone messages to the various headquarters and back; there should be less confusion if left hands knew what right hands were doing. It would be a step towards common boundaries for the various field workers' districts: there would be easier links with schools and with other agencies. Team-working would make more effective and economical use of staff. But, beyond this, the team was the embodiment of an attitude, built up from the concept of collective solution of problems at the point of impact.

This short account inevitably omits a good deal. Ideally it should have been accompanied by discussion of the place of the scheme in Liverpool's total concept of educational and personal services, for ventures of this kind are of little use unless they form part of a sensitive, comprehensive, and consistent approach towards redressing inequalities of educational and social opportunity throughout all an authority's services. But that would have meant going far beyond the scope of this chapter.

Nor has any attempt been made at evaluation. Space apart, there is a fundamental difficulty in assessing the value of any scheme involving such complex interactions: cause and effect are hard to identify. This is not to say that the attempt should not be made. For the practising administrator, the consolations of philosophy often have to compensate for the absence of the perspectives of research, but there is a consequent risk of automorphism and self-fulfilling prophecy unless some appraisal is attempted. The problem is how to do it.

The question arose shortly after the original team was launched. The Corporation's management consultants were sufficiently impressed to recommend that complementary teams be set up in the authority's personal health and social services branches. The education committee were enthusiastic about the early results, and agreed to expand the scheme to provide five teams that between them would cover the whole city. Yet there was a nagging doubt, expressed particularly by certain academic critics, about the apparently existentialist fashion in which the notion was being applied and developed. The critics were brought into the process and an attempt was made at evaluation.* This proved useful in indicating the gradations of deprivation that existed through the city and thus suggesting future priorities of remedial action, but it could not, of course, provide objective measures for assessing what had been, or what was likely to be, done.

It is still not clear – to me at any rate – what criteria can fairly be applied to such a venture, or who is entitled and qualified to apply them. The connection with education is itself a guarantee of relativism, and the concern with the complex interrelationships of handicap – social, psychological, physical, intellectual, environmental, the adjectives can be multiplied freely – elaborates the labyrinth. With this in mind, it seemed important to try to build the principles of self-analysis and capacity for change into the struc-

*It is described in *An Equal Chance*, by Derek Birley and Anne Dufton (Routledge & Kegan Paul 1971), a study of interacting educational and social problems and of some of the possible remedies.

ture of the social education scheme, so that the teams themselves could, if properly supported by sensitive administration, evaluate the scheme by the way they developed.

What has happened since reinforces the argument. 'Recent major organizational and functional changes in the Health and Social Services,' writes Kenneth Tucker, Assistant Director for Special Services in the Liverpool Education Department, 'have had considerable repercussions for teamwork in practice, and have emphasised the important co-ordinative role played by the Education Guidance Officers. The potential for successful team-work essentially turns on the extent to which opportunities are afforded to practitioners from the various agencies to become personally known to each other, to work together over reasonably lengthy periods of time during which they can establish norms and procedures of inter-action in face-to-face, collaborative working situations. The effect of some of the changes has been at best, to place field-workers in a looser network rather than closer team-work relationships and in consequence rich inter-play has had to be worked for that much harder.'

This reminder of the ecology of educational and social services (which is often distinct from the ecology of educational and social handicap) suggests that the quest for reform through improved administrative organization which has been the preoccupation of so many postwar advisory committee reports, White Papers, and the like, is at best a will o' the wisp. At worst, interprofessional rivalries, from which field workers themselves are not immune, can use any given administrative structure as a stalking horse. Tucker points out the snags that arise when protective barriers are removed: 'Changes in and confusion over what were hitherto, albeit superficially, distinctive field practitioner roles have imposed greater strains while problems centred on professional autonomies have become more overt.'

He also hints at a possible remedy. 'There is obviously a message here for interprofessional training.' This notion presently seems in danger of moving from the list of radical but utopian innovations to the formulary for educational advance without actually being implemented. Yet though the years, including a decade in an institution that tries to provide interprofessional training, have induced scepticism about the likelihood of success, they have done nothing to lessen my conviction that there will be no major or general advance in combating educational disadvantage until this becomes the normal method of training. The simple requirement is that teachers and all those with whom they must afterwards work should come together for some part at least of their initial and in-service education. Until that happens, social education teams and similar ventures will remain experiments.

CHAPTER 21

SECONDARY SCHOOLS AND NEIGHBOURHOOD WELFARE AGENCIES

Daphne Johnson

Taking further some of the questions relating to interdepartmental cooperation raised in the previous chapter, this paper offers a probing analysis of the relationships of teachers and social workers, based on the author's current research.

Introduction

Secondary education for all, the National Health Service, and the new system of social benefits were the first offspring of the welfare state in the mid-twentieth century. Thirty years on we are living with second-generation institutions. The health and social services have been drastically reorganized; the tripartite system of secondary education has been almost entirely replaced by comprehensive secondary schools. Have the education, health, and social services grown closer together, or further apart? To what extent can the schools and the social and health agencies work together as a unitary welfare network? What are the possible pathways for development? This chapter will debate these questions in the light of a recent major research.*

The central focus of our discussion will be the comprehensive secondary school and its relationships both actual and potential with particular agencies, including the education welfare, school psychological, and child-guidance services, social work area teams, school health and health education services, and the juvenile bureau of the police.

Teachers in the comprehensive schools are gaining experience of the strengths and weaknesses of their own institutions. At the same time, they

*The Schools, Parents and Social Services Project (1974-1977), funded by the DES. See References at end of chapter.

are becoming aware of the adjacent activities of the many agencies which also have a concern for their pupils. There is an undoubted tension for the schools in operating as an integral part of a welfare network, while also providing a specialist service of secondary education. To understand the source of this tension, we must identify those elements in the work of comprehensive schools which link them into the welfare network or insulate them from it.

Collaborative research with teachers in outer London confirmed that, like secondary schools of an earlier form, comprehensive schools try to provide for the social and affective well-being of pupils, as well as for their cognitive development.

Teaching a range of subjects to public examination level remains a central task of the comprehensive schools; but a number of factors have increased the complexity of academic provision in the new schools, compared with those of the tripartite era. The wider range of pupil ability, the raising of the school-leaving age, and advances in specialized knowledge, all press towards a curriculum which combines diversification with specialization. To meet the developing demands of the comprehensive curriculum, teachers must keep abreast of new teaching material, methods, and technology. Effective secondary school teaching is a task requiring considerable professional expertise and adaptability.

Another characteristic development in comprehensive schools, perhaps also stimulated by the size and range of ability of pupil population, has been the setting up of pastoral systems. This institutionalization of pastoral care, through the delineation of pastoral roles, makes formal provision for identifying and meeting the affective needs of pupils. It is through its pastoral work that the comprehensive school is potentially a part of the welfare network of agencies concerned with the care and control of young people of secondary school age.

Pastoral work and pastoral systems

When the concept of pastoral care is operationalized as pastoral work, carried out by role-holders in a pastoral system, a number of tasks become the province of pastoral staff. Teachers in pastoral roles who collaborated in our research acknowledged seven areas of pastoral work:

1 to provide a secure base to which the pupil can relate within a large school
2 to identify and respond to any problems the pupil is experiencing as an individual

3 to monitor and regulate the attendance, punctuality, behaviour, and progress of each pupil
4 to systematize the recording and communication of information relevant to the welfare of individual pupils
5 to make recommendations about special educational needs of individual pupils
6 to interact with the pupil's home regarding all aspects of pupil performance
7 to collaborate with the education welfare service and other agencies, so that pastoral care within the school and welfare provision and support outside the school complement one another

Each of these areas of pastoral responsibility entails some combination of the caring, disciplinary, and administrative functions which appear to become the lot of any pastoral system, once established. The different ways in which particular pastoral systems are organized to fulfil these functions provides a rich field of study which we have explored elsewhere (Johnson 1980). Here we consider only the *seventh* area of pastoral responsibility, and discuss some of the possibilities and problems of collaboration between schools and outside agencies.

In the schools studied, the slender resources available for pastoral work seemed ill-matched to the range of pastoral responsibilities which teachers identified. Role-holders in the pastoral system continued to teach a full timetable, time allocation for pastoral duties being scanty or nonexistent. Few teachers had any formal training for the pastoral roles they occupied. There was a tendency for disciplinary and administrative tasks to crowd out what most pastoral teachers saw as the prime objectives of pastoral care – getting to know the pupil and being alert to his problems.

Nevertheless, the spare time and goodwill of many teachers were being dedicated to making the pastoral system work. The pupils, and some less-experienced members of staff, were benefiting from the pastoral back-up to subject teaching which experienced teachers in pastoral roles provided. Although overburdened, these teachers appeared to enjoy exercising their responsibilities. Some of them were increasingly attracted to the social work aspects of the pastoral role, and would willingly have extended their area of experience by interacting with outside agencies. However, in almost every instance this was an unfulfilled ambition. The timetabled and school-bound nature of teachers' academic work in the classroom made it impossible for them to visit the agencies. The pastoral function of form tutors, heads of year, and heads of house could not be exercised beyond the confines of the school.

Teachers' evaluation of outside agencies

Although the majority of teachers with pastoral responsibilities within the school have no agency contact, they are, to a greater or lesser extent, aware of the agencies' existence and of their potential relevance for the pastoral concerns of the school. However, they have only limited experience on which to draw when evaluating the effectiveness and scope of particular agencies' work.

Teachers at one school studied in our research expressed some of the ambivalent attitudes to agency help which were common to all the schools we contacted, and which have also been noted by other investigators of school and agency relationships (Robinson 1978, Henderson and Welton 1979).

These teachers considered that some of their pupils had problems for which more specialized help was needed than they themselves could offer. Their inclination to refer such pupils to outside agencies was however tempered by a lack of confidence in the likely effectiveness of agency help. This tendency to mistrust agency capabilities was based partly on their perception that agencies did not value the information which schools had about their pupils. Despite the experience built up in the school through its dealings with the child over a number of years, this record was felt to be disregarded by agencies as irrelevant to agency assessment of the client's problem. Moreover, while teachers would, they contended, willingly supply information about pupils to agencies (even though it might be disregarded), agencies seemed to be mistrustful of the way teachers might handle reciprocal information.

Teachers were particularly irritated by the fact that they did not always know when pupils they were trying to help within the school were also the subject of social work involvement. They found it unsatisfactory to be made aware of the complementary or overlapping work of another professional through a casual remark by the child who was the object of their common concern.

These difficulties about the extent and mode of information exchange were perhaps less fundamental and more resolvable than the lack of congruence which teachers perceived between their own frame of reference for a child's problems and that used by the agency. Whereas for the teacher the child had to be handled and responded to as a member of a group, the social worker or the psychiatrist assessed and treated the client/patient in isolation.* Problems which might seem minimal in individualized therapeutic encounters were less tractable in a class group of thirty.

A more sympathetic though negative element in the evaluation which teachers made of agency capacity to help problem pupils was their perception of the understaffing of agencies. Social work teams were felt to be weakened by staff turnover, whether through resignation or secondment to training courses. The lengthy waiting lists for the child guidance clinic and the school psychological service, attributed to the low ratio of these agency practitioners to the pupil population, made the prospect of help from these sources so remote as to be irrelevant in the view of many teachers.

Although the work of the education welfare service was more closely aligned than that of other agencies with the concerns of the school, what the education welfare officer could achieve was also found to be severely limited by low manning of the service. Only the most serious cases of nonattendance could be followed up by the education welfare officer; whereas teachers considered that prompt enquiry at the first onset of untypical absence would also have been worthwhile. Those teachers who were aware of the welfare aspects of the officer's role perceived some overlap with the sphere of the social worker. Nevertheless, they found that the education welfare officer, like teachers themselves, did not always know when a social worker was involved with a schoolchild and his family.

Agency access to the school

Schools are not organized so as to be readily permeable from the outside. The design and resourcing of school buildings take more account of the self-sufficient specialist aspects of school functions than of the institution's place in a wider community. Reception facilities are often minimal or nonexistent, and a large school is likely to have far fewer telephone lines than a small business. Secretaries and administrative staff in schools sometimes interpret their role towards the outside world as one of gatekeeper rather than receptionist, warding off interruptions rather than facilitating meetings or delivering messages. And teachers themselves, whose working experience is often confined to the world of school, and follows immediately on their own years as pupil and student, tend not to be systematically alert to

*This frequently encountered teacher interpretation of agency/client relationship fails to take account of the fact that many agencies respond to the school-age client as a family member, rather than an autonomous individual.

the possibility that professionals outside the school may have reason to want to contact them.

Since the teacher cannot visit the agency, it is only when agency workers come to the school that teachers have a chance to meet them. But the exigencies of the timetable and of classroom management are such that the majority of teachers cannot be available to visitors during school hours. Our research affirmed that all visitors to the school, whether parents or agency workers, are more likely to be seen by senior members of staff who do not teach a full timetable. Certainly all teachers have occasional free periods when they are not timetabled to teach, but regular observation in schools revealed how frequently, in large schools, teachers have to spend their free periods supervising the classes of absent colleagues.

The head teacher and the deputy heads are in many schools the only teachers readily accessible during much of the school's working day. The pastoral head of house or year, and the form tutor, the teachers most likely to have personal knowledge of particular children, are usually in class when agency workers come to make enquiries and only learn of the visit at a later hour, if at all.

The differing priorities of teachers and agency workers

The practical difficulties which teachers and agency workers may experience in making contact with one another are readily recognizable and may be amenable to administrative action. The impediments to school/agency cooperation which arise from value conflicts or differing emphases of objectives are less obvious but nonetheless real. The differences in outlook of the teacher and the social worker are a case in point.

Teachers, as we have seen, sometimes see casework as an attempt to encourage the self-expression and self-realization of the individual, without regard to the group of which he may be a member. This evaluation overlooks the extent to which a social worker, for example, is an agent of control and socialization as well as of material and personal assistance. But although social work values may not be in conflict with the school to the extent that teachers sometimes surmise, social workers are more concerned to enable conformity to general social norms than to those of particular institutions.

One of the central norms of school life is the maintenance of regular attendance. If a school pupil is actually in the care of the local authority, so that the social services department, through a particular social worker, stands *in loco parentis* to the child, then the social worker (in place of the natural parent) has the statutory duty to send the child to school. In such circumstances, the school-agency relationship parallels the home-school relationship which, whatever the differences of interpretation, can assume some identity of interest in the child's education. However, as long as the social worker remains at one remove from the parental role, and works as adviser and facilitator for the welfare of the family as a whole, school attendance may well not take automatic priority over other family concerns.

Possible linking roles

Because of the many obstacles to effective collaboration between schools and agencies which we have described, the existence of some roles which link and interpret their work to one another seems highly desirable.

Traditionally, it is the head teacher who links the school with the wider community. The head teacher is probably still the most 'visible' figure from outside the comprehensive school. No matter how his responsibilities are subdivided and delegated within the school, it continues to be the head teacher who represents the school in dealings with the education authority and the board of governors, and he/she is the school's most frequent delegate at meetings, conferences, and courses. He may also hold some office outside the school, for example, that of magistrate. Such appointments recognize the experience gained as head teacher of a school.

Only the head teacher can legitimately and without special dispensation cross the school boundary in the execution of his normal duties – for his role requires him to maintain at least some personal contact with the education office and the director of education.

However, the welfare network seeks to attach and enlarge itself by more than one linking thread. Not all contact between, for example, a social work area team and the school can be mediated by the directors of the social services and the education department via the head teacher.

Within the school itself, one of the deputy heads may have overall pastoral responsibiility and seem the appropriate person for agency contact and school-agency interaction. However, as already indicated, pastoral systems frequently acquire disciplinary functions, and the titular head of pastoral care is likely also to be one of the most senior figures in the school's disciplinary hierarchy. While this may present no particular difficulty where control agencies such as the juvenile bureaux are concerned, some client-oriented social and medical agencies are more reluctant to deal with teachers who have direct responsibility for pupil behaviour. Such agencies try to identify some role-holder who can be for them 'our man in the school'; someone who not only has access to information about shared clients, but also some trained appreciation of the frames of reference within which agency diagnoses and initiatives are formulated. In the comprehensive schools we studied, the role which most nearly met this agency need was that of the *counsellor*.

The role of the school counsellor has been separately discussed in an earlier contribution to this book. For our purposes, we define counsellors as qualified teachers who have followed a course of training in counselling, and now hold full-time appointments as school counsellors. Our research showed that the scope of the counsellor's duties is considerably influenced by the organizational structure and the ethos of the particular school within which he works.* Here our concern is with the part played by the counsellor in linking the school with the welfare network. Child guidance psychiatrists and psycho-therapists saw the counsellor as an individual with training which equipped him, at least partially, to understand the vulnerability of disturbed children. Questions of professional confidentiality are of course at issue in all dealings between agency and school; but because the full-time counsellor could be related to as a fellow member of the helping professions, who shared the burden of possessing and responding to privileged information, it became easier for clinic and school to deal together.

Educational psychologists saw the counsellor as potentially easing the difficulties of their own approach to teachers, through his personal knowledge of the individuals concerned. Social workers considered that the trained counsellor could be expected at least to recognize the nature and potential of social work help and, in a favourable school climate, to call upon and cooperate with that help.

Juvenile bureau officers saw the counsellor rather differently but no less appreciatively. As a specialist member of the school staff without teaching responsibilities, the counsellor was able to undertake the swift information-gathering and reporting on individual pupils which the juvenile bureau required. His presence eliminated the need to use education welfare officers as information-gathering intermediaries, a procedure which could be time-consuming.

The counsellor, then, can act as the agencies' man in the school; but this may be at the expense of his working relationship with teaching colleagues,

*Teachers expressed a number of reservations about the usefulness of a counselling relationship with pupils which was developed in isolation from classroom pressures.

who may feel that he plays false to his own teacher-training by espousing too fervently the agency's interpretation of the child's situation. Alternatively, teachers aspiring to pastoral expertise and experience which transcends the school may resent what they see as the counsellor's attempts to insulate them from agency contact. A counsellor needs considerable reserves of tolerance for conflict and uncertainty, if he becomes the focal point of any tension which teachers experience between exercising their specialist professional skills and participating in the wider concerns of the welfare network.

In any case, whatever the difficulties of the counsellor's role as mediator, schools with counsellors are in a small minority. Some local education authorities try to bridge the gap between school and agency through work funded by the education office rather than the school.

The education welfare officer is at least potentially a link between school and agency. Although not a member of school staff, much of his work is directly necessary for and relevant to the school. In one of the schools studied, an education welfare officer who had been associated with the school for many years was defined as enabling the pastoral care system to extend into the surrounding neighbourhood.

From the point of view of the agencies, however, the role of education welfare officer was one of low status and limited discretion. The lack of professional training of the education welfare officer, and the bureaucratic administration of the education welfare service, meant that for other agency practitioners he was not acceptable as a liaison figure with the school.

An alternative arrangement for mediating between school and agency, which avoided using the education welfare officer and also kept the sanction-wielding senior teacher at one remove from the client-oriented agency professional, was for education departments to establish a middle-ranking administrative officer with special responsibility for liaison between mainstream schools and the agencies. Directly accountable to an assistant director of education, such an officer was several levels senior to the field education welfare officer, but unlike the member of teaching staff, he/she was not directly responsible for the behaviour of pupils. Although usually without specialized training, such an officer could, through experience, build up a knowledge both of the tasks and the personnel of agencies which could facilitate the school's attempts to enlist agency help.

A linking administrative role of this kind may help to transcend some of the practical difficulties of *contact* between school and agency. But difficulties of mutual *understanding* require a more analytic mediation, from a professional perspective. The role of the adviser is in many ways well suited to such a task.

While hitherto most advisers have been subject specialists, the role of general primary or secondary adviser is becoming increasingly important. General advisers, our research suggested, were in a good position for seeing the whole while understanding the complexity of the parts. Advisers were neither school nor office bound, and although the scope of their constituency would preclude detailed liaison regarding particular cases, they were well placed to visit and learn about the work of agencies and convey their analysis to class teachers through in-service training, thus promoting realistic interdisciplinary working and development between schools and the network of agencies. Even so, the adviser's first concern must be the internal organization and effective operation of the schools he visits. Like the teacher, the adviser feels the tension between the specialist and the more community-oriented functions of the school.

We have discussed at some length the practical and normative impediments to effective cooperation between school and agency, and the limitations to which mediating roles are subject. Before turning to the question of likely future developments, let us examine some of the ways in which, with or without the benefit of linking roles, and whatever the difficulties or potential for mutual misunderstanding, teachers and agency practitioners do currently work together.

Examples of working together

A casework practice which some schools have now adopted for internal use is the case conference, which brings together a number of professionals with a view to establishing a shared diagnosis and plan for treatment. In some areas, inter-institutional case conferences, bridging the school boundary, draw representatives from the school into agency deliberations which already bring together a number of disciplines. While the great range of information available to such conferences may make confident diagnosis and treatment more difficult, the inter-institutional case conference does ensure a move in the direction of responding to the 'whole child' and not just one aspect of his experience. This taking account of the whole individual, in all his complexity, is the avowed aim of many casework agencies, as indeed it is of many school-based pastoral systems. The inter-institutional case conference is a praiseworthy if not always successful attempt to move from rhetoric to action.

While the inter-institutional case conference, with its focus on the individual, is a mode of working together adapted from agency practice, agency workers sometimes make a reciprocal adaptation by assuming the role of teacher.

In the schools studied in our research, a number of agency workers made contributions to the curriculum, usually under the subject umbrella of social studies. Social workers, police, and health visitors were all intermittent contributors to teaching programmes. The subject of health education was in some cases taught to examination level exclusively by health visitors. This latter contribution to the work of the secondary school was organized by the health education service, and was intended to be an interim measure until full staffing permitted the absorption of the subject into the timetable of regular teaching staff. However, as a form of school-agency cooperation, the contributions which agency workers made to teaching were successful and enlightening for all parties. Unlike the case conference, the agency worker's teaching had to engage and allow for the class group rather than the individual. This extended the agency worker's experience to a wider range of young people than his clients could represent, and satisfied the schoolteacher that the agency practitioner was able to appreciate the particular challenges of class control and group learning.

A third development in work with young people which has brought teachers and agency professionals into working relationships during recent years has been the setting up of what are perhaps best described as 'extra-institutional zones'. Home tuition centres (a curiously contradictory label), special units, alternative schools, and intermediate treatment groups are all examples of arrangements made which are both extramural to established institutions and which attempt to employ interdisciplinary and cross-disciplinary working methods. A common factor in all these arrangements is that they tend to take place in premises which have the homeliness acquired through many years of use for a variety of changing purposes. More important for this discussion, however, is the fact that some of these special groupings are staffed and resourced jointly by the education and social services departments of the local authority. During the 1970s there has been a proliferation of such extra-institutional arrangements, the unit costs of which have often been disregarded in the interests of experimentation and the development of joint working skills.

Future prospects

Thus far, our discussion has taken stock of attitudes, policies, and practice which have prevailed in the 1970s. As we look to the 1980s, the insights derived from empirical research must give way to surmise. The two alternatives for developments in school and agency collaboration, like alternative projections of population trends, could lead to differing futures. Both, however, take account of the falling pupil rolls and economic retrenchment which seem likely to characterize the coming decade.

One possibility is that the tendency for the proliferation of special units, taking particular problem pupils out of the mainstream school, will be reversed. The schools would not only reabsorb fringe elements from their shabby but relaxed alternative environments, but might also extend a welcome to some pupils at present on the roll of more long-established special schools. This development would be in sympathy with the spirit of the Warnock Committee's Report (HMSO 1978), which advocated the recognition and satisfaction of a wider range of pupil needs within the mainstream school. It would have the further advantage of ensuring continued full use of the large school buildings which at present seem likely to be underused if falling rolls continue.

What would be the likely effect of such a development for school-agency relationships? In the first place, agency workers might become more visible in the school. Educational psychologists, for example, are at present familiar to a relatively small number of teachers in special schools and special units. The majority of the teachers in the mainstream schools have no contact with the educational psychologist, who may visit their school with some regularity but whose contact with pupils is arranged by senior teachers. Teacher experience would undoubtedly be extended by dealing with a wider range of pupil handicaps, even though the 'cots in the classroom' fantasies with which some teachers fuel their apprehensions go beyond anything that has so far been suggested.

The effect on schools' pastoral systems of repupilling the mainstream schools with children at present educated elsewhere is hard to predict. The sense of being part of the welfare network, with a perhaps more urgent need for the network's support, might increase. Or the pastoral teacher's own skills might perforce develop, with or without specialized training, so as to fill an increasingly challenging and perhaps an increasingly satisfying and rewarding role.

However, the alternative future projection is less dramatic in its predictions. This is the development envisaged by those who consider that pastoral systems and the tenuous links which schools have made with the welfare network have been only a temporary expedient, already becoming obsolete as comprehensive schools 'settle down' to a more confidently formulated and prepared-for role. Pastoral roles, in this view, were a useful face-saving device at a time when a number of senior teachers had to be absorbed into a smaller number of secondary schools; but senior pastoral appointments can be allowed to lapse as present incumbents retire. In this view, there is no real career ladder for the more junior teacher via the pastoral system, since so much of pastoral work is unremunerated and in any case does not call on the trained professional skills of the teacher. The only reputable professional specialization is in subject teaching, and the tasks of pastoral care must once again comprise part of every teacher's repertoire (as indeed some hold they always have).

Economies, in this alternative scenario, will not be the economies of size or full use of buildings, but the efficiency which derives from full use of the highest skills of expensively trained labour. Counsellors and other non-teaching teachers will become unfashionable anachronisms. Smaller pupil rolls will be taught by smaller staffs, and the competition for teaching posts will ensure more effective teacher performance. The definition and treatment of pupil problems will be in school terms, without recourse to agency interpretation. In any case, difficulties with pupils will decline as the school becomes more effective in its teaching task.

Both these alternative future prospects for our secondary schools have their attractive and their alarming sides. Our extrapolations have been chiefly in terms of likely implications for the relationship between schools and the welfare network, and cannot take adequate account of the many attendant implications for pupils, parents, and employers. The two formulations we have sketched out have party political resonances of a recognizable if oversimplified kind. The national politics of education will remain a vibrant field of activity, as in past years. But the local politics of education, and the stubborn diversity of particular educational institutions, are also factors to be reckoned with, and are unlikely to permit the bland skin of consistency to form over our secondary school system.

References

Henderson, G. and Welton, J. (1979), *Needs, Tasks, Professionalism*, Paper 1: Research in Progress. Home-School Links Project, University of Ulster.

Report of the Committee of Enquiry into the education of handicapped children and young people (1978), (The 'Warnock Report'), Cmnd. 7212, HMSO.

Johnson, D., Ransom, E., Packwood, T., Bowden, K., and Kogan, M. (1980), *Secondary Schools and the Welfare Network*, Allen & Unwin.

Robinson, M. (1978), *Schools and Social Work*, Routledge & Kegan Paul.

Schools Parents and Social Services Project (1974-1977). A three-year study of the relationships between secondary schools and welfare agencies, carried out by the Educational Studies Unit, Brunel University. Sixty teachers from four comprehensive schools in outer London, and a similar number of education welfare officers, social workers, juvenile bureau officers, clinical medical officers, health visitors, and members of child guidance and school psychological services, collaborated with the research team in an analysis of the work of the schools and the agencies, and their working relationships with each other. (See Johnson, D. et al. (1980), *op.cit.*)

CHAPTER 22

SCHOOL WELFARE ROLES AND NETWORKS

Maurice Craft

*In this field, with diffuse needs and numerous providing agencies, the range of specialists in home-school relations is now quite extensive. This chapter seeks to review the present pattern and to suggest some guidelines.**

Over the past twenty-five years, a now well-known series of reports and researches has sketched the outlines of educational inequalities in modern Britain. This was not a new discovery, but a situation about which we have become increasingly concerned, with accelerating national needs for skill, and with changes in our political and moral beliefs about individual opportunity. Waste of talent and rigidities in the opportunity structure are no longer so easily accepted (Craft 1974). In more recent years, researches have tended to move away from large-scale studies of educational opportunity and have begun to focus more upon 'educability' or responsiveness to schooling, the analysis of the complex *mechanisms* of disadvantage, and the definition of disadvantage itself (Craft 1970, Young 1971).

An accompaniment of these changing patterns of concern has been the development of a steadily growing network of welfare specialists based in and around schools. The Newsom Report, for example, was in no doubt about '. . . the need for a good deal of social work in connection with the pupils . . .' in what it called 'schools in slum areas', and recommended the appointment of teacher/social workers (CACE 1963). Plowden expressed similar anxieties, recommending a coordinated programme of support, and observing that, 'In schools with special difficulties, social workers may

*This is a revised version of 'The School Welfare Team', originally published in *Linking Home and School* (Longman 1972).

spend so much time in the schools as, virtually, to be members of the school staff' (CACE 1967). The fabric of supporting services, however, has grown piecemeal, and is very much a product of national traditions of problem-solving: the preference for decentralized decision-making, for down-to-earth practical solutions to social dilemmas rather than for large-scale reform, for consensus by compromise between competing interests, rather than for decision by hierarchy, and, above all, for gradualism rather than cataclysmic change.

School welfare needs have therefore tended to be met very largely on a local and pragmatic basis by numerous separate agencies, and the range of provision is accordingly extremely varied. A further complication is that school welfare provision serves a diversity of functions ranging from the largely 'educational' to the largely 'therapeutic'. Home visiting, for example, may be undertaken (by teachers) to sort out a problem relating to homework, or (by social workers) in rspect of an aspect of family breakdown. Clearly there is a large area of overlap between the two extremes, and although an unreal distinction in many ways, the educational/therapeutic dichotomy will be utilized below in discussing the range of welfare tasks now recognized, and of welfare strategies now to be found in British schools.

Present provision

The education welfare service, which grew from the school attendance officers of the 1870s, is still probably the most widespread form of school welfare provision, and its function may range from a relatively limited concern with school attendance, clothing, school meals, and transport, to a form of social casework (MacMillan 1977). In some areas, these staff are now known as school social workers. The school health service emerged in the early years of this century, and the extent of its functions now varies a good deal from region to region. But the role of the school nurse may be very significant, for many are also qualified health visitors and knowledgeable about local families; and they have a competence in health-related social problems such as drugs or child neglect, and may also contribute to health education and to counselling. School psychological services developed after the 1944 Act, and educational psychologists may spend their time advising teachers about individual children with learning or behaviour problems, working with individual cases referred by teachers, or testing children. These activities may often involve devising remedial teaching programmes,

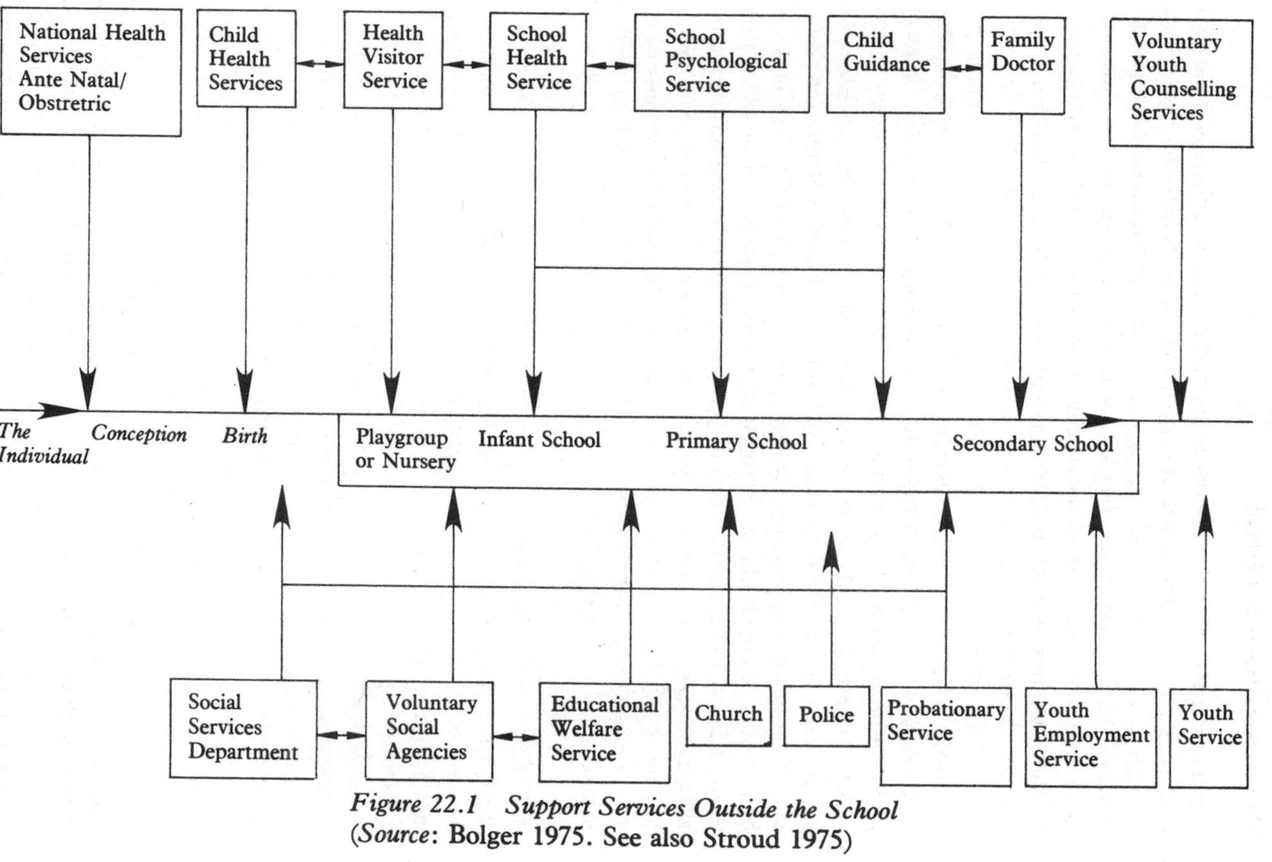

Figure 22.1 Support Services Outside the School
(*Source*: Bolger 1975. See also Stroud 1975)

liaising with parents, counselling teachers, and offering in-service training. The educational psychologist may also spend some time in the local child guidance clinic (part of the school health service), provision for which developed in the late 1950s, and which is staffed by an interdisciplinary team consisting of an educational psychologist, a psychiatric social worker, and a consultant psychiatrist, and is concerned mainly with children designated as 'maladjusted'.

These are the major school welfare services located outside the school, to which others such as the social services department (considered below), the youth employment service, and perhaps the probation service might also be added, as indicated in Bolger's excellent summary diagram (Figure 22.1).

But in recent years, these area-based specialists have been supplemented by a growing number of school-based specialists, teachers often with additional training whose roles may range very widely indeed. Some may be appointed to foster links with parents, to bring them up to date with curriculum changes, and to involve them more fully in the education of their children (McGeeney 1969, Cave 1970), and there have been numerous published accounts of experimental forms of parent-teacher cooperation (DES 1968a, Lang 1968, Haynes 1969, Midwinter 1972). In some cases, the 'home-school liaison teacher' (or teacher/social worker) may have a particular interest in 'parent education', discussing with parents the value of conversation, reading, and particular kinds of toys and activities at home, and perhaps going on to deeper aspects of child-rearing (Pringle 1970). In the case of preschool children, there have been experiments with 'educational home visitors' (Poulton 1975, Jayne 1977).

Another kind of specialist, the 'school counsellor', appointed to many LEAs in the past decade, may have an even more therapeutic function, requiring casework with individual children on personal problems and often involving their parents (Lytton and Craft 1974, Jones 1977). Usually an experienced teacher and having completed an advanced course of specialized training, the counsellor may often have a wide-ranging brief, as indicated later. All these kinds of welfare role can involve home visiting, and most are discussed elsewhere in this book.

Then there are welfare roles of a more instrumental sort which tend, on the whole, not to incorporate home visiting: careers teachers, for example, who may organize visits and work experience, provide careers information, and teach careers courses to ease the transition from school to work. Where a trained counsellor also undertakes work of this kind ('vocational guidance'), he may administer tests of ability, interest, and aptitude, and be responsible for an elaborate record system covering the whole of a child's school life and not simply the final year. Educational and vocational guidance then merge. Form teachers and house tutors are the traditional specialists in these areas and will continue to out-number counsellors and teacher/social workers in secondary education for many years to come. Most large comprehensive schools also have a remedial department, often staffed by specialists and making use of LEA advisers and of specialist remedial teachers based in the school psychological services and child guidance.

Some schools also have a *community* involvement through the appointment of a teacher/youth leader; or by designating themselves 'community schools' and creating a focus of cultural, recreational, or ameliorative activities (Poster 1971, Midwinter 1973). These links with the local community may generate much closer relationships with parents, social services, and employers, and may create additional flows of local knowledge of great value to the school's welfare function – especially in its preventive dimension.

Area variations

The total range of provision both within and outside the school is therefore quite extensive. But the pattern varies from LEA to LEA and from school to school, for traditionally, welfare services have depended not only upon the interests and abilities of individual heads, class teachers, and education welfare officers, but also of chief education officers and of their colleagues in other departments. This is not to argue against variety *per se*, or to suggest that freedom to experiment should be curtailed. But where experimental roles tend to be laid alongside or are superimposed upon existing ones there is always the possibility of stress, duplication, and inefficiency. As counsellors are appointed, for example, the precise role of the housemaster/mistress in a comprehensive school (or of the traditional pastoral function of the form teacher) will require some redefinition. Similarly with careers teachers, a fast developing group of specialists whose role is being increasingly regarded as complementary to that of the area careers officer, and not in conflict with it (Ministry of Labour 1965, Roberts 1970). At the LEA level, there have been numerous experimental patterns of provision. Liverpool, for example, established five area-based 'social education' teams through which school referrals are channelled, with each team coordinated by an 'educational guidance officer' and linking the child guidance and school psychological service, remedial teaching teams, and educational welfare officers (see the chapter by Derek Birley). Other LEAs, Southampton for example, have experimented with less formalized coordinating mechanisms (Luckhurst 1969). The ILEA have traditionally made use of voluntary workers through a school care service, and this element has remained within a unified education welfare service.

However, the central issue to have emerged in policy discussion relating to school welfare provision in recent years arose from the deliberations of the Seebohm Committee (1968), and from their proposal for a unified social services department in each local authority, embracing all neighbourhood welfare provision and including school social workers based in individual schools or serving groups of schools. The proposal argued that this pattern would considerably clarify channels of referral from the school outwards; but there was sharp disagreement among LEAs as to whether the new school social workers, recruited from the existing EWOs, should become part of the social services department or remain with the education authorities (Clegg 1968, Cook 1968), and the Local Authorities Social Services Act 1970 left this question open and for local authorities to decide. In due course, a number of authorities proceeded to incorporate EWOs into their new social services departments, but as the British Association of Social Workers' discussion paper subsequently reported

> Schools are generally unhappy with this development. They feel isolated and neglected and are resentful that their own welfare workers have been taken away from them. The social workers who have replaced them appear to them to place too low priority on this aspect of their work and in some respects even appear to collude with children and families against the school. (BASW 1974a)

The result was that the majority of local authorities reverted to the status quo, leaving only three – Cheshire, Coventry, and Somerset – where the social services department provides a social work service to schools. Even so, the powers of the EWO in relation to those of the new social services departments have diminished, and it is now more difficult to take families to court for nonattendance, a matter that has become a point of issue between the two professions. For social workers, poor attendance is merely a symptom of deeper unease, for teachers it represents the loss of a vital avenue to personal fulfilment and engenders the near certainty of more serious deviance.

The debate continues, and in their recent Report, the Association of

Directors of Social Services notes the '. . . unnecessary and destructive professional competitiveness' which exists at departmental policy levels, and calls for educational welfare to become the responsibility of qualified social workers – perhaps with additional specialised training (ADSS 1978). For their part, EWOs have endorsed the recommendation of the Ralphs Report that the Certificate of Qualification in Social Work should in future become the appropriate professional qualification for their service (Local Government Training Board 1973). However, regardless of this inter-professional conflict about the future role of the EWO, schools frequently have need to consult area social work teams, and on the evidence of Fitzherbert's account accessibility is often a problem (Fitzherbert 1977). The recent BASW discussion document (BASW 1979) argues for an early resolution of the matter, and proposes a more purposive expansion of school social work (area-based or school-based), either through the fuller development of the education welfare service or through some new provision of social service departments.

The school's welfare tasks

It will be clear from this brief review of the present range of school welfare provision and of area variations that, even allowing for terminology (i.e., different titles describing essentially the same role, or 'modernized' titles describing long-established roles), there remains a wide range of *tasks* which fall into the welfare category. Indeed, it is perhaps worth including Milner's summary diagram in which she indicates her assessment of the extent of a 'planned guidance programme' for a comprehensive secondary school (Figure 22.2).

There can be little doubt that this extensive group of welfare tasks which is now being undertaken by schools has grown enormously since the 1950s, and the reasons for this expansion are possibly to be found in the structural and ideological changes referred to earlier: the need for skill and concern for the individual, changes which have been reflected in the growth of an affective dimension to many professional roles (particularly teaching) and in the normal corollary of this – a splitting off of new welfare roles. Thus, while the average teacher is now expected to possess an expertise that is psycho-social as well as academic, it is recognized that specialization must occur in this as in other fields, leading, for example, to the appointment of counsellors, as well as of academic team leaders.

When we come to review the range of welfare tasks it is evident that not all

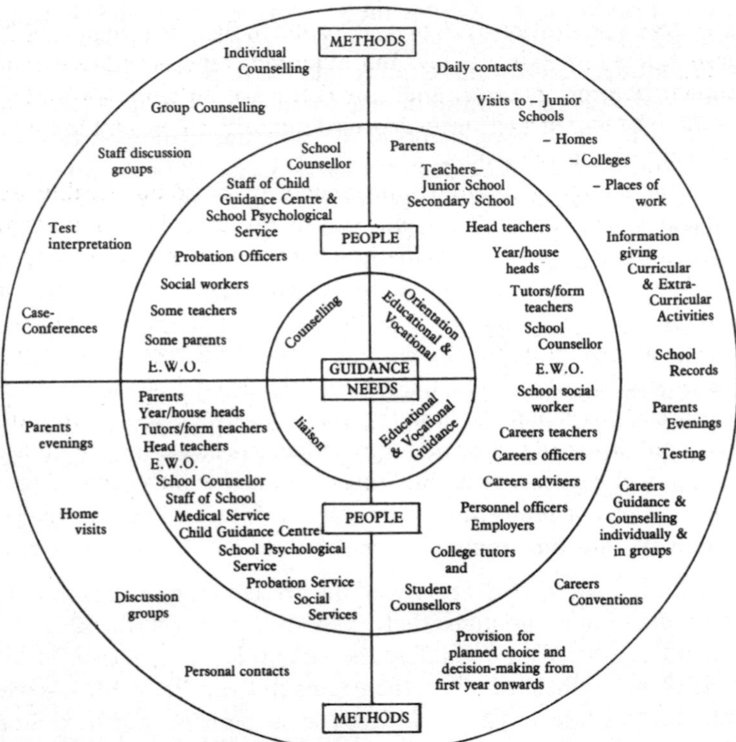

Figure 22.2 [*Source:* Milner 1974]

are alleviative. As suggested earlier, the distinction between 'educational' and 'therapeutic' roles is not always a clear one, but in the threefold classification suggested below this broad distinction is maintained for the purposes of argument. First, and perhaps foremost, school welfare provision seeks to offer effective systems for the identification of the *seriously disadvantaged*; and for their treatment or more skilled support, whether by referral to outside specialists, or as is more likely in many cases, given the general shortage of remedial and psychiatric facilities, by a supportive therapy within the school perhaps in consultation with outside agencies. For this group, welfare provision may also involve a compensatory curriculum, particular techniques of educational and vocational guidance (terms which are considered below), medical measures, and relationships with parents of a 'therapeutic' as well as an 'informational' kind often involving the social services. Whether this group of children 'at risk' comes from as large a proportion as 20 percent of all families, as Pringle (1970) has suggested, it is impossible to say. But numerous reports and researches in education, housing, poverty, and nutrition leave no scope for ambiguity about the existence of a seriously deprived minority whose children require special help within the schools.

Provision for these children immediately raises some sizeable issues, ethical and economic, which can only be touched upon here. For example, does the devising of more systematic school welfare provision imply the more effective adjustment of children to what is generally regarded as an intolerable social environment? Can the provision of special salary allowances, ancillaries, playgroups, nursery school and day nursery places, reception and language centres, and new school buildings in 'educational priority areas' be extended to meet the need, by Governments committed to reducing public expenditure? Is the urban land shortage, the preference for city living, and the consequent building of 'high-rise' flats going to provide new generations of problem children for the future? These wider policy issues are beyond the scope of a chapter concerned with the tactics of prevention at school level.

The second area of school welfare tasks is less obviously 'therapeutic', and concerns the needs not of a deprived minority but of the *overwhelming majority* of normal schoolchildren. Apart from health screenings, and perhaps some occasional remedial teaching, this consists very largely of the dual and interrelated category of educational and vocational guidance which seeks to identify abilities, interests, and aptitudes, and to provide for their fulfilment in school and beyond. Probably the majority of parent-teacher programmes fall into this second category. They are largely concerned to provide information about school progress, courses, and careers, and such 'parent education' as they involve is aimed at fostering supportive attitudes rather than at more basic matters of attitude change which may be entailed with deprived families. The comprehensive reorganization of secondary education and abolition of selection at eleven-plus in many LEAs has given rise to larger schools, more extensive curricula, and delayed and more flexible curriculum choice for an increasingly complex academic and commercial market, and these changes suggest the more obvious rationale for more elaborate systems of guidance to facilitate informed educational and vocational decision-making.

Thirdly, there are the normal stresses of *adolescence* and the need to provide personal counselling, a somewhat more 'therapeutic' service, for those children who seek it. This is a need which may sometimes be overstated by psychotherapists. Nonetheless, it is real enough for a number of children who could not be regarded as seriously deprived or disturbed, in a context of larger and more complex schools, smaller and more mobile families, and an accelerating rate of economic and social change which may foster an 'intergenerational gap'; and in an ideological setting in which the paradoxical commitments to individualism and to collective responsibility maximize freedom, but set the adolescent a major learning problem. With this third group, home-school relations might be more casework oriented.

Proposals for team functioning

So far this chapter has argued that the present pattern of school welfare provision is complex, first, because it has grown up piecemeal to meet the changing needs of a society which prefers local, gradual adjustments rather than large-scale, radical reform; and second, because it embraces a wide range of 'educational' and 'therapeutic' functions. It ought also to be added that the educational system of England and Wales with its 33,000 schools, situated in regions of differing levels of economic development, and divisible into numerous categories by age of pupils, type of curriculum, and form of government, is hardly likely to produce a tidy pattern. Nonetheless, this chapter has suggested that this range of school welfare functions can be grouped according to three broad categories of need: the needs of a small minority, the seriously disadvantaged; the need of the great majority of school-children for educational and vocational guidance; and the need of a minority of normal adolescents for personal counselling.

It will be obvious from this tentative grouping of welfare tasks that there are no neat divisions either of clientèle or of processes, in this field. 'Disadvantage' is a relative term and the size of this minority group fluctuates with time and place; and similarly with the proportion of young people who feel in need of help and advice as part of growing up. Secondly, the processes of guidance and counselling, themselves neither conceptually nor operationally distinct, can be applied to all three groups. However, this composite classification is felt to offer a workable basis for considering the shape of day-to-day machinery. This machinery, given the range of tasks, the growing size of secondary schools in particular, and rising standards of pastoral care, is increasingly being thought of in terms of a *team*, an idea that has been more widely implemented in the United States where the classroom teacher may be assisted, for example, by counsellors, a visiting teacher (or school social worker), a psychologist, and perhaps a psychiatrist, in a given school or school system (Arbuckle 1966, Strang 1968).

In Britain, the team notion is developing but slowly, and many of the proposals made so far relate more specifically to vocational guidance. The Albemarle Report on the youth employment service, for example, advocated closer cooperation between the youth employment officer (now called 'careers officer') and the careers teacher:

> The future of careers counselling in schools will be best served through the development of a *team* approach. . . . Guidance given by the Y.E.O. [careers officer] without relevant information from and consultation with the school is likely to be based upon an inadequate knowledge of the young person. Guidance given by a teacher without the cooperation of the Y.E.O. is likely to be based on too narrow a knowledge of the field of employment and the requirements of occupations. (Ministry of Labour 1965)

The CBI Report (1969) similarly recommended that each school should have a 'strong team of teachers' responsible for careers, working in conjunction with the careers officer who should 'supplement the careers teachers' understanding of the individual's personality, interests, and attainments, with a detailed knowledge of careers in all areas of employment and the physical and psychological requirements of particular occupations'. Hoxter (1964) proposed a slightly more elaborate team structure for vocational guidance. He suggested that each school should appoint a counsellor responsible for educational and vocational guidance who would be assisted by an area-based 'vocational guidance counsellor' (the equivalent of the present careers officer but with more specialized training), and by an LEA-appointed 'vocational guidance adviser' who would plan and coordinate the work of the school counsellors.

These different schemes place a varying emphasis upon the school-based and area-based elements in educational and vocational guidance. But although they argue for a *team* notion, the team they propose is to have fairly narrowly prescribed welfare functions. How are those needs which cannot be neatly classified as educational or vocational to be dealt with? With the Scottish Education Department's Report (1968) we have the recognition that, even if counselling for personal problems is offered by a school, the counsellor would still need the assistance of other staff to cover careers work; and Daws (1967a) draws the important distinction between *therapeutic* counselling on the one hand and *educational and vocational* counselling on the other. He argues that, together, both elements could comprise too demanding a role for a single welfare specialist and has elsewhere (1967b) considered a three-man team: careers teacher, careers officer, and counsellor, in which the counsellor would have a therapeutic concern. Clearly, this three-man team with its increased range would be likely to draw in form teachers, housemasters, and others on occasion (Daws 1968).

An additional dimension is added when the necessity to provide for home-school relations is taken into account. This adds yet a further role demand, a further caseload, and a further set of techniques to those of a counsellor who might already be trying to combine 'therapeutic' and 'educational/vocational' commitments; and it has led to the suggestion that this would be done by a school social worker (Fuller and Juniper 1967, Juniper 1967) and to the proposal for a four-man team: careers teacher, careers officer, counsellor, and school social worker (Daws 1968, Vaughan 1970). Lytton's (1968, 1974) notion of a four-man team is very similar: he sees educational and vocational guidance being carried out by teachers (with some additional training) working in collaboration with the careers officer; home-school links would be maintained by welfare officers rather like the present EWOs; and personal counselling, diagnosis, and referral to outside specialists would be the function of a 'pupil personnel worker'.

All these schemes are an improvement on those considered earlier, for they recognize and seek to provide for a wider range of needs than those which are strictly vocational. But none makes specific provision for remedial education. 'Educational guidance' would probably embrace a compensatory curriculum in the educational priority area, but what of the average suburban school? Here, remedial education is often a largely self-contained area of work; but in any overall review of school welfare provision is it justifiable for it to remain so, for there is certain to be a welfare dimension in the work of most remedial classes, and conversely, the work of welfare specialists will often have implications for remedial teaching. Secondly, none of these proposals for team functioning takes note of the contribution of outside specialists in the school health and psychological services, and in the neighbourhood welfare services. Nor do they speculate on the role of the EWO.

The Report of the National Association for Mental Health Working Party (1970), which also felt that school welfare is 'essentially a team function', put forward a more flexible and comprehensive team concept in which different members of staff and outside welfare specialists would be consulted by a school counsellor in particular cases. Thus, matters of 'educational choice' might involve consultations with departmental heads, parents, personal tutors or house tutors, and perhaps, the educational psychologist; 'vocational choice' would bring in tutors, parents, careers teacher, careers officer, and even employers; and 'critical developmental problems' would embrace the house tutor, form teacher, EWO, parents, and members of the child guidance team. Organizationally, the report suggests, this pattern might be achieved by provision at two levels. At a senior level within each school, a counsellor would be responsible for coordinating an *overall programme*, including liaison with outside agencies, and he might be one of two key assistants to the head teacher (the other being a senior administrative colleague). At the second level, there would be a number of assistant counsellors who would undertake *specific tasks* in the educational, vocational, and personal areas.

As the report suggests, this kind of scheme has the merit of providing a career structure for school welfare specialists; and it makes the important proposal that a single, trained specialist at a senior level should be responsible for coordinating a rational welfare policy within each school. As Hamblin (1974) has put it, the counsellor's role will include '. . . initiating contacts, linking up the people who are working with the pupil inside and outside the school in a constructive way . . . helping to work out viable strategies'.

Jones (1977) has described a somewhat similar pattern in her own school where as deputy head (and a former counsellor) she coordinated a team of teacher/social workers, with close links with the remedial department and with year tutors, form teachers, the school's EWO, and outside welfare and psychological services. Possibly few secondary schools would have as systematic an approach to 'team' functioning. But the DES (1977) Report on *Ten Good Schools* noted that, in their sample, the essential ingredient for effective pastoral care was staff collaboration and the use of pastoral committees or 'boards' where individual cases were discussed by head, coordinating tutors, EWO, and social worker. Hopefully, this kind of pattern will continue to become more widespread.

Interprofessional coordination

A major reason for the advocacy of a more coherent and coordinated pattern of welfare roles *within* the school arises from the still highly fragmented range of welfare services outside. The Plowden Report had drawn attention to this in relation to the needs of primary schools in deprived areas before the reorganization of neighbourhood welfare services had been undertaken, and Newsom had earlier recommended the appointment in secondary schools in difficult areas of '. . . additional members of staff who have special responsibilities for homevisiting, and who act as liaison officers with all the other medical, welfare and child care services in the district' (CACE 1963, 1967).

But even after the reorganization of local social services, coordination remains a serious problem, as was tragically illustrated in the case of Maria Colwell, who was battered to death shortly before her eighth birthday. Although several separate agencies had identified symptoms – teachers, EWO, social worker, and others – they failed to effect any joint action, and as the subsequent committee of enquiry observed, the greatest and most obvious failure of the system in this case was '. . . the lack of, or ineffectiveness of, communication and liaison' (DHSS 1974). The 1978 DES Report on truancy and behavioural problems in eighteen inner-city secondary schools similarly observed that '. . . much remained to be done to coordinate the work of schools and social agencies', and it continued:

> Links between the services were often haphazard and there were few regular meetings programmed for consideration of policy. Some of the best served schools were those with long-established members of staff who 'knew everyone' in the area and were happy to work on that basis. This was not, however, a sound basis for long-term cooperation, and in many schools effective systems still had to be worked out.

The recent report of the Association of Directors of Social Services (1978) states unequivocally:

> We think that it is only through the closest possible cooperation and coordination between the education service and the social services that the best results can be achieved in relation to the needs of those children who can be seen to be disadvantaged.

Their proposed solution is a unification of the education welfare service and the social services department. Fitzherbert (1977), however, discusses a more functional and possibly more fundamental solution, originally proposed by a BASW Working Party (BASW 1974b). This is the regular screening of whole class groups of children, initially by an interdisciplinary team comprising teachers, EWO, and social worker, in order to identify 'children at risk, not making normal progress or simply not thriving' (*op.cit.*), and then following this by further investigation and the involvement of other workers as required in individual cases. The BASW proposal claims that only in this way can genuinely shared decision-making – and its corollary, interprofessional cooperation – become possible.

Fitzherbert (*op.cit.*) comments that rather than wait until problems have become crises, *prevention* should be the objective, and regular multidisciplinary screening would seem to offer the best hope in this direction. She further notes that, 'There is no question that the school with its knowledge of the child as a whole is the place where such an assessment should begin and where it should be coordinated,' adding that parents ought also to be included in the assessment team when their own children are involved. The benefits to be derived when 'members of other professions visit the school regularly, make themselves at home in the staff-room and keep an eye on children with difficulties' include not only an enrichment of the school's capacity to cope with problems itself, but also a sharpening of teachers' perceptions of children's needs and of available strategies for meeting them (*op.cit.*). Lyons (1973) has made the same point in respect of her own experience as an education social worker as part of the London EPA action-research project.

It is also worth noting that in a recent report on the role of the school nurse, the Royal College of Nursing (1974) stressed the importance of regarding this specialist as 'a member of the school team' who must maintain close liaison with all others responsible for the health of the schoolchild.

But above all, there is the question of interdepartmental coordination and liaison at *policy* level, a point which was stressed in the BASW Discussion Document on social work in education (BASW 1979). This recommends the establishment of joint planning strategies and interdepartmental policy review committees, as a means of furthering the more effective coordination of local authority educational and social welfare services. We still have a long way to go in this.

Elements of team provision

The reorganization of primary and secondary education in the last decade has introduced an almost bizarre variety into the forms of British schooling, and it is clearer than ever that no single blueprint for school welfare provision could possibly meet the varied circumstances of more than a proportion of the schools. However, if the broad categories of need outlined earlier are accepted as valid, and if current trends in thinking (sketched in the previous sections) are any guide, it seems that three essentials in any future model must be, first, the establishment of a single, clear focus of welfare efforts, an *internal coordinator* or convenor, within each school; second, the elements, at least, of a *team* within each school; and third, the establishment of a *clear channel* out of the school to neighbourhood welfare services. Naturally, the interpretation of such a model would vary with local conditions. In some areas, the regular interdisciplinary preventive screening discussed by Fitzherbert would be a prime necessity, elsewhere it might be periodic. In one school the core team would need always to include the EWO and/or school social worker, in another it might be thought important to include staff concerned with careers.

In a large comprehensive school the internal coordinator or convenor might be a full-time (i.e., nonteaching) counsellor. Elsewhere, a part-teaching specialist might meet the need. Secondly, in large schools the range of welfare duties would obviously be too great and too conflicting for a single person to carry out alone, and the coordinator might therefore concentrate on the most demanding personal counselling while coordinating a *team* of part-teaching colleagues who were responsible for educational and vocational guidance, for home-school relations, and for remedial work; and responsible, above all, for acting in a consultant capacity to colleagues wherever required (Figure 22.3).

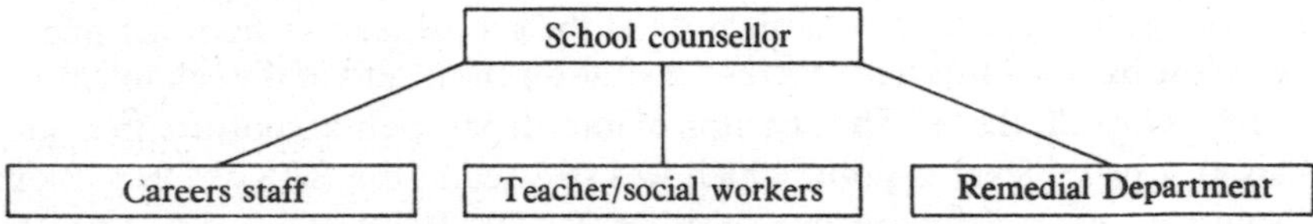

Figure 22.3 The school welfare team — some basic roles

In this model, appropriately trained careers teachers would be capable of administering psychometric tests as part of their work in educational and vocational guidance; but, if not, this could be done by the counsellor. Teacher/social workers (or 'home-school liaison teachers' as they are sometimes called) would foster links with parents, mainly in connection with educational and vocational guidance, and they would have a timetable adjusted to allow for this. Home visiting is so time-consuming that it is doubtful whether any of the other roles could be combined with it. In educational priority areas the teacher/social workers might also be involved in community work (Gulbenkian Foundation 1968), for this is a role which might lend itself to this line of development. In a small school, on the other hand, a teacher/social worker might have a less specialized role and might well be the internal coordinator. To these basic roles must be added the school's remedial teachers, and, of course, the outside specialists who would work with the team (Figure 22.4).

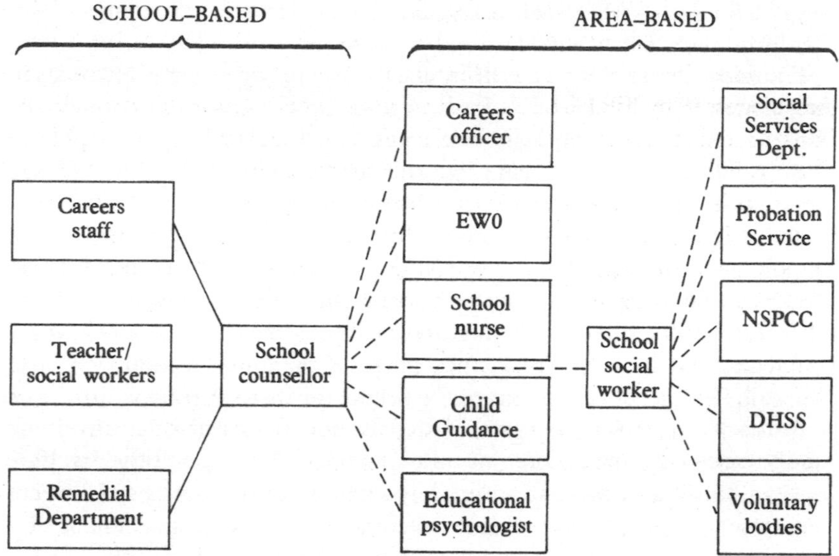

Figure 22.4 The school welfare team – internal and external specialists

The careers officer, school nurse, and EWO would each contribute a particular expertise, but as part of a coordinated team and not, as is so often the case at present, as visitors in isolation, occasionally granted a temporary foothold in the school. The school psychologist, like colleagues in child guidance, might well come to have a consultancy function in many areas, as suggested earlier. The traditional scheme of referral for specialized treatment combined with a supportive therapy in school may be the ideal relationship with area psychological and psychiatric services; but where these are seriously overstrained (if not actually nonexistent), 'the schools' (as the Schools Council Report, 1967, put it) 'have in large degree to contain their difficulties as best they can'. Where a school has a trained counsellor on the staff and the rudiments of a welfare team this containment could offer a constructive solution in many LEAs.

There would be much informal contact between members of the team and regular consultation with housemasters and other colleagues. The role of housemaster/year tutor would probably centre upon traditional administrative and extracurricular duties, facilitating the normative climate of a large school, and a pastoral concern at 'general practitioner' level with referral to the school welfare team wherever necessary. The coordinator would be responsible for calling regular case conferences/screenings which the outside specialists would attend as necessary.

The *internal coordinator* and the internal *team* are two essential elements in this model. The third is a *clear channel out of the school.* This might be thought to be the most ambiguous element, for Figures 22.3 and 22.4 have already indicated several channels: the relationship of the school-based members of the team with their area-based colleagues (i.e., careers officer, school nurse, EWO, psychologist, child guidance) will obviously be a flexible one and will embody clear and efficient channels as the occasion arises. Similarly, the teacher/social workers who will be involved in conveying information about courses and careers, discussing learning or behaviour problems, and in some areas, in aspects of parent education, will also maintain flexible 'channels' out of the school for these purposes. But when it comes to more serious cases of deprivation or disturbance involving family casework, probation, juvenile liaison, NSPCC, or other welfare services, this will be more appropriately a matter for the local social services department. The Seebohm Report recommended the establishment of a school social worker who would liaise between the schools and the department, and where such a role has been clearly designated this would provide the channel whereby referrals of this kind were made. The school social worker, school-based or area-based, would be responsible for convening case conferences of colleagues and might also be involved in casework with a child's family.

The need for a clear and effective channel in these more serious cases has often been stressed (e.g., Wedge 1965), and some have argued that the *counsellor* (in our model, the internal coordinator) could provide it (Lytton 1974, DES 1968b). This would certainly seem to be a logical solution in smaller schools. But in larger ones, the coordinator of a large team who is also carrying a personal caseload would hardly have the time to undertake liaison with a variety of outside specialists, nor would it be right for *him* to decide which was the appropriate point of contact.

Roles, networks, and welfare policy

Figure 22.4, it must be stressed, presents a purely hypothetical model, the purpose of which is to illustrate the range of functions involved in a modern conception of school welfare provision. It is not argued that each school should have this particular blend of components, it will vary according to local needs and resources. But *coordination, team* functioning, and a *clear channel* for referral are felt to be basic concepts. The more rational and coordinated pattern of neighbourhood social services to which we are hopefully moving will help little, if schools do nothing to rationalize *their* internal resources.

Secondly, it will be clear that this chapter has been mainly concerned with a tentative exploration of techniques. More basic organizational issues relating to role analysis, and a more theoretical concern with the social functions of schools and the social process of education have been largely left on one side. However, some theoretical assumptions have been made and these were referred to at the outset. Our society's growing need for skill and its ideological commitment to individual fulfilment have, particularly since 1945, contributed to the greater emphasis placed upon developmental aspects of the educational process. *All* teachers are being increasingly exhorted (and to some extent trained) to take on a wider and more diffuse range of tasks, including those of social welfare. But however desirable this may be thought to be, it is functionally impossible given the increasingly demanding pedagogic aspects of the teacher's role, and the wider range of 'educational' and 'therapeutic' tasks now included under the heading of school welfare provision. Although all teachers may therefore be expected to be capable of identification and referral at 'general practitioner' level, the emergence of school welfare specialists of one kind or another is inevitable, and in terms of functional efficiency, highly desirable.

Not all would necessarily agree with this theoretical orientation. Best et al. (1977) have expressed the view that the development of pastoral care structures may have more to do with social control (the containment of disruptive behaviour associated with the raising of the school-leaving age, for example), and with finding appropriate alternative posts of responsibility for staff displaced from senior departmental appointments in reorganized secondary schools. This is a perspective which certainly has validity and might, indeed, be applied to numerous other aspects of school welfare provision, interprofessional imperialism for example. But while quite rightly calling attention to the latent functions of welfare roles and networks, it seems doubtful that the manifest functions can all be so easily explained.

There remain many issues for research, and for educational and social policy. What the most functional team pattern should be for schools of different types and in different localities is clearly a foremost question, whether social workers should be school-based or area-based, and whether the front-line workers should be responsible as a team to the schools on the spot, or to a fragmented bureaucracy some way off. The findings of Rose and Marshall's (1974) seven-year research into counselling and social work in Lancashire tended to be pragmatic and to suggest that there are no definitive answers for the pattern of provision will vary according to the case. Overseas experience may often suggest helpful role models, but *coordination* appears to be also a central problem in all the states of Australia, for example (Craft 1977).

In the realm of professional training, the proposal that teachers and social workers should be trained alongside each other in an interprofessional setting has appeared in most major reports and commentaries in this field for many years, and it again found widespread expression in the recent reappraisal of teacher education (Craft 1971). Such a development might well enhance the school's preventive function, and now that a part of teacher education is located in interdisciplinary institutes of higher education and polytechnics, it seems nearer than at any time in the past. But this is very much a long-term proposal and cannot be relied upon as the only strategy for future school welfare provision.

Finally, this chapter has tended to assume that school welfare provision is largely a secondary school concern, and it would appear that the great majority of counsellors and other welfare specialists have been appointed to postprimary schools in recent years. But, as Moseley (1968) has argued, there are obvious grounds for claiming that preventive measures should most logically be sited in the *primary* school. This, too, is something which needs close scrutiny at a national level.

References

Arbuckle, D.S. (1966), *Pupil Personnel Services in the Modern School*, Allyn & Bacon.

Association of Directors of Social Services (1978), *Social Work Services for Children in School*, ADSS.

Best, R.E. et al. (1977), 'Pastoral Care: concept and process', *British Journal of Educational Studies*, Vol. 25, No.2, pp. 124-135.

Bolger, A.W. (1975), *Child Study & Guidance in Schools*, Constable.

British Association of Social Workers (1974a), 'Social work in relation to schools', *BASW News*, 21 March.

British Association of Social Workers (1974b), *Report of Working Party on Social Work in Relation to Schools*, BASW, Leeds and Mid-Yorks. Region.

British Association of Social Workers (1979), *Discussion Document on Social Work and the Education Services*, BASW, May.

Cave, R.G. (1970), *Partnership for Change: Parents and Schools*, Ward Lock.
Central Advisory Council for Education (1963), *Half Our Future* (Newsom Report), HMSO.
Central Advisory Council for Education (1967), *Children and their Primary Schools* (Plowden Report), HMSO.
Clegg, A. (1968), 'Seebohm: a sorry tale?', *Education*, 11 October.
Confederation of British Industry (1969), *Careers Guidance*, CBI.
Cook, D. (1968), Comment on Clegg (1968), in *Education*, 25 October.
Craft, M. (ed.) (1970), *Family, Class and Education: a Reader*, Longman.
Craft, M. (1971), 'A broader role for colleges of education', in Tibble, J.W. (ed.), *The Future of Teacher Education*, Routledge & Kegan Paul.
Craft, M. (1974), 'Guidance, counselling and social needs', in Lytton, H. and Craft, M. (eds.), *Guidance and Counselling in British Schools* (2nd edition), Arnold.
Craft, M. (1977), *School Welfare Provision in Australia*, Canberra: Aust. Govt. Pub. Service.
Daws, P.P. (1967a), 'What will the school counsellor do?', *Educational Research*, Vol. 9, No. 2.
Daws, P.P. (1967b), 'The guidance team in the secondary school', *Abstracts of the Annual Conference of the British Psychological Society* (Education Section).
Daws, P.P. (1968), *A Good Start in Life*, CRAC.
Department of Education and Science (1968a), *Parent-Teacher Relations in Primary Schools*, HMSO.
Department of Education and Science (1968b), *Psychologists in Education Services* (Summerfield Report), HMSO.
Department of Education and Science (1977), *Ten Good Schools*, HMSO.
Department of Education and Science (1978), *Truancy & Behavioural Problems in Some Urban Schools*, HMSO.
Department of Health and Social Security (1974), *Report of the Committee of Inquiry into the Care and Supervision Provided in Relation to Maria Colwell*, HMSO.
Fitzherbert, K. (1977), *Child Care Services and the Teacher*, Temple Smith.
Fuller, J.A. and Juniper, D.F. (1967), 'Guidance, counselling & school social work', in *Educational Research*, Vol. 9, No. 2.
Gulbenkian Foundation (1968), *Community Work and Social Change*, Longman.
Hamblin, D.H. (1974), *The Teacher & Counselling*, Blackwell.
Haynes, J. (1969), *Schools and the Community*, Kent County Council.
Hoxter, H.Z. (1964), 'Fresh thinking on guidance and counselling', in *Yearbook of Events, 1963-1964*, Institute of Youth Employment Officers (London and S.E. Branch).
Jayne, E. (1977), *The Deptford Educational Home Visiting Project*, ILEA.
Jones, A. (1977), *Counselling Adolescents in School*, Kogan Page.
Juniper, D.F. (1967), 'School social work', in *Abstracts of the Annual Conference of the British Psychological Society* (Education Section).
Lang, P. (1968), 'A school with a department for home/school relationships', *in Parents and Schools*, Vol. 2, No. 4 (CASE).
Local Government Training Board (1973), *The Role and Training of Education Welfare Officers* (Ralphs Report), LGTB.

Luckhurst, C. (1969), 'Experiments in welfare', in *Trends in Education*, January.
Lyons, K.H. (1973), *Social Work & the School*, HMSO.
Lytton, H. (1968), *School Counselling and Counsellor Education in the United States*, NFER.
Lytton, H. (1974), 'An integrated approach to counselling and social work', in Lytton and Craft (1974).
Lytton, H. and Craft, M. (eds.) (1974), *Guidance and Counselling in British Schools* (2nd edition), Arnold.
MacMillan, D. (1977), *Education Welfare; Strategy and Structure*, Longman.
McGeeney, P.J. (1969), *Parents are Welcome*, Longman.
Midwinter, E.C. (1972), *Projections: an Educational Priority Area at Work*, Ward Lock.
Midwinter, E.C. (1973), *Patterns of Community Education*, Ward Lock.
Milner, P. (1974). *Counselling in Education*, Dent.
Ministry of Labour (1965), *The Future Development of the Youth Employment Service* (Albemarle Report), HMSO.
Moseley, L.G. (1968), 'The primary school and preventive social work', *Social Work*, Vol. 25, No.2.
National Association for Mental Health (1970), *School Counselling*, NAMH.
Poster, C. (1971), *The School and the Community*, Macmillan.
Pringle, M.L. Kellmer (1970), 'Co-operation in child and family care', *Concern*, No. 5 (National Children's Bureau).
Poulton, G. (1975), 'Educational Visiting in England', unpub. M.A. (Ed.) dissertation, University of Southampton.
Roberts, K. (1970), 'The Youth Employment Service, the schools, and the preparation of social leavers for employment', *The Vocational Aspect of Education*, Vol. 22, No. 52.
Rose, G. and Marshall, T.F. (1974), *Counselling and School Social Work*, Wiley.
Royal College of Nursing (1974), *The Role of the School Nurse: Report of a Working Party*, R.C.N. (cyclostyled).
Schools Council (1967), *Counselling in Schools*, HMSO.
Scottish Education Department (1968), *Guidance in Scottish Secondary Schools*, HMSO.
Seebohm Committee (1968), *Report of the Committee on Local Authority and Allied Personal Social Services* (Seebohm Report), HMSO.
Strang, R. (1968), 'Guidance and the classroom teacher', in Noll, V.H. and Noll, R.P. (eds.), *Readings in Educational Psychology*, Collier-Macmillan.
Stroud, J. (1975), *A Guide to the Support Services*, Wark Lock.
Vaughan, T.D. (1970), *Educational and Vocational Guidance Today*, Routledge & Kegan Paul.
Wedge, P. (1965), *Preston Family Welfare Survey*, County Borough of Preston.
Young, M.F.D. (ed.), (1971), *Knowledge & Control*, Collier-Macmillan.

CHAPTER 23

STRATEGIES FOR PREVENTION

Katrin Fitzherbert

Part Five concludes with a review of the contribution made by each of the school welfare services, and a wide-ranging assessment of the need for a more conscious policy of interprofessional consultation and cooperation.

The school welfare network

The structure of our preventive services for schoolchildren is rather like the solar system. At the centre is the school; moving around it, each in its own orbit and at a varying distance from the school, are, in order of closeness, the education welfare service, the school psychological service, the school health service, and child guidance. Each service specializes in a different aspect of the child's development, yet all see it as part of their function to act as a link between home and school when needed. All are interested, or profess to be interested, in prevention.

While their statutory basis is different in each case, it is a fact that every nursery school, infant, junior, and secondary school in the country has a formal link with a branch of each of the four services; and every teacher, in every kind of school, has a valid claim on the help of a professional worker from each of the services if a child in his class is in trouble. This means a doctor, health visitor, nurse, psychiatrist, educational psychologist, psychiatric social worker, and education welfare officer. Completing the list of *dramatis personae* of the preventive network for schoolchildren are social workers. Although they also specialize in an aspect of child development and claim to be interested in prevention, the solar system model breaks down somewhat in their case, because their main responsibilities are outside the school's sphere of influence. Perhaps they fit the model best in the guise of rogue meteors, diving in and out of the school's atmosphere at odd times and for very specific reasons. Nevertheless, they have a statutory duty to provide social work for their catchment area, and a referral from a teacher is as valid as any other. Thus, the most important rule of the preventive network applies to them as much as to the specifically school-linked services, i.e., in case of a child in need, every teacher has a valid claim on the services of a professional social worker.

What, precisely, are the statutory obligations of the four preventive child care services as they affect the school? Taking the oldest first, the *educational welfare service* is a traditional, not a statutory service. Although it is responsible for carrying out some of the statutory functions of an education authority, no legislation specifies who must perform them. Traditionally clerical grade officers of education departments, many of them with a 'services' background, they have been made responsible for enforcing school attendance and other welfare obligations.

Despite their lack of legal status, it would be difficult to argue that they do not constitute a service in the true meaning of the word. Their professional association dates back to 1884; and their traditionally strong commitment to childrens' welfare and educational progress has possibly done more than official recognition could to give them the degree of respect they enjoy among teachers and, not infrequently, truants.

During the 1970s, the question of the EWO's position within the LEA suddenly became much more complicated. As a result of a work study done on them by the Local Government Training Board, and published in 1973, ('The Ralphs Report'), EWOs were in 1975 regraded and began to be paid as social workers. In the great majority of local authorities, however, they remained a part of the education department, within which training them as befits their new grading as social workers could clearly not enjoy a very high priority. Thus, in practice, they have continued to see themselves, and to be seen by schools, as responsible for the same limited range of duties – primarily attendance and welfare grants – as before. Their new pay, and their 'education social worker' title in some places, has made scarcely any difference to the way in which they work or to the kind of referrals schools give them.

Clearly a great opportunity for real preventive work with schoolchildren is being missed. While one can understand how administratively inconvenient it would be for an LEA to give its education welfare service the staff, training, and resources appropriate to a social work service, and not to do so if it can get away with it, it does not follow that teachers should join the same conspiracy. If they now have people called and paid as 'education social workers' attached to their schools, then they have a right to expect them to deal in greater depth and with a wider range of home-related problems than the traditional 'attendance' and 'free dinners'. If, having made such more complex referrals, it became evident that the EWO could not handle them without more support and training, then teachers, as constructive consumers of the education welfare service (or rather, 'education social service'), would seem to be under a moral obligation to point out this problem to their education authority and to press for appropriate action.

The *school health service* was established in 1907 to provide the first free health service for children. Its principal tools in the early years were routine medical inspection, free treatment, and the selection of children for special education. The social and economic changes of the first half of the century (including, in 1947, the introduction of the National Health Service), have changed the needs for, and the role of the school health service. Thus, although routine medical inspections are still being held in many area health authorities, they have not been statutorily required, but rather actively discouraged since 1956. The reason for this is that it seems wasteful for school doctors to spend their time inspecting large numbers of basically healthy children, when a small proportion of quite seriously handicapped and non thriving children who need their help is only too visible to all who know them. The currently most favoured school health service model is for a single, detailed medical examination for all children at school entry, followed by the annual screening of particular functions, such as eyes and hearing by a nurse or technician, backed up by regular meetings between doctors, nurses, and teachers whose selection of children who are not thriving is likely to be more accurate than that based on a four-minute routine medical.

Thus, according to the new philosophy, medical surveillance should be considered a joint activity between teachers and doctors from which each has much to gain. As the Warnock Report showed, the majority of physically handicapped children are already attending normal schools and being taught by teachers who have no special expertise or confidence in handling them. If school doctors and teachers could work more closely together, then teachers could be given guidance about the management of such handicapped and nonthriving children, while doctors would be given a short cut in the discovery of children with special medical needs.

The statutory basis of these recommendations is as follows. In 1907, all LEAs were statutorily required to establish a school health service with its own school medical officer responsible for medical inspections and treatment. Over the years these requirements were amended in various ways, culminating in 1956 with the replacement of statutory routine medicals by the more general and flexible system of medical surveillance described above. In the 1974 reorganization of the National Health Service, school health services were transferred from LEAs to the National Health Service, but there was a stipulation that their work should continue to the same standard as before. Since prior to that time child health had been the responsibility of three quite different branches of the health service – i.e., GPs, hospitals, and education departments – a committee of enquiry under Professor Court was set up to make recommendations for a more logical and effective pattern of health services for children. The results were published in 1976 in *Fit for the Future* (The 'Court Report'). This put forward a general philosophy of child health care in which the needs for interdisciplinary cooperation and prevention were greatly emphasized. This general philosophy has been broadly accepted by the Government, and recommendations for its implementation have been made to area health authorities in several documents, including two DHSS Circulars published in 1978.

As far as the school health service is concerned, these circulars recommend the general principles summarized above, with particular emphasis on the point that each school should have attached to it a named school doctor and nurse, so that good communications may be facilitated.

Little has been said of the school nurse's role. From the beginning of the school health service, the patch-based health visitor who knew most of the children in the area from the time they were born was the key person responsible for the nursing side. Since health visitors have become GP-attached, they have tended to retain nominal responsibility only for their school health work and to delegate most of the routine tasks to less well-qualified clinic nurses. This nominal attachment does mean, however, that the school can still call on its designated health visitor to provide information, or to make a home visit in relation to any medical problem in school. If the child concerned has another GP and health visitor combination, then the school health visitor will find out who is responsible and pass the case on.

Because of the development of the health visitor's role towards GP practices, the role of the school nurse has been recognized as increasingly important. The Court Report proposed that she should be specially trained for her job; that she should be available for self-referral by children from the earliest possible age; and that, by combining a programme of routine screenings with health education and personal counselling, she was in a key position to get the message of preventive health care across to children at all stages of their education.

Like education welfare, the *school psychological service* has no statutory basis as a service. It has grown up in response to legislation laying down statutory functions which LEAs could not carry out without expertise in educational psychology. The 1944 Education Act required LEAs to provide an appropriate education for children of all 'ages, abilities and aptitudes'. To do this, the accurate assessment of abilities and aptitudes was necessary. Although many LEAs were already employing psychologists prior to 1944, this Act virtually forced the remainder to equip themselves with educational psychologists.

The 1940s fashion for categorizing and labelling children into ability groups and segregating them accordingly has long been superseded by new beliefs about how we can help children to make the best of their abilities. In 1975 a DES Circular entitled *The Discovery of Children requiring Special Education and the Assessment of Their Needs* summed up new principles for helping children with special educational needs to make the best of their opportunities. Though these have changed the psychologist's role, it is no less important. The philosophy of the Circular is that a child's innate ability is only one ingredient of the complex mix which will determine his achievements. Aspects of his personality such as determination, competitiveness, resilience to stress and emotional stability, as well as physical endurance, will contribute to what he makes of his 'ability' and 'aptitude'. There are no scientific tests for these important character traits. The only way to discover them is to observe the child in a wide variety of situations, and no psychologist will ever have as good a chance to do this, as his mother, his class or his P.E. teacher.

Thus the emphasis in discovering a child's capabilities has changed from clinical testing to experimenting with different approaches to teaching and to seeing how the child responds. Does he need to be pushed, or does he go to pieces under pressure? Does he need reassurance and praise to keep him going, or does he like to be left to himself? In the words of the Circular, 'Assessment, in short, is inextricably interrelated with treatment and with education and is a continuing process.' Thus, as with doctors, the work of educational psychologists has become much more a question of collaborating and cooperating with teachers and parents, interpreting their experiences of a child, helping to deepen their understanding of a child's functioning, and supporting and advising their ongoing work.

The *child guidance service* is also based on the requirements of the 1944 Education Act. The 1945 Handicapped Pupil and School Health Service Regulations following this Act required local authorities to provide treatment for maladjusted children, one of the then eleven categories of educational handicap for whom special education was recommended. Since child psychiatry was a relatively undeveloped field at the time and many LEAs lacked the know-how needed to set about providing treatment for such children, a review of 'the medical, educational and social problems relating to maladjusted children, with reference to their treatment within the educational system' was commissioned in 1950 under the chairmanship of Dr. Underwood, the principal medical officer of the Ministry of Education.

The 'Underwood Report', published in 1955, suggested a structure for the treatment of maladjusted children which was widely followed and still operates in most LEAs today. This was based on a 'medical model' of maladjustment, in which the child is considered to be suffering from a malady which requires 'diagnosis' and treatment in a clinic. This model has not suited the majority of maladjusted children, who tend to lack the parental support needed to take them to the clinic or who are perhaps perfectly well 'adjusted' to an intolerable home or school situation. Although child guidance clinics have increasingly moved towards treating not only the child but his whole family as well, where appropriate, it nevertheless remains true that a minority of the known number of maladjusted children are benefiting from child guidance clinics.

This situation has been recognized, and in 1974 a joint Circular from the DHSS and the DES urged child guidance workers (who include child psychiatrists, educational psychologists, and psychiatric social workers) to develop a more flexible and out-reaching style of work, for example, seeking to help parents and teachers in the management of difficult children in their care for whom clinic treatment is not appropriate. The 1978 DHSS Circular commenting on the recommendations of the Court Report again took up this point and urged, 'Members of the team from all disciplines should spend a substantial proportion of time working with schools and other community agencies as part of a comprehensive service.'

A time for reassessment

A common thread links these brief accounts of the current state of the four services – education welfare, health, psychology, child guidance. All are at a turning point in their development and are having to question their traditional methods; all are the subject of official recommendations to change their work style; in every case the recommended direction is towards greater collaboration and more consultation with teachers (and, it should be added, with one another).

It is not surprising that these recommendations, some of them (e.g., regarding medical inspection) made more than twenty years ago, are very slow in being implemented. For in the relationship between schools and their support services, teachers ask for and receive the service; they are the hosts. If the recommended practice is for more communication and cooperation, how difficult for outsiders to impose this on teachers who don't necessarily have the same commitment to this objective? However evident to a doctor or psychologist that a teacher could benefit from discussions with them about her difficulties over a particular child, how can they get her to accept this, if she does not come to them to ask for help? And how can the school nurse launch a programme of combined health education and health counselling in a school which doesn't think the subject important enough to be given space in the timetable?

Thus, the widespread ignorance and lack of interest of the teaching profession in the role and potential of the child care services in education has for years proved to be an obstacle in their development. The problem is well illustrated by the following passage, taken from the NUT's submission to the Seebohm Committee on Allied and Personal Social Services in 1968:

> It has been traditional for teachers to believe that the total physical, mental and social wellbeing of the child is their concern, and that only when this is assured can education function effectively to promote the full development of the child. During the past decade or so, however, this belief of the teachers has been given scientific form and validity by much of the recent work in the field where sociology and education overlap, and has now found further full expression in the Plowden Report. It is now recognized that any form of social cultural and linguistic deprivation, equally with the more obvious effects of physical and mental handicaps, can have profound and far-reaching effects on the educational future of children. A more valuable part of the Plowden Report is its insistence on the close interrelation between the school and the community it serves, and the need for special measures to overcome the kind of handicap to which we are referring. The point that we wish to emphasise here is that no other institution is comparable with the school as the natural

> focal point for services of this kind. Only the school is in touch with almost all children. We are sure that our colleagues who provide one or other of the many important remedial services would agree that recognition that the problem exists is one of the most important factors in successful treatment. In the vast majority of cases the only other persons who are in a position to determine incipient problems are the parents themselves and, in many cases, perhaps particularly in those cases where problems are most likely to arise, they are unfitted to do so by lack of experience and by natural emotional involvement. . . .
>
> What, therefore, we are in effect saying is that the education service is the natural sector within which the various services should be gathered. We naturally do not suggest that, for instance, medical services should not remain under the control of the doctors, and similarly with other specialist non-teaching services; but we do suggest that only the education service can properly coordinate the various contributions that the services can offer and can involve them at the earliest possible moment. We are not able to suggest an organizational pattern through which this coordination can best be achieved but we do believe that it can be achieved through the education service and that this service should be given principal responsibility for such coordination.

This passage illustrates the deep confusion over the role and function of the child care services available to schools in the minds of teachers. Agreed, the school is 'the natural focal point' of health, psychiatric, psychological, and social services for children. But are all the services which could possibly be required not already present in the education sector? If 'only the education service can properly coordinate the various contributions that the services can offer and can evoke them at the earliest possible moment', what is stopping it from doing this? It is true that the services are not functioning as effectively as they could; but this is because to make them really come alive they need the very 'coordination' which 'only the education service can properly' provide.

That schools do not fully appreciate the potential of their support services, or give them the support they need to develop their potential to the full, illustrates the extent to which the whole question of child care and preventive work is an area of difficulty and confusion for the teaching profession. Not being strictly education, it has not been accepted as essential to the professional tasks of teachers. The whole question of the teacher's *in loco parentis* role, the ethics of intervening in family or personal problems, the use of the support services, none of these questions have really been thought through. When a child is in trouble or danger, is the teacher's task to teach? Is it to act like a parent? To care? To intervene? To delegate?

Where should the balance be struck between these alternatives? These questions have not been sorted out within the profession, nor in teacher education. Many courses do not discuss them at all. Young teachers often have no opportunity to work out their role about such questions until they are faced with a child in need, when they have to act one way or the other, often with nobody to share the problem (as, for example, with Maria Colwell's teacher).

Since, at present, each teacher has to make up his own mind about his role in this respect, there is considerable variation in what is considered acceptable practice. Some head and class teachers throw themselves wholeheartedly into child care work, making home visits, doing marriage guidance counselling with parents, and making medical appointments for children. These teachers play their role in this way because of their own inclination and personality, not because it is recommended practice for teachers. For every 'interventionist' teacher, there is another who profoundly disapproves of his 'interfering' colleague.

For similar reasons, considerable variation is found in the use different schools make of the preventive child care services. In her study of school nursing services in Hertfordshire, Thurmott (1976), for example, found that during one week, 63 of the 219 head teachers had discussed an individual child with their health visitor, 11 of them more than once. Eighty heads had not seen their health visitor during that week or the preceding 7 weeks since the beginning of term. Less than half the heads told their health visitors about children who were frequently ill or absent (but nearly all about children who had nits). One hundred twenty-nine schools gave their health visitors a list of the children in the school, 64 of them with the name of the GP, but 82 schools did not do this, thus clearly limiting what the health visitor could do for that school.

In 144 schools, visits to schools were arranged for the mutual convenience of health visitors and head teachers; in 24, health visitors dropped in when it suited them, but 46 could only visit a school when the head gave them a specific appointment. In 87 schools the health visitors were sufficiently part of the school to attend school functions; but in 109 schools no health visitor had ever been invited.

Another study looking at the use of child care services made by schools (unpublished, but reported at various educational conferences) concerned 20 secondary schools in one education authority. The HMIs who conducted the survey found that 2 of the 20 schools had produced 42 percent of all the referrals for learning difficulties made, as well as 39 percent of the contacts with social workers. These schools happened to have on their staff someone with an extra training in some aspect of child development or special education, and were clearly more aware of the potential of the services than the average teacher.

Interdisciplinary cooperation

It is high time that the teaching profession sorted itself out on these issues, and that some sort of consensus on the ethics, professionalism, and appropriate method of getting involved in social, health, and psychiatric care was reached. There is a real urgency about this matter.

First, research into child development in the last twenty years has established beyond any further doubt the interdependence between the different aspects of child development. The Isle of Wight study into the relationship between physical, educational, intellectual, and physical handicaps of the whole population of nine- to eleven-year-old children showed the extent to which a handicap in one area is likely to be accompanied by handicaps in other areas (Rutter et al. 1970).

The National Child Development Study has also shown the correlation between class, family composition, housing, family health, and school achievement (see, for example, NCDS 1979).

Findings such as these suggest that no profession concerned with child development can achieve the best results if it works in isolation from the others; that interdisciplinary cooperation is an important skill for all concerned with children. They also suggest that even if we cannot prevent disadvantage and handicap, then, by working together, we should at least be able to prevent one sort of disadvantage leading to another. Take the child with cerebral palsy. A much larger proportion of such children than of normal children develop behaviour and learning difficulties not related to their intelligence. Is this because of the emotional consequences of being handicapped? Is it because of attitudes towards handicap in teachers, parents, and other children? If so, then this is something we should be able to learn to handle very much better, so that secondary and tertiary handicaps may be avoided.

A second reason why teachers should develop a clear policy on this issue now is the state of indecision and crisis within all of the support services. In the current state of knowledge about child development, it has become clear that they cannot do their job properly without a clear commitment from teachers to work with them. A further reason is financial. In the present economic situation, none of the services, including education, are going to get all the resources they think they need. The only hope of improving services is to give better value for money by sharing resources and cooperating. After a decade in which the administrative structures of the education, health, and social services have grown steadily more separate and isolated from one another, this is not going to be easy.

In thinking through their role towards children whose needs fall outside their professional territory, teachers must distinguish between what they should do as teachers, and as caring individuals, i.e., between professional ethics and personal morality. There will never be a limit to the unmet needs of the children; and caring adults, whatever their professional training, will never be out of ajob. Propping up young mums and dads, running clubs for them, and so forth undoubtedly makes a difference to their lives and to their children, but they are not professional obligations for teachers. The teacher's job is to teach. Whatever energies he wants to devote to getting personally involved in family problems is his personal, not professional, concern.

In the last decade there have been various flirtations with the concept of 'teacher/social workers'. Indeed, inspired by the general philosophy of the Plowden Report, some of these were appointed to teach a class of children for part of the day and to turn their attention to individual problem children for the rest. Many teachers seem to find this combination of roles difficult. If your professional orientation is towards a group, it is very difficult to suddenly home in on a particular child's family crisis, and then to carry on teaching the child as just another member of a class of thirty. Neither does the brief vogue of ordinary teachers taking up informal home visiting with children who were failing educationally seem to have been altogether successful. There is often resentment in both parents and children for such interference, and a preference for keeping home and school separate.

Obviously these forays by teachers into doing social work themselves have been from the best motives – the realization that, for certain children, sorting out emotional and social problems is a necessary requirement for any sort of educational progress. However, the assumption that the best way to do this is via teachers themselves only follows if that school's supportive child care network is nonexistent or ineffectual, or if teachers are not using it properly. These three are usually closely connected.

Each of the child care professions has rapidly become more specialized, for each, more knowledge and more new methods need to be mastered to produce a competent practitioner. This also means that no one profession, including teaching, can any longer claim to be expert on every subject to do with children, or to be all things to all men in every sort of trouble. The role of teacher as confidante, support, and counsellor for a child or parent is more relevant and valuable than ever; but this is because the teacher is a respected individual who knows the family, not because he is by profession an expert on every subject.

Thus the most productive avenue for teachers to follow in sorting out a professional stance in relation to prevention and children with special needs is twofold: first, to concentrate on being good at their own thing, and second, to be intelligent and constructively critical consumers of the other child care services.

To begin with the first point. In the words of one London education welfare officer, 'the best form of social work with a deprived child is to get him to attend school'. To this must be added that, for many children, the best form of social work is to help them to acquire skills and knowledge. Being successful at school, whether academically, socially, or at sports, music, or handicrafts is a most valuable therapy for a child who is having to grapple with physical, family, or financial problems. A child who is neglected by his parents, suffers a physical disability, or is under another form of stress, who can develop self-esteem and confidence from his school progress, is well on the way to being equipped with the necessary means of overcoming his problems.

When the conventional educational techniques turn out not to work for a child, there is something else special to them that teachers can offer. The technique of working with groups is rarely found amongst social workers, health visitors, etc. For many of the children we are concerned about, children of broken homes, of harassed single parents who have little emotional energy to devote to their children, it is simply not going to be possible to make their home situation more satisfactory. If their emotional needs cannot be fulfilled at home, then regular therapeutic groups based on school could well be the most useful provision. Teachers are ideally equipped and placed to run such groups after school, and this is the area where their preventive energies might best be directed. The most satisfactory arrangement of all might be to do this in collaboration with the child guidance clinic or social services team.

On the second point, being intelligent consumers of the support services, it is often assumed that the use which teachers make of a service depends primarily on how good and effective it is. It is, however, just as true that how good the service is depends on the way in which teachers use it. All the support services discussed earlier have been neglected, misunderstood, or ignored by teachers for most of their existence. They have never got their share of resources in the general expansion of services for children and, as a result, have not developed their services to a quality or on a scale that would impress teachers. They have also become considerably demoralized.

Being intelligent and constructively critical consumers of the child care support services is as yet a realtively undeveloped skill in teachers. However, it is fundamental to any real progress in the field of preventive work. As the teacher is the only one of the child care specialists who sees the whole child functioning in an ordinary situation, he is the first and most reliable witness of unsatisfactory or abnormal development. Without him, early preventive work focussed on schoolchildren is, frankly, a nonstarter. We have seen how each of the support services has independently come to the conclusion that it can only do its work effectively by regular consultations with teachers. Teachers, in their turn, are now being asked to respond to this appeal and to see this as their principal contribution to preventive work.

How can teachers set about developing the skill of being responsible consumers of the support services? First, by being informed about the services available locally and getting to know the individuals involved. A good strategy for this might be to invite each of the professionals attached to a school to come and talk about their work in a lunch-hour or staff-meeting, so that teachers may obtain a clearer notion of their opportunities for making referrals. One point to bear in mind, however, is that there are as many different styles of being an educational psychologist or school doctor as there are of being a teacher. Having heard about the work of one individual should not be interpreted as knowing all that could be offered by that service. Thus, another skill required for being an intelligent consumer of the preventive services would be to keep up to date with developments in each of the professions, in so far as these affect their relationship with school and teachers and schoolchildren. This means expanding one's professional antennae as teachers to pick up developments, not only in reading techniques and systems of marking, but also to developments in education welfare and the rest of the services.

Distinguishing between variations in normal patterns of development, and recognizing physical, emotional, and social failure to thrive, are other skills which are important. Teacher training has a lot to offer here, in terms of understanding of concepts such as withdrawal, depression, and physical and emotional neglect. Theoretical learning is, however, not enough, and the best way of recognizing such needs is undoubtedly through sharing and learning with members of other professions who can throw a new light on symptoms which cause concern.

Working constructively with other professionals and learning how to share problems and how to use their expertise are also essential. At the West London Institute of Higher Education, we are experimenting with a project which is trying to develop all these skills. In three junior schools, a year-group of children is being screened by an interdisciplinary team made up of representatives of all the services mentioned. Any child who is identified by his teachers or another member as giving rise to concern is discussed at an interdisciplinary meeting, and each member contributes what he can to understanding the problem and, perhaps, to its solution. In this way, we are trying to forestall crises which might be pending for these children. A valuable by-product is the deeper understanding of child development and of one another's way of working which is coming out of this exercise in collaboration.

A final skill in teachers which would seem to be essential for school-based preventive work to develop to its full potential would be the skill of commenting on inadequacies in the support services and campaigning for improvements. As all the services are so small in comparison with main-stream teaching, social work and health services all need for their development to be backed up by a more influential party in the game of professional politics. Teachers are best placed to do this for them, and this could well be their most valuable contribution to preventive work with schoolchildren – second only, of course, to being good at teaching.

References

DES (1975), *Circular on The Discovery of Children Requiring Special Education and the Assessment of their Needs*, HMSO.

DES (1976), *Report of the Committee on Child Health Services*, HMSO, ('Court Report').

DES (1978), *Report of the Committee of Enquiry into the Education of Handicapped Children and Young People*, HMSO ('Warnock Report').

DES, DHSS and Welsh Office (1974), Joint Circular on *Child Guidance*, HMSO.

DHSS (1978), Circular on *Health Services Development*, HMSO.

DHSS (1978), Circular on *Prevention in the Child Health Services*, HMSO.

Local Government Training Board (1973), *The Role and Training of Education Welfare Officers*, HMSO ('Ralphs Report').

Ministry of Education (1945), *Handicapped Pupils and School Health Service Regulations*, HMSO.
Ministry of Education (1955), *Report of the Committee on Maladjusted Children Within the Education System*, HMSO ('Underwood Report')
National Child Development Study (1979), *Publications Arising*, National Childrens' Bureau.
NUT (1968), *Document for the Committee on Local and Allied Personal Social Services*, NUT.
Rutter, M., Tizard, J., and Whitmore, K. (1970), *Education, Health and Behaviour*, Longman.

PART SIX

Interprofessionalism

CHAPTER 24

INTERPROFESSIONAL TRAINING

J.W. Tibble

*Part Six takes up a theme which has emerged in several previous chapters, namely, the common ground shared by teachers and social workers. This chapter, previously published, by the late Professor Tibble, considers overlapping viewpoints and joint training.**

Some years ago, in 1958, there was held at Keele, thanks to the inspiration and energy of Professor Paul Halmos, a conference which brought together trainers of teachers, social workers, clinical and educational psychologists, and nurses, to consider the possible common ground in the content, aims, and methods of training in their respective courses. This first conference concentrated on the treatment of psychology in these courses. Three more such conferences were held at Keele, Leicester, and Nottingham, to explore the contributions of other basic subjects, such as sociology and philosophy, and to compare the techniques used in both study and practical training. The talks given at these conferences and some account of the discussion they provoked were published in a series of monographs.[1]

The committee set up to organize the conferences also arranged smaller working parties whose purpose was to consider practical outcomes and what steps might be taken to foster the development of courses of training in an interprofessional setting. In the field of teacher education, an interprofessional working party has since met from time to time to review developments, and in 1969, it sponsored a further national conference, at Bulmershe College of Education.[2]

*Reprinted from *Linking Home and School* (Longman 1972).

There are signs of a growing awareness of the need to bring the helping professions into a much closer association with the educational system. Dr. M.E.M. Herford, writing in *Education*,[3] makes a plea for a comprehensive counselling service for young people which would integrate the work of the schools, the health service, the youth employment service, youth clubs, and the probation service.

> The service for youth must be approached comprehensively. The Schools must be the base for action and exploration outside; they must be linked to the youth service in clubs and other centres. Creative use of leisure is part of education. The probation service, relatively isolated on the fringe, must become part of the counselling, preventive service for youth. There should, again, be suitable joint appointments as well as whole-time posts between schools, youth service, probation service. These would be mutually stimulating and provide a vigorous career structure, and cross-fertilizing influence. None of these services can any longer be considered as a private departmental concern. Each has a community function and is a community responsibility; they are organically interdependent and must be planned and organised comprehensively. Departmental planning can only isolate and destroy vitality.

Given this recognition of the need for integration, it seems obvious that the integration should operate at the level of both initial training for the professions concerned and at the level of postcertificate and postgraduate education. When the interprofessional conferences and working parties mentioned above brought together workers from the different fields, a good deal of the discussion revolved round what might be called interprofessional idiosyncrasies – the results of historical accident in the development of the respective training systems. As we are all products of these, it is difficult to discount the effects and adopt a viewpoint which ignores local colour and vested interest and tries to ask fundamental questions. We can say that the conference, and more particularly the working party discussions, did make good progress, once the inevitable initial professional defensiveness was overcome.

What has emerged so far has been a surprisingly large area of common ground on the one hand; on the other, certain differences have been seen to be not accidental and arbitrary, but fundamental. Common courses of education will have to provide for both similarities and differences. Comment on this can appropriately fall under two headings, content and process: for in the preparation of people for all these professions, it is generally agreed there are subjects, organized fields of study which are especially relevant to the profession in question; there are also specific skills to be acquired.

With regard to content, one difference between teaching and the rest quickly emerged: in preparation for teaching there is both a professional and a curricular content to be acquired. The former obviously may have an area of overlap with the professional content needed by the social worker, but the latter does not have a curriculum of subjects to be familiar with, through which in the teacher's case much of the relationship between teacher and child is mediated. Granted, curricular studies would have no counterpart in the social worker's education; but what did emerge from the discussion was that the study of a special subject or subjects 'for its own sake' by the student, as is now customary in courses of teacher education, might well be equally valid in the other courses of professional education and for the same reasons, i.e., it is part of the worker's equipment as a cultured, civilized human being.

The overlap in the area of professional studies is obvious enough, and once again recent developments in teacher education have brought the professional needs closer together. In the social work field it is a question of bringing together relevant contributions from a number of basic disciplines or forms of thought: psychology and sociology are obviously relevant and most people want to include some philosophic study dealing with values, ethical issues, and so on. This contributory approach to the study of what is described by Professor Paul Hirst as 'practical-theory' is now being advocated as the best formulation of the nature of education as a subject of study;[4] furthermore many of the topics chosen for study would obviously be common ground in the education for the different professions: the educative function of the family and the relation between home and school would be one of these common topics. It is further suggested that the advantage of having these common topics explored by groups with different professional biases would be considerable. Even in the areas of study where the professional interests would diverge, as in the study of the historical development of educational systems and institutions on the one hand and in the study of social administration on the other, there would be gain from the relating of these studies in mixed discussion groups. It is now being recognized, for example, in the field of education, that the history of education has been too narrowly conceived and will gain from a closer relating of this subject to the development of other institutions within the context of the welfare state.

Turning now from content to process, the working parties have in particular explored the possibility of common ground in practical work training, and acquisition of the special skills needed by teachers and social workers. Theoretically this involves the assumption of some common ground between education and therapy, as is indeed envisaged by Dr. Herford. This can be seen as arising from the fact that both education and therapy involve bringing about changes in a pupil or client which will enable him or her to fulfil needs and cope with problems more adequately. In both cases something has to be learned – knowledge, skill, attitudes – which is relevant to the need. The difference can perhaps most profitably be thought of in terms of education and reeducation, since the social worker is more likely to be specifically involved in repairing defects of knowledge, changing unsatisfactory attitudes, relearning of social skills, and so on. But clearly also many teachers need skills in remedial work, and have to cope with the effects of unsatisfactory home background and defective relationships between child and parent.

Another aspect of practical work which is being explored is that of the skills needed by the supervisor in the process of training the student teacher or social worker. The term 'supervision' is used in both contexts, but the discussion brought out very clearly that it described somewhat different practices. For example, the school practice supervisor normally operates by sitting in as nonparticipant observer on a lesson given by the student. The student has prepared the lesson and the lesson notes are available for comparison with the actual lesson. After the lesson the student has the benefit of the supervisor's criticism. There is a large element of judgement and assessment in this process, and it assumes a capacity in the student to identify with the supervisor's 'nonparticipant' point of view.

In the case of social work supervision, as it happens, it is often not possible for a supervisor to be present at the interview between social worker and client; it would be recognized as radically altering the situation for a third person to be present. Furthermore, it is more clearly recognized in this social work context that, for the student to benefit fully, the supervisor must start where he or she, the student, is, with the account of the interview produced by the student after the event. The supervisor's function is to help the student to explore in retrospect all the implications of the situation, to see more than he was able to see at the time, to develop further insights. It is suggested that teacher training would gain from making use of this other kind of supervision.[5] Certainly the traditional school practice procedures need reconsideration both from the point of view of determining what the specific role of the college supervisor is and to meet the demand from within the profession for more school-based training. It is suggested here that the respective roles have been rather more clearly defined and worked out in the field of social work training, and that teacher education would benefit from a greater awareness of this.

There are, of course, as many practical problems in achieving greater cooperation in training as there are in more closely integrating the professions as a whole. Different ministries and departments are involved, both locally and nationally. Different salary scales operate; changing jobs, or operating in two at once, is fraught with difficulties. Each profession has its own built-in habits of mind and established practice. Present exigencies, particularly in the field of teacher education, where an acute shortage exists, mean that it is difficult to get approval for the development of the multi-professional colleges envisaged in the Robbins Report. We must hope that in the long run solutions to the practical problems will be found, and that a broadly based and flexible system of interprofessional education will replace the present patchwork systems. Meanwhile it is important that experiments of the kind mentioned above should be instituted whenever it is practicable so that new ideas can be tried out in practice and the results assessed.

References

1. *Sociological Review Monographs* Nos. 1 and 2. *The Problems arising from the Teaching of Personality Development*, Keele, 1958, 1959.
   No. 3. *Moral Issues in the Training of Teachers and Social Workers*, Keele, 1960.
   No. 4. *The Teaching of Sociology to Students of Education and Social Workers*, Keele, 1961.
2. A review of interprofessional developments up to that time is summarized by M. Craft in 'Developments in interprofessional training', *Higher Education Journal*, Vol. 17, No. 3 (1969), pp. 11-14.
3. *Education*, Vol. 126, No. 3263, 6 August 1965, pp. 277-278.
4. For a full discussion of this see J.W. Tibble (ed.) *The Study of Education*, Routledge & Kegan Paul, 1966.
5. An account of an experiment in the use of this kind of supervision in teacher education appears in *Education for Teaching*, November 1965.

CHAPTER 25

THE OVERLAPPING PERSPECTIVES OF EDUCATION AND SOCIAL WORK

Margaret Robinson

This final chapter continues the discussion of overlapping aims, viewpoints, and skills presented by Professor Tibble in Chapter 24, and comments further on the complementary and shared roles and responsibilities of teachers and social workers.

In 1978, the Association of Directors of Social Services published their policy document on *Social Work Services for Children in School.* For them, this policy document was the culmination of their concern about the role and function of the education welfare service, which though considered as an integral part of the social work service by the Seebohm Committee 1968, had not been included in the subsequent Parliamentary legislation which had promulgated the structure and responsibilities of the present-day social services departments. Instead, the Local Authority Services Act (1970) had made no recommendations about social work services to schools, although the Government of the day invited local authorities to consider whether or not they wished to use their discretion to include the education welfare service within the new departments. In fact very few did so, and a number of these reverted to their more traditional patterns of organization in the subsequent amalgamation of their authorities in 1974.

But the formation of the now large local authority social services departments, with their considerable statutory responsibilities in relation to child care, highlighted the division of responsibilities as regards the care of children at risk, and led to increasing boundary skirmishes between the new departments and those of the longer-established education departments. How had such a situation come about, when it had been less than a hundred years previously that the devastating results of the industrial revolution had led many like-minded people to concern themselves with the needs of children? In this comment on the overlapping perspectives of education and social work I shall hope to consider various aspects of this matter, firstly by means of a very brief historical note. Secondly, and in more detail, I shall attempt to draw out the current role and responsibilities of education and social work, and to demonstrate how they do in fact overlap, particularly as regards children who are in difficulties, or who may be at risk. Finally, I shall try to indicate some of the shared ways in which both the similar and the distinctive knowledge and skills of teachers and social workers can complement each other, and be used cooperatively in shared initiatives, so as to be of most benefit to the children who are of common concern.

The background

An historical review of developments in education and social work could perhaps be briefly summarized in the following way. The struggles of the working man to gain a political voice led to the demand for education for his *children*, and this was the major preoccupation of the nineteenth century. During the twentieth century, when education was by now compulsory, there was increasing interest and concern with those socialist ideals of equal opportunity for all, which led to a preoccupation with the quality of schooling, and the nuts and bolts of education. Social work, on the other hand, while developing from a similarly inspired concern for *families* who had fallen on hard times, began to concentrate on supportive and substitute care for children, as part of its broader focus on helping individuals and families in need.

The subsequent debate on care or control for deprived and delinquent children has reflected society's general concern as to whether to provide relief or punishment for those adults who fail to subscribe to its mores. Thus, education has primarily focussed on the access to and the quality of schooling for all children; while social work has developed, as part of its brief, the provision of care for families in need, with the provision of substitute care for children as the last resort. It is in the area of preventive work with children at risk that both education and social work meet, as I hope to show in the next section, but also in drawing the lines between when prevention has failed and remedial action is required. It is therefore, perhaps, unsurprising that the education welfare service should be the territory for the struggles between social work and education. As I have described elsewhere (Robinson 1978), the history of the education welfare service demonstrates an evolution from a 'kid catching' role in which the major task was to get the children into school, to a social work service, and one which has an increasingly important role as a bridge and a mediator between the school and the families of schoolchildren.

The responsibilities and current roles of education and social work

The major shift within education in the past decade or so has been towards the implementation of comprehensive education for all secondary school children, regardless of the background from which they come, although special schools have been retained for children with particular difficulties and handicaps. Social work, as well as establishing large new local authority departments, has been endeavouring to recapture and develop the child care skills (so evident in children's departments in the 1950s and 1960s), in response to various public enquiries following the death from nonaccidental injury to children such as Maria Colwell.

All the most recent legislation relating to children, culminating in the advent of the 1975 Children Act, states that the first consideration should be given to the welfare of the child. This principle has to some extent emphasized as statutory the right of children to be considered as individuals, separate and distinct from their parents. Both social work and education must work within the legislative framework which prescribes their responsibilities and legitimates the actions for which those in the public sector are accountable to the State. Within these overall guidelines, however, there is a good deal of room for the exercise of discretion, and also for the manoeuvres of various interested groups. In the present financial situation, and because all our social institutions reflect the uncertainties of current political climates, both schools and social work are the subject of considerable public attention and criticism. It is therefore perhaps not surprising that both, at times, are reduced either to defensive postures, or to activities of mutual blaming for society's failure to provide the wherewithal to care for its casualties and rejects.

The role of the school in modern society is to provide education for all children of school age, that is from five to sixteen. Compulsory education, originally introduced to protect children from unscrupulous employers and exploitative parents, has now taken on a new dimension, whereby the education system is criticized by some for forcing children to attend schools which fail to teach them adequately much that they need for their adult lives, and to assist them to realize their full potential. Schools are nowadays considered to have two main responsibilities towards children, who are required to spend at school approximately six hours daily for five days a week, over roughly three-quarters of the year, for eleven years of their lives. Firstly, schools are expected to develop the cognitive abilities of their pupils, to teach them specific skills such as reading, writing, and arithmetic, and to impart general information considered useful to everyone. Most children arrive at infant school with some basic everyday knowledge which has been imparted to them within their early family life, and it is the task of the school not only to build upon this rudimentary knowledge, but also to develop the child's potential for thinking and learning, and to inculcate in him a desire to learn. Later in the school life of the child at primary school, but particularly at secondary school, the emphasis of his cognitive development becomes more specialized into discrete subject areas, and also specialized according to his aptitudes and interests. The debates around the areas of cognitive learning centre on the learning competence of the children, the skills of the teacher, and the selection of subject matter for the curriculum.

Secondly, and much more controversially than that of children's cognitive development, there is the school's role as a socialization agent. Socialization is the development of the person both as a social being and as a participant in society; it is a process which begins within the family network with the acquisition of language and of self-hood, the learning of social roles and the moral norms which are the basis of that particular family system. Whilst families are generally regarded as being the primary agents of socialization, schools are recognized as having a major role to play as secondary agents. It is within the schools that children are taught the cultural goals and values which are considered to be endemic within a given society. As part of these secondary socialization processes, schools are expected to provide role models and guidance to children for the parts they will be expected to play in adult life. Schools have these two major responsibilities for *all* children of compulsory school age who are educated within the state system; and the balance between cognitive and social education and the forms in which they are taught is achieved within the curriculum.

'The secret garden of the curriculum' (as Sir David Eccles called it in the 1960s) is a highly political matter. Lawton (1979) considers the curriculum legally to be the responsibility of the local education authorities and school governors, although in practice decisions about the content and teaching methods, and so on, are usually left to the head teachers and their staffs. The political nature of the curriculum is also stressed by Maurice Kogan (formerly secretary to the Plowden Committee) who writes that:

> Men wish to improve themselves for several reasons. The first is an innate desire to be more powerful and competent, and more in control of their own powers, for the sake of psychological comfort and self esteem. This purpose of education . . . of giving pupils a sense of autonomy relates quite closely to those of enabling pupils to be economically self sufficient and to contribute their share to the formation of family or national wealth . . . it is this individual objective of education that gives fierce dynamic to education as a political force. . . . These individual objectives are closely tied to social objectives with which they may conflict . . . school is an important centre for social learning. In another sense too, education is socialising in that it transmits the dominant culture to new generations by inculcating norms of language and ideas. Much of this socialisation is implicit . . . but debates about the curriculum and how it is taught are central to educational politics. (Kogan 1978)

In amplifying this point about the struggle over curriculum and standards Kogan comments:

> It is true that reformers have tried to influence secondary schools with the best of the primary school traditions. These attempts were evident in such documents as the Newsom Report (1963) on the less able secondary pupil. The primary zone at its best, used to embody . . . the 'progressive concept' whilst the secondary selective system again at its best embodied the idealist concept of education. The one relied primarily on the interaction between the pupil and teacher for the development of the child's potential. The other assumed that there were educational patterns, skills and categories of knowledge existing in an ideal world outside the school and able to be transmitted from one generation to another. Part of the controversy about the introduction of comprehensive education is concerned with ending that gentle truce between the progressivism of the primary school and the rigourism that many had hoped to see in the secondary school. Those who believe in comprehensives also believe in inducing the best aspects of the primary school into the secondary stage. For one thing, of course, primary schools are themselves comprehensives because there is no selection by ability into different schools.

Critics accuse schools of basing their curriculum and teaching methods on 'middle-class values', which, it is alleged, are inappropriate to the large mass of their working-class pupils. Furthermore, it is also said that this emphasis on middle-class educational aspirations acts as a disincentive to disadvantaged children who may respond by underachievement, or even by delinquency as compensation for their lack of success. The work of Power

(1970) and Hargreaves (1970) adds support to this view. But the struggle over the curriculum is not only about the values on which it is based; it is also about who should decide which are the paramount and prevailing values. As the report of the enquiry into William Tyndale Junior and Infants School (1976) showed, differing and conflicting opinions were held about whose views should prevail, by the teachers, by some of the parents, and by the managers (some of whom were active in involving the local Labour Party of which they were members).

The latest work of Rutter et al. (1979) draws some interesting conclusions on schools as social organizations. They found

> that secondary schools in the Inner London Area differ markedly in the behaviour and attainments shown by their pupils. This was evident in the children's behaviour whilst at school . . . the regularity of their attendance, the proportion staying on at schools beyond the legally enforced period, their success in public examinations and their delinquency rates. . . . Those differences in outcome between schools were systematically related to characteristics as social institutions. Factors as varied as the degree of academic emphasis, actions in lessons and the availability of incentives and rewards, good conditions for pupils and the extent to which children were able to take responsibility were all significantly associated with outcome differences between the schools. All these were open to modification by the staff rather than fixed by external constraints.

Because of these and other findings they finally conclude that there is a

> strong probability that the associations between school process and outcome reflect in part a *causal* process. In other words, to an appreciable extent, children's behaviour and attitudes are shaped and influenced by their experience at school, and, in particular, by the qualities of the school as a social institution.

The role of social work in modern society is to provide a service for that proportion of the population who are either self-referred, recommended, or compulsorily sent by those who have particular concern and responsibilities for them, whether these are statutory or otherwise. Social work clients characteristically come from among the socially deprived segment of the general population, but this is not necessarily so. Many are, however, likely to be demonstrating signs of social failure in the management of their own lives, or towards those for whom they are responsible. Others are dependent, whether through immaturity, age, or ill health, and appear to be being neglected or ill-treated by those on whom they are dependent.

Social work does not necessarily take place within a particular institutional setting in the way that schools are concerned with education. Much of social work practice takes place in the homes of the recipient. It is generally organized so as to be the responsibility of various welfare agencies, which may be situated within the public or the private sector. The independent, or voluntary agencies, as they are usually called, are usually concerned with particular groups or clients with similar problems, and they are financed by donations, subscriptions, and various state subsidies.

Until recently the public sector agencies were also organized to serve particular client groups – the delinquent, the mentally ill, the physically handicapped and elderly, and families where the children were deprived, delinquent, or variously at risk. The probation service is still responsible for the social work for the courts, whether this might be for social enquiry reports for those before the courts, or for probation and prison after-care for those who have been convicted of criminal offences. They may also provide welfare reports on children who are the subject of custody disputes, and on occasion act as guardian *ad litem* in adoption cases. However, since 1970 nearly all the public sector social work has been amalgamated into one large social service department. This department has considerable statutory responsibilities emanating from various pieces of legislation relating to specific groups; but most particularly for children. As has already been mentioned, only a few social service departments include the social work service to schools, the education welfare service, within their organizational structure. This service, like the hospital social work departments, is carried out from within institutions established for other purposes and in this sense social work is a secondary task, focussed on assisting the patients or pupils to have the benefit from what is available to them whether it is diagnosis and treatment or education.

There is considerable debate, at times acrimonious, but no general agreement about what actually is the role of social work. However, one way is to distinguish two main aspects as this will facilitate the comparison with education and highlight the areas of overlap. Firstly, it could be said that social work also has responsibilities for the socialization of its clients, though these are both less clear and more controversial than those connected with the socialization role of education. This role is unclear because the responsibilities of social work are not towards the whole population at the same time in their lives, but to certain specified members of the population who are considered to be in difficulties or to be deviant. While the role of education is concerned with minors who are still legally considered to be dependent on their parents or guardians, many of the clients of social work agencies are adult and parents themselves, although others are children or dependent because of the state of their physical or mental health. The controversial aspects of the socialization responsibilities of social work are twofold. Firstly, because some social work clients are seen to be in difficulties which are not of their own making, they are viewed sympathetically and perceived as unfortunates who are worthy of assistance; others are often seen as immoral, scroungers, or positively antisocial. Secondly, social work has statutory responsibilities towards some groups of potential clients (notably children and the mentally ill), which are accompanied by the power in certain circumstances, and subject to certain legal constraints, to cause their clients to be removed from their home and admitted to one of a variety of forms of custodial care. I have elsewhere described the cumulative effects of such intervention and its sequelae (Robinson 1978). It is important to stress that the process of becoming the client of a social worker is often both perceived and experienced as lowering self-esteem, while compulsory school attendance is not viewed as perjorative to the child. However, there is no doubt that as the social work role also includes aspects of socialization then this implies that both the primary and secondary agents of socialization, that is, the family and the school, may have failed to achieve their own task of socialization.

The second aspect of the social work role is that of assisting clients to gain access to resources for which they are eligible. In our welfare state the ways of obtaining benefits are often complex; others are discretionary and also scarce and some form of 'rationing' exists, such as waiting lists for council accommodation. Social workers assist their clients through the maze of complexities regarding benefits such as discretionary needs payments or applications for free school meals. At times they may act as powerful advocates for their clients, arguing on their behalf. Within social work itself there is discussion about how much social workers should work towards helping their clients to obtain the resources to which they are entitled for themselves, and how much and when they should undertake advocacy on their behalf. But there is considerable disagreement about when social work directed towards resource-getting should be particularized in relation to individual clients, and when clients who have similar needs should be aggregated and encouraged to voice their corporate requests, complaints, or even demands. This particular form of work is usually known as community work which may, for example, be undertaken on behalf of particular client groupings, such as ethnic minority groups or claimants of supplementary benefits; or it may be carried out at neighbourhood level, perhaps on a particular estate.

It will be apparent by now that social work too is a political matter, though it is not easy to discern a parallel to 'the secret garden of the curriculum'. The equivalent to the curriculum is possibly the policies of various social work agencies, and these of course are considerably influenced by the statutory responsibilities which are carried by them. Kogan has stated that there is not only considerable debate about what should be included in the curriculum, but also about who should decide and control what is taught. All children go to school, but those who become the clients of social workers are often already differentiated into one of two categories: those regarded as in need of care, and those who are delinquent and in need of punishment. It could be said that neglected or ill-treated children need care in the form of compensatory socialization, while the naughty children who commit offences which would be regarded as criminal if committed by an adult need punishment in the form of resocialization. But as was indicated in the previous section, children who are 'deprived' also behave in ways which might be considered 'depraved', and so the whole care/punishment debate once more bedevils not only the schools but also social work. Despite the attempts of the somewhat ill-fated 1969 Children and Young Persons Act to clarify the situation, and to imply that all children in trouble are in need of caring control, rather than punishment, public opinion (which of course includes social workers, teachers, parents, and even children) stubbornly continues to attempt to distinguish between naughty and neglected children and to propose their own solutions to the problems.

This makes the social control aspects of the social work role particularly controversial. Social control is that part of the socialization process which is directly or indirectly concerned with the maintenance of moral norms. In a rapidly changing society such as our own, these moral norms are in a constant process of redefinition; but it is argued that moral imperatives must be maintained for the well-being and continuance of society. There are, of course, informal sanctions and controls which exist in families, kinship groups, work groups, and communities, and these may or may not conflict with those contained within the school curriculum. While there are elements of social control within the role of education, these are even more pervasive and controversial within social work. Both social workers and teachers have socialization responsibilities towards children which involve elements of social control; but those of social workers (in social service departments) are based on statutory responsibilities which are ultimately backed by the power to remove from home a child who is believed to be being ill-treated or neglected. Though they can only do this under certain circumstances and for a brief period of time, because it is the juvenile court which has the ultimate power of making a supervision order or a care order as the result of properly constituted legal proceedings, this power is perceived with considerable ambivalence, not only by society generally, but also by the social workers themselves. Their duties at times involve attempting to distinguish between the welfare of the child and the rights of the parents, where these may be in conflict.

It is the aspect of social work which is concerned with assisting their clients to develop a community voice in connection with resources to which they should be entitled which tends to make social work a demonstrably political activity. There are particular problems which arise from social responsibilities becoming extended in this way. Firstly, that in their role as compensatory or resocialization agents to groups of clients, they inevitably come upon other agencies such as schools, which are perceived as failing to carry out their responsibilities. Thus, some social workers consider that it is part of their task to involve themselves as resocializing agencies, and indeed writers such as Goldstein (1973) consider that this is a legitimate part of the social work role. Clearly this is debatable, as social workers have no statutory mandate to carry out such activities; obviously the strength of their success depends very much on the manner in which such resocialization is carried out. In fact, much of the work now generally regarded as being part of the role of the education welfare service, though it is described as 'interpreting the school to the family' or 'mediating between the family and the school', amounts to resocialization, when the attempt is made to find a consensus between the groups involved. It is when the attempts at resocialization are by means of conflict strategies that difficulties arise.

The second problem is whether or not it is legitimate for social workers to claim such a mandate. Just as the Tyndale Inquiry (1976) revealed that there were differing perceptions as to who in fact controlled the curriculum, so there are differing views between community workers, social workers, councillors, and others regarding social work when it becomes overt political activity. No one could gainsay that teachers and social workers may be politically active as private individuals; the debate is around whether or not they also have a responsibility politically, to educate their pupils or to politicize their clients. The debate becomes particularly heated when education or social service department employees are in effect encouraging public criticism of the policies of the very council which employes them. If, indeed, such activity is a legitimate aspect of the socialization and resocialization responsibilities of teachers and social workers, then there remains a further question which requires to be debated. That is, how in a society which is committed to open government can ways be found to constrain individual public employees from using the power of their role to indoctrinate vulnerable groups in society with their own political ideologies?

The children at risk or in difficulties

In spite of the overlap between education and social work in the process of socialization, whether secondary, compensatory, or resocialization, there is still a need to distinguish failures in the process as early as possible whether the failure is located within the family or the individual child. This may in any case be a matter of perception, the school emphasizing the plight of the individual child, and the social work agency recognizing the conflict of needs within the family. The political aspects of both education and social work have been discussed, and it will be apparent that for outsiders entering the inner life of the family it is a very delicate matter indeed, even when there is general agreement that children should be both educated and protected.

Leaving these problems aside for the moment, we need to consider the question of which families with children might fall prey to such a degree of social failure that some form of remedial or corrective measures are found to be necessary. In fact a good deal is already known, and Kellmer-Pringle (1975) has identified five groupings of families who are particularly vulnerable:

1 the socially and culturally underprivileged
2 those where personal relationships suffer from some degree of impairment or where there is some emotional neglect
3 those where there is serious mental illness or disabling handicap
4 single-parent families
5 those affected by sudden and disrupting crises

Holman (1970) pointed out that the families who were at risk from poor social conditions resulting from poverty, inadequate housing, and overcrowding often live in the twilight zones of the inner-cities which compound any other problems such families might have. I have developed a model of the stages of family life (Robinson 1978), suggesting when families with children appear to be more than usually preoccupied by the natural psychological tasks associated with the multiple role changes which occur in all families. I pointed out that there were two peak stress periods when families might be particularly vulnerable: the first when the children in young families are beginning to attend school, and the second when the adolescent children leave school and perhaps begin to think of leaving home also. Simple screening procedures carried out at this time might enable contact to be made with families who are at an early stage of social failure, whereas, at present, families with children who are at risk or in difficulties only come to light when the problems are seriously entrenched.

The concern expressed by the directors of social services, which was referred to at the beginning of this chapter, appears to be well-founded. But what can be done? They rightly draw attention to the role of the education welfare service, pointing out, among other issues, the confusion about the role of the education welfare officer and the preoccupation with school attendance to the exclusion of other problems. The directors emphasize the need of a social work service for children in schools and, in summarizing the history of the various reviews of need for such a service, they make particular reference to the views expressed by the Newsom, Plowden, and Seebohm Committees (1963, 1967, and 1968). Each of these in turn pointed to the necessity for the closest cooperation between teachers and social workers, and that 'first and foremost it is essential to consider, and if necessary deal with the child in his total environment which includes his family and neighbourhood as well as his school'.

How is this to be done? The directors stress the value of an integrated and fully professionally qualified service which does not lead to waste of resources by duplication. Many of the points they raise to support this integration I have also discussed with particular reference to the organizational issues (Robinson 1978); but on balance and *at the present time*, I have concluded that there are certain advantages in retaining a social work service which is exclusive to schools. There are of course historical, organizational, financial, and political grounds for the retention of the education welfare service, some of which have been discussed in this chapter, though my own view is that they are unconvincing. There are also two strong arguments for maintaining a reformed *education social work service* which is exclusive to schools, and also a third which is currently particularly relevant. Firstly, it should be possible for an education social work service to act as a screening and early warning system, to locate families with children who are beginning to get into social difficulties before actual social failure becomes obviously apparent. Such a service would also have the power to switch resource priorities to helping such families, without deflecting them from other groups in greater need. However, such a service would only be possible if staffed by properly qualified social workers, and if accorded appropriate status and respect from within the education system. This in itself calls for a considerable change of attitude in a service which has long been both teacher-dominated and oriented, and would require resources to be geared accordingly.

An important factor would be to find a way in which the creation of an organizational structure, whereby the directors of education social work area services would be accorded comparable status to that of head teachers. Should such a change of attitude prove realistic rather than utopian, then it might become easier for teachers to refer children at risk earlier than they appear to be able to do at present. Secondly, the families themselves would have more choice about the type of social work service to which they go for help. The directors make the point that there are families who are against the authority of the school; but there are also those who are deterred from referring themselves to social services because they fear the powers which the local authorities possess to remove children from home.

It is not only important for clients to have some choice about the service to which they go for assistance, it is also necessary to try to find ways in which the stigma which accompanies the referral to the statutory social work services might be diminished. These attitudes, which may stem from ignorance of what social workers actually do, might of course be alleviated by informed education and information which is readily available; but while social workers have the power that they do, it is unlikely that the stigma will disappear. In some ways, therefore, it is understandable that teachers are somewhat reluctant to make early referrals of children in difficulties, although their hesitancy might be reduced if they could have easy contact with well-trained education social workers with whom they were in regular contact.

Finally, in view of the current financial constraints which have not only resulted in a worsening of problems, but also a reduction of resources, it seems that the social services departments are in danger of being overwhelmed by the enormities of the statutory work for which they are responsible. It is not realistic to expect them to develop the early warning service which has been described; and yet if some similar service is not given priority, it will not be possible to try to develop ways in which family failure can be alleviated in its early stages.

Innovative developments

The knowledge base of both teachers and social workers is derived from the social sciences, particularly from psychology, sociology, and social policy. Teachers, of course, are also expected to study a main subject which may later form their own specialism. Social workers on the other hand are expected to study some general and psychiatric medicine, as well as aspects of law, particularly the professional law which is relevant to them. In some universities and institutions of further and higher education, experiments are beginning in which teaching and social work students share at least some courses; and such developments are welcomed. The core courses of both teachers and social work education and training are those connected with what Evans (1976) has described as 'practice theory'. This is knowledge which has slowly been accumulated and built up from the profession's practice wisdom, which has been gained in day-to-day work, carried out within schools or social work agencies. This practice theory has often been devalued by pure academics (including those whose subjects form part of the knowledge base of both professions), on the grounds that it is 'applied' rather than 'pure'.

Both teachers and social workers are expected to undertake practice experience under special conditions in the institutions within which they will subsequently work. What is not generally recognized is that some of the skills which they struggle to acquire are not as dissimilar as they have been led to believe. Before discussing these skills, however, it is important to recognize that both professions require initiates to develop a personal style which is relevant to either teaching or social work. Inevitably, the personal style is influenced by the values and characteristics of the person as well as those of the profession. Both teaching and social work require more than basic knowledge, personality, and good commonsense which is often attributed to them, particularly towards each other!

Firstly, social workers and teachers alike need to acquire skills in relationships, although they may use them differently according to the tasks they undertake. Teachers, for example, spend more time in relating to classes of twenty–thirty children than they do in individualized relationships with individual children. They must develop skills in controlling such a large group of children in order to gain and hold their attention. Social workers, on the other hand, tend to work with individuals or small groups of children, who are often either in trouble or in pain and sometimes both. This requires considerable skill and sensitivity in understanding and helping children to confront and deal with their difficulties at their own pace. Teachers who move to this more individualized and intense way of relating, often comment on the pain which this engenders in them, and how difficult it is to gauge the pace of helping the child confront the painful reality. Thus, both teachers and social workers must develop skills in understanding and in relating to children, which are congruent with the tasks and responsibilities which they undertake.

Another area of skills which are common to social workers and teachers are communication skills, though again they are often used differently. Teachers must learn to communicate clearly to groups of children, so that what they are saying, whether they are communicating knowledge or giving instructions, can be understood by all the children in the class – not just the most able, or those who are most articulate. Social workers too require skills in communication, but these are more likely to be individualized for particular children with whom they may need to communicate on a number of different psychological levels simultaneously.

It is worth reiterating that teachers are expected to be able to develop skills to teach all children in the particular kind of school which they have chosen, whether it be an infant, primary, or secondary school; and that even those teachers who specialize in teaching particular *subjects* have to develop generalized skills in teaching. Social workers, on the other hand, while developing skills in working with children who are in difficulties of one kind or another, also have to develop skills in working with families and with other groups of clients, although they too may specialize.

Skills in relationship and communication, when combined with a compassionate attempt to emphasize and understand what is happening to specific others so that they might be helped thereby, are known as counselling. Teachers and social workers are not the only members of the helping professions who need to develop counselling skills; but they are among those who have to combine counselling skills within a framework of statutory responsibilities towards their clients or pupils. It is in ways in which they are able to use their shared skills (such as counselling) as well as their distinctive ones (such as the conveying of information and knowledge of resources) that both teachers and social workers might work together.

Within the past few years there have been some interesting developments in which teachers and social workers have been using their shared concern and interest in children at risk, to find ways of working together. Often these have been projects which have been developed under the intermediate treatment schemes whose development was encouraged during the debates leading up to the 1969 Children and Young Persons Act. The aim of IT projects, as they are called, is to provide developmental opportunities for young people who are already known to be in difficulties of one kind or another, but who given intensive and appropriate help remain with their families rather than being taken into care. IT projects are based within education and social services departments, and also within voluntary agencies; and sometimes are a cooperative venture. These schemes nearly all involve some kind of residential experience, but also regular small group meetings where children undertake shared activities or discussions. One such scheme has been described by Ward and Pearce (1979), a probation officer and a teacher. A group of seven boys who had been before the juvenile court for offences which they had committed together were invited by the leaders to meet as a group in the school which they all attended (infrequently), after school hours. The leaders invited them to devise a programme, and stressed the democratic emphasis of the group. After initial mistrust, a programme of alternate activities (swimming and football, and a visit to a discotheque, etc)., together with discussions, was worked out, and there were also camping excursions. The boys were also helped to find jobs and supported over the period of transition when they left school. Three years later, four of the boys had not reoffended, though the major success the authors considered was 'breaking down the professional barrier of the school gate'.

As I hope has been shown, the overlapping perspectives of social work and education have been an integral part of the growth of both the services. It may have been inevitable that they should have developed so separately, in order to emphasize the distinctive aspects of their tasks. Perhaps it might now be possible to use the advent of a crisis of public confidence in both education and social work to demonstrate cooperatively that the 'garden of the curriculum' is not to be secretly set apart from the rest of society; and that social work and its clients are not social outcasts to be cast away on some social refuse heap, which because it is often out of sight is also out of the public mind, until there is a scandal!

References

Association of Directors of Social Services (1978), *Social Work Services for Children*.

Auld, R. (1976), *Report of the Inquiry into William Tyndale Junior and Infants Schools*, ILEA.

Central Advisory Council for Education (1963), *Half Our Future*, HMSO.

Central Advisory Council for Education (1967), *Children and their Primary Schools*, HMSO.

Children Act, 1975.

Children and Young Persons Act (1969), HMSO.

Evans, R. (1976), 'Some Implications of an Integrated Model of Social Work for Theory and Practice', *British Journal of Social Work*, Vol. 6, No.2.

Goldstein, H. (1973), *Social Work and the Unitary Approach*, University of South Carolina.

Hargreaves, D. (1970), 'The Delinquent Subculture and the School', in Carson and Wiles, *op.cit.*

Holman, R. (1970), *Socially Deprived Families in Britain*, Bedford Square Press.

Kellmer Pringle, M. (1975), *The Needs of Children*, Hutchinson.

Kogan, M. (1978), *The Politics of Education*, Fontana.

Lawton, D. (1979), *The End of the Secret Garden: A Study in the Politics of the Curriculum*, University of London Institute of Education.

Power, M. (1970), 'Neighbourhood, School and Juveniles before the Court', in Carson, E.F. and Wiles, P. (eds.), *Crime and Delinquency in Britain*, Martin Robertson.

Report of the Committee on Local Authority and Allied Personal Social Services (1968), (Seebohm Report), HMSO.

Robinson, M. (1978), *Schools and Social Work*, Routledge & Kegan Paul.

Rutter, M., Maughan, B., Mortimore, P., and Onslow, J. (1979), *Fifteen Thousand Hours*, Pelican.

Ward, D. and Pearce, A. (1979), in *Social Work Today*.

AUTHOR INDEX

SUBJECT INDEX

The Harper Education Series has been designed to meet the needs of students following initial courses in teacher education at colleges and in University departments of education, as well as the interests of practising teachers.

All volumes in the series are based firmly in the practice of education and deal, in a multidisciplinary way, with practical classroom issues, school organisation and aspects of the curriculum.

Topics in the series are wide ranging, as the list of current titles indicates. In all cases the authors have set out to discuss current educational developments and show how practice is changing in the light of recent research and educational thinking. Theoretical discussions, supported by an examination of recent research and literature in the relevant fields, arise out of a consideration of classroom practice.

Care is taken to present specialist topics to the non-specialist reader in a style that is lucid and approachable. Extensive bibliographies are supplied to enable readers to pursue any given topic further.

Meriel Downey, General Editor

New titles in the Harper Education Series

Mathematics Teaching: Theory in Practice by T.H.F. Brissenden, University College of Swansea

Approaches to School Management edited by T. Bush, J. Goodey and C. Riches, Faculty of Educational Studies, The Open University

Linking Home and School: A New Review 3/ed edited by M. Craft, J. Raynor, The Open University, and Louis Cohen, Loughborough University of Technology

Control and Discipline in Schools: Perspectives and Approaches by J.W. Docking, Roehampton Institute of Higher Education

Children Learn to Measure: A Handbook for Teachers edited by J.A. Glenn, The Mathematics Education Trust

Curriculum Context edited by A.V. Kelly, Goldsmiths' College

The Primary Curriculum by A.V. Kelly and G. Blenkin, Goldsmiths' College

The Practice of Teaching by K. Martin and W. Bennett, Goldsmiths' College.

Helping the Troubled Child: Interprofessional Case Studies by Stephen Murgatroyd, The Open University

Children in their Primary Schools by Henry Pluckrose, Prior Weston School

Educating the Gifted Child edited by Robert Povey, Christ Church College, Canterbury

Educational Technology in Curriculum Development 2/e by Derek Rowntree, The Open University

The Harper International Dictionary of Education by Derek Rowntree, The Open University

Education and Equality edited by David Rubinstein, Hull University

Clever Children in Comprehensive Schools by Auriol Stevens, Education Correspondent, The Observer

Values and Evaluation in Education edited by R. Straughan and J. Wrigley, University of Reading

Middle Schools: Origins, Ideology and Practice edited by L. Tickle and A. Hargreaves, Middle Schools Research Group